Economic Progress, Private Values, and Public Policy

ESSAYS IN HONOR OF WILLIAM FELLNER

Economic Progress, Private Values, and Public Policy

ESSAYS IN HONOR OF WILLIAM FELLNER

Edited by

BELA BALASSA
The Johns Hopkins University

and

RICHARD NELSON
Yale University

1977

NORTH-HOLLAND PUBLISHING COMPANY
AMSTERDAM · NEW YORK · OXFORD

ISBN North-Holland: 0 7204 0515 7

Publishers:

NORTH-HOLLAND PUBLISHING COMPANY
AMSTERDAM · NEW YORK · OXFORD

Distributors for the U.S.A. and Canada:

ELSEVIER NORTH-HOLLAND INC.
52 VANDERBILT AVENUE
NEW YORK, N.Y. 10017

Library of Congress Cataloging in Publication Data
Main entry under title:

Economic progress, private values, and public policy.

Includes index.

CONTENTS: Reynolds, L. G. Development theory in classical economics. – Ranis, G. Economic development and financial institutions. – Nelson, R. R. and Winter, S. G. Dynamic competition and technical progress. [etc.]

1. Economics – Addresses, essays, lectures.
2. Economic development – Addresses, essays, lectures.
3. Economic policy – Addresses, essays, lectures.
4. Fellner, William John, 1905–

I. Fellner, William John, 1905– II. Balassa, Béla, 1899– III. Nelson, Richard R.
HB34.E24 1976 330 76–20719
ISBN 0–7204–0515–7

PRINTED IN THE NETHERLANDS

Dedication

The authors of the essays in this volume have been greatly influenced in their thinking about economic issues by William Fellner as teacher and colleague. They dedicate the volume to him, one of the leading figures of his generation who through his articles and books has made significant and manifold contributions to economic knowledge.

The essays deal with themes Fellner has developed, which gives a certain unity to the volume. The approaches taken to the major themes, and the methodologies, are diverse, which also is reflective of Fellner's work that has ranged from exploration in pure theory to analysis of contemporary policy issues, from tightly structured formal analysis to rich and sweeping essays. Fellner has been one of the most complete economists of his generation in the range of the topics, techniques, and perspectives.

Part I of the volume is concerned with the processes and measurement of long-run economic progress: a topic to which Fellner has returned again and again. Reynolds' essay takes a contemporary look at the writings of the classical economists regarding economic development. The role of financial institutions in the economic development process is the topic of Ranis' essay. Nelson and Winter present a Schumpeterian model of competition and economic growth. Watts focuses on the investments involved in bringing up and educating the next generation. Finally, Dorfman is concerned with assessing the impact of economic change on environmental values.

The rich textured and complex view of the process of long-run economic progress that comes through in these essays stands in contrast with the simple starkness of the growth models that were fashionable a decade ago. Yet it is impressive the extent to which Fellner's own work on growth recognized the empirical, analytical and normative issues that the much of the profession is only now beginning to perceive.

The subject matter explored in Part II – the equilibrium generated by the interaction of economic units pursuing their interests as they see them, and the consonance or disconsonance of this equilibrium with public values – also is one to which Fellner has contributed often and in many different ways. While the essays in this part tend to be more theoretically formal and deductive than those in Part I, they also lead to applications in public policy-making.

Among the authors of these papers, Friedman focuses on an area where Fellner's own work has been of major importance – oligopoly theory. The Schelling and Kurz papers are concerned with "externalities" broadly defined, another topic to which Fellner has made pioneering contributions. Schelling's focus is on the formation of groups based on individual preferences. Kurz is concerned with the explanation of altruistic behavior in society and determination of norms of conduct. The Phelps' paper focuses on some implications of a Rawlsian concept of distributive justice on optimal taxation schemes, while Balassa examines the desirability and the modalities of introducing income distributional considerations in decisions on public investment.

The essays in Part III are focused specifically on questions of macroeconomic policy. Apart from his concern with the contribution that analytical work might make to abstract and purely intellectual understanding, throughout his career Fellner has been concerned with the policy relevance of economic analysis. Over the past decade a significant fraction of his publications have been about policy problems per se, and involvement in economic policy-making process has absorbed a large fraction of his time. The essays in this part aim to further our understanding of problems Fellner has dealt with at one time or another.

The Brainard and Tobin essay is concerned with asset markets and the cost of capital. Lawrence and Sonia Klein present an empirical analysis of signals which foreshadow inflation. The Wallich paper is an eclectic look at the evolving blend of Keynesian and quantity theory that seems to be taking shape in the analysis of monetary and fiscal policy variables. Haberler is concerned with the coexistence of inflation and high levels of unemployment that has marked the past half decade, and attempts to trace its causes and affect its cures. Triffin presents data on what has happened to international monetary reserves during the 1970–74 period along with an assessment of causes and implications.

The hallmark of Fellner's writings and teaching has been an open-minded and non-dogmatic search for a better understanding of a complex and variegated economic reality that perhaps never can be completely comprehended. This perception of the nature of economics, the role of economists, and the fruitful method of economic research, has had a profound influence on us. The authors of these essays – students, colleagues, admirers of William Fellner – fondly dedicate this volume to him.

BELA BALASSA – RICHARD NELSON
Editors

Contents

Dedication v

Part I – Economic Progress: Process and Measurement

1. Development Theory in Classical Economics 3
LLOYD G. REYNOLDS, *Yale University*

2. Economic Development and Financial Institutions 27
GUSTAV RANIS, *Yale University*

3. Dynamic Competition and Technical Progress 57
RICHARD R. NELSON and SIDNEY G. WINTER, *Yale University*

4. A Model of the Endowment of Human Wealth or Let's Look at Social Policy Through the Eyes of the 21st Century's Adults 103
HAROLD W. WATTS, *Wisconsin University*

5. Towards a Social Index of Environmental Quality 121
ROBERT DORFMAN, *Harvard University*

Part II – Private Equilibrium and Public Values

6. Cournot, Bowley, Stackelberg and Fellner, and the Evolution of the Reaction Function 139
JAMES W. FRIEDMAN, *Rochester University*

7. Segregation on a Continuous Variable 161
T. C. SCHELLING, *Harvard University*

8. Altruistic Equilibrium 177
MORDECAI KURZ, *Stanford University*

9. Linear "Maximin" Taxation of Wage and Property Income on a "Maximin" Growth Path 201
EDMUND S. PHELPS, *Columbia University*

10. The Income Distributional Parameter in Project Appraisal 217
BELA BALASSA, *The Johns Hopkins University*

Part III – Macroeconomic Policies

11. Asset Markets and the Cost of Capital 235
JAMES TOBIN and WILLIAM R. BRAINARD, *Yale University*

12. Early Warning Signals of Inflation 263
LAWRENCE KLEIN and SONIA KLEIN, *University of Pennsylvania*

13. From Multiplier to Quantity Theory 279
HENRY C. WALLICH, *Federal Reserve Board*

14. Size, Sources and Beneficiaries of International Reserve Creation: 1970–74 297
ROBERT TRIFFIN, *Yale University*

15. Stagflation: An Analysis of its Causes and Cures 311
GOTTFRIED HABERLER, *Harvard University* (Emeritus)

Appendix – William John Fellner: Selected Writings 331

Author Index 337

PART I

ECONOMIC PROGRESS: PROCESS AND MEASUREMENT

Chapter 1

Development Theory in Classical Economics

Lloyd G. REYNOLDS

Development economics is concerned with the acceleration of economic growth in a previously near-static economy. Population and national output may have been growing slowly for a long time before such acceleration occurs. But at some point, and for reasons which doubtless run beyond the domain of economic analysis, the time trend of output per capita turns perceptibly upward. Such an inflection point can only be identified well after the fact, because it takes time to distinguish secular trends from cyclical or random fluctuations. Development economics attempts to analyze the growth of an economy during the period of, say, two to three generations surrounding such an inflection point.

While there is an element of autonomous scientific development in economic theory, there are also cycles of interest induced by exogenous economic and political events. It is thus not surprising that the first wave of interest in economic development occurred at the time and in the countries which were experiencing growth acceleration. In England, this acceleration occurred in the decades following 1740; in France and the predecessor German states, in the decades following the end of the Napoleonic wars in 1815; and by the 1850's, several other European countries had been drawn into the broadening current of economic growth. The writers considered here, most of whose work appeared between the *Tableau Économique* in 1758 and Mill's *Principles* in 1848, set out to explore the principles underlying long-term growth, including the question whether this growth could be expected to continue indefinitely in the future.

It is particularly appropriate to re-examine these writers in a volume honoring William Fellner, who had a profound and lifelong interest in the development of our discipline. For many years he introduced Yale undergraduates to economics through a course which treated modern economic analysis in historical perspective; and from this course emerged a book filled with penetrating insights into classical economic thought – Fellner (1960).

In treating the classical writers as development economists, we do not imply that this was their sole concern. Their work is enormously rich, containing pieces of economic history, the rudiments of modern microeconomics, a theory of international trade, and much besides. Our task here is not to assess the full range of their concerns, but simply to consider what they had to say about matters which would be recognized today as central to development economics: the definition of national accounting concepts; the division of the economy into producing sectors; intersectoral flows of income and product; the conditions governing the long-term growth of capital stock, population, and per capita income; the question whether such growth can continue indefinitely or must end in stagnation; and the political and institutional prerequisites for sustained growth.[1]

1. François Quesnay: Agriculture as Centerpiece

The group of *physiocrat* writers, the first to be labeled *les économistes*, was dominated by François Quesnay – physician, courtier, friend of Madame de Pompadour – whose court position helped to make his views the rage of the salons and to give them an influence on public policy. Around him grew up a fervent and singleminded group of disciples which included Dupont de Nemours, who moved to America during the revolutionary disturbances and whose sons founded the Dupont industrial empire. Most of their writings were published in the years 1760–1770, and by 1780 their views were largely forgotten. But for several reasons they are worth recalling today.

When we open the macro section of any principles textbook, we find a diagram of the "wheel of wealth" – goods flowing in one direction, money flowing in the other. The physiocrats originated this concept. They viewed the economy as a general equilibrium system, involving a circular flow among a few major sectors. In lieu of the piecemeal economics characteristic of much earlier discussion, they took an aggregative approach. One can speculate that Quesnay's medical experience (he had written on the circulation of the blood) may have had something to do with his development of circular flow concepts in economics. He also explained the necessary equality of income and output, a key feature of modern national accounting.

How did the physiocrats sector the economy? They distinguished *landowners*; *farmers*, whom they thought of as large, well-capitalized

[1]The most extensive previous discussion of these matters can be found in Lord Robbins (1968).

tenants renting land from the landowners; and *everyone else* – artisans, traders, soldiers, servants. Broadly, the division is between agriculture and non-agriculture, resembling that in contemporary dualistic models of economic development.

The central position of agriculture in the physiocrat system was natural in the circumstances. Agriculture was much the largest sector of the French economy. An active process of agricultural improvement was already underway in England and was widely discussed in France, though less widely practiced. Beyond this, the physiocrats regarded agriculture as primary in the sense of indispensable. Non-agriculturalists are dependent on agriculture for both food and industrial raw materials. In addition, agriculture is the only economic activity which produces a *net product.*

To appreciate this concept, we must recall that physiocratic principles related, not to the actual economy, but to "the natural order", an ideal system whose outlines were self-evident to any thoughtful observer. They used a Weberian "ideal type" or, as we would say today, a model. A key feature of the natural order was *laissez faire*, the sweeping away of governmental restrictions, leading to a regime of universal competition. Now under pure competition, the amount which manufacturers and other non-agriculturalists receive for their product is entirely distributed as wages of labor or interest on capital. There is nothing left over.[2]

But in agriculture, there is something left over. The farmer, after covering his labor and capital costs, has a surplus which he pays as rent to the landowner. This net product, attributable to land, is the only true surplus in the economy.[3] The physiocratic policy prescriptions follow directly from this doctrine. First, agricultural development should be promoted in order to make the net product as large as possible. This is reminiscent of contemporary development literature from about the mid-sixties onward, which has placed increasing emphasis on the need to raise agricultural output. Second, all government revenue should be derived from a single tax on land rent. A tax imposed anywhere else in the system will in any event be shifted to the landowners, who possess the only available surplus. They realized that an increase in land taxation would impose a capital loss on present landowners; but anyone purchas-

[2]The term "sterile classes" which the Physiocrats applied to the non-agriculturalists was not meant to denigrate their activities, which were recognized as necessary to the economy. It is simply an analytical concept, identifying those whose labor yields no net product.

[3]As Schumpeter (1954, p. 238) points out, there is a similarity here to Marx: "Exactly as Quesnay let land alone be productive of surplus value, so Marx let labor alone be productive of surplus value. Neither construction allows any productivity to capital – meaning plant, equipment, and material – which is indeed a conductor or embodiment of surplus value created, respectively, by land or labor but does not add to it."

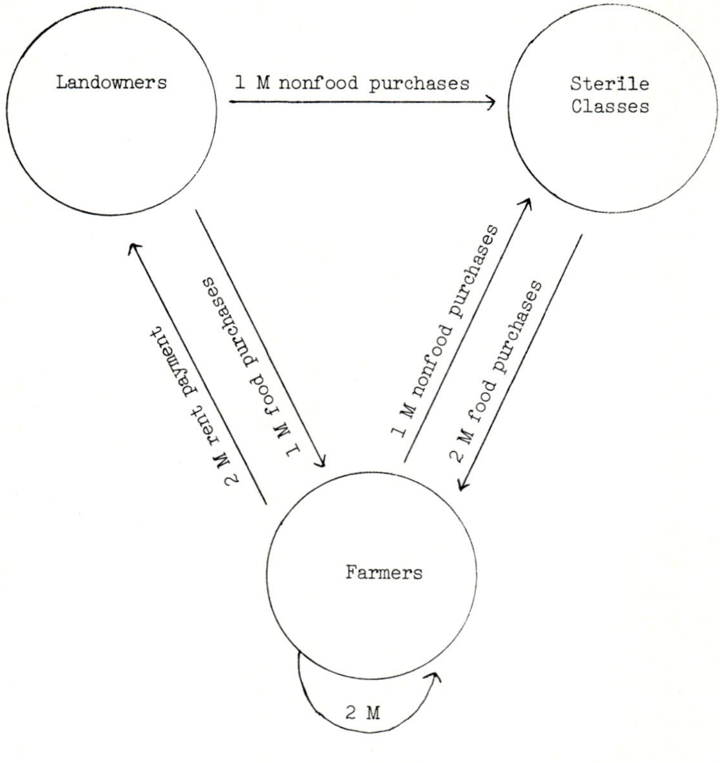

FIGURE 1. Money flows in the physiocrat system.

ing land thereafter would not suffer, since the tax would be reflected in a lower purchase price.

The flows of goods and money in the physiocrat schema are outlined in Figure 1. The figures, in milliards of francs, are those used by Quesnay, which he believed corresponded roughly to actual magnitudes in contemporary France.[4] Farmers, the productive class, produce 5 milliard francs of output. Of this, 2 milliard is consumed on the farm and 3 milliard is marketed. Of the sales proceeds, 2 M goes as rent to landowners and 1 M is spent on non-food products. The "sterile classes" buy 2 M worth of food and raw materials from farmers, financing this by selling 1 M of

[4]"This movement of commerce from one class to another, and the conditions which give rise to it, are not mere hypotheses. A little reflection will show that they are faithfully copied from nature." [Quesnay (1758, p. 60)].

non-food output to farmers and an additional 1 M to landowners. The landowners, who produce and sell nothing, divide their 2 M of rent receipts equally between food and non-food consumption.

This schema is simplified, but in ways which could readily be remedied. The sterile classes presumably consume some of their own output, which would add an extra loop to the diagram. Further, under the physiocrat single-tax program, the landowners would pay part of their rent income to government. (The physiocrats thought that one-third would be a reasonable proportion.) This tax revenue would support those of the "sterile classes" employed by government, who would respend it on foods and non-foods, thus maintaining balance in the circular flow.

A limitation of the model is that the circular flow is static, with no provision for enlargement over time. Farmers and other producers replace the circulating capital used during the year, and make good the depreciation of fixed capital. But they do no net saving, and neither do the landowners. True, the physiocrats urged increases in agricultural output in order to increase the net product, and this implies an increase in the capital stock. But capital accumulation does not figure in their formal system.

2. Adam Smith: The National Income of Nations

Despite its precursors, Smith's great work is rightly regarded as the first systematic treatise on economic development. By the *wealth* of nations Smith meant the *income* or, as we would say today, the GNP of nations. He sets forth clearly, and for the first time, the concept of *income per capita* as the criterion of economic progress.[5] He shows that national income and output must be equal, distinguishes gross from net concepts, and separates out the main components of capital. His treatment of capital, indeed, is in some ways superior to later practice. He includes explicitly "the acquired and useful abilities of all the inhabitants", which has recently been re-discovered as "human capital"; and excludes housing, treating it as a consumer durable.

The largest component of capital is circulating capital or "stock", (or "advances to labor", or "the wages fund"). Crudely, a capitalist farmer

[5]The first paragraph of *The Wealth of Nations* – Smith (1776) – "The annual labor of every nation is the fund which originally supplies it with all the necessaries and conveniences of life which it annually consumes . . . Accordingly, therefore, as this produce . . . bears a greater or smaller proportion to the number of those who are to consume it, the nation will be better or worse supplied with all the necessaries and conveniences for which it has occasion."

advances "corn" to his laborers for subsistence during the growing season. When the crop comes in it is sufficient to repay these advances and other production expenses, plus a profit to the farmer and a rent to the landowner. Similarly, the advances by a manufacturer to his employees are eventually repaid with a profit.

It is not correct to say, as sometimes is said, that capital in Smith is *only* circulating capital. The workmen to whom wages are advanced may work either on consumer goods or on capital goods. Smith recognized and approved of fixed capital – "machines which facilitate and abridge labor, and enable one man to do the work of many". The employer is assumed to divide his resources between fixed and circulating capital in the most profitable way, given existing technology. The fact that machinery substitutes for labor and appears *prima facie* to reduce employment did not concern him, though it did later concern Ricardo.

A word should be added on the famous distinction between "productive" and "unproductive" labor. This can be regarded as essentially a distinction between saving and consumption. Smith visualizes an employer receiving an income more than sufficient for his basic consumption requirements. This surplus income he can either put back into the business as (primarily) circulating capital, where it will employ additional workers, leading to further increases in output, profit, and saving; or he can spend it on servants and retainers, whose work leaves no material trace. The latter are "unproductive", and so are soldiers and civil servants. This is not primarily a judgment that output of material goods is more useful than output of services (though it did harden into that form in the Marxian variant of classical thought). Rather, it is a judgement that saving, which adds to the stock of circulating capital, is socially more productive than individual or government consumption.[6]

With these preliminaries, we may proceed to Smith's definition of economic sectors and his analysis of economic growth.

2.1. Economic Sectors

Smith agreed with the physiocrats that the basic sectoral division is between agriculture and non-agriculture, and that the interchange of commodities between them is of central importance.[7] As regards the

[6]See the similar interpretation by Hicks (1965, p. 37): " . . . productive labor plays the same part in his system as gross investment does in ours. It is unproductive labor which corresponds to our consumption sector."

[7]"The great commerce of every civilized society is that carried on between the inhabitants of the town and those of the country . . . The country supplies the town with the means of subsistence, and the materials of manufacture. The town repays this supply by sending back a part of the manufactured products to the inhabitants of the country." (Book III, ch. 1).

agriculture–industry terms of trade, he thought that urban producers typically have an advantage because, being fewer in number, they can more readily conspire to fix the prices of their products. They also have disproportionate political influence, and can secure restrictions on entrance to industry, tariffs against competing imports, and other measures which benefit them at the expense of the farm population. Smith also estimates, however, that the "corn price" of wool cloth and other key manufactures had fallen considerably in England over the previous century.

Smith also shared the physiocratic view that agriculture should be preferred over other sectors. It is particularly productive, because "nature labors along with man". He believed that both the capital/labor ratio and the capital/output ratio are lower in agriculture than in manufacturing.[8] Further, agriculture is the basic industry, on whose growth all others must depend. The city depends on the country for subsistence, for raw materials, and for a market for its products.[9] The "functions" of the agricultural sector in a developing economy have never been more clearly expressed.

Smith breaks with the physiocrats, however, in their treatment of manufacturing as a "sterile" activity yielding no surplus.[10] The manufacturing worker produces not only the equivalent of his wages, but also returns a profit to his employer; and this profit can be saved and contribute to capital accumulation, which will employ more labor in the future. The outcasts of Smith's system are menial servants and other service workers whose "services perish in the very instant of their performance, and seldom leave any trace or value behind them . . .".[11] Nor did Smith believe that manufacturing should be discouraged by public policy. On the contrary, manufacturing development benefits the agriculturalists by cheapening the goods which they buy.

The flow of income and output in the Smithian economy is sketched in

[8]"The capital employed in agriculture, therefore, not only puts into motion a greater quantity of productive labor than any equal capital employed in manufacture, but in proportion too to the quantity of productive labor which it employs, it adds a much greater value to the annual produce of the land and labor of the country, to the real wealth and revenue of its inhabitants. Of all the ways in which a capital can be employed, it is by far the most advantageous to the society." (Book II, ch. 5).

[9]"It is this commerce which supplies the inhabitants of the town both with the materials of their work, and the means of their subsistence. The quantity of the finished work which they sell to the inhabitants of the country, recessarily regulates the quantity of the materials and provisions which they buy. Neither their employment nor subsistence, therefore, can augment but in proportion to the augmentation of the demand from the country for finished work; and this demand can augment only in proportion to the extension and improvement of cultivation." (Book III, ch. 1).

[10]His critique of the physiocrats appears in Book IV, ch. IX.

[11]Book II, ch. 3.

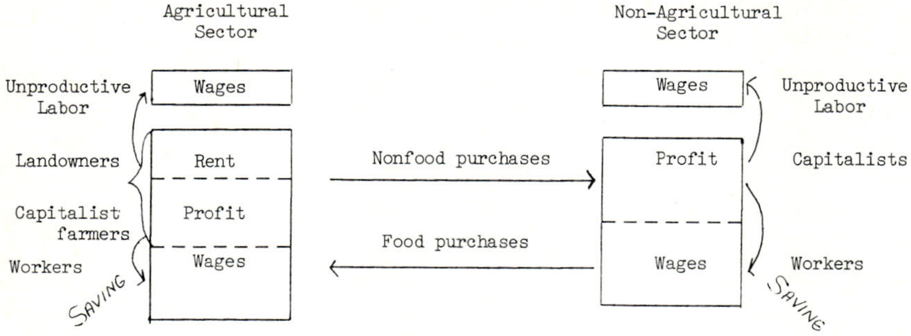

FIGURE 2. Income flows in the Smithian economy.

Figure 2. The "great commerce" between the agricultural and non-agricultural sectors appears in the middle of the diagram. (There is also, within each sector, a substantial consumption of its own output – farmers eating food, town dwellers consuming manufacturers – and only the surplus above this enters into the exchange flow.) Within the agricultural sector, income produced is divided among wages, profit, and rent; within the non-agricultural sector, between wages and profit. The principles governing this distribution, a central subject in classical political economy, will be examined in a moment. Wage-earners spend all of their income on consumption. But rent and profit recipients divide their income among material consumption, hiring of unproductive laborers, and saving which adds to the wages fund.

2.2. The Growth Process

The growth of output depends on capital accumulation, on growth of the "stock" which can be advanced to productive laborers. The classical writers tended to regard landowners as a prodigal class, spending their income on retainers and high living. The real savers are the capitalists in both the agricultural and non-agricultural sectors. The savings rate thus depends on the size of the profit share of income, and on how this is divided between saving and employment of unproductive laborers. Capital accumulates through reinvested profits, as in the Lewis model which, as Lewis himself emphasized, is a revival and elaboration of classical thought.

Growth depends also on correct allocation of capital. This issue, prominent in contemporary development theory, is also a central theme in the *Wealth of Nations*, developed in a chapter on "the natural progress of opulence". Smith was of course pre-marginal, and the concept of equating yields at the margin was foreign to him. Rather, he regarded some sectors as superior to others in an absolute sense. One should pour capital into the socially most profitable sector until it is, as it were, "filled up". Then capital should spill over into the second-best sector until it is full; and so on.

His ranking of sectors is based on the amount of labor which will be employed by a unit of capital. The "best" sector is that with the highest L/K ratio which, if one assumes no intersectoral difference in output per worker, would also mean the highest Y/K ratio. The use of capital which contributes most to output will also contribute most to capital accumulation, and hence to continued increase of output in the future. The real criterion is not employment *per se*, but rather the contribution which a particular use of capital makes to future growth.

The best sector, as already noted, is agriculture. Manufacturing ranks next in labor-absorbing capacity (one must remember that English manufacturing at this stage was still almost entirely handicraft production, with a high labor/capital ratio). Wholesale and retail trade, which use little labor relative to the capital employed, are least advantageous. Smith believed that this ranking based on social profitability corresponded with the ranking in terms of private profit and that, if government did not intervene unwisely, capital owners would be led "as by an invisible hand" to allocate capital in the proper sequence.

He observed, however, that in France and England the historical sequence of investment had been almost the reverse of that which he prescribed. The low level of investment and productivity in agriculture he blamed mainly on faulty tenure arrangements – large landholdings owned by unprogressive landlords, share rentals amounting to as much as half of the total produce, insecurity of tenure – as well as to heavy and erratic government levies on agriculture. All this is reminiscent of contemporary discussion.

To return to the central theme: as the capital stock grows, more labor is employed. Where does this labor come from? There is no clear concept of "surplus labor" in Smith, though British economic historians seem agreed that there was at this time a labor surplus in both town and country. Rather, Smith relied on population growth as the main source of additional labor.

Smith shared with his classical followers an essentially cost-of-production theory of labor supply. In a stationary state, the worker earns only a subsistence wage, defined as one which will enable him to rear enough children to maintain the labor force intact. If the demand for labor now rises through capital accumulation, the market rate of wages will rise above this "natural" level, and labor supply will respond. Population will grow, mainly through fewer children dying prematurely. If and when labor supply begins to rise as rapidly as the capital stock, wages will level off; and if labor supply should rise faster, wages would be driven down again toward subsistence level, retarding the rate of population increase.[12] In Smith's model population cannot rise more rapidly than capital stock over the long run; and the capital/labor ratio in production is fixed, a natural assumption given the interpretation of capital as primarily circulating capital.

But with capital and labor increasing proportionately, how can output per capita grow? Part of the answer is that, as total output rises, there is increasing opportunity for specialization and exchange – "the division of labor is limited by the extent of the market". Increases in labor productivity arising from greater specialization are a key force raising per capita income.

A second source of higher labor productivity is growing mechanization of production. This also stems from division of labor because, as tasks become more finely subdivided, they are also more readily mechanized. Finally, Smith believed that a higher real wage will by itself raise the productivity of labor,[13] leading to a "virtuous circle" of cumulative upward progress. The hypothesis of a backward-bending supply curve of labor was firmly rejected.[14]

Formally, then, Smith's model includes output as an increasing function of capital and labor inputs, capital as a (implicitly, though not clearly specified) function of output, and labor supply as a function of capital stock. This yields three equations in three variables. But Smith's insights are more important than the technical completeness of his model.[15]

What is the long-run tendency of the system? Smith believed that the rate of profit tends to fall over time, though his explanation of this is not very convincing. (His most explicit statement is that, as more and more capital crowds into the same industry, competition will reduce the level of prices and profits. But this is surely not adequate at a macroeconomic

[12]The market wage level thus depends, not on the size of the capital stock, but on its *rate of increase.* "It is not, accordingly, in the richest countries, but in the most thriving, or in those which are growing rich the fastest, that the wages of labor are highest. England is certainly, in the present times, a much richer country than any part of North America. The wages of labor, however, are much higher in North America . . ." (Book I, ch. 8).

[13]"A plentiful subsistence increases the bodily strength of the laborer, and the comfortable hope of bettering his condition, and of ending his days perhaps in ease and plenty, animates him to exert that strength to the utmost. Where wages are high, accordingly, we shall always find the workmen more active, diligent, and expeditious than where they are low; in England, for example, than in Scotland . . ." (Book I, ch. 8).

[14]"That a little more plenty than ordinary may render some workmen idle, cannot well be doubted; but that it should have this effect upon the greater part, or that men in general should work better when they are ill fed than when they are well fed . . . seems not very probable." (Book I, ch. 8).

[15]For an effort to formalize the Smithian system, see Adelman (1961).

level.) Eventually, profit will fall to a level which discourages further net saving. The concept of the "fully stocked" economy in which accumulation has ceased – China is the favorite illustration – recurs at several points in the book. When an economy has been in this situation for some time, population growth must eventually reduce wages to subsistence level, after which population growth will also cease.[16]

There is no clear picture of the stationary state in Smith, however, and he obviously regarded it as (for England) a distant prospect. The general tone of the book is optimistic. Smith asserted that per capita income in England had been rising gradually for several centuries, and he obviously expected this to continue for the foreseeable future.

2.3. Growth and Trade

Smith's views on this subject have been analyzed by Hla Myint,[17] and little need be added here. Smith believed that a nation benefits from international trade in two ways, which differ from each other and also from the classical theory of comparative costs. First, trade enables an industry to expand beyond the confines of the domestic market, which makes possible a finer division of labor with a resulting gain in productivity. This is different from the gain posited by comparative cost theory, which results entirely from resource reallocation after the opening of trade, with *given* production functions.

Second and more novel is Smith's "vent for surplus" doctrine, which views trade as providing an outlet for production which otherwise could not find a market.[18] In order for such a (potential) output surplus to exist, there must be a surplus of productive resources not presently in use. If these can be mobilized to meet a foreign demand, the imports received in return are a net gain to the economy. (This is reminiscent of recent writings on mobilization of "surplus labor" for economic development.)

But why should unused resources exist in the first place? In a

[16]"...it is in the progressive state, while the society is advancing to the further acquisition, rather than when it has acquired its full complement of riches, that the condition of the laboring poor, of the great body of the people, seems to be the happiest and most comfortable. It is hard in the stationary, and miserable in the declining state." (Book I, ch. 8). *Progressive*, *stationary*, and *declining* are to be interpreted in terms of the size of the capital stock.

[17]Myint (1958).

[18]"It carries out that surplus part of the produce of their land and labor for which there is no demand among them, and brings back in return for it something else for which there is a demand. It gives a value to their superfluities, by exchanging them for something else, which may satisfy a part of their wants..." [Myint (1958)].

developed economy, apart from cyclical disturbances, this is not easy to explain; and Smith does not really provide an explanation. As Myint points out, however, Smith's argument does fit the situation of many sparsely-populated countries of Africa and Southeast Asia during the nineteenth century. In these initially isolated economies, basic food requirements could be met by using only part of the available labor time and arable land. As communications developed with other economies, peasant exports of rice, coffee, cocoa, palm oil, and other products grew rapidly. This was accomplished by drawing additional land into cultivation and by additional labor inputs per capita. The new export production was simply added to the previous subsistence production rather than substituting for it.

None of this, however, is relevant to the England of Smith's days. He did refer to timber and iron ore in northern Europe, which could find an outlet only through trade. His vent for surplus concept perhaps related mainly to such natural resource products rather than to manufactures.

3. Rise and Fall of the Population Problem

Population behavior, like economic growth, has undergone wide fluctuations of interest. In classical thought, the race between population growth and food supply played a central role. After about 1850, when the spectre of food deficits seemed to have vanished, population also vanished for a century from economic discussion. But the period 1850–1950 now appears as a special episode in history, marked by a once-for-all mobilization of land reserves in the land-rich countries, and by a demographic transition in the developed industrial countries which reduced their rate of natural increase. Today, with population rising rapidly in the less developed countries and pressing hard against food supplies, population economics has been rediscovered and has moved back to the center of the stage.

Adam Smith, as we have seen, defined a "natural" or subsistence wage rate which would enable a husband and wife to replace themselves with two surviving children. This kind of Z.P.G., unlike the contemporary version, involved unchecked fertility accompanied by high infant mortality rates. But in an "advancing" economy, where capital accumulation is raising the demand for labor, the real wage will rise above subsistence, more children will survive, and population will grow. This disequilibrium situation, Smith thought, could continue for a long time – he never indicated just how long – before a slackening of capital accumulation would eventually force wage rates back toward subsistence. Food supply *per se* does not seem to have troubled him. The English population was growing only slowly and England up to 1750 was still a grain-exporting country.

When Malthus wrote around 1800, however, population was growing at about 1 percent a year, and the previous food surplus had turned into a food deficit. He was impressed by the potential speed of population growth (his illustrations usually show it doubling in a generation), and by the strength of diminishing returns to agriculture in a fully-settled country. Unlike Smith, he thought that population growth would *quickly* offset any tendency for the market wage to diverge above subsistence, and would drive it back down to the Z.P.G. level. He did, however, admit one loophole. A sustained improvement in real wages was possible if, as wages rose, workers held the birth rate in check through "moral restraint". By this he did not mean contraception, which as a clergyman he opposed. Moral restraint meant simply abstinence, reinforced by late marriages. But he did not expect this check to be very effective in practice.

Malthusian population theory was a pillar of Ricardo's system, with its eventual tendency toward a stationary state. By the time of Mill, however, the future already appeared brighter. Contraception was accepted by progressive thinkers and this, in addition to Malthus' preventive checks, seemed to provide a basis for family planning. Subsistence was re-defined, not as a wage corresponding to zero population growth, but as any conventional living standard which workers are willing to defend by curbing fertility. It thus became possible to visualize a "ratchet" movement of living standards. Wages rise above subsistence because of rising labor demand, as Smith explained. Workers become accustomed to this higher level, and curb reproduction in order not to endanger it. Continued increase in labor demand raises wages again, workers adjust their expectations and their reproductive behavior to the new level; and so on.

The English birth rate did in fact peak in the 1820's, and then began a sustained decline. And after the Corn Law repeal of 1846, wheat came flooding in from the new world at a rate which removed the food problem from the realm of practical discussion. Population passed from the main text into footnotes, and from there to virtual oblivion. Roughly a century was to pass before population discussion revived in a different empirical context.

4. David Ricardo: Rent and the Stationary State

If Smith impresses by his wide historical knowledge and sharp policy insights, Ricardo impresses by the tightness of his analytical system. He professed little interest in the *size* of national income,[19] asserting that the central problem is what determines the *distribution* of national income among "the three classes of the community" – landowners, capitalists, and wage-earners. But distribution here must be interpreted in a historical sense. The problem is how factor returns tend to *change over time*, and whether their projected movement is consistent with continued economic progress. This is clearly a problem in growth theory.

Consider first the evolution of land rent. As population grows, agricultural production is pushed harder on both the intensive and extensive margins of cultivation. Because of diminishing returns, the amount of labor needed to produce an additional bushel of corn rises steadily. Since there has been no change in the amount of labor required to produce industrial products, the relative price of corn must rise. The internal terms of trade move against industry. Rent per acre of land, and the rent share of national income, rise continuously over time.

The wage rate is the price of labor and, like any price, depends on the amount of labor required to produce the article in question – in this case, the amount of labor required to grow enough food to support a worker at subsistence level. This Ricardo defines as the *natural* level of wages.

There is also a *market* level of wages which depends, as in Smith, on the relative rates of increase in labor supply and in the stock of (circulating) capital which governs the demand for labor. If capital is growing more rapidly, the market wage rate will diverge above the natural rate. On Malthusian reasoning, however, the rate of population growth will in time overtake and exceed that of capital accumulation, and the market wage will then fall toward the natural level.

If the natural rate is of dominant importance, the crucial question is how this rate changes over time. In real terms, it does not change – the amount of food required for the worker's subsistence is constant. But the money wage required to buy this amount of food rises over time. The reason, already noted, is that the relative price of food is rising because of the operation of diminishing returns in agriculture.

[19]In a letter to Malthus, cited by Robbins, he says: "Political economy you think is an enquiry into the nature and causes of wealth – I think it should rather be called an enquiry into the laws which determine the division of the produce of industry among the classes who concur in its formation. No law can be laid down respecting quantity, but a tolerably correct one can be laid down respecting proportions. Every day I am more satisfied that the former enquiry is vain and delusive, and the latter only the true object of the science." The letter appears in the Sraffa edition (1951, vol. 1, p. 5) of Ricardo.

This tendency, usually termed "the Ricardian food bottleneck", puts a squeeze on industrial profits. Consider a cloth manufacturer. He is faced with a rising wage bill for the reason just noted. But the value of his cloth has not increased, because there has been no change in the amount of labor required to make it. Rising labor costs with no increase in product prices must reduce the profit share of value added.[20] Here is the basis for a secular decline in profit, which Smith forecast but did not adequately explain. Moreover, since competition must lead to the same profit rate in all industries, this decline will extend throughout the economy.

These secular tendencies can be summarized as follows:

	Rate per unit	Total amount	Percent of national income
Rent	+	+	+
Wage	+	+	?
Profit	–	?	–

Profit could conceivably fall to zero. But at some point before this the incentive to net saving will vanish and the capital stock will become constant. With the lag necessary for population to catch up, the market rate of wages will fall to the natural rate, after which population (and output, and output per capita) will also remain constant. This is the Ricardian stationary state. Ricardo recognized the possibility of technical progress as a counteracting tendency; but he thought that it could do no more than slow down the eventual arrival at the stationary state.

The other section of the *Principles* which might be regarded as verging on growth theory is a chapter on machinery, added in the Third Edition. Here Ricardo suggested that the "freezing" of circulating capital into larger quantities of fixed capital might, by diminishing the wages fund, cause growing unemployment of labor over time. The argument is rather confused, however, and did not provide a useful starting point for later speculation about technological unemployment.

Until recently the Ricardian system seemed interesting merely in antiquarian terms. But in today's less developed economies, the Ricardian food bottleneck is no historical figment. The agriculture–industry terms of trade are central to contemporary development models. The pressure of rapidly-growing population on food supplies has already turned the

[20]To repeat, the worker's "corn wage" has not risen – he eats no more than before. But to provide him with this fixed amount of corn, the employer must give up more and more cloth, since corn prices have risen relative to cloth prices. The worker's "cloth wage", his share of value added, has risen. The essence of the matter is that the terms of trade turn increasingly against industry on account of diminishing returns.

domestic terms of trade in favor of agriculture in some countries, and threatens to do so in others; and as Ricardo predicted, this tends to choke off industrial development.

5. John Stuart Mill: The Dawn of Victorian Optimism

Mill was the first great systematizer of economics, the first textbook writer to break the 900-page barrier. His *Principles*, published in 1848, remained the standard text for British and American students until well after 1900.

While Mill built upon Ricardo's theoretical system, he made important new contributions. He anticipated Marshall in using the *ceteris paribus* technique. His chapter[21] on the effect of economic growth on factor prices first analyzes the consequences of population growth in isolation from any other change in the economy, then the effect of capital accumulation acting alone, and then the effect of technical progress by itself. This is about what we have been doing ever since. He distinguishes nicely between the effect of land-saving improvements and labor-saving improvements in agriculture. And he distinguishes between cost reductions in the production of goods consumed by workers ("wage goods", as we would now say) and "luxuries" consumed by the population at large. The latter benefit consumers generally, but do not affect income distribution. Improvements in producing wage goods, however, influence the behavior of Ricardo's natural rate of wages, and so do influence distribution.

Mill's treatment of profit is also more elaborate than that of earlier writers. He decomposes profit into: (a) the pure rate of return on saving, (b) a risk premium appropriate to the degree of risk involved in a particular venture, and (c) the wage of management, an appropriate item in an era when ownership and management were usually indistinguishable. Components (b) and (c) fall gradually in a growing economy, as the supply of management grows and the success of past ventures makes future investment appear less risky.

The pure return to saving also tends to fall as capital accumulates; but this cannot continue indefinitely. Like his predecessors, Mill believed that there was some low, positive rate of interest at which net capital formation would fall to zero. Indeed, he believed that if capital continued to accumulate in a country like Britain, and if nothing else happened, the profit rate would quickly reach this floor level. His discussion is reminis-

[21] *Principles* (Book IV, ch. 3). This Book contains most of Mill's systematic reasoning on long-term growth.

cent of the "secular stagnation" writings of the nineteen thirties. But the evil day is postponed, if not averted, by several things: the possibility of capital exports to other countries; waste of capital by government as well as by unsuccessful private investors; technical progress, which permits new investment without lowering the rate of return; and the possibility of cheap food imports (much clearer in 1848 than in 1820), which retards the rate of increase in money wages and reduces the Ricardian squeeze on profits.

Even if one had no data on the capital formation rate in mid-nineteenth century England, one could infer from Mill's writings that it was substantial. He clearly believed that saving responds flexibly to investment opportunities and that, far from inadequate saving being a barrier to economic growth, the real danger was a possible glut of capital. This view led him to interesting policy conclusions. For example, government borrowing for productive purposes is no danger, even if it encroaches temporarily on private capital formation. The potential supply of saving is so ample that the reservoir will soon be refilled, and private capital formation will be as high as before. At most, there may be some diversion from overseas investment to home investment. Again, while he accepts Ricardo's view that "freezing" circulating capital into fixed capital will reduce employment, this effect will be only temporary. Saving will quickly rebuild the stock of circulating capital to its previous level, and employment will be as large as before.

By 1848 Britain's economic success was assured. So it is not surprising that Mill's book is more optimistic than Ricardo's a generation earlier. Mill is impressed with the importance of technical progress and other dynamic changes which postpone the consequences of the Ricardian model. We are always within sight of the stationary state, but the horizon recedes as we approach it. Nor would eventual arrival at the stationary state necessarily be undesirable. In an interesting chapter,[22] Mill argues that a (high-level) stationary state would probably be more pleasant than any other. The sight of people trampling over each other in the race for progress, the intense concentration on money-grubbing (to which he considered Americans particularly addicted!) was not edifying to a man who at heart was a moralist and a political philosopher. The tone is reminiscent of some of today's anti-growth arguments.

Mill offers numerous side-comments on how other countries can hope to attain the prosperous position of Great Britain. One example, addressed to "the various nations of Asia", may suffice:

"... the desideratum for such a country, economically considered, is an

[22]Book IV, ch. 6.

increase of industry, and of the effective desire of accumulation. The means are, first, a better government: more complete security of property; moderate taxes, and freedom from arbitrary exaction under the name of taxes; a more permanent and more advantageous tenure of land, securing to the cultivator as far as possible the undivided benefits of the industry, skill, and economy he may exert. Secondly, improvement of the public intelligence: the decay of usages or superstitions which interfere with the effective employment of industry; and the growth of mental activity, making the people alive to new objects of desire. Thirdly, the introduction of foreign arts, which raise the returns derivable from additional capital, to a rate corresponding to the low strength of the desire of accumulation; and the importation of foreign capital, which renders the increase of production no longer exclusively dependent on the thrift or providence of the inhabitants themselves . . . These considerations apply more or less to all the Asiatic populations, and to the less civilized and industrious parts of Europe, as Russia, Turkey, Spain, and Ireland."[23]

Clearly, Mill is talking about things which are still central in development discussion: a rational tax system; improvement of land tenure; development of education; encouragement of saving; stimulation of personal incentives through "the demonstration effect"; international transfers of technology and capital. He took it for granted that economic development would be essentially *private* development; and that, beyond improving institutions and providing infrastructure, government should not intervene in resource allocation. The classic statement of this principle by Smith[24] was subscribed to in all essentials by later writers.

6. Karl Marx: The Great Dissenter

It is currently fashionable to urge that social scientists should not be "narrow specialists" but broad-ranging, multi-disciplinary scholars. The

[23]Book I, ch. 13; in the Ashley edition (1909, pp. 189–190).

[24]"What is the species of domestic industry which his capital can employ, and of which the produce is likely to be of the greatest value, every individual, it is evident, can, in his local situation, judge much better than any statesman or lawgiver can do for him. The statesman, who should attempt to direct private people in what manner they ought to employ their capitals, would not only load himself with a most unnecessary attention, but assume an authority which could safely be trusted, not only to no single person, but to no council or senate whatever, and which would nowhere be so dangerous as in the hands of a man who had folly and presumption enough to fancy himself fit to exercise it." [Smith (1776, Book IV, ch. 2)].

classical economists certainly followed this pattern. The outstanding example is Karl Marx – philosopher, historian, political theorist, and Old Testament prophet. It is easy enough to poke holes in Marx's technical economics, and to show that his predictions were not validated by events; but this is not the most important part of his total system.

In Marx's view, social structure is rooted in the material conditions of production. To a particular stage in the development of the "productive forces", there corresponds an appropriate economic organization, and a political and ideological superstructure which serves to rationalize and defend this organization. The essence of this structure is the division of society into a dominant, exploiting class and a subordinate, exploited class – the feudal lord and the serf, the capitalist and the laborer. For the natural harmony of interests posited by mainstream thinking, he substituted a doctrine of inevitable conflict of interests which could be resolved only by revolutionary struggle.

Government is the instrument of the dominant class. Its function is to protect the dominance of that class and confirm the exploitation of the oppressed. The bland prescription of Smith and Mill that government should abstain from direct intervention in economic affairs, and should content itself with caretaker functions promoting the "general interest", he dismissed as a bourgeois fiction designed to veil what was actually going on. It is in his politics rather than his economics that Marx breaks most completely with the liberal economists.

Post-Marxian controversy has focussed heavily on his prognosis of the eventual breakdown of capitalism. But this is not the part of Marx which is relevant for our present purpose. A country in an advanced stage of capitalist development is scarcely a less developed country. Our concern here is with how growth acceleration occurs in a pre-industrial, primarily agricultural economy, i.e., with the *emergence* of industrial capitalism rather than its eventual fate. The relevant part of Marx's schema, therefore, is his analysis of the transition from the feudal to the capitalist stage of development.[25]

Where did the capitalists come from, and how did they accumulate the capital needed to launch large undertakings? Some of them were initially small artisans, who gradually took on employees and expanded their scale of operation.[26] Large initial capital, however, was usually accumulated

[25]The fullest statement of his views is in Part VIII of Volume I of his *Capital*, which should properly be read as the introductory rather than the concluding part of that volume.

[26]"Doubtless many small guild-masters, and yet more independent small artisans, or even wage-laborers, transformed themselves into small capitalists, and (by gradually extending exploitation of wage-labor and corresponding accumulation) into full-blown capitalists." [Marx (1867, vol. I, ch. XXXI)].

either through money-lending or commerce, the latter often associated with exploitation of overseas colonies. Once this capital has been converted to employment of industrial workers, further capital accumulation presents no problem. It occurs naturally and cumulatively through reinvestment of profit ("surplus value") extracted from the laborers. Along with other classical writers, Marx believed that industrialists have a natural passion for accumulation, and will not waste their income in prodigal living. As in other classical writings, too, continued accumulation drives down the rate of profit, so that the capitalists must accumulate ever more frantically to maintain the same *total profit*.

Where does the new class of industrial workers come from? Since agriculture is the dominant industry, they must come mainly from agriculture. In contemporary development models, this rural–urban flow of labor is a voluntary movement induced by a substantial wage gap. In Marx, on the other hand, small farmers are forcibly evicted by large landowners, with the cooperation of government, and turned into landless proletarians against their will. His description of this process doubtless reflects elements of reality. The large landholdings which had developed in England by the eighteenth century were achieved partly through land consolidation and displacement of small farmers and cottagers. Enclosure of the old common lands, depriving small men of living space and rights to fuel and pasturage, contributed to this enforced movement. Marx does appear, however, to overstate the conscious malevolence with which landlords and government collaborated to drive the dispossessed into the arms of the waiting capitalists. Nor does this "English model" have much relevance to the small peasant producers who dominate the agriculture of contemporary Nigeria or Thailand.

A secondary source of labor supply is the extinction of the artisans, who are outcompeted by the more productive capitalist enterprises. The small handicraft producer is separated from direct contact with the means of production, and is forced to sell his labor power to the capitalist who now owns those means. Marx regarded this process as inevitable, and even as desirable. Small workshops do not permit the division of labor and mechanization required for high productivity. Modern technology *requires* large-scale enterprises, and history, ever-responsive to technological imperatives, obligingly brings them into being.[27]

[27]"... this petty mode of production ... attains its adequate classical form only where the laborer is the private owner of his own means of labor set in action by himself; the peasant of the land which he cultivates, the artisan of the tool which he handles as a virtuoso. This mode of production presupposes parcelling of the soil, and scattering of the other means of production. As it excludes the concentration of these means of production, so also it excludes co-operation, division of labor ... and the free development of the social productive powers. It is compatible only with a system of production, and a society, moving within

It cannot be over-emphasized that, in Marx's view, the capitalist stage of development serves a necessary historical purpose. This is to concentrate capital in ever-fewer, ever-larger production units through competition among capitalists ("one capitalist kills off many"), which permits a steady increase of specialization, mechanization, and productivity.

These enterprises eventually reach a scale at which their socialization is technically easy and, indeed, essential for further progress. Capitalist resistance to socialization provokes a revolutionary struggle, in which the capitalists are overthrown and socialism ushered in. This Marxist vision of history does not really depend on the technicalities of absolute and relative surplus value, variable and constant capital, and the like which have consumed so much misspent intellectual labor over the past century.

If the capitalist stage is essential, how can a country undertake to skip it? How can countries like China,[28] Cuba, or North Vietman move directly from an agrarian economy to full-blown socialism? What would Marx have said of such un-Marxian behavior?

A contemporary less developed country which launches directly into socialism is starting from a different position than that which Marx visualized. In agriculture, small-scale, owner-operated farming is often the dominant tenure form. Yet for reasons already noted, the Marxian tradition is deeply hostile to such a "backward system". Farm sizes must be enlarged, the peasant must be uprooted; and, since the capitalists have not accomplished this in a prior stage of history, the socialists must now set about doing it. This outlook, which has been translated into policy in most socialist countries, does not ease the problem of raising agricultural productivity.

---

narrow and more or less primitive bounds. To perpetuate it would be, as Pecqueur rightly says, 'to decree universal mediocrity'. At a certain stage of development it brings forth the material agencies for its own dissolution. From that moment few forces and new passions spring up in the bosom of society; but the old social organization fetters them and keeps them down. It must be annihilated; it is annihilated. Its annihilation, the transformation of the individualized and scattered means of production into socially concentrated ones, of the pygmy property of the many into the huge property of the few, the expropriation of the great mass of the people from the soil, from the means of subsistence, and from the means of labor, this fearful and painful expropriation of the mass of the people forms the prelude to the history of capital." [Marx (1867, vol. I, ch. XXXII)].

[28]In contemporary Chinese doctrine, to be sure, there is a "capitalist epoch", which began with the forcible intrusion of the Western powers in the early nineteenth century and lasted until 1949. But this was largely mercantile capitalism. Factory industry was little developed, and certainly had not by 1949 served the historic purpose of concentrating "the social production powers" into huge modern units.

7. Yesterday and Today: What Remains of Classical Thought?

On re-reading the classics, the dominant impression is not of what they overlooked but of how much they anticipated. They dealt with most of what are now regarded as leading issues in development economics. Most, though not all. They underrated technical change, and particularly the potential of technology as an offset to diminishing returns in agriculture. They would have been surprised to hear that, in the United States over the past several decades, output per man-hour has risen faster in agriculture than in any other sector except electric power production. They could scarcely foresee the decolonization of most of Asia and Africa, the emergence of new centers of political and economic power, the increased volume and changed pattern of international trade, the marked increase of "official" capital flows relative to private capital movements. They would have been surprised also to see some of today's poor countries undertaking to skip the capitalist stage of development.

This having been said, one is impressed by how many of today's central issues were central also in classical economics. Brief listing of these may serve to summarize the preceding discussion:

- the determinants of population growth, and the importance of relative rates of increase in population and food supply;
- the functions of the agricultural sector in a growing economy, as food supplier to the towns and as a market for industrial products;
- the importance of the intersectoral terms of trade, and the possibility that a continued movement of the terms of trade in favor of agriculture may choke off industrial development;
- the forces governing long-term trends in relative factor prices and in the functional distribution of national income;
- reinvestment of capitalist profits as the dominant mechanism for capital accumulation;
- the issue of optimal allocation of capital among economic sectors;
- the potential contribution to domestic growth of participation in international trade;
- the importance of government economic policies in stimulating (or possibly impeding) economic development.

These issues are perhaps discussed more precisely in contemporary development theory. But the increasingly narrow and technical character of modern economics has involved loss as well as gain. A comment of Joan Robinson's concerning Marx could be broadened to include other classical writers: "The orthodox economists have been much preoccupied with elegant elaborations of minor problems, which distract the attention of their pupils from the uncongenial realities of the modern world, and the development of abstract argument has run far ahead of any possibility of empirical verification. Marx's intellectual tools are far cruder, but his sense of reality is far stronger, and his argument towers above their intricate constructions in rough and gloomy grandeur." [Robinson (1957, p. 2)].

The classical writers worked close to the earth. They had a rich understanding of the economic process. Nor did they hesitate to talk demography, psychology, politics, and ethics. Instead of worrying about how far they could go before transgressing the boundaries of their discipline, they asked how far they must go to reach the boundaries of a problem. In this, as in other respects, we can still learn from them.

8. References

Adelman, I., 1961, Theories of economic growth and development (Stanford University Press, Stanford, CA).

Fellner, W., 1960, Emergence and content of modern economic analysis (McGraw-Hill, New York).

Hicks, J. R., 1965, Capital and growth (Oxford University Press, New York and Oxford).

Marx, K., 1867, Capital, German edition. First English edition edited by F. Engels, 1887. Many subsequent editions.

Mill, J. S., 1848, Principles. Many subsequent editions, of which the most widely used is: W. J. Ashley, ed., 1909 (Longmans, Green & Co, London).

Myint, H., 1958, The 'classical theory' of international trade and the underdeveloped countries, Economic Journal LXVIII, June, pp. 317–337. Reprinted in: H. Myint, 1971, Economic theory and the underdeveloped countries (Oxford University Press, London and New York).

Quesnay, F., 1758, Tableau économique (Paris).

Ricardo, D., 1817, The principles of political economy and taxation. Many subsequent editions, including the recent and definitive by: P. Sraffa, 1951, The works and correspondence of David Ricardo, vols. 1–10 (Cambridge University Press, Cambridge).

Robbins, L.C., 1968, The theory of economic development in the history of economic thought (St. Martin's Press, New York).

Robinson, J., 1957, An essay on Marxian economics (Macmillan, London).

Schumpeter, J., 1954, History of economic analysis (Oxford University Press, New York).

Smith, A., 1776, The wealth of nations. Many subsequent editions, of which the most commonly used is the Modern Library edition edited by Edwin Cannan, 1904 (6th ed. in 1950).

Chapter 2

Economic Development and Financial Institutions

Gustav RANIS

1. Introduction

There has been relatively little effort in the literature to systematically deal with the role of financial institutions and policies in the context of development.[1] Not unlike conventional macro-economics focussing on the mature industrial world, such considerations customarily assume their place in the sun mainly when we enter into discussions of the short run but are relegated to a separate and unequal status in considerations of the long run. Admittedly, business cycle problems rear their ugly head in both the rich and the poor countries; but their importance in the supply-constrained Say's Law environment of the developing world is surely much smaller – and thus the cost of the relative neglect of the financial dimension much larger.

We can perhaps achieve agreement on this without too much difficulty; but where to start and how to insert the analytical scalpel is quite another matter. This paper is not so presumptuous as to attempt a specific answer; it is intended to do little more than suggest one possibly fruitful avenue of approach. The heart of that approach is a plea for more historical and typological sensitivity. There is, we believe, relatively little mileage in analyzing the role of financial institutions in "the" developing economy irrespective of time or place. In fact, an awareness of such typological and/or historical differences may be an essential ingredient if we are to be in a position to treat the financial sector as an integral part of the development problem rather than as an isolated, if fascinating, after-thought.

We take as our starting point Kuznets' apt definition of the development problem as an attempt at transition from a long epoch of agrarianism to a long epoch of modern growth. Such a transition, if successful at all, is likely to last 20 to 50 years or more and is itself, moreover, likely to be composed of a number of distinct sub-phases during which the develop-

[1]For some of the few exceptions, see Goldsmith (1969), Gurley (1967), McKinnon (1973), Patrick (1966) and Shaw (1973).

mental characteristics of the society undergo substantial change. Specifically, developing societies seem to first move out of dependent (or colonial) agrarianism into independent (or post-colonial) primary import substitution; from there into either secondary import substitution or export substitution; and finally, if successful, into modern growth. Each phase or sub-phase, moreover, has differing requirements, if transition is to be achieved, with reference to the nature of the appropriate financial institutions and policies.

This is the basic framework within which we will be operating. We hasten to reassure the reader on two counts. One, we do not believe in any "inevitable" historical stages of growth; however, if one does observe marked changes in endowment, in the pattern of resource utilization, and in policy over time indicating gradual changes of the rules of the game, there is no reason to permit the ghost of Rostow to forever scare us off. Secondly, we recognize that "natura non facit saltum" – not even when countries would like to – and that the movement from one sub-phase of growth to another must be viewed not as a quick orderly switch but rather as a gradual and irregular transition over a period of years, with many characteristics remaining unchanged, with others changing randomly, and only the behavioral center of gravity undergoing predictable variation.

In Section 2 we briefly describe the main outlines of the typical LDC transition process in the ideal sense and then attempt to relate it to the idealized changing role of financial institutions and policies. Historical Japanese and contemporary Taiwanese experience will be viewed as a proto-type. Section 3 is devoted to an analysis and explanation of the preponderance of real world deviations from this ideal pattern – on both the real and financial fronts. Philippine and Brazilian experience will be cited. Section 4, finally, is devoted to a summary of findings and to the conclusions for policy emanating from the analysis.

2. The "Deviant" LDC in Transition

The curtain of historical development may be arbitrarily raised on the so-called colonial agrarian epoch when the overseas territories have already been impacted by the investment, trade and (sometimes) political and military presence of the (then already advanced) Western world. The essential, necessarily caricatured, characteristics of that period include the existence of a raw materials or minerals intensive export-oriented enclave, complete with ancillary services and (limited) auxiliary industrial activities, side by side with a relatively large and relatively stagnant food-producing agricultural hinterland. The proceeds of this natural resources-based export activity are deployed in part to finance the luxury consumption needs of the domestic and foreign elite, in part to provide industrial consumer goods to help pull workers out of subsistence agriculture and into enclave activities, and in part reinvested in the further expansion of these activities – or reinvested abroad.[2]

The financial structure to accommodate the requirements of such a dependent economic system are as quickly summarized. With respect to the larger, relatively stagnant, agricultural hinterland, any system approaching the "circular flow" of the physiocrats makes minimum demands on financial institutions and policies. This is not to deny that the absolute volume of traditional finance for traditional purposes may be substantial in toto. To the extent domestic trade gradually expands, the demand for capital other than of the traditional wages fund variety, of course, also expands, e.g., for roads, transport, marketing facilities, etc.[3] But while the money economy is bound to be gradually displacing pure barter, to the extent little is happening on the real side, little is required on the financial side, either to lead or to accommodate.

Most of the dynamic activity – both real and financial – is focussed in the export enclave and those services and industrial activities which facilitate its functioning and expansion. An important component of that accommodating service sector activity is, in fact, the banking function, sometimes tied up with management and enclave operations in the form of the East India Company proto-type – as a forerunner of the modern multinational corporation – more often an expatriate specialized bank at the service of the exporting and investing elite, foreign and domestic.[4]

For our purposes the colonial agrarian epoch is of interest mainly by way of contrast with what follows. Once political independence is achieved – after World War II in most developing countries, earlier in Latin America – governments almost invariably attempt to restructure colonial production and trade patterns to facilitate national development. This effort most often takes the, by now well-known, form of a primary import substitution sub-phase. The overriding objective becomes the creation and/or expansion of the industrial sector, especially in previously imported consumer goods, and of the services and overheads required to

[2]Whether or not net foreign investment takes place, or capital is repatriated, depends mainly – aside from political considerations – on the foreign demand prospects for the enclave product, relative to other opportunities facing the foreign investor. Moreover, as McKinnon (1973) has pointed out: "insofar as indigenous individuals in the colony participated in the process of bank intermediation, they were depositors rather than borrowers."

[3]See Fei and Ranis (1969).

[4]Foreign branch banks were integrated exclusively into the system of the metropole [see Nevin (1961)].

facilitate that expansion. The main tool is government's acquisition of control over the traditional export earnings and their reallocation to industry and overheads via exchange controls and licensing. These are the bare essentials of import substitution. Usually they are accompanied by substantial protection of the fledgling industries, either via tariffs, more often via import quotas, accompanied by expansionary fiscal and monetary policies and associated with inflation and an increasingly overvalued exchange rate – all intended to drive complementary domestic resources into the same hands.

Much has been written in criticism of the import substitution policy syndrome in developing countries.[5] We do not wish to add to it here. But, faithful to our historical perspective, we will simply assert that such a sub-phase is likely to be an important ingredient for a successful transition to economic maturity whenever entrepreneurial capacity is initially weak and physical (especially rural) infrastructure deficient. In other words, we believe that an infant industry/infant entrepreneurial argument in general has merit and that much of the criticism of import substitution along the Little–Scitovsky–Scott lines is really – and quite properly – directed towards the question of how much, what kind, and for how long.[6]

If that is the case, we can proceed to the question of the appropriate role of financial institutions and policies in the context of the primary import substitution sub-phase of transition. The banking system clearly represents an important additional instrument in the government's effort to shift resources, domestic as well as foreign, into the hands of the nascent industrial entrepreneurial class (or possibly into the government's own hands wherever the public sector is involved in overhead construction and/or in directly productive activities). It accomplishes this, in part, by holding government debt and assuming the role of docile partner to government deficit financing efforts. Floors are often placed under banks' holdings of "safe" low interest government bonds and ceilings on their holdings of other "unsafe" assets to accomplish this purpose. In this nominal sense financial institutions accommodate the government's needs, usually in the absence of an adequate fiscal capacity, to force some saving via the process of inflation and to simultaneously shift the functional distribution of income in favor of profits.

Interest rate policy represents another important instrument in the arsenal of import substitution. By keeping official rates low (often

[5]See, in particular, Little, Scitovsky, and Scott (1970). Also Cohen and Ranis (1971).

[6]For a fuller statement, see Ranis (1972), as well as the exchange with Eckstein, Ruggles and Stolper which follows.

negative in real terms) governments claim to be encouraging overall investment (which, given the customarily high marginal efficiency of capital, is doubtful) while channeling the limited credit available into the hands of the new industrial elite. The Central Bank similarly shifts the foreign exchange proceeds, which must now be surrendered, to the same favored class at artificially low (overvalued) rates of exchange. There is an attempt to bring in as much foreign capital as possible – initially, aid and, increasingly with time, private capital on very favorable terms.[7] The financial system thus serves the import substitution regime's main purpose of shifting resources and providing unearned profits to the new consumer goods industries.

During this period there clearly exists a premium on "getting things done", with relatively little concern with its level of efficiency or inefficiency. It is the brute act of saving and its redirection which is the overriding objective, not the finer points of efficient allocation and management. Traditional raw material exports – supplemented by foreign capital – continue to provide the main foreign exchange fuel for the primary import substitution industrialization process. Domestic saving emanates from the direct reinvestment of industrial profits and from the surpluses generated by agriculture. Even the less extreme import substitution policy packages, if not single-mindedly industry-oriented, tend to discriminate against domestic food producing agriculture – e.g., via unfavorable terms of trade, infrastructural neglect, overvalued exchange rates, etc.; consequently, the contribution of agricultural saving, the main source of household saving, is likely to be limited.

More modest or flexible manifestations of primary import substitution, such as experienced by Japan in the latter half of the nineteenth century,[8] or by Taiwan in the 1950's, are, on the other hand, quite consistent with substantial increases in agricultural productivity and the substantial contribution of agricultural saving from the beginning. Nineteenth century Japanese agricultural surpluses, either captured by the government via the land tax or channeled through private hands, provided the lion's share of the system's investment funds, especially in the early years.[9] But the heavy Japanese attention to food producing agriculture, even during

[7]The incentives given to private capital during this period often far exceed what is required to attract it, and carry the seeds of later dissatisfaction and conflict. For a fuller analysis, see Ranis (1976).

[8]The "mildness" partially enforced by extraterritoriality which restricted Japan's ability to maintain high protective tariffs. And, perhaps luckily for Japan, Schacht had not yet been born.

[9]The land tax, for example, provided more than 70% of total government revenue in the 1870's and 1880's and rent, mostly non-consumed, close to 60% of net agricultural output. [See Ranis (1959).]

import substitution, transmitted also to her colonies, seems to be rather unique.

Private saving in agriculture, if it does make a contribution, will, of course, continue to do so mainly in the form of direct investment in tangible assets such as the improvement of land via levelling, draining, etc., and the construction of other mini-infrastructure. As in the Robinson Crusoe case, in the absence of much agricultural/non-agricultural sector interaction, the preponderance of financial intermediation in this sub-phase is likely to proceed via the individual himself, or his family, and substantially back into agricultural activity. If food producing agriculture is relatively dynamic, as in Japan, some of these savings will flow into non-agricultural rural activities, for example, into silk production, cotton weaving, etc., which constituted more than 30% of the income of Japanese farmers by the end of the 19th century. In either case, the financial intermediation effort is focussed on the quantity of savings–investment, not on its quality. After all, we do not know how good Crusoe was at constructing his first fishing rod.

As is well known, this primary import substitution sub-phase of transition growth is bound to run out of steam sooner or later as LDC domestic markets for consumer goods are gradually exhausted. It is at this juncture that the society typically faces the crucial decision of whether or not to gradually shift to a non-traditional industrial export orientation, or to persist with import substitution, this time of the secondary variety – including capital goods, consumer durables and processing industries.

If recent LDC history is any guide, the majority of developing societies seem to prefer remaining on an import substitution course – if at all possible. Especially if the natural resources base is sufficiently strong to continue to provide the fuel for this ever more capital and technology intensive process, such a societal choice is very understandable since it presents the path of least (especially political) resistance. Strong vested interests such as the new urban industrial class benefitting from the high temperatures of the import substitution "hot house", and the civil service whose power (and sometimes income) derives in large part from the typical control system are naturally loath to give it up. As long as the natural resources don't give out – either on the (domestic) supply or (foreign) demand side – growth can thus be maintained, even though, at least for the labor surplus economy, it becomes ever more inefficient. However, the costs of continuing this strategy in terms of such other increasingly important development objectives as the reduction of under-employment and income redistribution, may rise over time.[10]

[10]Much more could be said on this important subject but this essay is not the place. See, however, Chenery et al. (1974).

In Section 3, we intend to further analyze the situation in the preponderant (non-deviant) majority of contemporary developing countries which seem to have chosen secondary import substitution. But first it is, we believe, instructive to deal with the path a few deviant countries have taken at the end of their primary import substitution sub-phase, namely that of export substitution, or a shift to non-traditional exports of the labor-intensive industrial type. Japan in an earlier day and Taiwan more recently undoubtedly chose this path, mainly under the pressure of their fundamental long-term natural resources scarcity. It is this direction which we consider "ideal" for at least the garden variety of labor surplus developing countries – even those, like the Philippines, and much of Latin America, with a substantially better natural resources base – and which requires, in turn, "ideal" changes in their financial institutions and financial policy framework.

The export substitution sub-phase is most easily – and briefly – described in relation to the presumed change in the economy's capacity to participate in international trade on a more competitive basis. If the major intended purposes of import substitution have indeed been achieved, i.e., the maturation of a newly emerging industrial entrepreneurial class and the construction of missing infrastructure, e.g., in agriculture, in the field of financial intermediation, and elsewhere, the economy should now be ready to increasingly expose itself to competition in the international markets for industrial consumer goods.

Such changes cannot realistically be effected overnight, nor are zigzags of policy and performance likely to be avoided; but the overall tendency is clear; if the infant industry argument has merit, the labor surplus economy should increasingly be in a position to shift from traditional land-based to non-traditional labor-based exports in its foreign trade and to a substantial increase in the level of mutual interaction between agriculture and non-agriculture on the domestic front.

The changes in the general policy package required to accommodate this change in the production and trading pattern are equally clear: gradual liberalization of a number of markets previously controlled, directly or indirectly, by government, mainly on behalf of the new industrial class. Specifically, we would expect foreign exchange controls to yield to tariffs, and tariffs in turn to be gradually lowered, while the exchange rate is initially devalued and then maintained at a more realistic level (if necessary, by frequent quasi-routinized, e.g., quarterly, adjustments); simultaneously we would expect there to be less need for deficit financing as both the government's tax base and fiscal capacity and the system's voluntary saving potential increase – hence a reduction of inflationary pressures; finally, and most important from the point of view of this paper, we would expect monetary reform to take place, focussing on substantially higher rates of interest and the consequent reduction of subsidies and the role of credit rationing in investment decisions.

With the reduction of inflation and monetary reform yielding more realistic real rates of interest, the differentials between official credit markets and the unofficial or "parallel" markets are bound to diminish, and the scope for an expanding network of financial intermediation likely to increase substantially. With domestic credit as well as foreign capital now priced more realistically, the market can be expected to have a larger (though still by no means exclusive) hand in determining allocations and enterprise survival patterns.

All this, of course, depends on the existence of the proper dynamically flexible institutional framework – whether it is to lead or to accommodate the increased desires of households and unincorporated businesses.[11] Government intervention, in fact, shifts from the force-feeding of designated industrialists, via the assignment of unearned profits, to the subsidization of a more and more varied and sophisticated institutional construction program by the public sector. Increasingly as the real economy becomes more export and efficiency oriented, the brute act of saving, fairly well served by intermediation through the family in agriculture and by the reinvestment of industrial profits in both rural and urban industry gives way to the need for greater efficiency in the allocation process. This is tantamount to the increased need for a specialized financial intermediation network serving the ever more demanding requirements of differentiated industrial activities. To return to our homely Robinson Crusoe analogy, interdependence in a competitive inter-island market would sooner or later require him to seek out efficient investors to match his saving effort.

If markets, especially foreign, are to be continuously expanded, the system will require an equally expanding and increasingly specialized financial intermediation network. Specialized banks, insurance and pension funds, savings and loan institutions – finally even bond and stock markets – can be expected to increase in importance as the portfolio needs of savers become more and more sophisticated and the distance between them and the equally more sophisticated investors grows. Thus, the relationship between money, quasi-money and GNP and that between the assets of all financial institutions and GNP, Goldsmith's financial intermediation ratio, are all likely to rise in periods of rapid LDC growth, as the economy makes its way through export substitution to economic maturity. While Goldsmith is not sure about the direction of causality, he

[11]See Patrick's (1966) distinction.

has found that the rate of growth of financial intermediation is positively associated with the rate of growth in real terms.[12]

Japan's historically mild import substitution during the early Meiji period gave way to an increased export orientation, accompanied by a larger role for market forces, near the turn of the century. While raw silk was the main export crop initially, cotton textiles constituted 35% of her total imports, and Japan did not become a net exporter of cotton yarn and cloth until about 1900. The policy shift from government ownership of major industries and the favoring of large-scale private industries via subsidies and preferential interest rates took place during the same period. Japanese experience illustrates that, if the period of protection under mild import substitution is used well, much of the infrastructure required for later successful export substitution will have been laid and can continue to be gradually expanded thereafter. One example, of course, is in agriculture where early public sector irrigation, research and education investments had a substantial and sustained pay-off. Another is in the area of the creation of an appropriate financial infrastructure. Postal savings were organized early in the Meiji period, taking advantage of the well-understood (and trusted) functions of an integrated national postal system. Small savers in large numbers (if not large amounts per capita) were attracted by this form of intermediation which, along with the land tax, helped finance government infrastructural expenditures. Increasingly in the course of the 19th century, public and private commercial branch banking was established in rural areas,[13] savings banks spread, government bonds were issued to households (instead of only to banks) and an increasingly diversified banking system took shape. Special banks were created for foreign trade, for longer-term investments in overheads, in industry and in the colonies. As Patrick has pointed out: "between 1868 and 1914 Japan's financial system . . . developed rapidly into a modern, pervasive, variegated system, providing a wide spectrum of financial services."[14]

The effective channelization of agricultural surpluses, aided by substantially positive real rates of interest (see Table 1), continued to be important in Japan after the turn of the century. The agricultural sector remained a substantial net contributor to non-agricultural investment and,

[12]See Goldsmith (1969, p. 48).

[13]Sometimes in the form of "quasi-banks" which were multi-purpose institutions growing out of trade and cash crop related credit advances.

[14]Patrick (1967). This seems to be borne out in current unpublished research by Goldsmith. See also the high level of monetization (not including time deposits) reflected in column 1, Table 1.

TABLE 1
DATA FOR JAPAN; 1887–1935.

5-year moving average centered on	M / GNP (current) (1)	Real GNP growth rate (2)	Rate of non-agricultural labor absorption (% change from previous year) (3)	Inflation (% price change from previous year) (4)	Interest on 6-month time deposits (avg.) (5)		Interest on secured loans (avg.) (6)		Gross saving rate (% of GNP) (7)
					Nominal	Real	Nominal	Real	
1887			3.9	−0.3	5.3	5.5	9.8	10.1	12.6
1888		3.6	3.8	1.1	5.0	3.9	9.6	8.5	12.6
1889		4.4	3.7	2.6	4.9	2.3	9.7	7.1	13.0
1890		2.7	3.6	0	4.8	4.8	9.6	9.6	13.7
1891		3.4	3.5	0.5	4.7	4.2	9.0	8.5	13.5
1892		3.0	3.4	0	4.8	4.8	8.8	8.8	13.5
1893		4.9	3.3	0.6	4.8	4.5	8.8	8.2	15.7
1894		2.8	3.2	3.4	4.9	1.5	8.7	5.3	16.5
1895		2.9	3.1	7.1	5.2	−1.9	9.1	2.0	16.5
1896		2.5	3.0	8.5	5.7	−2.8	9.9	1.4	16.8
1897		3.0	3.0	6.8	6.0	−0.8	9.8	3.0	17.0
1898		1.5	2.9	7.3	6.3	1	10.1	2.8	14.9
1899		2.4	2.9	4.9	6.7	1.8	10.6	5.7	14.0
1900		2.3	2.8	3.4	6.9	3.5	10.6	7.2	13.6
1901		1.6	2.8	2.7	6.7	4.0	10.1	7.4	13.1
1902		2.4	2.8	4.3	6.5	2.2	10.0	5.7	11.3
1903		1.8	2.7	2.6	6.3	3.7	9.7	7.1	9.7
1904	0.224	1.0	2.6	3.4	5.9	2.5	9.1	5.7	9.6
1905	0.230	2.1	2.6	4.7	5.6	0.9	8.7	4.0	10.1
1906	0.231	2.5	2.5	3.1	5.7	2.6	8.9	5.8	10.4
1907	0.238	0.8	2.5	1.8	5.6	3.8	8.9	7.1	12.1
1908	0.241	3.0	2.4	1.1	5.4	4.3	8.6	7.5	14.2
1909	0.240	3.3	2.4	2.2	5.1	2.9	8.2	6.0	14.5
1910	0.237	2.6	2.3	1.2	5.1	3.9	8.1	6.9	14.3
1911	0.235	2.2	2.3	2.5	5.1	2.0	7.9	5.4	14.2
1912	0.233	1.8	2.2	1.7	5.3	3.6	8.0	6.3	14.4
1913	0.227	1.7	2.2	0.3	5.4	5.1	8.2	7.9	15.3
1914	0.227	3.1	2.1	0.4	5.4	5.0	8.3	7.9	17.4

1915	0.227	4.9	2.1	3.9	5.2	1.3	8.2	4.3	20.8
1916	0.230	6.5	2.0	10.2	5.0	−5.2	7.9	−2.3	23.6
1917	0.226	7.3	2.0	18.4	4.9	−13.5	7.7	−10.7	24.6
1918	0.233	6.7	2.7	20.6	5.2	−15.4	8.1	−12.5	24.8
1919	0.245	5.7	2.7	17.3	5.5	−11.8	8.6	−8.7	22.5
1920	0.260	3.4	2.7	12.4	5.9	−6.5	9.0	−3.4	19.5
1921	0.276	0.7	2.7	5.3	6.1	0.8	9.5	4.2	16.3
1922	0.293	2.2	2.7	−1.1	6.3	7.4	9.8	10.9	15.1
1923	0.297	1.8	1.9	−1.8	6.3	8.1	9.7	11.5	13.9
1924	0.291	0.6	1.8	−1.0	6.3	7.3	9.6	10.6	13.8
1925	0.287	1.8	1.8	−1.0	6.3	7.3	9.6	10.6	13.8
1926	0.282	4.0	1.8	−1.6	6.1	7.7	9.4	11.0	14.3
1927	0.282	1.6	1.7	−2.2	5.8	8.0	9.1	11.3	15.0
1928	0.285	2.4	1.7	−4.5	5.5	10.0	8.6	13.1	15.2
1929	0.291	2.4	0.4	−5.9	5.2	11.0	8.1	14.0	14.9
1930	0.290	2.6	0.3	−5.3	5.0	10.3	7.7	13.0	14.3
1931	0.287	3.4	0.8	−4.0	4.7	5.7	7.2	11.2	14.2
1932	0.283	5.1	1.8	−3.2	4.5	7.7	6.8	10.0	13.8
1933	0.275	5.9	2.2	−0.7	4.3	5.0	6.5	7.2	14.2
1934	0.265	6.3	2.7	2.1	4.1	2.0	6.2	4.1	15.2
1935	0.262	6.7	2.9	3.4	3.8	0.4	5.8	2.4	15.6

(1) $M \equiv$ cash currency + deposit currency.
Cash currency = currency in circulation − cash holdings by financial institutions.
Deposit currency = demand deposits of all banks − checks, etc., held by banks.
(Source: *Historical Statistics of Japanese Economy*, Bank of Japan, 1962 [*HSJE*].)
GNP (current): at market prices.
(Source: *Estimates of Long-Term Economic Statistics of Japan Since 1868*, vol. 1, K. Ohkawa et al., eds., Tokyo, Toyo Keizai Shinposha, 1974 [*LTES*].)

(2) [*LTES*].

(3) Refers to those employed less those engaged in agriculture and forestry.
(Source: *Hundred-Year Statistics of the Japanese Economy*, Tokyo, Bank of Japan, 1966.)

(4) Change in consumer prices from previous year [*LTES*, vol. 8].

(5) Tokyo banks [*HSJE*].

(6) Tokyo banks (through 1929: "loans on deeds" [*HSJE*]; from 1930: "loans on bills" [*HSJE*]).

(7) Series disregards statistical discrepancies [*LTES*]. GNP (current) as in (1).

increasingly, industrial profits as well were committed to financial intermediation, especially via banks, in place of the virtually exclusive pattern of the reinvestment of industrial profits of the 19th century. On the other hand, we may note that securities markets and corporate bonds played no major role until after World War II.

The successful overall performance of the Japanese economy during this period is well known. Agricultural labor productivity increased in a sustained, if unspectacular, fashion throughout the period, as did GNP (see Table 1), keeping well ahead (low rates of) population growth. Saving rates, initially modest, rose to more than 20% by World War I; the sustained, if unspectacular, nature of this balanced export-oriented growth path yielded rates of labor reallocation sufficiently rapid to culminate in the end of the labor surplus condition by that time.[15]

Turning to Taiwan, the case of a contemporary LDC moving along a more sharply delineated "ideal" path, we may note (see Table 2) that typical, relatively low, real interest rates in official markets – along with a much higher informal market – were adhered to during the import substitution sub-phase of the 1950's, though nominal rates were set higher than in most post-war LDC's in the effort to curb the inflationary psychology. At the same time productivity in agriculture increased consistently, while land reforms and infrastructural investments combined to prepare the ground for fuller participation later on.

The shift from import to export substitution, accommodated by major changes in the policy package, occurred in the early 1960's. Stabilization and a decline in the rate of inflation was followed by devaluation coupled with import control liberalization and a substantial increase in the nominal rate of interest. As a consequence, the real rate of interest rose from an average of 10% in 1958–1960 to close to 15% in 1963–1965. At the same time the interest rate in the unofficial or "parallel" markets, deprived of some of their monopoly content, declined from levels of 50% on average in the late 50's to the vicinity of 25% per annum in the 60's.

While elements of credit rationing, of course, persisted, such changes in interest rate policy – even sharper in the case of South Korea where the policy changes occurred a few years later – do imply a much enhanced role for private saving via official intermediation channels and greater scope for the use of government monetary policy. As both Taiwan's and Korea's experience in the 60's showed, once saver confidence has been reestablished, the relationship between interest and saving rates probably weakens, saving becomes more closely tied to changes in the level of income, and interest rates safely decline somewhat again.

[15]At least in agriculture. The controversy on the date of the "turning point" need not detain us here. [See Minami (1968).]

At the same time (i.e., the 60's), the institutional structure of financial intermediation became more diversified and sophisticated, and household savers for the time had really viable alternatives to the unhappy choice between direct investment and acceding to the government as a monopoly borrower. As a consequence, the gross saving rate for Taiwan, less than 10% in 1954–1958, rose to more than 20% by the end of the 60's. Of this remarkable total, 70% came from household saving, more than 80% of which, in turn, made its way through financial channels.

During this period, the real performance of the economy picked up considerably. Agricultural labor productivity spurted (from 2% to 4% plus); the rate of labor reallocation, as indicated in Table 2, increased substantially; and the growth rate moved from 7% to approximately 10% annually. While overall exports grew at rates in excess of 30% annually by 1970 – with more than 25% of the GDP exported – what is even more interesting is the tremendous shift in composition from traditional land-based to non-traditional labor-based commodities. By 1970, labor-intensive industrial goods constituted more than 80% of total exports, in contrast to 25% in the early 1950's. This major restructuring of output and export patterns meant that, by the end of the 1960's, employment in the industrial sector had increased at such a rate that, in spite of still substantial (if declining) population growth, the surplus labor conditions came to an end, as indicated by rapidly rising unskilled real wages after that point.

A well-developed growing network of rural financial intermediation, via cooperative banks, farmer associations and commercial branch banking was, moreover, extremely helpful in ensuring that much of the industrial sector growth followed an efficient low cost pattern, much of it directed towards the expansion of rural industries, especially in food processing and in subcontracting for larger, including export-oriented, firms. It is a striking characteristic of the Taiwanese industrialization pattern that it remained efficiently labor-intensive through most of the 60's providing employment to some of the poorest farmers; as a consequence, more than 50% of farm family income was derived from non-agriculture by the end of the 1960's and the distribution of income in Taiwan remained one of the best in the world during this period of rapid growth.[16]

In the (milder) case of historical Japan as well as in the contemporary case of Taiwan, we may thus note some approach to the idealized pattern

[16]The Gini level near 0.3 is remarkably low by LDC standards – mostly in the 0.5 range. Even more interesting is that the initial rise anticipated by Kuznets did not take place. This contrast, for income distribution, of a secondary import substitution vs. export substitution choice is currently under study but cannot be dealt with here. [See, however, Fei, Ranis and Kuo (1975).]

TABLE 2

DATA FOR TAIWAN; 1954–1971.

3-year moving average centered on	$\frac{M_2}{\text{GDP (current)}}$ (1)	Real GDP growth rate (2)	Rate of non-agricultural labor absorption (% change from previous year) (3)	Inflation (% price change from previous year) (4)	Interest on deposits (average of 6-month and 1-year rates) (5)		Interest on secured loans (6)		Gross saving rate (% of GDP) (7)
					Nominal	Real	Nominal	Real	
1954	0.114	8.5	4.1	10.1			26.9	16.8	8.4
1955	0.121	7.0	2.1	7.4			24.6	17.2	8.7
1956	0.130	6.8	0	9.3			23.1	13.8	9.3
1957	0.157	6.2	7.5	6.4			22.4	16.0	9.6
1958	0.183	7.1	5.0	6.5	16.4	9.9	21.0	14.5	9.7
1959	0.200	6.7	4.0	10.1	15.9	5.8	20.3	10.2	10.4
1960	0.217	6.9	3.4	12.3	14.7	2.4	18.9	6.6	11.5
1961	0.241	6.9	3.4	9.6	13.5	3.9	18.0	8.4	12.7
1962	0.279	8.1	3.4	4.1	12.0	7.9	16.5	12.4	14.1
1963	0.310	9.7	4.9	1.5	10.9	9.4	15.7	14.2	16.2
1964	0.337	11.1	3.3	0.6	10.2	9.6	15.0	14.4	18.4
1965	0.364	10.8	2.2	0.6	9.7	9.1	15.0	14.4	20.1
1966	0.391	10.1	4.7	1.8	9.4	7.6	14.7	12.9	21.2
1967	0.408	9.4		3.9	9.1	5.2	14.4	10.5	22.3
1968	0.420	9.4	5.1	4.9	9.1	4.2	14.2	9.3	23.0
1969	0.433	9.7		5.0	9.1	4.1	13.6	8.6	24.1
1970	0.473	10.4	3.1	3.7	9.0	5.3	12.9	9.2	26.0
1971	0.531	11.2	12.1	3.7	8.5	4.8	12.0	8.3	

(1) M_2 = line 34 (money) + line 35 (quasi-money) + line 45 (time and savings deposits).
(Source: *International Financial Statistics*, various issues.)
GDP (current): book value, at current prices. 1972 GDP used in calculations is preliminary estimate.
(Source: *Taiwan Statistical Data Book, 1973* [*TSDS*].)

(2) Same as for GDP (current) in (1); 1972 GDP used in calculations is preliminary estimate.

(3) Not 3-year moving average; is % change from previous year only. For 1952–1966: refers to those employed (aged 12 and over) less those aged 12 and over engaged in agriculture. For 1967–1972: refers to those employed (aged 15 and over) less those aged 15 and over engaged in agriculture, forestry, and fisheries (since 1969, including servicemen). [*TSDS*].

(4) % consumer price change in year [*TSDS*].

(5) Average of 6-month time deposits at banks (year-end interest rate per annum).
(Source: The Republic of China, *Taiwan Financial Statistics Monthly*, April 1975 [*TFSM*].)
1957–1958: one-year preferential time deposits.
(Source: A. G. Chandarvarkar, *IMF Staff Papers*, 1971, 18:83.)
1959–1969: one-year savings deposits in banks at year-end (assumed compounding monthly at the monthly interest rate for year-end).
1970–1972: one-year savings deposits in banks (year-end interest per year) [*TFSM*].

(6) Nominal rates; effective rates may be higher. 1953–1955: secured time loans in banks at year-end (assumed compounding monthly at the monthly interest rate for year-end) [*TFSM*]. 1956–1969: same as 1953–1955, except "secured loans" instead of secured time loans. 1970–1972: secured loans at banks (year-end interest rate per annum).

(7) [*TSDS*]. GDP (current) as in (1).

described earlier. On the real side we encounter a gradual shift from land-intensive exports fuelling import substitution, to labor-intensive exports, with agriculture finally participating more fully via sustained productivity increase, and labor being reallocated, until the economy's labor surplus condition is ultimately exhausted and the transition to modern growth has been successfully negotiated. On the financial side, this requires the continued growth of a more and more complex financial intermediation system accommodating – and/or inducing – the generation and channelization of the agricultural surpluses, with organized money markets gradually reeducing the importance of parallel or dual markets, especially in rural areas, and providing fairer access to all comers. During this relatively market oriented export substitution sub-phase, we can thus expect the economy not only to obtain a higher level of efficiency but to be able to support a larger total effort, whether measured in terms of labor reallocation, rates of saving, or growth.

3. The "Non-Deviant" LDC in Transition

While the above export substitution path approaches some sort of idealized sequence, it has, in fact, been followed by only a small minority of so-called "deviant" LDC's. Most contemporary developing economies can be said to have more or less maintained their import substitution policy syndrome after the inevitable end of their primary import substitution subphase of development. As was pointed out earlier, the choice of secondary import substitution at this point essentially means "more of the same" – except more so. What is required basically is continuity of the policies previously in vogue – including with respect to financial institutions and policies. Specifically, in non-agriculture it means satisfying the ever increasing appetite, for capital and technology, of the new capital goods, durable consumer goods and processing industries – especially, of course, those in the hands of prime borrowers – and continuing to accommodate to the rising requirements for overheads of the public sector; in agriculture, it essentially means maintenance of the force-feeding of subsidized credit to large farmers, with relatively little attention to the effects on participation, on agricultural productivity, on default rates, or the generation of inter-sectoral saving.

We, of course, recognize that these "choices" of growth paths, and of accompanying policy packages, are never quite as clear-cut as all this in real life, but tend to fade into each other at the edges. But while there certainly exist substantial elements of both secondary import substitution and export substitution in the overall production and trade structure of most LDC's, the contrasts painted here are both meaningful and instructive. The performance of such "typical" countries as Brazil and the Philippines is sharply differentiable from the deviant minority we were discussing in the last section.

A labor surplus LDC which continues to persevere in traditional exports-fuelled secondary import substitution long after its changing endowment would seem to render it capable of beginning to shift to non-traditional industrial exports is likely to encounter ever increasing capital and technology requirements along the way. This means, in turn, that the burdens placed on the system's financial institutions, especially in terms of the quantity of saving which must somehow be generated and channeled, are substantially increased. The capital requirements for processing, durable consumer and most capital goods industries are generally substantially larger than those applicable to non-durable consumer goods. Lumpiness is more pronounced and public sector overhead and urbanization costs likely to increase. With the financial intermediation network, on the other hand, retaining, more or less, its import substitution characteristics previously described, the supply of domestic saving is not likely to increase *pari passu*. In fact, the resulting continued state of "financial repression", as Shaw calls it, means that neither the increased participation of households and of other medium and small savers nor the higher quality of allocation forced by greater competitive pressures is likely to occur as long as the official policy of artificial low deposit and lending rates persists. Instead, there is an even greater likelihood of resort to inflationary financing, public and private, at home, plus even more fervent attempts to attract capital from abroad, via special tax treatment and favored access to domestic loan capital. Consequently, both the choice of technology and of output mix are likely to become more and more distorted in terms of a basic endowment which can be expected to shift only gradually from its labor-abundant/capital-and-skill-short characteristic.

The accompanying relative neglect of food producing agriculture frequently leads not only to non-support from that sector – either via the domestic saving or foreign exchange route – but to the need to divert resources to the importation of foods. Ultimately, unless the outlook for the further expansion of natural resources-based exports is good – and/or foreign capital inflows make up the difference – customary rates of growth may not be long maintainable. And even if they are, increasing problems of maldistribution and unemployment in the more and more capital-intensive labor surplus economy are bound to create more and more social and political stress and strain. Thus, for one reason or another – and possibly both – even countries which have been navigating "successfully" through secondary import substitution waters, i.e., at 6–8% growth rates, may sooner or later find themselves in difficulties.

The post-World War II experience of the Philippines (see Table 3) may be viewed as representing one such case in point. Primary import substitution which started seriously after the war began to run out of steam by the end of the 1950's. Faced with a sharp deceleration in industrial growth and the inability to depend on a sluggish primary export sector to provide the necessary foreign exchange, the Government initially opted for devaluation and decontrol in the early 1960's. However, for a number of reasons, including the failure of food producing agriculture to provide the necessary support in the form of productivity and saving increases, and government unwillingness to provide for real import liberalization by tackling the highly protective tariff structure, this incomplete venture into export substitution proved unsuccessful. Largely as a consequence, decisions, especially after 1968, can be said to have taken the Philippines firmly down the secondary import substitution path. Two decades of heavy protection have thus left the Philippines with an increasingly capital-intensive geographically highly concentrated industrial structure relying for its continued – if every more costly – growth on the expansion of traditional exports. In spite of respectable overall growth rates, in excess of 6% in most years, not only social but even private rates of return in the industrial sector have been declining. Even more significant has been the increase in underemployment and the worsening distribution of income.

The strikingly dualistic characteristic of Philippine development extends as well to its financial institutions and markets. A highly organized official market catering mainly to the large-scale urban industrial sector, on the one hand, and plantation-style export crops, on the other, exists side by side with unorganized markets serving small industrial enterprises (rural and urban) and food producing agriculturalists. Nominal annual rates of interest at saving banks, governed by usury laws, remain in the vicinity of 12–14% (with effective rates somewhat higher) while interest rates in the informal markets vary between 60 and 400%.[17] Interest rates offered to depositors are also regulated and even more in disequilibrium. Within the official market, small savers can obtain no more than 6–8% nominal, but larger savers do have access to both commercial and government deposit substitutes which earn substantially more. In addition to the disequilibrium low levels of both organized sector deposit and loan

[17]Contrast this with an estimated real rate of return (before taxes) on assets in manufacturing around 15% by the end of the 1960's leading to an average nominal rate of return of between 20% and 25% minimum [see Ranis (1974)].

rates, we may thus note the large legally induced "spread" creating what must be regarded as a regulated banking oligopoly.[18]

The growth of financial institutions, measured either by the Goldsmith financial intermediation ratio or the (easier to obtain) relationship between M_1, M_2 and GNP, first accelerated and then (by the late 60's) reversed direction. The banking system became more diversified and non-bank financial institutions grew substantially, but most of the growth, qualitative and quantitative, continued to affect the two enclave sectors. An examination of the distribution of loans actually made by the official banking system illustrates this further. Between 1958 and 1967, for instance, the smallest 20% of the loans absorbed less than 1% of the loans made, while the largest 20% of the loans absorbed more than 90% of loan value.[19] Little financial intermediation was directed towards extending the capillary activities between these and agricultural plus small-scale (including rural) non-agricultural activities.[20] The gross saving rate rose steadily towards a peak of 21% in the late 60's but has declined more or less consistently thereafter (19% in 1972). Yet the increasingly capital-intensive and skill-intensive character of the industrialization process has heightened capital requirements and lowered the (social and even the private) rate of return. Increasingly, in its efforts to prolong the import substitution regime, the Philippines has been forced to try to find new raw material sources (e.g., bananas and now oil). In the absence of a major break-through by virtue of the bounty of nature, we can thus anticipate an increasingly costly industrial development pattern, with the terms of trade deteriorating further and, given the secularly stagnant food producing agricultural sector, an increasing proportion of export proceeds having to be diverted to the importation of food. Moreover, given the inherently labor surplus condition of much of the Philippines, continuation along the present narrow growth path would, even in the advent of a new natural resources bonanza, be politically difficult to maintain in terms of the negative employment and distributional outcomes which can be expected.

[18]The argument by the banks that the present "spread" is necessary as compensation for services rendered as financial intermediaries must be judged to be largely spurious. Banks needing such a spread must be operating highly inefficiently, and the economy would generally stand to benefit from the elimination of same, which would result from the more competitive behaviour of the group.

[19]Default rates, among farmers, in the Philippines were in the 50–75% range in the mid-60's [see Gimenez (1965, p. 47)]. Contrast this with the 5% level for Taiwan [see Shen (1970, p. 205)].

[20]The fastest growth was recorded in investment houses, trust funds and finance companies, less subject to fixed interest rate policies, but which effectively exclude participation by potential small savers. The same thing is true for such short-term papers as bankers' acceptances and Central Bank certificates of indebtedness, a market which serves institutional investors and wealthy families only.

TABLE 3

DATA FOR THE PHILIPPINES; 1954–1971.

	3-year moving average centered on	$\frac{M_2}{\text{GDP (current)}}$ (1)	Real GDP growth rate (2)	Rate of non-agricultural labor absorption (% change from previous year) (3)	Inflation (% price change from previous year) (4)	Interest on deposits (average of 6-month and 1-year rates) Nominal (5)	Interest on deposits Real (5)	Interest on secured loans Nominal (6)	Interest on secured loans Real (6)	Gross saving rate (% of GDP) (7)
[A]	1954	0.182	8.7		−1.5					11.9
	1955	0.186	7.7		2.1					11.8
	1956	0.195	5.7		1.9					12.6
	1957	0.198	5.1	1.5	2.2					13.1
	1958	0.205	4.8	−4.7	0.3					13.7
	1959	0.207	4.7	7.3	2.1					13.4
	1960	0.217	4.7	1.2	3.0					15.1
	1961	0.234	2.7	8.0	4.4			7.8	3.4	16.9
	1962	0.250	5.0	3.5	5.7			8.0	2.3	19.2
	1963	0.253	4.5	7.6	7.7			8.0	0.3	20.1
	1964	0.244	6.1		6.3			8.3	2.0	20.3
	1965	0.241	4.9		5.2			8.8	3.6	20.2
	1966	0.257	3.9	6.2	4.7	5.8–6.3	1.1–1.6	9.4	4.7	20.0
	1967			−2.3						
[B]	1968	0.282		6.7	3.6	6.0–6.3	2.4–2.7	9.9	6.3	21.3
	1969	0.285	3.1	−7.0	8.5	6.3–7.0	−2.2– −1.5	10.4	2.1	21.4
	1970	0.277	5.1		16.3	6.5–7.7	−9.8– −8.6	11.0	−5.3	21.1
	1971	0.265	4.8			6.5–8.0		11.4		20.8

(1) M_2 = line 34 (money) + line 35 (quasi-money) + line 45 (time and savings deposits).
(Source: *International Financial Statistics*, various issues.)
GDP (current): at current prices.
(Source: [A] *Statistical Reporter*, 1969, Vol. 13, No. 1 [*SR*]. [B] N.E.D.A., *The National Income Accounts 1967–1972*, Manila, 1973 [*NEDA*].)

(2) Same as for GDP (current) in (1), for [A] million P of 1955, for [B] million P of 1967.

(3) Not 3-year moving average; is % change from previous year only. "Non-agricultural" refers to employed persons in labor force not engaged in agriculture, forestry, hunting and fishing.
1957–1968: figures are for October.
(Source: *1971 Statistical Handbook of the Philippines*, Bureau of the Census and Statistics, Manila.)
1969: figure calculated from May 1968 to May 1969.
(Source: *The BCS Survey of Households Bulletin*, May 1968, no. 25 and May 1969, no. 27.)

(4) 1953–1957: % consumer price change in Manila (December to December).
1958–1971: % consumer price change for Philippines (December to December).
(Source: *Statistical Bulletin*, Central Bank of the Philippines, various issues.)

(5) Interest on time deposits in commercial banks at year-end.
(Source: *Philippine Financial Statistics*, Central Bank of the Philippines, December 1973.)

(6) Nominal rates for commercial banks (average for year); effective rates may be higher.
(Source: *Sharing in Development: A Programme of Employment, Equity, and Growth for the Philippines*, ILO, Geneva, 1974.)

(7) Same as for GDP (current) in (1).

TABLE 4

DATA FOR BRAZIL; 1961–1971.

3-year moving average centered on	$\frac{M_2}{\text{GDP (current)}}$ (1)	Real GDP growth rate (2)	Inflation (% price change from previous year) (3)	Finance company interest rate for borrower (4)		Finance company bill of exchange yield (5)		Gross saving rate (% of GDP) (6)
				Nominal	Real	Nominal	Real	
1961	0.282	8.4	43.2	23.9	−19.3			
1962	0.271	5.7	60.1	28.6	−31.5			19.9
1963	0.255	3.2	74.8	35.2	−39.6			21.0
1964	0.250	2.4	69.2	37.8	−31.4			22.2
1965	0.238	3.6	54.9	37.8	−17.1			21.1
1966	0.240	4.2	32.6	34.9	2.3	72.8	40.2	20.3
1967	0.239	6.4	29.6	34.3	4.7	65.3	35.7	21.8
1968	0.255	7.7	23.5	33.9	10.4	57.0	33.5	23.2
1969	0.264	9.3	21.6	33.1	11.5	55.1	33.5	
1970	0.275	9.9	19.6	31.0	11.4	53.8	34.2	
1971	0.301	10.4	18.6	28.4	9.8	52.4	33.8	

(1) M_2 = line 34 (money) + line 35 (quasi-money) + (time and savings deposits at end of year). Figure for 1965 savings deposits not known.

(Source: Lines 34 and 35 from *International Financial Statistics*, various issues. Time and savings deposits from *Boletim do Banco Central do Brasil*, January 1974, vol. 10, no. 1.)

GDP (current): at current prices.

(Source: *Conjuntura Economica*, 1973, vol. 27, no. 12 [*CE*].)

1969–1972: preliminary estimates.

(2) [*CE*] 1969–1972: preliminary estimates.

(3) Refers to General Price Index (aggregate supply) – (December to December change) [*CE*].

(4) To 1966 [NESS].

1967–1970: (Rio de Janeiro) 180-day loans for working capital compounded monthly at the average December monthly interest rate.

(Source: *Boletim do Banco Central do Brasil*, 1974, vol. 10, no. 9 [*BOLETIM*].)

1971–1972: (Rio de Janeiro) 360-day loans for consumer credit compounded monthly at the average December monthly interest rate [*BOLETIM*].

1967–1970: (Rio de Janeiro) 180-day maturity; compounded monthly at the average December monthly interest rate [*BOLETIM*].

1971–1972: (Rio de Janeiro) 360-day maturity (year-end % interest rate per annum) [*BOLETIM*].

(5) To 1966: refers to 6-month exchange bills.

(Source: W. L. Ness in *Economic Development and Cultural Change*, 1974, vol. 22, no. 9 [*NESS*].)

(6) Flow of funds savings estimate [*NESS*].

The post-war experience of Brazil (see Table 4) may be viewed as representing another historical illustration of the path most LDC's have, in fact, chosen. After transiting from primary to secondary import substitution in the 50's, Brazil by the early 60's was experiencing all the previously stated symptoms of increased industrial inefficiency accompanied by increased financial "regression". On the real side we may note increasing industrial capital–output ratios and stagnant, if high, saving rates – with the contribution of households, given severe inflation, minimal. Financial intermediation remained relatively stagnant, with Goldsmith's financial intermediation ratio falling from 70% in 1948 to 55% in 1963.[21]

By the early 60's (see Table 4), even the rate of growth, fuelled by the reinvestment of industrial profits, the effects of public sector deficit finance and increasingly reluctant foreign investors, was becoming somewhat anemic. By the mid-1960's corporate self-finance amounted to more than 8% of GNP. Brazil's balance of payments problems had begun to mount and her inflation seemed out of control.

In the post-1964 period a new (military) government initiated a series of reforms, including devaluation of the exchange rate and partial abrogation of the anti-usury laws, which permitted a modest increase in the nominal rate of interest along with other components of a so-called export substitution or liberalization oriented policy package. At the same time, both the relative size and degree of diversification of the financial intermediation network increased significantly, accompanied by a narrowing of the interest rate spread between official and unofficial markets, on the one hand, and between lending and borrowing rates, on the other. Real interest rates gradually became substantially positive for the first time (see Table 4) as inflation declined from 70% levels to around 20% and nominal rates of interest rose as high as 50% for the case of finance company instruments.[22] Saving and loan associations and other specialized intermediaries assumed real importance for the first time – as witnessed by the fact that commercial banks were responsible for 94% of all loans to private borrowers in 1964, but for only 61% of a much larger total by 1972. Government bonds, previously sold almost exclusively to the banking system, now began to attract private customers – especially after the so-called monetary correction was introduced in 1968.[23] Both the

[21]In fact, Goldsmith found that less than 3% of gross national saving was channeled through these intermediaries. For a relevant discussion of the Brazilian case, see Montoro (1975).

[22]By using the device of letters of exchange whose legal return was fixed but which could sell at a substantial discount.

[23]This permits the indexation of government bonds along with many other monetary instruments. The overall role of indexation is a most interesting but large subject and cannot really be dealt with in the context of this paper.

M_2/GDP ratio and the saving rate reversed trend as a result of the reforms. What followed was a marked improvement in growth performance and, though we lack annual data, the rate of surplus labor absorbed in non-agricultural activities undoubtedly increased. Much of this additional labor absorption was reflected in such labor-intensive areas as footwear and related to a substantial export boom in recent years.

Nevertheless, as in the case of the Philippines in the early 60's, it is not at all clear whether Brazil has really determined to gradually shift to an export substitution type of growth path, whether she is backsliding or simply experiencing random oscillations in policy. Certainly, the experience of the most recent past provides room for doubt. Perhaps most important is the fact that the level of effective protection of Brazilian industry has undoubtedly again increased substantially, that more than 60% of the spectacular increase in exports in the early 70's was in primary products, and that an increasing proportion of her industrial exports was in the durable consumer and processed goods area and heavily subsidized.[24] Certainly Brazil's current emphasis on high technology and capital-intensive industries, e.g., in petro-chemicals, atomic energy, etc., in the presence of a still very substantial overhang of surplus labor, seems to argue in favor of the interpretation that the center of gravity may be shifting back towards a policy of secondary import substitution – if somewhat milder than in many other direct-controls-oriented LDC's. Growth rates are beginning to decline again; but, perhaps more significant is Brazil's unfavorable, and apparently worsening, income distribution record.[25]

4. Summary and Conclusions

As we have tried to show in an admittedly somewhat heuristic fashion, the appropriate developmental role of financial institutions and policies cannot be satisfactorily assessed independent of time and place. Instead, for the typical labor surplus economy, we have tried to differentiate among the functions to be performed in each phase of the transition process. This, in turn, has permitted us, with the help of some real world illustrations, to differentiate between an idealized or "deviant" and a

[24]Such subsidies are provided by the government in terms of differential interest charges, tax exemptions, rebates, etc. Moreover, multinationals are asked to export below cost in return for continuing to enjoy guaranteed high profits in the domestic market. Such "pushing out" of industrial exports may be termed "export promotion" to distinguish it from the more organic dynamic resource endowment-sensitive process of "export substitution".

[25]See Fishlow (1972).

more realistic or "non-deviant" pattern in the actual evolution of financial institutions and policies in the contemporary developing world.

The contrasts between these two sets are substantial and instructive. The deviant LDC utilizes its primary import substitution sub-phase not only to protect its fledgling entrepreneurs but also to construct the financial and physical infrastructure required subsequently, pays due attention to agricultural productivity increase, and transits before long into export substitution. It requires the help of a policy reform package and a financial intermediation structure flexible with respect to the changing tastes for real and financial assets as well as changing investor competence. The non-deviant LDC elects to move from primary to secondary import substitution, a move which implies an increasingly capital and skill intensive growth path and pressure for a continuation and, in fact, intensification of the existing policy package. This includes the relative neglect of agriculture and, with low participation by households and relatively narrow official intermediation markets, heavy reliance on public, corporate and foreign saving in satisfying rapidly growing industrial capital requirements.

Both sets of countries may show relatively good growth performance, but the first as a consequence of a gradual shift to fuller human resources utilization, the second via enhanced reliance on the natural resources base and/or foreigners. Pronounced differences are likely to appear even for those blessed with really abundant natural resources, i.e., in the income distribution and unemployment dimensions of development; and certainly for those not quite so lucky there arise questions as to the longer-term prospects of maintaining a satisfactory rate of growth itself – at least without incurring a prohibitively high structure of foreign debt.

If all but the really exceptional cases (e.g., the oil countries) are thus likely to run into increasing difficulties – as they, in fact, have – why, it may well be asked, does the majority of LDC's not shift their policies towards export substitution and away from secondary import substitution?[26] A large part of the answer is, we believe, that it is politically difficult to do so. The changes contemplated threaten not only the unearned profits of the new industrial elite but also the controls-related power (and incomes) of the bureaucracy. Small wonder that policymakers – who are presumably just as human as the rest of us – would prefer to avoid taking the unpleasant medicine of devaluation, credit and import liberalization if it can be avoided. The actual (or putative) availability of a friendly Mother Nature – and/or foreign donors – is

[26]It could, of course, be because the reasoning underlying this paper is seriously deficient; but this possibility is arbitrarily excluded.

ideally suited to strengthening the natural temptation to leave things more or less as they are. Policy-makers in our "deviant" minority group of LDC's, it should be noted, are not necessarily smarter or more virtuous, but rather more "up against it", without recourse to the same pleasant alternatives. Thus while, in theory, additional resources – whether via the bounty of nature or foreign lenders – should be all to the good, i.e., provide an additional potential advantage to a country contemplating a painful transition from one sub-phase to another, it may, in fact, not work that way in the realm of political economy. This is, in fact, akin to a generalized version of the so-called "Kuwait effect" on a country's exchange rate and balance of payments.

All this, of course, does not imply, that the majority of contemporary LDC's do not consider exports – especially industrial exports – highly desirable and are willing to go to some lengths to achieve a better performance in this regard. Even such strong proponents of import substitution strategies as Prebish have substantially moderated their views in recent years. But the difference is that the exports being generated by and large result from policies which "push out" exports artificially without a basic change in the import substitution environment. Notice, for example, that a substantial portion of the industrial exports of such countries as Brazil and Mexico in recent years has not been in the field of relatively labor-intensive non-durables but in such capital and skill-intensive areas as durable consumer goods. This attempt at an export orientation – which may be called "export promotion" – is thus not to be confused with "export substitution" caused by the gradually evolving play of comparative advantage, as liberalization replaces infant industry protection – but is rather the result of policies intended to subsidize industrial exports while maintaining the hot-house temperatures of import substitution.

Institutional devices are often created to help promote exports, e.g., the use of interest rate differentials and "special windows". Fiscal incentives are given and, finally, companies, including the multi-nationals, are pressured directly to export a certain portion of their output, even if below cost, in exchange for the guarantee of the maintenance of high unearned profits on the rest of their output in the protected domestic market. Thus the increased value of industrial exports by itself does not necessarily signal a switch to a more endowment sensitive growth path, nor does the establishment of additional specialized financial facilities to encourage industrial exports. An examination of value added at international prices will indicate that "crimes" committed in the name of export promotion can be just as costly as those committed in the name of the no longer as fashionable import substitution. As long as the golden goose of natural resources abundance doesn't give out – and/or the political problems attending a worsening distributional outcome can be handled – negative value added on both fronts can be "afforded". In any case, without the – often admittedly painful – changes in policy described earlier, the transition to a more efficient, broadly participatory growth path cannot be effected.

What is required, in short, is an uncommonly high degree of statesmanship. Mobilizing the rural sector early and in a sustained and persistent fashion; building the financial infrastructure required for the effective channelization of the resulting surpluses; and, finally, permitting the industrial sector to help finance its own future growth via export substitution all imply government actions challenging old habits and deeply entrenched interests. Small wonder that the greater the opportunity provided by natural resources or foreign capital the greater the temptation to use it instead to help postpone the day of reckoning.

Navigating towards economic maturity via some approximation to the idealized path sketched here – both real and financial – thus requires both technical competence and the political will to secure the necessary agreement among the various parties to the social contract. That some groups, e.g., small farmers, medium-scale entrepreneurs, and other economically disenfranchised elements would be likely to benefit from the proposed change of strategy is clear enough. But the fact that even the landlords and large-scale industrialist class stands to benefit, over the longer term, from a more rational interest rate policy, for instance, is less obvious. Such a change in the environment will call for a change in the *way* profits, or rents, are earned but not necessarily in the volume or even in the relative shares. A shift from monopoly to earned profits is likely to mobilize substantial underutilized entrepreneurial, managerial and innovative resources for the first time and thus lift the entire performance of the system onto new tracks. The alternative may well be that, in spite of all efforts to prop up declining rates of return, dwindling domestic markets and the increasingly difficult process of fuelling import substitution while pulling along a recalcitrant agricultural sector, will eventually boomerang for the very urban industrial class it is intended to protect.

5. References

Chenery, H., M. S. Ahluwalia, C. L. G. Bell, J. H. Duloy and R. Jolly, 1974, Redistribution with growth (Oxford University Press, London).

Cohen, B. and G. Ranis, 1971, Import liberalization and growth: The second post-war restructuring, in: G. Ranis, ed., Government and economic development (Yale University Press, New Haven, CT).

Fei, J. C. H. and G. Ranis, 1969, Economic development in historical perspective, American Economic Review, May.

Fei, J. C. H., G. Ranis and S. W. Kuo, 1975, Growth and the family distribution of income by factor components: The case of Taiwan, Economic Growth Center Discussion Paper no. 223 March, revised edition April (Yale University, New Haven, CT).

Fishlow, A. 1972, Brazilian size distribution of income, American Economic Review, May.

Gimenez, M. E., 1965, Credit delinquency, The Rural Banker XIII, no. 9–10.

Goldsmith, R. W., 1969, Financial structure and development (Yale University Press, New Haven, CT).

Gurley, J. G., 1967, Financial structures in developing economies, in: D. Krivine, ed., Rehovoth Conference on Fiscal and Monetary Problems in Developing States (Praeger, New York).

Little, I., T. Scitovsky and M. Scott, 1970, Industry and trade in some developing countries – A comparative study (Oxford University Press, New York).

McKinnon, R. I., 1973, Money and capital in economic development (Brookings, Washington, DC).

Minami, R., 1968, The turning point in the Japanese economy, Quarterly Journal of Economics, Aug.

Montoro, A. F., 1975, Some aspects of the recent development of the Brazilian financial system, Dissertation draft (Yale University, New Haven, CT).

Nevin, E., 1961, Capital funds in underdeveloped countries: The role of financial institutions (St. Martin's Press, London).

Patrick, H. T., 1966, Financial development and economic growth in underdeveloped countries, Economic Development and Cultural Change, Jan.

Patrick, H. T., 1967, Japan, 1868–1914, in: R. Cameron, ed., Banking in the early stages of industrialization (Oxford University Press, New York).

Ranis, G., 1959, Financing Japanese economic development, Economic History Review XI, no. 3.

Ranis, G., 1972, Relative prices in planning for economic development, in: D. J. Daly, ed., International comparisons of prices and output (NBER, New York).

Ranis, G, ed., Sharing in development: A programme of employment, equity and growth for the Philippines (International Labour Office, Geneva).

Ranis, G, 1976, The multinational corporation as an instrument of development, in: L. Goodman and D. Apter, eds., The multinational corporation and development (Yale University Press, New Haven, CT).

Shaw, E. S., 1973, Financial deepening in economic development (Oxford University Press, New York).

Shen, T. H., 1970, The Sino-American Joint Commission on Rural Reconstruction: Twenty years of cooperation for agricultural development (Cornell University Press, Ithaca, NY).

Chapter 3

Dynamic Competition and Technical Progress

Richard R. NELSON and Sidney G. WINTER*

1. Introduction

The concept of competition employed in formal economic theory suffers from anemia. Having been carefully bred over the years to emphasize the traits approved in the arena of formal theory, it seems to have lost most of the vigor that characterizes the verb "to compete" in the natural environment of everyday usage. The connotations of contest, rivalry and struggle have been suppressed; the resulting concept thrives only under equilibrium conditions, when the contest is over and has resulted in a tie. Many economists have lamented the change of meaning, arguing that it has not only deprived the concept of much of its positive content, but also has tended to obfuscate discussion of the normative significance of competition. In particular, the formal concept is very limited in scope; it identifies the state of competition with the limits of pricing discretion, to the exclusion of other aspects of firm strategy. It has been argued that competition, in the broad sense, may be both more vigorous and of greater social consequence in certain non-price dimensions. In his *Competition Among the Few*, William Fellner[1] comments as follows about the nature of competition among oligopolists:

> "While oligopolistic firms typically live in a state of quasi-agreement, quasi-agreements do not typically cover the entire range of the market variables . . . Quasi-agreements frequently allow the participating firms to handle certain variables on an individual-competitive basis, and these variables are apt to be more nearly associated with inventiveness than are the variables regulated by the quasi-agreement. The lowering of costs of production, product variation, and gains from advertising

*The authors are much indebted to Stephen M. Horner and Richard Parsons for research assistance and valuable suggestions. Financial support for this research was provided by the National Science Foundation under Grant SOC-705529 and by the Institute of Public Policy Studies at the University of Michigan; this support is gratefully acknowledged. A preliminary version of this paper was presented to the Econometric Society in December, 1974.

[1]Fellner (1949, p. 183).

are more nearly related to inventiveness than pricing. Inventiveness is the faculty of improving the conditions under which one is operating, by adopting methods which are unpredictable."

We will not review here the history of the complaints and rebuttals. We do want clearly to identify the central issue, *viz.*, whether it is appropriate to assume that choice sets are given and the outcomes of any choice known. If choice sets are given and the consequences of any choice known, the only function of competition is to get – or help get – the signals and incentives right. This is, indeed, the neoclassical position. But assume, contrary to present orthodoxy, that choice sets are not given, nor the consequences of choices known. While some choices may be clearly worse than others, there may be no choice that is clearly best, *ex ante.* On this assumption, one would expect to see a diversity of firm behavior in real situations. Firms facing the same market signals would respond differently, and the more so if the signals were relatively novel. Indeed, one would *hope* for such a diversity of response in order that the range of possible behaviors be adequately explored. One function of competition, in the structural sense of many firms, is to make possible that diversity. Another function of competition, in a more active sense, is to reward and enhance the choices that prove good in practice, and to suppress the bad ones. Over the long run, one would hope, the competitive system should promote firms that choose well on the average, and eliminate, or force reform upon, firms that consistently make mistakes.

On this view, the market system is (in part) a device for conducting and evaluating experiments in economic behavior and organization. The role of *ex ante* calculation by individual actors appears smaller than in the orthodox perspective; the manner in which market institutions structure the feedback to actual choices appears correspondingly more significant. The meaning and merit of competition must be appraised accordingly. Our use of the term "dynamic competition" is intended to distinguish the object of this appraisal from the narrower concept prevailing in orthodox theory.[2]

It should be obvious, given this portrayal of the central issue, that the analytical tools of orthodox theory are ill-suited for the study of dynamic competition. Those tools – founded as they are on the assumptions of well-defined choice sets and identifiable best choices – are predicated on the non-existence of the experimentation task that the dynamically competitive system performs. What is needed is a theoretical scheme

[2]Examples of the literature on dynamic competition include Schumpeter (1950, 1955), Clark (1955) and McNulty (1968), as well as the Fellner volume cited above.

within which firms act sensibly – but not necessarily optimally, and definitely not *identically* – in the pursuit of profit. And the scheme should permit a focus on the dynamic interactions of the firms, and the shaping of those interactions by market institutions and other forces.

These requirements are fully consistent with the orientation of our recent work on evolutionary theory. In the present paper, we examine some aspects of dynamic competition from an evolutionary point of view. We are concerned with modeling the influence of various considerations upon the level and rate of change of productivity within an industry. More specifically, we set forth a model and some simulation results bearing on the "Schumpeterian hypothesis" – the claim that the static allocational disadvantages associated with market power may be more than offset by the greater technical progressiveness of larger firms.

2. The Schumpeterian Hypothesis

The hypothesis involves considerations of both "supply" – i.e., the conditions of production of new technical knowledge – and "demand" – i.e., the incentives to produce it. Under both headings, the issues raised by Schumpeter and in subsequent discussion are multifaceted and complexly interrelated. The hypothesis has, thus far, resisted statement in a precise analytical form that would properly relate all the causal mechanisms that have been discussed.[3] At the level of ultimate policy implications, the situation seems to be more clearly defined than it is at the level of causal mechanisms: anything that indicates that an industry would be more progressive if organized into a few large firms rather than many small ones is regarded as pro-Schumpeterian evidence. As our analysis below makes clear, even this formulation is subject to ambiguities, and does doubtful justice to Schumpeter. The size distribution of firms is endogenous to the entire dynamic process, and cannot reasonably be regarded as subject to direct and continuous policy control. The formulation does have the virtue of simplicity, however, and we employ a modified version of it in this paper.

On the supply side, the considerations adduced in favor of the hypothesis include increasing returns to scale in the conduct of research and development, and the financial and risk-spreading advantages of the large firm. The returns to scale issue itself involves a number of disparate sub-issues. One is that at least some types of research and development

[3] Fisher and Temin (1973) have recently attempted a clarification of the issues. In our view, the attempt is not entirely successful.

output are characterized by indivisibility, hence there may be minimum input levels that are necessary for any output at all. Another is that some types of research and development *input* come in indivisible units – e.g., scientists with particular specialties – and thus the larger research and development team has the advantages of finer division of labor and broader coverage of esoteric areas of competence. A possible offset to these considerations is the difficulty of providing adequate incentives and flexible administrative control in a larger organization.[4] Theoretical analysis of these matters has been limited in extent and fairly inconclusive, in part because of the difficulties of conceptualizing research and development activities and their fruits; it is hard to formulate a precise notion of returns to scale in the absence of a precise notion of output. In the present analysis, since our principal concern is with the demand side of the problem, we adopt the "neutral" assumption that returns to scale in R and D are, in a precise sense, constant. Our particular formulation of the constant returns assumption is, we think, of some independent interest.[5]

As for the financing and risk-spreading aspects of the problem, they too play a precise role in our analysis. However, that role is shaped very strongly by our evolutionary approach, and we would not claim to have accurately captured the meaning of these considerations as they are presented in the literature.

In analyzing the demand side, it is first of all necessary to recognize the fundamental distinction between the degree of monopoly of specific technical *information* or capability and the degree of monopoly in the market for the *product* to which the information relates. The returns to innovation are related to both, but in quite different ways. Arrow, in his important 1962 paper, made this distinction and went on to analyze the case of cost-reducing innovation. He proposed that pre-innovation monopoly in the product market diminishes the incentive to innovate, *assuming* that the information monopoly (i.e., property right) is absolutely secure. The point is basically simple: the gross value of a method for reducing unit costs is proportional to the output to which it is applied; the costs of innovation are largely independent of output; competitive output is larger than monopoly output.

The patent system, and secrecy, provide a degree of monopoly power with respect to specific technical information. However, property rights

[4]See the discussion in Kamien and Schwartz (1975, pp. 9–10) and Scherer (1972, pp. 353–354).

[5]The same conceptualization could be used, of course, in formulating increasing or decreasing returns assumptions.

in information are both limited in scope and difficult to defend. Patent protection is almost totally ineffective in the area of strict process improvements – of "disembodied" technical change. It is of limited value in some areas of new product development, where it is relatively easy to "invent around" a patent, once the possibility and profitability of meeting a particular need have been demonstrated. In the absence of effective legal power to prevent unauthorized use, the marketer of a technical secret faces the problem of certifying the value of the information without disclosing it, along with the problem that a sale automatically produces an alternative source of the information for future buyers. Under these circumstances, the gross value of superior technical information to a firm may be just the value associated with its use in that firm, for as long as the secret is kept. To the extent that firm growth rates are bounded, and the information monopoly tends to leak away with time, the return to possession of such information will be directly related to the size of the innovating firm. Given the size of the market, firms will be larger in a relatively concentrated industry than in a fragmented one. This is the situation in the model we analyze – the returns to cost-reducing innovation exist only because imitation occurs with a lag, and output price thus remains temporarily above cost for the innovating firm. Financial constraints limit firm growth rates, and thus the size of an innovating firm at the time the innovation is made is a powerful determinant of the returns the firm will reap.

Emphasis on the *transient* rewards to innovation, and on the relationship between these rewards and size or market position, is fully explicit in Schumpeter's discussion in *Capitalism, Socialism, and Democracy.* A review of the antecedents of that discussion in *The Theory of Economic Development* will establish beyond doubt the central place of these transient profits in Schumpeter's vision of capitalist evolution. It is therefore curious that so much of the literature purporting to discuss the "Schumpeterian hypothesis" focuses on supply-side issues, particularly on the advantages of large scale and protected position as a "base" for innovation. While passages in this vein can be found in Schumpeter, and these ideas play a role in our own discussion below, it should be plain that "the process of creative destruction" does not extol the virtues of the quiet life for monopolists. Perhaps some of the contributors to the "Schumpeterian hypothesis" literature had actually been reading Galbraith, or perhaps the distortion is explained by the difficulties of dealing with transient profits within the framework of conventional theory. In any case, we hope that the present paper will clarify the issues.

3. A Model of Dynamic Competition: Overview

Before proceeding to the specifics of our formulation, we sketch the economic situation with which the analysis is concerned. Imagine an industry in which a number of firms produce a single homogeneous product. The firms do not collude; however, a firm with a large market share is capable of recognizing that it does not face a perfectly elastic demand, and will engage in some form of output restraint. With given technical knowledge, production is characterized by constant returns to scale. Input prices facing the industry are constant. It is possible to discover lower cost methods of production by two methods – by doing research which draws on the general fund of relevant technical knowledge (which is independent of events in the industry), and by imitating the production practices of other firms. To obtain information from either of these sources is a costly, time-consuming and uncertain business – but once a firm has acquired new technical information it can apply it to its entire capacity without further cost.

Each firm faces the problem of deciding how much to invest in efforts to obtain new techniques by the two available methods. Assume, however, that the "fundamental paradox of information demand" [Arrow (1962)] holds in a strong form: A firm cannot know, without expending resources on research and imitation, either the technical information it would acquire if it *did* make the expenditures, *or* the cost levels that this information would make possible. It is entirely plausible for the firms to be thus ignorant: So far as research is concerned, the "general fund of relevant technical knowledge" may be changing over time according to unknown laws. The fruits of imitation effort, on the other hand, depend on the research policities of other firms in general – which a firm cannot know *a priori*, and which also may be changing over time. In keeping with our earlier characterization of dynamic competition, the firms in the model are fundamentally ill-informed about their choice sets.

We assume, also, that capital markets are imperfect and firms must rely heavily on internal funds to finance investment. This is the only natural assumption in this context since lenders are presumably even less knowledgable about the payoffs to alternative firm strategies than are the firms themselves. Even if an optimal strategy existed, and were in fact displayed by some firm, the impossibility of knowing that this is the case would imply that lenders would be unwilling to make indefinitely large loans at fixed terms. Thus, whatever a firm's desired expansion rate may be in a given situation, its achievable expansion rate will be bounded by financing constraints.

The theoretical question is, what determines the technical progressiveness of such an industry? And what are the roles of firm size and market power in determining that progressiveness? From an orthodox point of view, we have pretty much barred the way to useful analysis of this problem by insisting that the firms do not have the ability to see through it. When the individual economic actors are baffled by their problems, so is the orthodox analyst.

4. An Evolutionary Approach

Real firms, however, do not have the problem of obeying the elaborate canons of rationality that economists generally ascribe to them. They only have the problem of taking action. Suppose, therefore, we abandon the attempt to build subtle models of a complex future into the "minds" of our theoretical firms, and design instead some rough and ready firms that are able to make decisions, and sometimes money, in a world they do not really understand. We can then ask how a firm of this sort will fare in an industry environment, involving other similar (but not identical) firms and specified exogenous conditions. We can ask how the industry will develop over time, and whether strong forces will develop that tend to suppress certain types of behavior and promote others. And we can seek to determine how the evolutionary patterns would be affected by changes in the initial conditions and exogenous environment, including changes that might be brought about by policy measures.

In taking this approach to the dynamic competition problem posed above, our central assumption is that firms establish long-term policies with respect to the effort devoted to obtaining new technical information. These long-term policies serve as the "genes" for an evolutionary process. Given an initial population of firms of varying genetic makeup (but in other respects identical) and given a characterization of the exogenous environment, we can ask what sorts of selection pressures arise and tend to modify the distribution of policies in the population. Specifically, we can ask how research-oriented, innovative firms tend to fare compared to imitative ones.

The notion that policies toward information acquisition have a quasi-genetic character is, we think, behaviorally plausible. It is supported by the fact that there are good reasons to discount the relevance of past experience when attempting to judge the appropriate level of effort. There is first of all the uncertainty and time-consuming character of research effort – the experience from the past may just be an unrepresentative sample, and the sample size does not increase very fast. Furthermore, the historical character of the process makes inference difficult – at any time, something novel may appear in the exogenous technical environment that is of high relevance to the industry, and past experience may reveal little about the probabilities of such occurrences. Thus, ideas about how important it is to be technically progressive, or up to date, are (quite rationally) resistant to modification by experience. Also, organized research efforts have high set-up and adjustment costs; even if short-term fluctuations in the payoffs to such efforts were readily discernible, it would not pay to respond to them.

The firms in our theoretical scheme have, of course, other policies besides those related to technical information. They make short-run output decisions and investment decisions. They have accounting practices that provide an information base both for their own decisions and for those of the institutions from which they borrow. None of these policies and practices would get particularly high marks from an economist or operations researcher who carefully scrutinized them for internal consistency or "optimality". The policies do, however, have a plausible responsiveness to the main forces in the situation.

We describe below the structure of our evolutionary model. Since the present paper is only a preliminary report, and presents only illustrative simulation results, we will not attempt a complete characterization of the models' logic in either the analytical or computer program versions. We omit, in particular, discussion of the mechanisms of adaptive adjustment of research and imitation policies, the rules of entry and exit, and the features of the model that permit the treatment of cases where there are costs of changing technique (i.e., costs in addition to the costs of discovering the new techniques). None of these mechanisms and features are operative in the simulation runs presented.

Latent Productivity. A key feature of the model is the theoretical representation of the exogenous influence that we have hitherto called "the general fund of relevant technical information". Advances in knowledge relevant to an industry's technology can take the form of improved understanding of basic physical laws, or (at the other extreme) of invention of specific devices that can be incorporated in the industry's products. They might also take the form of additions to the stock of research methods, or of problem-solving "heuristics". The richness of this externally-supplied fund of ideas and devices, together with something like its "proximity" or "average applicability" to the industry's problems, must be a major determinant of the fruitfulness of research efforts conducted in a particular firm. It is this sort of notion that is invoked when, for example, interindustry differences in the intensity of research effort are attributed to differences in the degree to which the industries are "science-based".[6] And the same general concept is involved when the time-path of an industry's development is attributed to the "maturing" of its technology, i.e., to the gradual depletion of the fund of research opportunities.

It is plainly a hopeless task to model *in detail* the way in which such an externally-determined "fund" influences the success of attempts to achieve specific, economically significant advances. Indeed, one can view an industrial research project as being itself an attempt to trace out a portion of this relationship; effort is required to achieve advances precisely because the "givens" of the research problem bear no obvious relationship to its solution. On the other hand, it is equally clear that some theoretical representation of the role of the "fund" is needed if we are to obtain any valid insights into the ways that other considerations (including policy variables) influence the rate of technical progress. It is easy to believe, for example, that a patent life of seventeen years has a very different meaning in an industry based on a rapidly-advancing science than in one that lacks such a base.

Our response to this dilemma is to focus the entire analysis of technical progress on a single, easily understood measure – the average productivity of inputs. At each point of time, the production technique in an individual firm is characterized by a productivity level. This is expressed as output per unit capital; however, it is assumed that input proportions are fixed and productivity change is Hicks-neutral, i.e., proportional changes in productivity are identical for all inputs. The object of a firm's research efforts is to raise its productivity level. The *effectiveness* of these efforts in a given time period is determined, in part, by the level of "latent productivity". Latent productivity summarizes all the influences from outside the industry that affect the fruitfulness of research efforts in the industry, aggregated and expressed in the same terms in which individual firm techniques are expressed – average productivity of capital. Similarly, borrowing of technology from the other firm in the industry is here treated as a direct borrowing of the productivity level the technology makes possible.

In our terminology, efforts that draw on information sources external to the industry are called "research"; efforts to borrow from other firms are called "imitation". Implicitly, we are assuming that research and imitation are disjoint efforts, performed by different sets of people. In fact, the activity ordinarily called "research" or "research and development"

[6]See, for example, the discussion in Nelson, Peck and Kalachek (1967, p. 73) and Scherer (1970, pp. 373–376).

involves both what we call "research" and what we call "imitation". Also, it is probably true that all firms draw to some extent on both information sources, even if they have no organized research and development activity at all. Henceforth the terms "research" and "imitation" should be understood in the special sense just described.

Latent productivity does not strictly determine the results of research efforts; rather, it is a parameter of a stochastic process that generates those results. For a given research effort, a firm will tend to achieve larger productivity gains, the lower its productivity is in relation to the current level of latent productivity. But this is only a tendency: firms that are lucky – or, equivalently, that have a special research competence that is too subtle to model – will do better than those that are unlucky (or incompetent).

Firm State Variables. In its structure, as in its theoretical motivation, our dynamic competition model has much in common with the ones we have developed in other work. It is a Markov process in a set of industry states, where an industry state is specified by listing the states of individual firms and the level of latent productivity. The probability distribution of the industry state at time $t + 1$ depends on the state at t in a highly structured way; many of the critically important economic assumptions of the model appear as state transition rules. In very broad terms, the following features of this structuring are noteworthy: (i) The probability distribution for latent productivity at $t + 1$ depends only on the value of latent productivity at t (and perhaps on t itself) and is independent of other features of the industry state at t. (ii) The distribution of the next-period state for a given individual firm depends very directly on the current state of that firm, but other firms influence a given firm only through their impact on a small number of intervening variables, e.g., the market price of the industry's product. (iii) Price changes from period to period in inverse relation to industry output.

A "firm state variable" is a variable that is indexed by firm number and time, and that plays a causal role in the system. In the version of the dynamic competition model employed here, there are four such variables,[7] although there are many more firm-and-time indexed magnitudes that can be calculated as functions of the state variables and of parameters that remain constant over a realization of the process. Here, we will briefly describe the four variables and their roles, keeping details to a

[7]Actually, in the simulation experiments reported, two of the four state variables (R and IM) are constant over time, one (IM) is constant over firms. In this specific context, therefore, they could be regarded as parameters rather than state variables. But in our conceptual scheme, and in the computer program, they are definitely state variables, and we treat them as such here.

minimum. The state of firm j in time t is characterized by:

K_{jt}, *its capital stock.* Capital serves as *numéraire* in the system, so the unit of capital is "a dollar's worth". Depreciation is deterministic, as a constant proportional rate. Capital is fully utilized in every time period.

A_{jt}, *its productivity.* This has the dimensions "output per period per unit capital", equivalently, "output per period per dollar of capital". Thus, the output of firm j in time period t is $Q_{jt} = K_{jt}A_{jt}$.

R_{jt}, *its research policy.* A research policy is a commitment to a certain level of research expenditures per unit of capital. Thus the dimensions are "dollars per period per dollar of capital", hence "pure number per period".

Productivity growth increases output per unit of capital. Since costs per unit capital is constant by assumption, price will tend to fall (in a given state of competition) at the rate of productivity growth. Thus dollar sales per unit of capital will tend to be constant, and our research policy will tend to correspond to a policy of preserving a relatively constant ratio of research expense to sales – a policy that many firms actually seem to follow for extended periods.[8] What a firm buys with its research expenditure ($R_{jt}K_{jt}$) in a given period is a probability of sampling, in that period, on a distribution of productivity levels whose central tendency is determined by latent productivity. Specifically, the probability of a draw from the research distribution in a particular period is *proportional* to research expenditure, and it is in this sense that research is conducted under constant returns to scale.[9] When a research draw occurs and turns up a productivity level superior to the firm's current one, the firm moves to this superior productivity level in the following period. Diminishing returns therefore prevail in research *results* because, given the level of latent productivity, the expected gains from another draw become smaller as the achieved level of productivity increases. Thus, the metaphor runs: The more you spend, the more you get to look at the possibilities implicit in the current state of knowledge, and more you look, the more likely you are to see things that constitute an alternative productive technique. Given the level of your current technique, the more you see in the way of alternatives, the more you are likely to see something that is better than what you've got. However, the better what you've already got, the less

[8]See, for example, Mansfield (1968, ch. 2).

[9]The factor of proportionality and firm scales are so chosen that the upper bound of probability one is not encountered. We think of this scheme as a binomial approximation to a Poisson scheme in which the expected number of draws per period is proportional to research expenditure. The latter scheme would, of course, accommodate the possibility of multiple draws by a single firm in a single period, and would not involve any restriction on research expenditure.

likely it is that any given collection of alternatives will contain something that is better still.

IM_{jt}, its imitation policy. This is similar to R_{jt} in all respects, except that the distribution on which the sampling is done is not determined by latent productivity, but by the actual productivity levels of firms in the industry in the current period. Specifically, in the version employed here, imitation expense buys a probability of a "look" at current "best practice" technique, i.e., a probability of being able to switch to the highest productivity technique currently in use.

It has often been noted, in discussion of the "Schumpeterian hypothesis", that with a given research policy, a large firm will spend more than a small firm, hence will be closer on average to the frontier of knowledge. It has been less noted that for a given imitation policy a large firm will spend more than a small firm and thus on average will imitate faster other firms' innovations, and be closer to best practice. The significance of this point for the relationship between concentration and the degree of internalization of the returns to innovation has, we believe, been overlooked by others. Indeed, we had overlooked it ourselves until analysis of our simulation results forced us to think about it.

5. Industry Dynamics

Overview. Starting with a particular industry state, the flow of events in the model may be divided into four phases; at the completion of the fourth phase a new industry state is established. In the first phase, latent productivity changes in a manner that, as noted previously, is independent of the firm states. In the second phase, industry output is determined by summing individual firm outputs ($Q_t = \Sigma_j Q_{it} A_{jt}$), and the price of output is determined by a demand-price function. Various accounting magnitudes for individual firms, such as sales, production cost and research expense are also determined in this phase; these magnitudes are given functions of the firm state, the output price, and various constant parameters. In the third phase, the research and imitation processes yield the new value of productivity, A, in each firm.

Phase four involves the determination of investment, hence, the next-period capital stocks. Desired net investment is determined by the relationship of price and average production cost and by the firm's perception of its market share. However, investment is also subject to financial constraints, and cannot exceed a certain ratio to retained earnings. Since research and imitation expense reduce retained earnings, it is possible for a firm to be "research poor" – to be technically advanced, yet to be incapable of expanding because of the burden of its research and imitation costs.

The foregoing brief statement summarizes the causal links of the system that are reflected in the period-to-period transition rules. However, as the same rules are reapplied period after period in the dynamic sequence, feedback relationships arise that relate all the variables in the system to each other (with the exception that latent productivity affects, but is not affected by, the other variables). In particular, the total research expense of the industry will vary, with individual firm policies held constant, as a consequence of the differential capital growth of firms with high and low values of R.

Specific Transition Rules: Productivity (A_{jt}). With probability proportional to $R_{jk}K_{jt}$, firm j gets a research "draw". A draw is a sample of one on a log normal distribution, with the mean of the logs equal to the log of latent productivity. In addition, with probability proportional to its imitation expense $IM_{jt}K_{jt}$, the firm gets an imitation draw. In the present case, such a draw gives the firm the highest of the productivity levels displayed by firms in period t. The actual value of $A_{j(t+1)}$ is then determined by a comparison aimed at determining the largest of the three values A_{jt}, the result of the research draw (if any) and the result of the imitation draw (if any).[10] However, the comparison is subject to random error and the firm will not always pick the best of these alternatives.

Capital (K_{jt}). Firm investment policies are based on a target markup rule. The target markup factor, MU, is an increasing function of the firm's output share. If the current price exceeds the target markup factor times the firm's unit production cost, the firm will desire to make a positive net investment. Specifically, *desired gross* investment, $DESIN_{jt}$, is determined as follows:

$$DESIN_{jt} = \left[DEPR + KADJ \cdot \left(1 - \frac{MU \cdot UNCOST_{jt}}{PRICE}\right)\right] K_{jt},$$

where $DEPR$ is the (constant) depreciation rate, $KADJ$ is an adjustment coefficient, and $UNCOST_{jt}$ is the firm's production cost per unit of output. The latter is in turn determined by the firm's *next-period* productivity and by cost rate constants:

$$UNCOST_{jt} = \frac{RATE + DEPR + VCFAC}{A_{j(t+1)}}.$$

[10] We are assuming, in effect, that technical change is entirely "disembodied" and there is no scrapping of equipment or conversion cost involved in a switch to a new technique. This assumption eliminates from our model the problem of determining when an available new technique should be introduced, which was examined by Fellner in *The Influence of Market Structure and Technological Progress* (1951).

RATE is an interest rate, and *VCFAC* is the rate of variable input cost per unit capital, both taken as constants. So total production cost per unit of capital is constant, and cost per unit of output varies inversely with output per unit of capital.

Note that a firm's desired investment is not directly influenced by its research policy. If it can produce output at a marked-up cost that is below the prevailing price, it sees an opportunity to make profits by expanding capital and output. Its research policy may call for an increase in research spending, linked to this increase of capital. But the prospect of this expense does not deter the firm from expanding to take advantage of a profitable production opportunity.

A word should be said about the basic function relating target markup to the firm's share. Specific forms for this function can be derived, or rationalized, by familiar sorts of arguments. Suppose, for example, the demand function facing the industry is of constant elasticity *ELAS*. Then the rule

$$MU = \frac{ELAS}{ELAS - SHR},$$

where *MU* is the ratio of price to unit production cost, corresponds essentially to the Cournot reaction function, except that the adjustment is conceived of as relating to long-run capacity determination rather than short-run output determination. A firm in capital stock equilibrium, using this markup rule and the associated investment rule, is in long-run profit-maximizing equilibrium if the profitability of output changes is calculated on the assumption that all other firms hold output constant. In particular, the rule agrees with the ordinary monopoly solution at $SHR = 1$ (assuming $ELAS > 1$), and it agrees with competitive price-taking behavior in the limit as $SHR \to 0$.

Actual gross investment is bounded below by zero, and above by a financing constraint. The latter reflects a dividend payout rule that says that interest and dividends must add up to $RATE \cdot K_{jt}$; thus the firms actually pay out, in every period, the going rate of return times their assets. This implies that what is available to finance gross investment is the *excess* return, or economic profit, plus depreciation, plus borrowing. Borrowing consists, in effect, of the issue of consols; debt is never refinanced or retired. Maximum borrowing in a period is a proportionality constant *BANK*, times the excess return, NET_{jt}, provided the latter is non-negative, but zero otherwise. Thus, a firm can invest more than its excess return if *BANK* is greater than zero, which we assume throughout the paper. The implication is that a firm with a negative economic profit, NET_{jt} will necessarily have gross investment less than depreciation, and thus a smaller capital stock in the following period. A profitable firm can, if it desires, borrow to finance investment in excess of retained earnings. With $GRIN$ = gross investment, FIN = the amount that can be financed, and DEP = depreciation = $DEPR \cdot K_{jt}$, we have

$$\begin{aligned} GRIN_{jt} &= 0, && \text{if } DESIN_{jt} \leqq 0 \text{ or } FIN_{jt} \leqq 0, \\ &= \text{Min}\,(DESIN_{jt}, FIN_{jt}), && \text{if } DESIN_{jt} > 0 \text{ and } FIN_{jt} > 0; \end{aligned}$$

$$\begin{aligned} FIN_{jt} &= (DEP_{jt} + NET_{jt}), && \text{if } NET_{jt} \leqq 0, \\ &= (DEP_{jt} + (1 + BANK) \cdot NET_{jt}), && \text{if } NET_{jt} > 0. \end{aligned}$$

It should be noted that balance sheet considerations, as such, play no active role in the model. We keep track of the balance sheet implications of firm decisions, but the decisions themselves do not depend on, for example, the level of *DEBT* or the level of *CASH*. The model's exit rule (which is not operative in the simulation runs) is based on a minimum scale requirement, not on net worth. The only role of our simple capital market is to enhance, on a period to period basis, the growth rate of the more profitable firms. The exclusion of balance sheet considerations from the causal structure is obviously the sort of assumption that is justified primarily by the great simplification it effects. On the other hand, treatment of the capital market as a mechanism to magnify growth rate differentials is a natural, and in our opinion valuable, feature of the evolutionary perspective.

6. Behavior of the Model in Special Cases

Although the principal results reported in this paper derive from a computer simulation study, we will mention here some basic features of the model's behavior that can be established by direct analysis of its assumptions. This background will be helpful in interpreting the simulation results.

Consider first the behavior of the model when firms make no efforts to obtain new techniques, i.e., R and IM are set to zero in all firms. If entry is impossible, or is restricted to being strictly imitative of firms in business, the model's behavior becomes independent of latent productivity. Also, since the only stochastic features of the full model are associated with the occurrence of technical change, the circumscribed model is fully deterministic.

Suppose that R and IM are zero, entry is prohibited, and the target markup factor is defined for all values of SHR ($0 \leqq SHR \leqq 1$), equal to one at $SHR = 0$, continuous and strictly increasing in *SHR*. Since research and imitation expense are the only non-production costs, positive net investment can always be financed if price is above unit cost. If all firms have identical productivity and unit cost levels, there will be equilibria in which *N* firms share the market equally. The equilibrium markup factor will, of course, be that given by the target markup factor schedule at $SHR = N^{-1}$. For sufficiently small values of the adjustment coefficient, *KADJ*, these equilibria will be at least locally stable.

The picture is more complex if the firms have different unit cost levels. If *N* different firms have *N* different cost levels, but the differences are small, there can be equilibria in which all *N* firms survive, but output shares are ranked inversely with unit cost levels. At the other extreme, suppose there are N_1 firms at the lowest cost level. Consider this lowest unit cost marked up by the markup factor corresponding to $SHR = (N_1)^{-1}$. If this value is below the next-to-lowest unit cost, then the "natural selection" process will operate unimpeded by the output restraint of the lowest cost firms: They will drive the others entirely out of the market, and wind up sharing the market among themselves. This result will necessarily occur if N_1 is sufficiently large, since the markup factor tends to one as *SHR* tends to zero.

Now suppose that, while *R* values remain zero, all firms display the same positive *IM* value. The effects of the selection mechanism will be supplemented by imitative search. Ultimately, all surviving firms will display the same unit cost level, which will be the lowest of those displayed in the initial conditions (assuming that no mistakes are made in technique comparisons). The number of surviving firms (and hence the equilibrium markup) will depend on the entry and exit specifications.

If we now admit positive *R* values, the link to latent productivity comes into play, and things become a great deal more complicated. Much depends, obviously, on the relation between initial firm productivity levels and latent productivity, and on the time path of latent productivity. Radically different patterns of "historical" development of the industry are implied by the different assumptions, and we contend that these differences are worthy of analysis, and suggestive of possible interpretations of real events. For present purposes, however, the temptations of steady-state analysis are irresistible: Let us discuss what happens when latent productivity is advancing at a constant exponential rate.

Consider, specifically, the simplified model that arises if the investment mechanism (as well as entry and exit) is suppressed and firms remain the same size forever. This makes productivity behavior independent of price and profitability. Each firm will have characteristic (positive) levels of research and imitation expenditure, constant over time. Asymptotically, the average rate of increase of productivity in each individual firm will equal the rate of increase of latent productivity. In other words, each firm's productivity level will fluctuate around a particular long-run average ratio to latent productivity. Of course, the larger the firm's research and imitation expenditures, the higher that ratio will be. But any maintained rate of expenditure – no matter how small – will yield, asymptotically, the same growth rate. This is because the expected productivity gain from a research or imitation draw keeps increasing as the firm falls farther behind latent productivity, and ultimately is sufficiently large to compensate for the long average interval between draws.

If we abandon the simplifying assumptions that individual firms stay the same size, and entry is barred, the phenomena that appear include not only those of differential firm growth – which are central to our evolutionary analysis – but also certain gross responses to demand by the industry as a whole. Assuming that demand is constant over time, a demand function of constant unitary elasticity has special significance: A given percentage increase in productivity produces the same percentage decrease in unit cost and price, leaving the industry capital stock in the same state of equilibrium or disequilibrium it was before. That is, with unitary elasticity of demand, the advance of productivity does not, of itself, produce a trend in industry capital. By contrast, if demand elasticity is constant and greater than unity, productivity advance raises the price–cost ratio (at a given capital stock), and thus leads to an increased capital stock. Since information-seeking efforts are proportioned to capital, this mechanism tends to produce an increase in the ratio of realized to latent productivity over time. The corresponding implications of inelastic demand, or of demand growth or decline, should be obvious.

7. Simulation: Assumptions

Our experiment explores how the evolutionary contest between "researchers" and "imitators" is affected by the number of firms in the contest. The "researchers" seek new techniques both through costly research and through imitation; the "imitators" only imitate. Latent productivity is advancing at a rate of one per cent per quarter, and research draws are distributed around latent productivity with a standard deviation of about five percent. (The standard deviation is 0.05 in the logs.) The demand curve facing the industry is of unitary elasticity.

Cost parameters are set so that the ratio of capital to the value of output is about 6 quarters, or 1.5 years. Values of R, for R firms, are in the neighborhood of 0.02 per unit of capital per quarter. This corresponds to a research-to-sales ratio of about 0.12 – which, by empirical standards, is high. (This high value was chosen to assure that the cost impact of research would stand out clearly.) Imitation is ten times more effective than research, in terms of draws per unit of expense. Values of *IM* are twenty times lower than the *R* values, which makes imitation essentially negligible on the cost side. Since imitation expense is ten times as effective as research expense in yielding draws, and twice as many firms are imitating as are doing research, the expected number of imitation draws is initially the same as the expected number of research draws – about 0.5 per period in the industry as a whole.

With the benefit of hindsight, based on many repetitions of the industry's history, we know that the above parameter settings characterize a regime in which research is somewhat unprofitable on the average. It is not so clearly unprofitable, however, as to make it patently unreasonable to assume that firms continue to pursue it. In future work, we will explore the implications of a variety of different regimes of latent productivity increase and research cost. In this first reconnaisance with the model, we will confine ourselves to exploring the specific regime just described.

Five different sets of initial conditions are examined, with 2, 4, 8, 16 and 32 firms in the industry. In each condition, half the firms are researchers, or "*R* firms" and the other half are imitators, or "*IM* firms". All the firms are of equal size initially, and have the same productivity level, which is equal to the level of latent productivity. The initial total capital stock is chosen so that desired net investment is zero. This means that total capital is larger, and initial price is lower, the larger the number of firms. The levels of *R* and *IM* are adjusted to compensate the difference in initial capital, so that the initial levels of total research expense and total imitation expense are the same in all runs. Thus, the initial expected values of research draws and imitation draws are the same under all initial conditions; in this sense, the industry is initially equally progressive under all initial conditions. If systematic differences in technical progress emerge, therefore, they are associated with the difference in the number of firms. We simulate the industry's evolution for 100 periods (25 years) of change.

In addition to differences in the number of firms, the experiment also explores the effect of changing a single model parameter, *BANK*. As noted above, *BANK* determines the borrowing limit of a firm in each particular period. In half of our runs, $BANK = 1.0$; in the other half, $BANK = 2.5$. There are ten different experimental conditions in all (two *BANK* levels times five number-of-firms levels), and each condition is run five times. Other details of the simulation set-up are displayed in Table 1.

TABLE 1

SUMMARY OF ASSUMPTIONS AND PARAMETER SETTINGS FOR SIMULATION RUNS.

---

(1) Latent Productivity

Rate of latent productivity increase = 0.01 per quarter.
Standard deviation of log(A) around log(latent productivity) = 0.05.

---

(2) Demand-Price Function

$$PRICE = \frac{67}{QSUM}.$$

$$QSUM = \sum_j K_{jt}A_{jt}.$$

---

(3) Production Cost Parameters

$DEPR$ = depreciation rate = 0.03 per quarter.
$RATE$ = interest rate = 0.03 per quarter.
$VCFAC$ = variable cost per unit capital = 0.10 per quarter.

---

(4) Research and Imitation Draws

Probability of a research draw for firm j in period t = 0.125 (research expense) = 0.125 $(R_{jt}K_{jt})$.

Probability of an imitation draw for firm j in period t = 1.25 (imitation expense) = 1.25 $(IM_{jt}K_{jt})$.

---

(5) Accounting

$$NET_{jt} = (PRICE \cdot A_{jt} - RATE - DEPR - VCFAC - R_{jt} - IM_{jt})K_{jt}.$$

$$NETW_{jt} = \text{net worth} = NETW_{j(t-1)} + NET_{j(t-1)}, \qquad (NETW_{j1} = 0).$$

---

(6) Target Markup Factor

$$MU = (2 - SHR)/(2 - 2 \cdot SHR).$$

Corresponds to profit maximization on assumption that demand elasticity is one and remainder of industry responds along a supply curve of elasticity one.

---

(7) Investment

$$KADJ = 1.$$

$$BANK = 1.0 \text{ or } 2.5.$$

$$UNCOST_{jt} = (RATE + DEPR + VCFAC)/A_{jt} = 0.16/A_{jt}.$$

$$DESIN_{jt} = \left[DEPR + \left(1 - \frac{MU \cdot UNCOST_{j(t+1)}}{PRICE_t}\right)\right]K_{jt}.$$

$$FIN_{jt} = (DEP_{jt} + NET_{jt}), \quad \text{if} \quad NET_{jt} \geqq 0$$
$$= (DEP_{jt} + (1 + BANK) \cdot NET_{jt}), \quad \text{if} \quad NET_{jt} > 0.$$

$$GRIN_{jt} = \text{Max}[0, \text{Min}(DESIN_{jt}, FIN_{jt})].$$

$$K_{j(t+1)} = K_{jt} - DEP_{jt} + GRIN_{jt}$$
$$= (1 - DEPR)K_{jt} + GRIN_{jt}.$$

TABLE 1 (*contd.*)

(8) Initial Conditions

No. of firms:	2	4	6	16	32
Variable: *K*	139.58	89.70	48.85	25.34	12.89
A	0.16	0.16	0.16	0.16	0.16
*R**	0.0287	0.0223	0.0205	0.0197	0.0194
IM	0.001433	0.00112	0.00102	0.00099	0.00097

**R* firms only. Latent productivity = 0.16.

(9) Implied Initial Values of Industry Variables

No. of firms:	2	4	8	16	32
Variable: *KSUM*	279	359	391	405	412
QSUM	45	57	63	65	66
*PRICE**	1.500	1.167	1.072	1.033	1.015
RESXI	4.00	4.00	4.00	4.00	4.00
IMXI	0.40	0.40	0.40	0.40	0.40
RNETI	0.064	0.015	0.000	−0.006	−0.008

RESXI = total industry research expense.
IMXI = total industry imitation expense.
RNETI = industry average rate of excess return.
*Initial unit cost is 1.00 in all runs. Hence, *PRICE* = *MU*.

8. Results

The simulation runs yielded a large and diverse set of data, describing individual firm histories and the behavior of many industry aggregates over the twenty-five year period, iterated fifty times. In this section we present a survey of these quantitative results, focusing primarily on the effects of the ten different experimental conditions on a number of variables characterizing the industry state at the end of the run. We make only a few interpretive comments in the course of this survey, deferring systematic discussion of significant patterns until after we have sketched in the picture as a whole. As we have already noted, one important feature of this general picture is that the imitators tend to be more profitable than the researchers; only seven of the fifty runs are exceptions to this pattern. A firm that does not do research, but only spends enough on technical information to enable it to imitate what other firms are doing, saves a lot of money, and in general does not lag drastically behind the research firms in productivity level.

Figures 1–14 show average values of various variables over the five runs under each of the ten experimental conditions. (Precise numerical

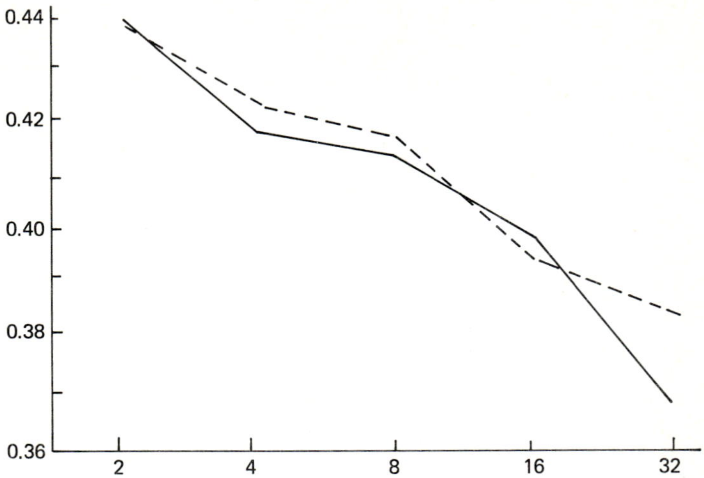

FIGURE 1. Average productivity. *Note*: In all figures, values shown are at end of run (period 101), and are means over five runs. Broken lines represent the *BANK* = 1.0 condition, solid lines the *BANK* = 2.5 condition. See Table 2 for precise numerical values.

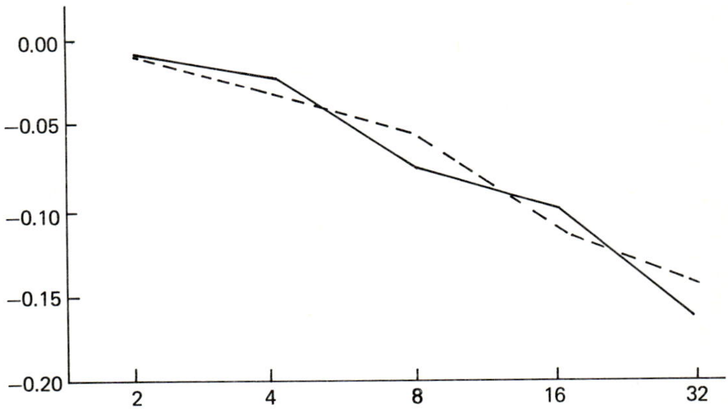

FIGURE 2. Average productivity gap.

values for these means, and the standard deviations, are in Table 2.) The solid lines connect observations under the *BANK* = 2.5 condition, while the broken lines represent the *BANK* = 1.0 condition.

One striking result is the clear and systematic tendency for average productivity (Figure 1) to be higher at the end of the run in situations where firms were few in number than where they were numerous initially. The same story is told by the average productivity gap display in Figure 2.

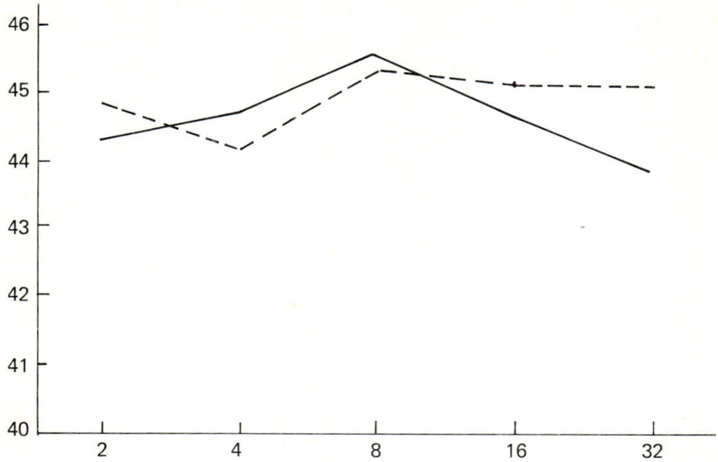

FIGURE 3. Best practice productivity.

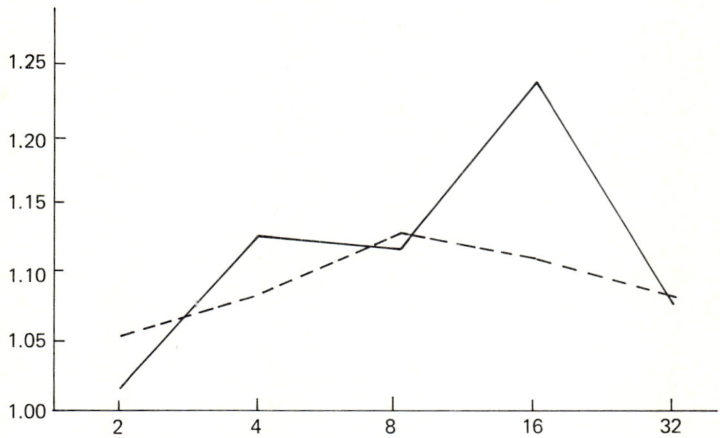

FIGURE 4. *R/IM* productivity ratio.

The gap is defined as the geometric mean, over time, of the ratio of average productivity to latent productivity, minus 1. In the duopoly runs the gap is close to zero. Latent productivity is tracked almost exactly (recall however that it is *a priori* possible to have a positive gap). In the 32-firm cases, productivity runs about 15% below latent productivity. Figure 3 shows that this result does not obtain for "best practice" productivity, which appears relatively insensitive to the number of firms. Thus, the large numbers cases were marked by a higher ratio of best practice to average productivity than the small numbers cases.

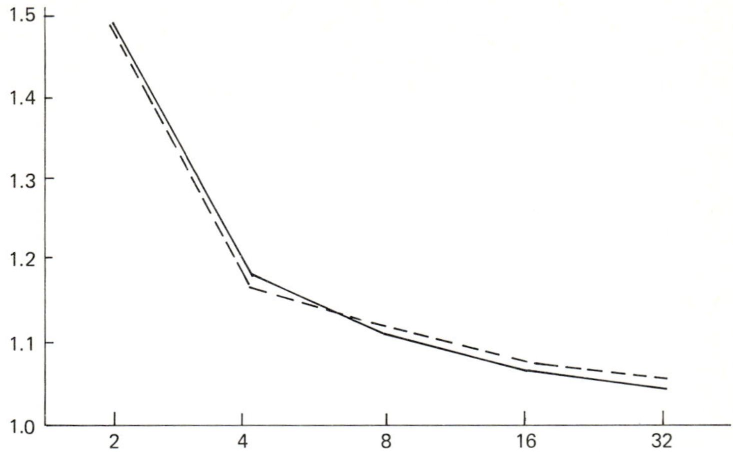

FIGURE 5. Average markup factor.

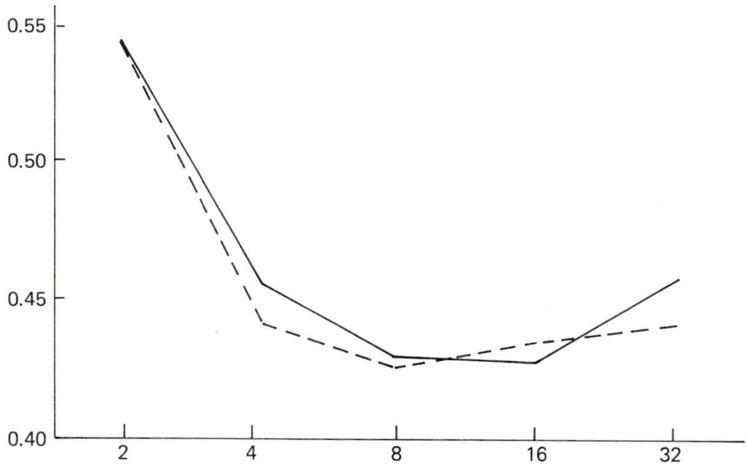

FIGURE 6. Price.

Figure 9 presents the research expense recovery rate. This is a simple descriptive measure of the extent to which firms that do research recapture, in transient profits derived from superior productivity, the funds they expend on research. The measure is defined as the difference between the final net worths of researchers and imitators, divided by cumulative research expense, plus one. A value of 1.0 for this measure corresponds, obviously, to a case in which the final net worths of

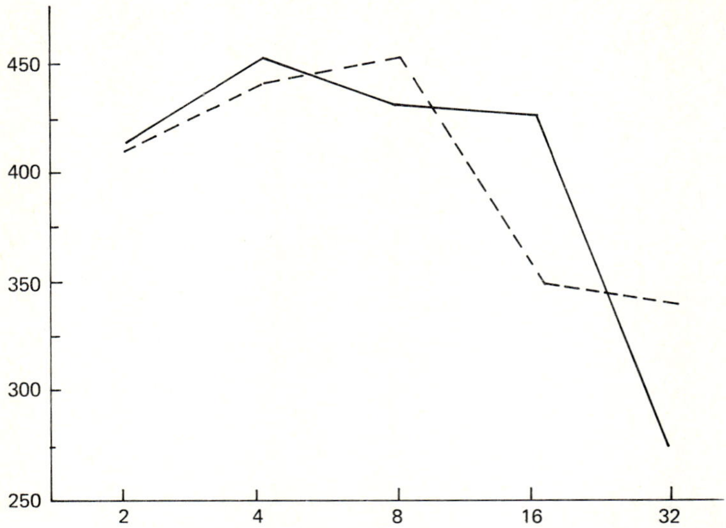

FIGURE 7. Cumulative research expense.

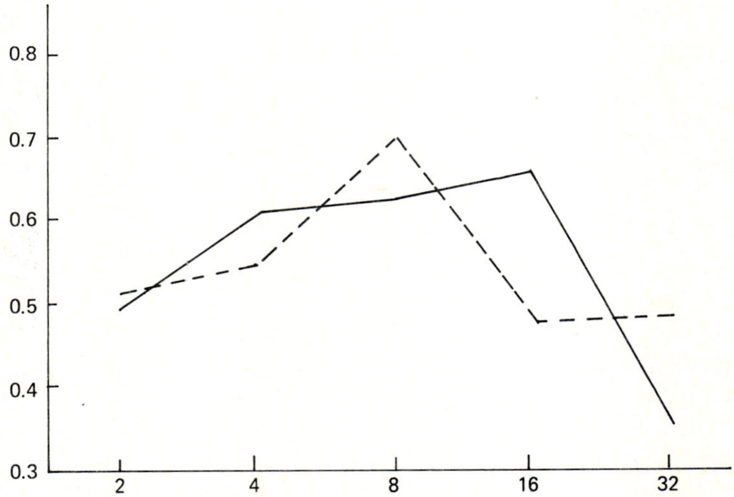

FIGURE 8. Researchers' capital share.

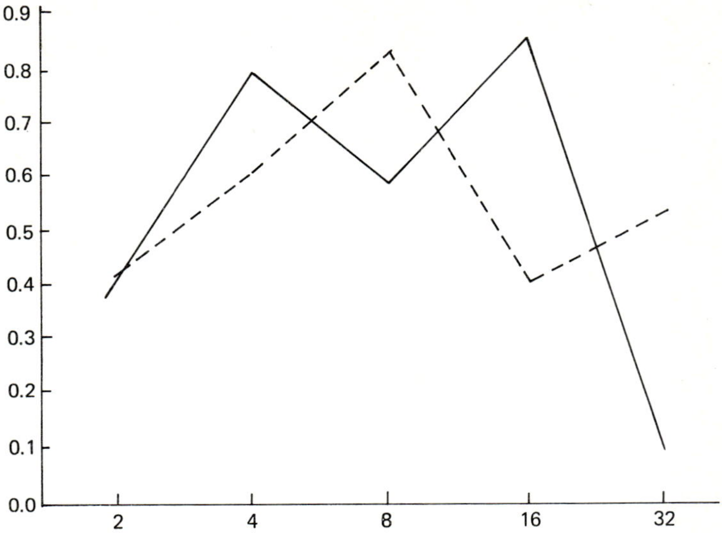

FIGURE 9. Research expense recovery rate.

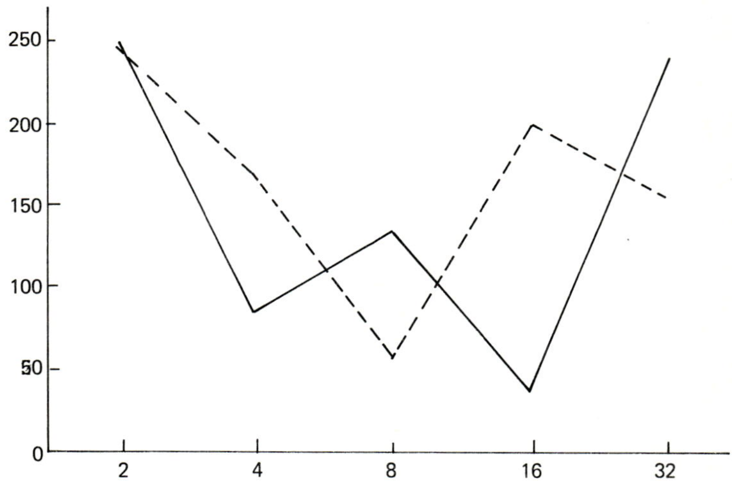

FIGURE 10. *IM* − *R* net worth difference.

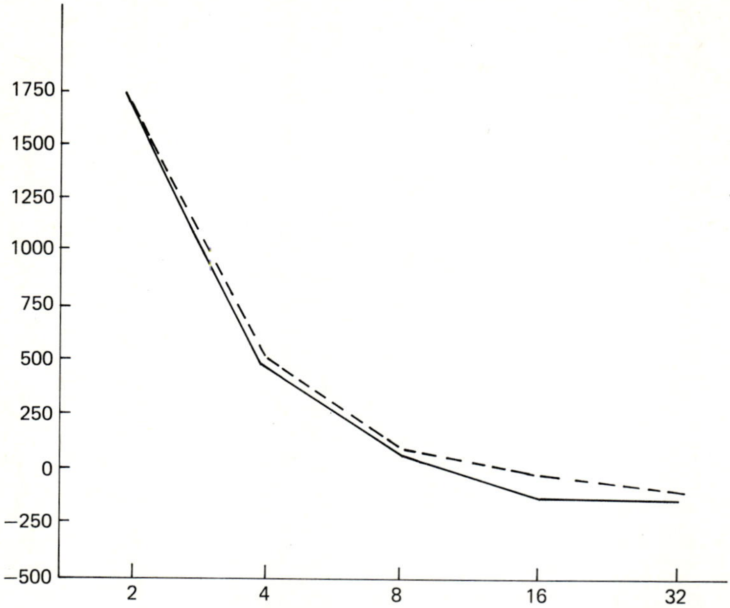

FIGURE 11. Total net worth.

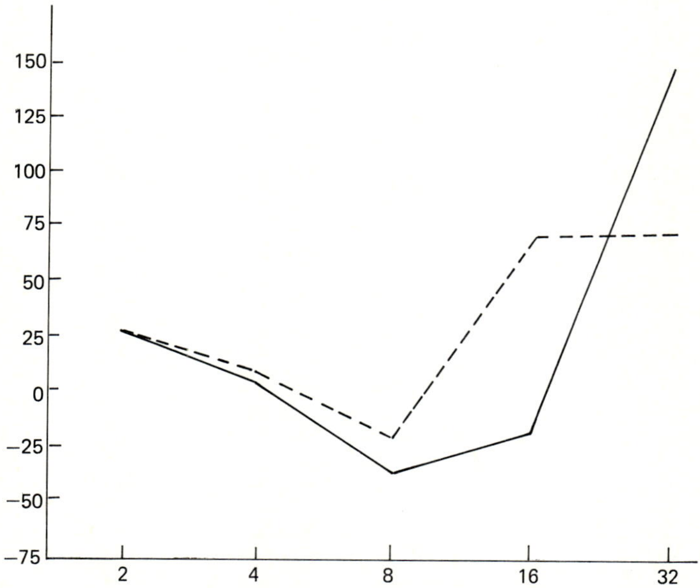

FIGURE 12. *IM* − *R* borrowing difference.

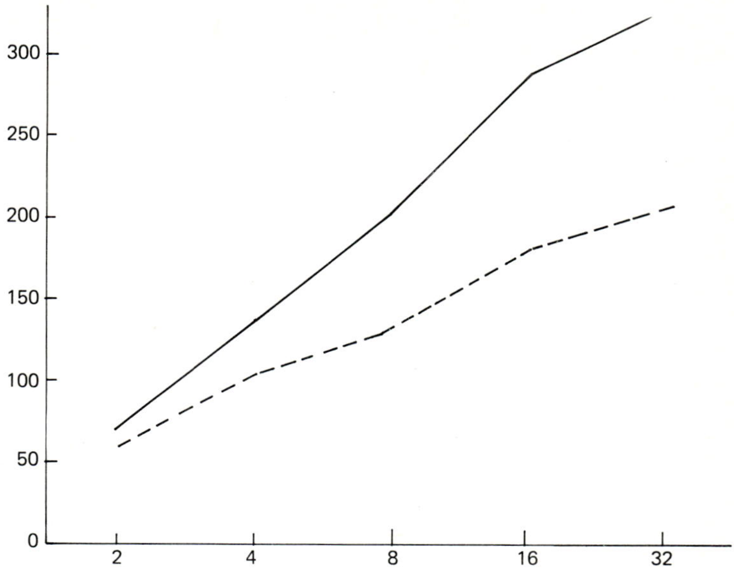

FIGURE 13. Cumulative borrowing.

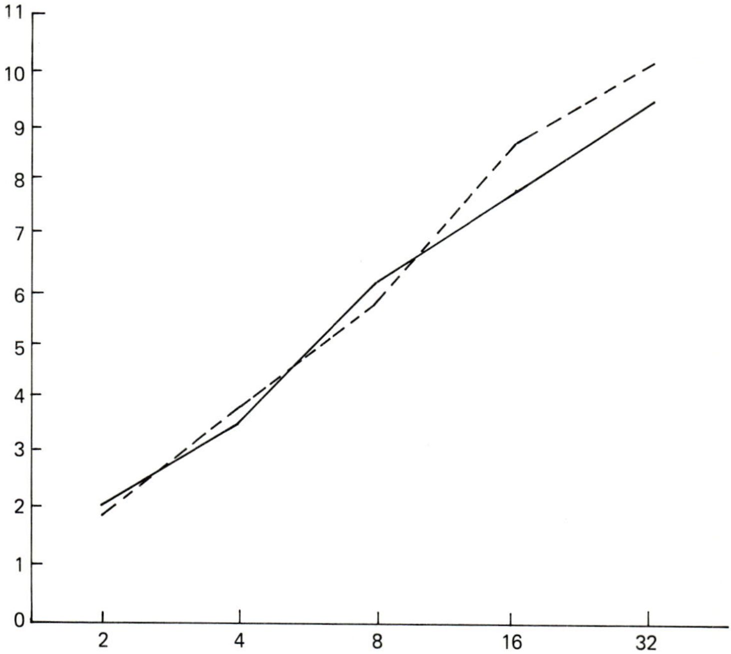

FIGURE 14. Entropy numbers equivalent.

TABLE 2

MEANS AND STANDARD DEVIATIONS OF 5 RUN SAMPLES (VALUES AT END OF RUN).

Variable	Bank	Number of firms 2	4	8	16	32
(1) Average productivity	1.0	0.4381 (0.0096)	0.4231 (0.0138)	0.418 (0.0066)	0.395 (0.0210)	0.385 (0.0126)
	2.5	0.439 (0.0195)	0.417 (0.0130)	0.414 (0.0130)	0.398 (0.0107)	0.368 (0.0130)
(2) Average productivity gap	1.0	−0.0091 (0.0075)	−0.0440 (0.0121)	−0.0573 (0.0083)	−0.1155 (0.0095)	−0.1445 (0.0074)
	2.5	−0.0074 (0.0130)	−0.0283 (0.0086)	−0.0688 (0.0147)	−0.0981 (0.0090)	−0.1570 (0.0145)
(3) Best practice productivity	1.0	0.449 (0.0154)	0.442 (0.0127)	0.454 (0.0248)	0.451 0.0254	0.451 (0.0163)
	2.5	0.443 (0.0137)	0.447 (0.0148)	0.456 (0.0263)	0.446 (0.0190)	0.438 (0.0184)
(4) *R/IM* productivity ratio	1.0	1.054 (0.0849)	1.086 (0.0669)	1.130 (0.0514)	1.111 (0.1020)	1.088 (0.0544)
	2.5	1.018 (0.0367)	1.129 (0.0895)	1.120 (0.0978)	1.246 (0.1765)	1.085 (0.1075)
(5) Average markup	1.0	1.492 (0.0341)	1.175 (0.0132)	1.115 (0.0091)	1.073 (0.0143)	1.068 (0.0203)
	2.5	1.496 (0.0101)	1.188 (0.0163)	1.110 (0.0139)	1.061 (0.0258)	1.044 (0.0159)
(6) Price	1.0	0.545 (0.0235)	0.444 (0.0137)	0.427 (0.0059)	0.435 (0.0263)	0.444 (0.0190)
	2.5	0.546 (0.0277)	0.456 (0.0173)	0.429 (0.0117)	0.427 (0.0168)	0.456 (0.0157)
(7) Cumulative research expense	1.0	412.8 (0.61)	441.7 (5.73)	445.7 (48.03)	353.9 (53.37)	343.9 (21.57)
	2.5	413.1 (0.40)	456.1 (14.15)	435.0 (78.34)	432.8 (53.34)	278.6 (27.31)

TABLE 2 (*contd.*)

MEANS AND STANDARD DEVIATIONS OF 5 RUN SAMPLES (VALUES AT END OF RUN).

Variable	Bank	Number of firms 2	4	8	16	32
(8) Researchers' capital share	1.0	0.504 (0.009)	0.564 (0.027)	0.716 (0.110)	0.478 (0.160)	0.484 (0.091)
	2.5	0.500 (0.007)	0.618 (0.055)	0.628 (0.164)	0.666 (0.093)	0.344 (0.114)
(9) Research expense recovery rate	1.0	0.4174 (0.0754)	0.6176 (0.0560)	0.8474 (0.2795)	0.4180 (0.3728)	0.5564 (0.2256)
	2.5	0.4024 (0.0530)	0.8020 (0.2499)	0.5992 (0.5236)	0.8742 (0.2398)	0.1242 (0.3034)
(10) Net worth difference $(IM - R)$	1.0	240.5 (30.8)	168.7 (22.7)	59.0 (114.6)	191.0 (123.4)	151.8 (72.1)
	2.5	246.7 (21.7)	87.4 (114.2)	132.9 (175.4)	45.2 (82.9)	237.6 (63.6)
(11) Total net worth	1.0	1744.8 (5.55)	515.4 (19.40)	118.5 (63.27)	−21.1 (51.06)	−103.2 (73.94)
	2.5	1741.3 (4.85)	500.4 (40.23)	71.3 (75.44)	−126.7 (26.30)	−159.4 (38.74)
(12) Cumulative borrowing difference $(IM - R)$	1.0	0.75 (7.18)	−15.79 (12.86)	−32.35 (33.47)	46.82 (46.34)	49.28 (31.10)
	2.5	1.10 (11.59)	−20.33 (21.13)	−60.01 (75.87)	−42.22 (56.34)	150.06 (58.88)
(13) Cumulative total borrowing	1.0	55.1 (12.45)	100.7 (8.80)	135.4 (22.84)	186.4 (11.73)	212.4 (12.33)
	2.5	65.2 (11.16)	136.4 (19.47)	207.8 (34.97)	289.3 (15.02)	326.6 (26.16)
(14) Entropy numbers equivalent	1.0	1.996 (0.009)	3.854 (0.161)	5.806 (0.697)	8.696 (0.699)	10.146 (1.268)
	2.5	2.000 (0.000)	3.698 (0.150)	6.264 (1.050)	7.706 (0.648)	9.526 (1.385)

researchers and imitators are equal.[11] In this case any productivity advantages gained from research are just offset by the cost of research. Although there are individual runs in which the research expense recovery rate exceeds 1.0, Figure 9 shows that this is never the case for the five run averages. Given the parameter settings of these runs, research typically does not pay. In particular, it does not pay for large firms. Interestingly enough, it is less of a losing proposition in the intermediate numbers cases than either for large numbers or for small. The net worth differences between research firms and firms that do no research are displayed in Figure 10. Generally, they mirror the results of the previous figure.

While research was not in general profitable for the firms, it is apparent that selection pressures against researchers differ strikingly in different industry structures. Figure 8 shows the share of industry physical capital held by research firms at the end of the run. For the duopoly cases, there apparently was no strong selection pressure against the researcher. The capital share of the researcher tends to remain at its initial value of 0.5. In the 32-firm cases, selection pressures against research firms apparently operated much more strongly. Their share of capital tended to decline sharply. It is interesting, and a puzzle that we will have to deal with, that in the middle three cases the researchers tended to grow relative to the imitators. Since research policies imposed constant ratios between research expense and researchers' capital, the level of research expense at the end of the run follows the researchers' capital share almost exactly. Cumulative research expense over the entire run is displayed in Figure 7, and also follows the pattern of being higher in the 4 to 16 firm cases.

Figures 12 and 13 describe the borrowing behavior of the firms over the run as a whole. Recall that the $BANK = 1.0$ case corresponds to one in which firms can, if they wish, invest twice their net earnings; in the $BANK = 2.5$ case positive net earnings have even greater leverage on possible investment. The comparison between imitators and researchers, in Figure 13, is broadly consistent with the "enhancement of growth rate differentials" interpretation of our simple capital market. That is, a

[11]It should be noted that, under the prevailing payout rules and accounting procedures, the final net worth of a firm is simply the sum of all excess returns earned in the course of the run, without regard to the date at which the returns are earned. Interest received or paid in the firm's "cash" account is assumed to be reflected in dividends. As noted previously, a model firm's behavior is independent of its balance sheet, so the implicit treatment of dividend behavior is significant only insofar as it affects the usefulness of the balance sheet figures for descriptive and analytical purposes. To accumulate interest in the cash account would be to give more weight, in the description, to what happened early in the run. Given the fact that it is the long-term *results* of different initial conditions we are seeking to describe, not the initial conditions themselves, this seemed inappropriate.

comparison of Figures 8 and 12 shows that borrowing differentials mirror the movement of the final capital share. We expected that the bigger credit line (*BANK* = 2.5) would lead to a sharper capital share movement, but in the same direction as the *BANK* = 1.0 case, and also that the borrowing differential would increase in absolute magnitude but maintain its sign. As Figure 8 shows, these expectations are not entirely borne out. But they are clearly correct for the 32-firm cases, which we have already noted as illustrating strong selection pressures. The borrowing differential, already in favor of imitators in the *BANK* = 1.0 case, is much larger when *BANK* = 2.5. And it is plain, from Figure 8, the role the greater borrowing is playing is to enhance the growth of imitators relative to researchers.

Figures 5, 6 and 11 show that some of the old verities do prevail in our newfangled model, and with great clarity and force. Concentration, and the associated ability to affect prices, does make it possible for firms to make more money. Figure 11 portrays the systematic effect of concentration on industry net worth at the end of the run. Put in other terms, market structure strongly influences the extent to which productivity gains are passed on to consumers. Figure 6 shows average values of price in the final period. From the consumer point of view, the superior productivity performance of the small numbers case is more than offset by high markup (Figure 5). Prices are highest, by far, when the industry is a duopoly. However, output restraint is negligible when there are 8 or more firms, and productivity performance becomes the dominant influence on price.

Concentration itself is, in part, endogenously determined in the model. While runs that started with a highly concentrated market structure tended to remain concentrated, there was a marked rise in concentration in the runs with an unconcentrated initial structure. Figure 14 displays end-of-run values of the "entropy numbers equivalent". This is a measure of output concentration in the industry; intuitively, it is the number of firms in an industry of equalized firms that has the same degree of concentration as the actual industry. Thus the fact that the entropy numbers equivalent is very close to 2.0 in all the duopoly cases is a reflection of the fact that the two firms do remain very nearly equal in size in these cases. In the four-firm cases, there is a slight tendency for concentration to increase over the run. This tendency becomes pronounced beginning with the eight-firm cases. In the ten runs with thirty-two firms, the largest final value for the entropy numbers equivalent is 12.35 – a level of concentration comparable to the consequences of the disappearance of well over half of the firms initially in business, if the remainder were of equal size.

It is also evident, on inspection of the standard deviations in Table 2, that the number of firms strongly influences the degree of run-to-run variability in the values of some of the variables. A particularly striking case is cumulative research expense: The standard deviation is almost one hundred times larger in the sixteen-firm cases than in the two-firm cases.

9. Interpretation

We now attempt to explain some of the more significant patterns in the simulation results. In one sense, of course, such explanation is redundant: The results are the logical consequence of the model's assumptions, parameter values, and initial conditions – which we have already described – together with the outputs of the random number generators – for which there is no interesting explanation. But reference to the assumptions, parameter values and initial conditions does little to improve understanding of the forces at work in the model situation, and without such understanding one can say very little about the possible relationship between the model's behavior and real events. For the latter purpose, and to provide a basis for further theorizing, we must attempt to find simple and satisfying explanations for the patterns displayed by simulation runs.[12]

Three interrelated puzzles confront us. There is, first, the fact that researchers expand or hold their own relative to imitators, in all but the 32-firm cases, although there seems to be decisive evidence in the final net worth figures that research does not pay. The second puzzle is that there is a relatively weak connection between productivity performance and research expenditure, but a much stronger one between productivity performance and the number of firms. According to the (demand-side) Schumpeterian hypothesis, the influence of the number of firms was supposed to operate by way of internalization of returns, and thus on the level of research expenditure. Finally, there is the "internal maximum" problem, i.e., the fact that both the level of research expense and the return to it seem to be higher in the intermediate numbers cases.

Taking up the first puzzle, it is instructive to begin with the results in the two-firm runs. The capital share of the researcher hovers close to 0.5 throughout all of these runs, while the research expense recovery rate

[12]We cannot adequately convey, in the discussion below, the extent to which the interpretations given constitute "discoveries" stimulated by confrontation with specific numerical examples of the model's logic.

varies from 0.3 to 0.5. What is happening here is that research is essentially a "slack" activity, something the researcher can afford by virtue of being a rich duopolist, but that really does not pay. The transient productivity leads it confers are not sufficient to offset its costs. Figure 4 shows, for example, that average productivity of researchers averages about $3\frac{1}{2}\%$ above that of imitators at the end of the run, in the duopoly cases. But when research outlays are accounted for, costs per unit capital are about 18% higher for the researchers, and hence costs per unit output are about 14% higher for the researchers. But this unfavorable balance is reflected only in the profitability indicators, and not in firm size. No financial constraint on investment arises, because of the excess returns associated with duopoly. Desired investment is determined by production costs (as explained above), which are generally lower for the researcher. With lower production costs, the researcher will aim at zero net investment only when he has somewhat more than half the market. That the capital shares stay close to equal, rather than favoring the researcher, is a reflection of two facts: (i) With the prevailing imitation parameters the imitator has the same technique as the researcher a significant fraction of the time, and whenever this is the case the two firms move toward equal size. (ii) Under the assumed markup rule, the "equilibrium" share of the duopolist with lower costs increases slowly with the cost differential; e.g., a firm with a 10% cost advantage must produce 53.6% of output if both firms are to desire zero net investment, and it does this with 51.2% of capital.

Consider now what happens as the number of firms of each type is increased. On the desired investment side, this means that firms have smaller target markups, hence invest more vigorously when their costs are below prevailing prices. (In the limit, with infinitely many firms, each firm desires an infinite expansion whenever price is above unit production cost.) However, the smaller markups and larger industry capital also mean that excess returns are smaller. The financial constraints on investment must ultimately (as the number of firms increases) become binding. The constraint will bind first on the firms with the higher unit costs inclusive of research costs, and this tends to be the firms that do research. Thus a different type of "equilibrium" sharing of the market arises – one in which the imitators are large enough to desire markups high enough so that the researchers can break even. Of course, it may happen that there are enough imitators so that the researchers are entirely driven out before such an "equilibrium" arises.

The foregoing account obviously abstracts from many of the dynamic complexities, in particular, it does not deal with the fact that the development of concentration within the researcher and imitator categories affects markups and the impact of research and imitation. But the account does explain co-occurrence of researcher capital shares greater than one-half with low research profitability. Table 3 displays illustrative calculations of the share of industry capital held by researchers on the assumption that researcher's productivity is 6.25% higher than that of imitators. After allowing for the way R varies with the number of firms, this implies that unit total cost of researchers is about 11% higher in the two-firm case, and 5.5% higher in the 32 firm case. The calculations assume that firms are the same size within each group. The "desired" column shows the share of industry capital that researchers would have to have if both researchers and imitators were to desire zero net investment. The "constraint" column shows the share of industry capital at which researchers would wind up if they engaged in positive net investment whenever they could finance it (while imitators' behavior continues to reflect the desired investment function). In this illustrative calculation, the financing constraint becomes binding between the four- and eight-firm cases. Thus, the true investment function is reflected in the first two numbers in the "desired" column and the last three in the "constraint" column. The resulting series – 0.508, 0.564, 0.549, 0.181, 0.0 – is broadly consistent with the capital share pattern in the simulation, in the sense that one could accept these values as characterizing the asymptotes toward which the system is headed.

We turn now to the second puzzle, which involves the behavior of the average productivity gap (*AVAGAP*). Regression analysis confirms the impression created by the figures: The number of firms (J) is a powerful determinant of the average gap. Specifically, a regression of *AVAGAP* on *BANK* and $\log_2(J)$ produces the following result:

$$AVAGAP = \underset{(4.91)}{0.0309} + \underset{(0.57)}{0.0014}\, BANK - \underset{(-26.40)}{0.0356} \log_2(J),$$

TABLE 3
"EQUILIBRIUM" CAPITAL SHARES OF RESEARCHERS.

No. of firms	Desired	Constraint
2	0.508	0.813
4	0.564	0.738
8	0.686	0.549
16	0.940	0.181
32	1.000	0.000

with $R = 0.937$.[13] Given this single result, considered in isolation from the rest of the data, one might be tempted by an explanation in terms of influences on the level of research spending. Research is the source, or at least the vehicle, of productivity growth. While rapid imitation may make research unprofitable, the market environment is at least more permissive to research spending when the number of firms is small. Hence (one would argue) productivity performance tends to be better when the number of firms is small.

This argument quickly becomes untenable as other features of the simulation results are taken into account. First of all, research spending is tightly linked in the model to the capital share of researchers, and we have just discussed the fact that this share is maximal in the intermediate-number cases, not in the small-number cases. Secondly, the argument's emphasis on research spending would lead one to expect that research spending itself would be the best predictor of productivity performance, and the independent influence of the number of firms would be negligible. The following regression result, with cumulative research expenditure included as an independent variable, shows that this expectation is far from correct:

$$\underset{}{AVAGAP} = \underset{(-1.33)}{-0.0214} + \underset{(3.47)}{0.001}\ CUMREX + \underset{(0.58)}{0.0013}\ BANK \underset{(-22.4)}{-0.0327}\log_2(J), \quad (R^2 = 0.950).$$

When $\log_2(J)$ is dropped as an explanatory variable, and *CUMREX* retained, the R^2 falls to 0.4. Thus, the independent influence of the number of firms on productivity performance is firmly established.

In retrospect, it is clear that the relationship between the average size of firms and productivity performance is quite complicated in our model, and perhaps also in the real world. Even if the size (or number) of firms had no influence on total research spending, the size distribution would affect average productivity. Research effort yields, from time to time, superior techniques. But the immediate effect of a technical change on industry average productivity depends on the size of the innovator relative to the industry (as well as on the size of the advance represented by the innovation). Similarly, each successive imitation of the new technique has an impact on industry average productivity that depends on

[13] Figures in the parentheses are t-ratios. We have taken the number of firms variable to be the log to the base 2 to facilitate comparisons of the experimental conditions; e.g., in the result above, we see that each doubling of the number of firms makes the average productivity level fall another $3\frac{1}{2}$ percent behind latent productivity.

the size of the imitator relative to the industry. In the model, the rate at which acts of imitation (i.e., imitation draws) occur is roughly independent of the industry structure. Thus, the lessened effect of each individual act, when the number of firms is large, is fully reflected in industry average productivity. For a given level of industry research spending, the productivity associated with "best practice" technique should be independent of industry structure. (As Figure 3 shows, there is little or no systematic relationship between best practice productivity at the end of the run and the number of firms.) But the gap between best practice technique and average productivity (and hence the gap between latent productivity and average productivity) should be greater when there are many small firms than when there are a few large ones.

The explanations offered for the first two puzzles are also relevant to the third. The capital share of researchers, and hence the level of research spending, is higher in the intermediate numbers cases because (or partly because) of the way investment responds to market shares and financing constraints. And the analysis of the average productivity gap behavior has revealed some of the complexities in the relationship between market structure and imitation rates. But we still need to provide an explanation for the fact that the net worth figures and research expense recovery rates reveal research to be more profitable in the intermediate-number cases.

The cost of a single innovation, in the sense of expected research expense per research draw, is a constant in our model, and thus obviously independent of the number of firms. What about the return? The (undiscounted) return can be thought of as the product of three factors. The first is the size of the advance, in terms of the increase in revenue per unit capital. Revenue per unit capital tends to be approximately constant over the run – in the large-numbers case it is approximately 0.16, the constant value of production cost per unit capital – so the size of the advance is proportional to the percentage increase in productivity it involves. The second factor is the duration of the lead, the length of time that passes before output price reflects the adoption of the innovation by the rest of the industry. More precisely, we should consider the expected time to full adoption, and recognize that the size of the innovator's profitability advantage over the rest of the industry declines from its initial value to zero over this period of time. Finally, there is the size of the innovating firm, i.e., the amount of capital to which the innovation is applied. The problem now is to characterize, at least approximately, how these three factors are influenced by a change – e.g., doubling – of the number of firms. For this purpose, it will be necessary to consider how things would turn out in situations simpler than that of the actual model.

Assume that the number of firms is "very large" and the rate at which innovations appear is "very low". By the former assumption, we mean that the impact of the innovator's productivity advance on industry price is negligible (i.e., until some imitation occurs); by the latter we mean that a given advance is typically fully imitated well before the next one appears. At a given level of industry research expense, and hence a given rate of research draws (innovations), the growth rate of best practice productivity will come ultimately to equal that of latent productivity. And because of the simplifying assumption of a "very low" innovation rate, productivity will typically be at best practice levels in all firms before the next innovation occurs. Then, the average percentage increase in the innovating firm's productivity resulting from an innovation is simply the percentage increase in latent productivity over a period equal to the average time interval between research draws. Under these assumptions, the average size of an advance depends on the level of research expense and the rate of increase of latent productivity, and not on the number of firms.

The situation with respect to the duration of the lead has already been suggested in the discussion of the second puzzle. Smaller firms apply the fruits of imitation effort on a smaller scale, just as they apply the fruits of research effort on a smaller scale. In general, the resulting slowing of imitation will be at least a partial offset to the smaller scale of application of research results, as the average size of firm decreases. In the present simplified context, with the additional crucial assumptions that the total imitation effort remains constant and that the change in concentration is negligible, it is demonstrable that the expected duration of the lead is precisely doubled by a doubling of the number of firms. Intuitively, since each imitation draw converts half as much capital, the amount of time required to convert all the capital is doubled.

The impact of doubling the number of firms on the average size of firms is obvious, if it is only the immediate impact that is considered. Thus, if there were no firm growth mechanism, and the experimental doubling of the number of firms were the only influence on firm size, we would have reached our answer. Doubling the number of firms leaves the average size of an advance unaffected, doubles the time required for given amounts of imitation, and halves the amount of capital to which an advance is applied, leaving the gross return to an innovation unaffected. But the change in the number of firms has more remote effects on firm sizes, as well as the direct effect. One such is the decline in desired markups and the associated increase in total capital, but that effect is negligible in the present context because we have assumed the number of firms is already "very large".[14] The remaining major effect can be seen clearly if we ignore for a moment the costs of research. Then the innovating firm will grow

[14] Also, in our experimental set up, we have compensated for the influence of this effect on research and imitation effort levels by adjusting R and IM.

relative to the industry, while its lead lasts, at an average rate over that period corresponding to that associated with half the profitability advantage produced by its innovation. The duration of that period of growth is longer, the slower imitation occurs – which means that it is longer, the larger the number of firms. If research were free, the "fitness' of researchers – their growth rate relative to imitators – would be proportional to the number of firms, given all the simplifying assumptions now in force. Alternatively, if we think simply in terms of the average size of the firm in which an innovation is applied, the relevant average is *not* reduced by as much as one-half when the number of firms is doubled. Hence, the return to an innovation is increased when the number of firms increases.

Of course, research is not free in our simulation runs. In fact, it is so costly that the relative fitness of researchers is negative, not positive, when the number of firms is large. The technical leader always desires relative growth, but often cannot finance it. When the number of firms is small, the researchers' desired relative growth *can* be financed – out of the excess profits that stem from monopolistic behavior. When the number of firms is doubled – from two to four or four to eight – the profitability of research is enhanced (although in general it still is negative), but overall average productivity in the industry falls. As the number of firms increases further – to sixteen or thirty-two – the diminution of market power brings the financing constraint on investment into play, and relative prosperity becomes decisive for relative growth. This feeds back as an adverse influence on the profitability of research, since, when researchers are in decline, the amount of capital to which an innovation is applied is in decline as well.

There are, of course, a great many other effects occurring simultaneously in the simulation runs. Concentration is increasing, the gap between average productivity and latent productivity is changing, and the level of total research expense is changing with the relative capital share of researchers. We cannot prove, now, that our explanations of the three puzzles are correct. They are, at least, consistent with the results, and, in our view, interesting. Their validity will be explored with further work, using both analytic and simulation techniques.

10. Further Analysis

There are many other patterns in the simulation output, besides those discussed in connection with the three puzzles. We will comment briefly here on some of the more significant ones.

First, it is very obvious that the results of our twenty-five-year simulations do not provide a picture of the steady-state behavior of the model, except perhaps in the two- and four-firm cases. When we impose on our model industry an initial structure involving a large number of small, equal-sized firms, the data loudly proclaim the artificiality of this supposition. All measures of the degree of concentration show strong upward trends in the sixteen- and thirty-two-firm cases. The assumed amount of imitation effort is simply inadequate to sustain such an atomistic structure.

The relevance of this observation to the Schumpeterian hypothesis is clear. Whatever the advantages of a more atomistic structure, the viability of such a structure is quite doubtful, given the uncertainties associated with technical change. In our model, the only forces making for concentration are the stochastic character of research and imitation, and the economies of scale in information use. We assume no economies of scale in the production of output or of new knowledge. The strategies of the model firms do not include the deliberate pursuit of greater market power; in fact, the output restraint exercised by large firms is a major influence tending to *limit* concentration. In spite of these factors, the drift toward concentration is very pronounced. Thus, if atomistic structure were deemed desirable in our model industry, a policy to achieve it could not consist of a single episode of breaking up the larger firms. It would either have to involve periodic attacks on large firms, starting the competitive race anew, or continuously operating measures to cut the link between profitability and growth.[15] Needless to say, analysis of such policies should reflect recognition of the fact that firm decision rules might be modified in response to them.

There are other respects in which the simulation results depict transient rather than steady-state behavior. For example, firms started at the same level of productivity, equal to latent productivity, in all runs – but only in the duopoly cases did this relationship between actual and latent productivity prove to be roughly maintained. In the other cases, the data typically show that the ratio of actual to latent productivity first falls, then fluctuates or rises again. The larger the number of firms, the more systematic is the downward drift, the lower the level reached and the clearer the recovery. The recovery is no doubt the reflection of rising concentration, and the associated rise in the capital affected by research and imitation draws. Table 4 provides illustrative data for two experimen-

[15]Williamson (1972) provides a balanced discussion of the antitrust policy problem posed by dominant firm positions achieved through "business acumen or historic accident". Our simulation results may be taken as suggestive of the possible strength of the tendency of concentration to increase for those reasons.

TABLE 4

MINIMUM AND FINAL RATIOS OF AVERAGE TO LATENT PRODUCTIVITY.

	1	2	3	4	5
Min (period)	0.94 (45)	0.91 (60)	0.92 (34)	0.91 (78)	0.90 (100)
Final	1.00	0.96	0.96	0.93	0.93
Min (period)	0.80 (32)	0.75 (55)	0.75 (77)	0.79 (101)	0.81 (40)
Final	0.85	0.86	0.85	0.79	0.86

tal conditions, showing the minimum and final values of the average–latent productivity ratio, and the period at which the minimum occurred.

Another noteworthy feature of the results is the structure of the variation in outcomes. There is, as we noted previously, a strong relationship between the number of firms and the run-to-run variability in certain descriptive measures. Our duopolists lead very quiet lives; their investment/pricing policies result in a dynamic system that is quite tolerant of cost differences between the two rivals (as was explained in connection with the first puzzle). Also, their size implies a considerable reduction in the uncertainties associated with technical change; they are, so to speak, capable of self-insurance with regard to the risky outcomes of their research and imitation policies. For a quantitative illustration of these effects, consider the share of capital held by researchers at the end of the run. Over the ten-duopoly cases, this variable ranges only from 0.49 to 0.52. In the thirty-two-firm runs, it ranges from 0.17 to 0.58. Or consider the research expense recovery rate: Over the ten-duopoly cases, the range is 0.29 to 0.48. Over the thirty-two-firm cases, it is −0.17 to 0.80.

Since it is the technical change process that is stochastic in the model, it is not surprising that, within each experimental condition, there tends to be more variation in variables that relate more closely to the technical change process. For example, the difference between the net worth values of researchers and imitators reflects the stochastic outcomes of the research and imitation processes. On the other hand, total industry net worth is primarily influenced by the deterministic processes of capacity adjustment, and is quite closely determined once the number of firms is specified. (Compare Figure 10 and 11 for an indication of this.) Of course, the stochastic events do affect the development of concentration, and hence the degree of output restraint – but this effect is relatively weak, compared to the differences produced by the initial number of firms.

Finally, variation in profitability and growth among firms with the same policy, in a given run, reflects the same factors that produce run-to-run variation. If the experimental condition is one that results in large run-to-run variation (i.e., large numbers of firms), firms with the same policy will have very different fates. For example, in the four-firm runs, the larger researcher typically has less than 20% more capital than the smaller one. In the thirty-two-firm cases, the largest researcher is typically 20–100 *times* as large as the smallest one. A similar pattern holds for imitators, although, interestingly, the size discrepancy for the imitators appears to be systematically larger than that for the researchers in the four-firm runs.

The extent of the run-to-run and firm-to-firm variations in outcomes from our model may seem unrealistically large. Can it really be the case that two firms, initially identical and pursuing identical policies, can have such different luck that they wind up differing in scale by a factor of 100 after twenty-five years? (Such a differential corresponds to a relative growth rate of about 20% per year.) Of course, we do not claim to have calibrated the model with respect to the size of the stochastic elements – or, for that matter, with respect to the number of firms, which is so important a determinant of the size of the growth differentials. But before dismissing this sort of result as a consequence of a poor model or faulty parameter setting, the reader should recall that intuitions about the character of *cumulative* effects in random processes are notoriously faulty and are biased specifically toward underestimation of the probabilities of long runs and the persistence of leads.[16] Recall, furthermore, that the model used in the experimental runs contains no bankruptcy or exit mechanism, i.e., nothing that eliminates from the system the firms that suffer long runs of bad luck. If our simulations do overstate the extent to which initially identical firms can have different histories, it may be because the model does not truncate the histories of the unfortunate ones the way the real world does.

If the variation in the model's behavior in the large-number cases is not wildly unrealistic, the implications are somewhat sobering with respect to the utility of simple economic models. We do not have the opportunity to keep running the real world's history over and over again until we have located the central tendency of the effect of some policy. We get only one realization to examine, and the character of that realization may not be very closely determined by the policy choices and the operation of the main economic forces, as compared with the total effect of a very large number of minor considerations. In attempting to understand, as the single realization unfolds, the structure of the system that generates it, we may have a virtually irrestible tendency to overinterpret, and to ascribe definite causes to outcomes that are important to us. A warning against

[16]See Feller (1957, ch. 3) and Alchian (1950).

this tendency is certainly one of the lessons that simulation can teach. To spin a plausible story about the patterns revealed in a given run is amusing and relatively easy – the difficulties start when you look at another run generated by the identical conditions.

There is another way to read the same lesson. One can think of the random elements in the process as corresponding to considerations that are at least observable, and perhaps even predictable, but do not reflect the working of strictly economic laws. On that interpretation, the lesson says that detailed prediction of economic events may require knowledge of a large number of specific facts, including non-economic facts, as well as of economic "laws" (theories). This proposition is fully consonant with our own conception of the role and utility of economic theory, but is at odds with prevailing doctrine and practice.[17]

The simulation results can, of course, be approached in this spirit. It is plain enough that the random events in the model are, collectively, the source of the random variation in outcomes. But which random events matter most to particular outcome variables and by what chains of causation do the effects arise? What would one have to know to be able to predict specific features of the outcomes? We have one example of a partial answer to such a question: The effectiveness of imitation – as measured in our model by the randomly varying number of imitation draws occurring in the first half of the run (*JDIM*) – seems to bear importantly on the results of the researchers–imitators struggle. The following regression explaining cumulative research expenditure,

$$\begin{aligned} CUMREX = \underset{(10.2)}{464.3} - \underset{(-3.67)}{5.35\,JDIM} - \underset{(-0.132)}{0.98\,BANK} + \underset{(4.62)}{94.3\log_2(J)} \\ - \underset{(-6.19)}{20.7\,[\log_2(J)]^2}, \end{aligned}$$

has an R^2 of 0.68. Without the imitation draws variable, *JDIM*, the R^2 is 0.58. Note that the number of imitation draws in the first half of the run is essentially exogenous random input to the model: Since all firms have the same imitation policies, and these are adjusted as the number of firms varies to compensate the change in the industry capital, the only systematic endogenous influence on *JDIM* is the decline in the capital stock resulting from rising concentration. This is a negligible influence on the expected value of *JDIM*, compared to the purely random variation in *JDIM* around its expectation. [The mean of *JDIM* is about 22, the standard deviation (run-to-run) is about 4.]

[17]The proposition is, however, entirely consistent with the position taken by Leontief in his presidential address (1971).

The most straightforward explanation of this effect is this: the more imitation draws there are in the first part of the run, the smaller the profits produced by the research draws. The smaller those profits, the smaller both desired and financable investment of researchers tend to be, and hence the smaller the researchers tend to be. Events in the first part of the run appear to be particularly significant, because an initial shift of capital share toward imitators seems to produce a cumulative process in that same direction. The average productivity lead of researchers dwindles, and even becomes negative, as the number of their research and imitation draws declines. This "slippery slope" effect is involved in the "research debacles", i.e., the runs in which the *gross* return to research is negative.

11. Summary and Conclusions

Let us review the basic elements of our conceptualization of the process of technical change. We have treated the process as one of "tracking" the potential for productivity improvement that is implicit in the exogenous advance of knowledge relevant to the industry's practice. We have assumed that firms are significant institutional units in the dissemination of technical information; the mechanisms by which information moves from firm to firm are costly and uncertain, but once a firm has acquired information, it can apply it on an arbitrary scale without further cost. We have represented firm policies toward research and imitation as long-term, quasi-genetic strategic commitments, linking effort to the size of the firm. And finally, in experimenting with different industry structures, we have held total resource commitments to information acquisition constant. Of course, no one of these elements is an axiom, immune to empirical overthrow, or to adaptation to the purposes of some different inquiry. Together, however, they are the basis for a coherent analytic model that is clearly more appropriate to the study of the Schumpeterian hypothesis, and other phenomena of dynamic competition, than models in the neoclassical tradition.

The particular numerical results obtained in our simulation experiments are not, in and of themselves, of great theoretical or practical interest. Different parameter settings would lead to different numerical results. Some of the parameter values that bear most critically on the phenomena of interest are ones for which it is most difficult to provide an empirical basis; specifically, this is the case with the parameters that translate research and imitation expenditures into expected "draws", and ultimately into techniques discovered. These parameters also determine the extent of stochastic variation in the research and imitation outcomes –

which, as we have shown, is a major determinant of some of the most striking qualitative features of the results. Furthermore, we have conducted our experiments only in a single demand environment, characterized by a stationary demand curve of unitary elasticity, and a single latent productivity environment, characterized by steady advance at a particular geometric rate. The quantitative assumption regarding the cost and effectiveness of research and initiation, together with the assumed rate of latent productivity growth, turned out to define a regime in which research is somewhat unprofitable.

Although the scope of our specific results in this study is narrow, the theoretical issues raised and clarified are, we think, of general significance. As is often the case, the clarification of issues involves recognition of the importance of certain distinctions. It matters whether the standard of progressiveness" in an industry is the level of average productivity, or the productivity of best practice technique, or the price of the product. Whether large scale enterprise confers advantages in progressiveness or not depends not only on how one defines progressiveness, but also what specific structural condition of the industry as a whole represents organization into large scale enterprises. And, of course, it matters what specific policy measures are to be used to affect the structure of an industry, when that structure may be subject to rapid change by endogenous mechanisms.

Our results provide illustrations of the possible importance of these distinctions. These are "possibilities" not merely in the sense of being logically possible, but in the sense of being possible in the context of a specified economic selection environment, in which the success of any particular policy or firm is linked to and limited by the other policies and firms in that environment. Let us review a few of them: Although large size confers advantages on an innovating firm, in terms of the ability to appropriate the returns from innovation, that advantage may be cancelled if rivals are also large, and able to respond more quickly for that reason. A concentrated structure may result in an industry achieving higher productivity levels at each point of time, but the output restraint associated with the concentration may more than offset this advantage from the buyer's point of view. A more atomistic structure may result in poorer average productivity performance because it diffuses innovations more slowly, but for that very reason it may offer higher returns to innovation and thus result in superior performance as measured by best practice technique. If the profitability of research is low or negative, but some firms are research-oriented nevertheless, the persistence of research efforts may be contingent on a degree of market power. A relatively concentrated structure may tend to be much more stable, in the face of the uncertainties associated with technical change, than a relatively concentrated one.

This is a rather complex array of possible mechanisms and behaviors, all illustrated by what is basically a very simple model. It is obviously much *too* simple, in the sense that it is easy to compile a long list of significant features of reality that are not represented in it. But, as we have emphasized elsewhere, we make no apologies for constructing and studying simple models of economic evolution. We claim the usual prerogative of dividing the difficulties. We also claim that the particular difficulties we have chosen to attack are, at least, worth conquering.

12. References

Alchian, A. A., 1950, Uncertainty, evolution and economic theory, Journal of Political Economy 58, June, pp. 211–222.

Arrow, K. J., 1962, Economic welfare and the allocation of resources for invention, The rate and direction of inventive activity (Princeton University Press for the National Bureau of Economic Research, Princeton, NJ).

Clark, J. M., 1955, Competition: Static models and dynamic aspects, American Economic Review 45, May, pp. 450–462.

Feller, W., 1957, An introduction to probability theory and its applications, vol. 1, 2nd ed. (Wiley, New York).

Fellner, W. J., 1949, Competition among the few (Alfred A. Knopf, New York).

Fellner, W. J., 1951, The influence of market structure on technological progress, Quarterly Journal of Economics 65, Nov., pp. 556–577.

Fisher, F. M. and P. Temin, 1973, What does the Schumpeterian hypothesis imply? Journal of Political Economy 81, Jan.–Feb., pp. 56–70.

Kamien, M. I. and N. L. Schwartz, 1975, Market structure and innovation: A survey, Journal of Economic Literature 13, March, pp. 1–37.

Leontief, W., 1971, Theoretical assumptions and nonobserved facts, American Economic Review 61, March, pp. 1–7.

Mansfield, E., 1968, Industrial research and technological innovation (W. W. Norton, New York).

McNulty, P. J., 1968, Economic theory and the meaning of competition, Quarterly Journal of Economics 82, Nov., pp. 639–656.

Nelson, R. R., M. J. Peck and E. D. Kalachek, 1967, Technology, economic growth and public policy (Brookings Institution, Washington, DC).

Nelson, R. R., S. G. Winter and H. L. Schuette, 1976, Technical change in an evolutionary model, Quarterly Journal of Economics 90, Feb., pp. 90–118.

Scherer, F. M., 1970, Industrial market structure and economic performance (Rand McNally, Chicago, IL).

Schumpeter, J. A., 1950, Capitalism, socialism, and democracy, 3rd ed. (Harper & Brothers, New York).

Schumpeter, J. A., 1955, The theory of economic development (Harvard University Press, Cambridge, MA).

Williamson, O. E., 1972, Dominant firms and the monopoly problem: Market failure considerations, Harvard Law Review 85, June, pp. 1512–1531.

Chapter 4

A Model of the Endowment of Human Wealth

OR

Let's Look at Social Policy Through the Eyes of the 21st Century's Adults

Harold W. WATTS

"The fundamental fact about society as a going concern is that it is made up of individuals who are born and die and give place to others; and the fundamental fact about modern civilization is that it is dependent upon the utilization of three great accumulating funds of inheritance from the past, material goods and appliances, knowledge and skill, and morale. Besides the torch of life itself, the material wealth of the world, a technological system of vast and increasing intricacy and the habituations which fit men for social life must in some manner be carried forward to new individuals born devoid of all things as older individuals pass out."

Frank K. Knight (1921)*

1. Introduction

The essay that follows represents an attempt to provide a framework for understanding an important part of the process that gives continuity and sometimes progress to a society. It is a framework that may unify or at least envelop a number of concepts and sub-models which have developed in the micro-economics of the household during the past decade, and perhaps give some guidance about where future analysis would be especially fruitful.

But there is another motivation behind this attempt at system-building. One important aspect of our social policies, active or passive, lies in their effect on children – on how they grow and develop into future adults and parents of succeeding generations. While there is a clear and generally acknowledged validity to the primitive notion that there is something

*Knight, F. H., 1921, Risk uncertainty and profit (Houghton Mifflin, Boston) p. 375.

uniquely important about children and their development, there is not a comparable framework of analysis that elucidates or demonstrates that importance. It is not difficult for an orator to incite emotional assent to the proposition that our children are our only social legacy and few legislators are able to resist supporting programs (however symbolic and unproved) which promise to brighten the lives of deprived children. But when we, as economists, come to analyze existing or proposed policies, we do not have a theory which explicitly distinguishes children from "people in general" or which yields an explanation of why children and the process of their nurture and rearing may deserve the rapt attention of orators and political representatives. This essay will indicate a possible approach to the development of such a theory, and thereby provide a more coherent analytical structure for considering current issues of policy.

I have become convinced that children do form a useful category of humanity for economic analysis or public policy and the main burden of this essay is to pass that conviction on. The critical link is the concept of human wealth – that cornerstone of permanent income theory which has already done so much to revitalize our thinking about the dynamic behavior of households. Clearly childhood is when a great deal of capital-formation is happening. I would interpret experts in child-development as saying that some kinds of human capital can *only* be acquired in childhood and that some part is analogous to the "infra-structure" kinds of physical capital that are required if subsequent investment is to be fruitful. Hence policies toward children are, from an economic point of view, the primary instruments by which the endow-ments of human capital to successive cohorts of adults can be altered. The variety and malleability and inequality of that capital endowment as distributed to individuals is, in turn, an important component of both the potential productivity of a cohort and its contribution to future social and political stress.

It is perhaps useful to recognize that present groups of "children" (0–18 years) will be 25–43 at the close of the 20th century. Our present college students will mostly have found their level of mediocrity and will be striving to consolidate it, while they pay for educating *their* children. The vital and innovative cohorts as we enter the 21st century are now on our laps and in our schools. How, we might ask, will they view their legacy of human capital, again in terms of variety, malleability and inequality? Will they wish that less human potential had been wasted, will their social policies be pre-occupied with immense disparities in earning capacities, will they find themselves vulnerable to skill obsolescence or "structural" unemployment, etc.?

A part of what I want to urge is that this process of working backward from a desirable end point or steady state can give us useful guidance for present-day policies. The possibility of such insights is hardly in question, and the techniques of dynamic programming give some hope that explicitly stated problems can be solved. But my present objective is much more modest than the explicit calculation of an efficient sub-space. I want to assert and explore the proposition that an appropriate economic specification of the problem of choice among policies toward children should focus on how alternative policies affect the endowment of wealth in a cohort of children and on how that endowment – with all the potential and problems it contains – promotes or hinders that cohort's individual and collective efforts to achieve societal goals.

There are many issues of policy facing our society which have a relatively direct impact on children and many others which are indirect but no less powerful. We have allocated resources to compensatory education but we do not have a satisfactory basis for judging whether such policies should be abandoned or intensified. How higher education should be financed is another live issue and the confusing area of day care and preschool education is moving toward some sort of (probably) massive public involvement. But these are among the policies which have an immediate effect on children. Consider the grand macro-issues as well since the effects of unemployment and diminished purchasing power do not fall equally on childless and childed families, nor even on the parents of young vs. older children. Here the chances for full development of many children may be diminished well beyond our ability to compensate. Likewise, other conditions of employment – hours, occupational hazards and compulsory relocation – may be unnecessarily harmful to parental effectiveness.

In sum, this essay will attempt to outline an improved theoretical framework which can provide a crucial and dynamic perspective on the role and possible effects of alternative programs, and at the same time encourage more efficient inquiry into human behavior and the effects of alternative institutions and policies.

2. Parts of the Model that Now Exist

As already mentioned the basic concept is human wealth – a concept which has been thoroughly introduced. I will here recognize a difference between human wealth which is a value aggregate, and human capital which is the real "commodity" and may take a variety of forms and dimensions. The price of types of human capital may change causing a change in wealth without a corresponding change in those human capacities which we think of as capital. For the most part I will be considering issues of investment in capital – building capacities out of potentials – without reference to the aggregate of wealth or the prices which define it. But expectations about those prices do condition the choices considered later, and the eventually realized "wages" are the ultimate arguments of the social welfare function we can argue about.

The development in recent years of a "New Home Economics", as named by Nerlove, has produced a large amount of theoretical and empirical work that is directly relevant. This line of inquiry has been the subject of three National Bureau Conferences and is, at this point, a very significant fraction of ongoing economic research and publication. A central concept in this work is the value of human time – a variable which effects and is affected by fertility choices and which is also central to most household production, labor supply, and consumption choices. The relation of that time value to human wealth should be clear – it is simply the flow that corresponds to that wealth stock. When we observe behavior that implies the value of time has increased we should infer that human wealth has increased by a similar proportion.

It would not be far-fetched to propose that the value of time is a welfare indicator of a more relevant and meaningful sort, than is, say, per capita GNP or consumption of market goods. The value of time is not dependent upon how the time is allocated to market and non-market uses and, subject to the qualification of involuntary unemployment, gives a better notion of the range of choices available than does realized income.

We already have a well developed set of measures and arguments about how the income distribution might enter a social welfare function. What we do not have is a very happy solution to the concept of income we would like to measure and argue about. The general emphasis of the framework developed here will suggest strongly that is the distribution of human wealth or the value-of-time among individuals at the point of achieving emancipated adulthood – 22–25 years, say – which should be a major focus of policy along with monitoring of how that distribution is changed by unforeseen price or policy changes as the cohort becomes older. We should not be so concerned with the outcomes of *voluntary* choices about how time of a given value is utilized *except* where those choices prejudice the full development of the time value of someone in a succeeding generation.

A further point and possible conflict having to do with aggregate wealth and the output flow it produces ought to be noted here. Most people would favor policies that promote "full" development of the potential capacities of children – few favor deliberate stunting or maiming. Such development of course, increases individual and aggregate real human wealth in the sense that someone at least is capable of performing more and/or more valuable services. Assuming that people will want to exercise at least part of their increment in productive potential, and that we want to provide employment for all who desire it, we must expect to observe economic growth – both in terms of potential and realized output. Those who propose a no-growth society should carefully consider how they want to depress either the development of human capacities or the freedom to utilize those capacities once acquired.

3. What are the Determinants of an Individual's Human Wealth?

As a first step in developing the theory it may be useful to list and categorize the influences that bear upon the amount and value of human capital which an individual brings into adulthood. Frank Knight characterized the process as "... a world where individuals are born naked, destitute, helpless, ignorant and untrained, and must spend a third of their lives acquiring the prerequisties of a free contractual existence." Let us consider further what determines the outcome of that "gestation period".

To begin with we must recognize some biological inheritance and immediately admit that we know very little about how or even whether genetic factors enter the process of acquiring the learned responses we associate with human capital. Certainly there is some genetic determination of purely physical attributes (and no small amount of environmental influence as well) that affect human capital (height, lung capacity, etc.). It is certainly possible that some cognitive capacities and affectional dispositions are similarly "innate". But there are no direct measures for these at birth, and their reflection in measurable behavior, which is inevitably learned by interaction with an environment, remains quite ambiguous. There can be no ambiguity, however, about the importance of environment in the development in children of human capacities. The fact that I am quite unemployable as a TV repairman has very little to do with the genes I inherited but a great deal to do with the history, including chance elements, of my growing up and formal education. We can't know, and surely will never experience, how much inequality of human capital of various kinds would exist if environmental factors were absolutely constant. But given the unquestionable leverage of environmental influences, there is not much operational significance in the question to begin with. Similarly we have no reason to think that any constant or variable innate capacity limits have been reached by our halting gropes toward optimal human development and there is always the possibility of completely unexplored human potentials awaiting eventual discovery and exploitation.

But let us reserve the possibility, some would say likelihood, that there is a substantial genetic influence on an individual's potential for development of various capacities, and turn to the environmental influences where we have both evidence of potency and a better chance of purposeful change. Most of the early influence comes via the family – involving parents or surrogates in the absence of parents. This nurture is an intensively private and individual activity. The child-rearing household can be thought of as a productive organization capable of producing the goods and services – shelter; nutrition; security; physical, psychic and intellectual interaction and stimulation, etc. – that serve as inputs to a child's development. The human wealth of the parents or other adult members of a child's family is an important determinant of the quantity and quality of nurture that the child will receive. Clearly two parents well endowed with human capital will be able to provide ample material inputs without using up all of the parents' time and energy, and leaving enough of both to provide the direct labor and affection input required to nourish, stimulate, and protect a developing child. One parent, or two with low human wealth, will find it much more difficult to provide a satisfactory level of nurturing services.

Household technology is also an important influence on the amount and kind of nurturing a household is able to provide. This applies both to "hard-goods" technology such as appliances, textile innovations, and convenience foods, and to the softer technology of know-how and technique in the production of the services needed by developing children, or in the judicious use of outside services available for either routine or emergency use.

From the testimony of psychologists and others specializing in child development it appears that a great deal of a child's future personality and approach to learning are determined in the earliest years of childhood. Certainly those are the years when an enormous range of responses and behaviors are learned, and the predominant influence comes from the parent or parents and the human and material elements of the immediate family setting. Even during later years when schooling takes up a part of the day for a part of the week for part of the year, we should remember that a great deal of the "input", whether it be food for thought or for the belly, still originates in the family and parental circle.

To these considerations we should add the evidence from the "Coleman Report" that family background is a more important determinant of variation in school achievement than is the quantity and quality of school inputs. We could also note that attempts to secure durable changes in cognitive achievement among children who are "behind" their peers, have been successful mainly where some modification has been made in the amount or quality of a child's stimulation in the home and/or from his parents. A relatively conventional conclusion is suggested – namely that influences originating in the family and especially in the child's interaction with parents, are tremendously important influences on a child's development.

It should be explicitly noted that a suspicion about *where* a large amount of the capital-formation happens is a long way from knowing just how it happens and what can be done either by parents or by legislation to affect the detailed outcomes. We may be able to use weak average correlations to suggest that where greater amounts of input (parental time, material goods, qualitative factors) are available the children develop greater amounts and/or varieties of capabilities and hence end up with greater human wealth. I would argue that "weak" results of this sort are about the most we can hope for and that much further study and analysis is needed to establish quantitative reliability even for such aggregate tendencies. More detailed causal models providing foolproof blueprints for producing standard or "customized" adults seem so far beyond the reach of our understanding that the problem of what to do with such power is not worth much discussion. We can nevertheless recognize family and parental influence as being the source of much variation not amenable to further explanation and an additional portion that is due to parental response to influences that can be manipulated exogenously.

Moving outside the family-household sphere, but not too far outside, the child encounters the immediate neighborhood and community (if any). A number of important influences derive from that setting. Other people, and especially other children are met mainly in one's neighborhood and the perceived "suitability" of those persons is probably the main criterion for a parent in judging the quality of a neighbourhood. There are also institutions, especially schools, but also libraries, day care facilities, clinics, churches, etc., which are present in greater or lesser density and together form an important part of the influences absorbed by a child and also determine the availability of services that the child's parent may require in the provision of nurture. Here is where encounters with organized society begin and where the survival value of skills and procedures learned at home can be tested and perfected.

The schools, as part of the neighborhood influence need little emphases as important inputs into the development of a child's human capital. The question may be whether schools should be treated as a separate major category. The answer is that schools, because they exist solely for the purpose of doing something with or to children, are most often *over*-emphasized. The knowledge and skills that the schools are somewhat specialized in providing are very important as components of human capital and in some part crucial to further development of some kinds of capabilities. But it is too easy to forget the many things that are being learned and the amount of coincidental experience that comes outside the school during the years of compulsory attendance. Both the home and the wider neighborhood make large inputs to a child's development and these surely interact in complex ways with experiences at school.

As for understanding of the causal process involving these neighborhood influences, we are at least as uncertain about the specifications of optimality as we are for the family inputs. Some neighborhoods are simply physically dangerous, and others may be too stimulating for some children and still others may be so bland and homogeneous that understimulation is a problem. We are probably able to place some "lower bounds" or identify some generally harmful conditions, but beyond that we must again recognize individual variations in both children and parents in their interaction with a given neighborhood environment. But we must also insist that the "richness" and variety of intellectual, physical and emotional stimulation offered by the community is a substantial influence on a child's development and also protest against the supposition that such activities are monopolized by the schools.

A final category of influences must be mentioned, involving a somewhat broader ecology than the neighborhood. One can think of society as a whole; or the state, nation, or world, but it is perhaps more fruitful to consider how these broader contexts are conveyed to the child.

Consider instead communication, transportation, and mobility as the more immediate source of influence. Clearly television has had a substantial effect on how children spend their time and no doubt on their conception of the world outside their home and community. As for an assessment of television's impact of the development of human capital, there is not much conclusive evidence to date. The usual situation holds of being able to gain some agreement on a few features of television that are "bad" or "harmful" and for the rest falling back on individual variation in the absence of any clear criterion of optimality.

Of course, the other mass media also share in bringing a wider range of experience to children, and it may be correct to include the recording industry here along with written and broadcast "messages".

The ease of transportation and the fact of geographic mobility of families affects the likelihood that a child will directly experience different environments or, at the very least, will encounter age peers who have originated somewhere else. This is another way in which information and broadened competence can be imparted, both of which augment the fund of human capital.

To review, we have enumerated the sources of influences that affect a child's development of the capacities we term human capital. Starting with a biologically given bundle of potentials for development, the parents and family are seen as the prime source of the nurturing goods and services and probably the major source of variation in the final result. The neighborhood and community become more important for children as they become older and begin to interact with a wider society of age peers and others in schools and less organized settings. Finally the television and other media augment personal or "eyewitness" sources of information and experience about the world beyond the immediate family and neighborhood (the reliability of the image of that world is not being considered here).

4. What Are the Basic Mechanisms in the Process of Building Human Capital?

In the discussion of influences the primary inputs to human capital formation have been mentioned implicitly if not explicitly. Now it is time to consider how imputs are allocated and what are the potentials and limitations of various policy approaches for changing the level and/or distribution of human capital. This will be approached by reviewing first the critical choices which are made privately, usually within a family and constrained by prices and incomes. This is followed by a discussion of general areas of public choices that either affect child development directly or operate through incomes, prices, etc. on family and parental decisions.

Our society leaves a great many of the detailed choices that are relevant to a child's development in the hands of the parents. Indeed, the choice of whether a child will be conceived (and increasingly, if conceived, whether born) is essentially a private choice. Hence, if we regard the gross additions to a social human wealth aggregate as a function of the quantity and quality of the annual cohort of new adults, we see that the cumulative decisions of their parents over the past 20–25 years comprise a very large part of the "causal" influence on that gross investment.

Our economic models of household behavior, including the "New Home Economics", generally analyze parental choices as current consumption – which may be appropriate from the parents' point of view – rather than as a wealth transfer which would be a more appropriate category from the viewpoint of the "developed" child entering his/her own adulthood. Whether that future wealth status of the child is fully internalized as a source of present satisfaction for the parents is an open question. But regardless of the characterization of the motivations of parents – selfish, hedonistic, altruistic, sacrificing – they have the authority and responsibility for allocating resources within the family between functions which accumulate the elements of human capital in their children and other possible uses. It may be useful to consider some of the major parental choices which seen likely to affect the child's development.

The decision to become a parent (and how many times and at what intervals) is one of the most basic choices. While the degree of control of fertility on the part of individuals may have been subject to qualification and debate in past decades, there is no longer much question that the means for such control are quite generally available and the knowledge and disposition required for their use is spreading rapidly as well.

A great deal of analytical talent has been devoted to the study of human fertility by economists and demographers and some promising hypotheses and models are available. But the interest in such models for our purposes lies in their use to determine important aspects of the environment in which a given child develops. Clearly the relationship between income and birth probabilities affects how many children are born into families with scanty material resources and how many into relative abundance. Again, holding constant the earning rate of the parents, the number and spacing of siblings directly affects how many shares must be made from available resources at various times during childhood.

The number and spacing of children in a family also has a great deal to do with the sharing of human services expended within the family. In larger families the time, effort, patience and affection of a mother and/or father simply have to be spread over a larger number of children. At the same time, the interactions among siblings and the possible substitution of sibling services for parent services suggest that the relation of fertility rates to the availability of inputs for child development is a bit more complex than simple division of a fixed pie among available mouths.

Another decision of parents is crucial to at least the nature, if not the outcome of the child rearing process. This is how parents deploy their time in outside activities for purposes of earning income. The "classical" nuclear family in which the father specializes in work outside the home and the mother specializes in work inside the home can no longer be regarded as a norm, but it is still quite prevalent and is useful as a point of departure because speculative thinking about families usually presumes that model. The most common departure is for the mother also to engage in outside employment – usually as a "secondary" earner. Clearly this departure from the stereotype is a matter of degree depending on which the mother works full or part-time, and for how much of the typical year. But it is becoming more and more common for mothers, especially in small families to work at some time during their child's developing years, although it is still relatively uncommon while the children are infants, or when there are many children in total.

The other major departure is the single parent family. There is no possible division of labor within such families and the solitary parent must usually choose between some sort of dependency (welfare) status that allows full-time parenting, or independence achieved through outside employment in combination with most of the burdens of parenthood. Of course, for many single mothers the choice is severely constrained by limited earning capacity and/or opportunity.

In either case the departures from the cozy stereotype involve some need for alternate care-takers for children on a regular basis. This need is met in a variety of ways: intra-family arrangements using older children and spouses; extended family members enlisted as "sitters", hired "nannies"; day care homes, or organized day care centers. From the point of view of the child's development, this involvement of non-parents is a significant departure from the pattern we associate with the "Dick and Jane" stereotype.

While this choice of in-home versus out-of-home activities is most salient for mothers at the present time, movements toward sex equality may come to involve more fathers in the same allocational process. But in any case, the issue of quantity and quality of the direct human service input to a child's development is related to the choices parents make about their own time. It should not be assumed that there is any simple conclusion about whether more or less personal parenting is "good" for children. Surely there is a great deal of individual variation in parental ability and disposition, and we should always expect a wider choice, exercised with judgement, to lead to a happier, if not "better" result.

Still another area of decision-making appears critical from a number of points of view – the choice of residential location. A large number of services are not distributed uniformly, and certainly the nature of the physical environment is location-specific, and hence the choice of location is a determinant of a lot of other influences on a child's development. As mentioned above with regard to neighborhood influences, we can feel reasonably confident that some environments are generally "bad" ones for child-rearing – e.g., no positive features of lead paint and cockroach infestations have been proposed. Fewer people than in the past are now inclined to promote the benefits of a rural setting without qualification. Certainly, a reasonable preparation for adulthood in the urban setting, which will be the destiny of most children, ought to include something beyond vocational agriculture. There is, of course, plenty of room for individual differences since there are lots of locations and lots of children.

This leads into yet another area of choice, one which to some extent subsumes all of the others – that of "style" of upbringing. There is no one dimensional measure of "style" of course. But there is some sense in which the tradition expressed in the parents' own upbringing is modified, adapted or departed from in the pattern adopted for their own children. In part these elements of style or strategy will be expressed in the choices about becoming a parent, decisions to work, where to live, etc. But even within family size, type and location categories, there will remain substantial variation in the way in which parents interact with children and prepare them for eventual adulthood.

The existence of substantial amounts of variation in the way children are raised might itself be interpreted as evidence against any simple prescription for optimal child development. It should rather suggest that there are a lot of ways to "succeed" both in the sense of many ways to secure a given goal, as well as a great many possible goals. Put another way, the production function and the output set are both extremely complex. We must recognize this complexity and appreciate how preferences, talents and opportunities may interact in a given parental choice process which yields one or several new entrants in upcoming cohorts of new adults.

Much has been said above about the choices made by parent-households that bear on the development of children. So far we have not considered the constraints on the choices. There are first of all the conventional constraints of an economic nature – the choices available to a poor parent are simply more restricted. The disparities among children in terms of the income available to their parents is very wide indeed, and a much larger fraction of all children are below the poverty threshold than is the case for non-aged adults (currently 14% versus 8%). Certainly the over-all resource constraint is the most pressing one for most parents but there are other constraints that should be noted. One has to do with unequal availability of services – some areas are doctor-poor even for those who can pay for them. Similar situations have been claimed for child care services. Lack of information and/or uncertainty probably restricts further the choices perceived by parents.

5. Public Choices

By contrast, the choices available to shapers of social policy for affecting human wealth formation seem relatively weak and indirect. There is very little that public policy can do directly with the very young child so long as the basic autonomy and dominance of the parents and the family is maintained. The primary exception is, of course, compulsory education for children between 6 and 16 (usually). Here services are provided directly and (largely) free of charge. Children are required to accept the services or secure a certified equivalent at added expense. No doubt the compulsory feature could be extended to other services or ages, but there does not seem to be much enthusiasm for such an extension.

But public choices also include direct provision of goods or services on a non-compulsory basis. Kindergarten and the final years of high school are two examples. Health services are generally not compulsory (except for some immunizations) and this is an area of increasing collective activity. There is also a wide variety of social services that can be and, in various places and times, are being provided free of charge or on some means-tested fee schedule.

Short of full subsidization it is possible to change the effective relative prices of goods or services by partial subsidies. It is possible to view food stamps in this way – a reduction in the relative price of one important category of goods aimed at improving nutrition. In the case of food stamps the degree of subsidization or price reduction is also graduated by income. However food stamps are not available in freely variable quantities and this makes their effect more like a simple income subisdy combined with a side condition of minimal food purchase.

Direct income subsidies have been available for children via a number of public programs for many years. Much of the early activity concerned the child deprived of a male breadwinner by death, divorce, or abandonment. So far there has been a decided reluctance on the part of legislators to subsidize intact families with an employed breadwinner. Unemployment and in some cases underemployment of a father has recently become an acceptable basis for subsidizing children in low income families, and the Food Stamp Program – regarded as an income subsidy – is conditioned only on income and allows low-wage intact families to benefit. Of course, the provisions of the personal income tax grants an exemption for children – one that is most valuable for high-income tax payers and also allows deduction of child care expenses for low- and middle-income parents where these are costs of earning income. Finally the medical expenses of children (as well as adults) may be deductible if they are a large fraction of income. These items are a partial list of the provisions which accomplish income redistribution both from the rich to the poorer and from the childless to the childed family units. In both dimensions this is one of the most important and pervasive ways that public choices affect child development. Besides the provision of free or subsidized services and the redistributional activities, public policies in the form of family law (marriage, divorce, adoption); regulations concerned with employment conditions (including government's role as a major employer); and regulation of broadcasters, drug manufacturers, etc. form yet another category of policies which use the coercive powers of the state to prohibit or promote activities which may have a bearing on children. In the spirit of general equilibrium, all policies must have some impact of course, but it is possible to rank some as of greater apparent importance in changing the conditions in which children grow up – in their families, in their neighborhoods, and in their contacts with the broader reaches of society. Clearly we must look beyond those programs which have "child" somewhere in their title.

6. Elements of the Model

It may be useful to regard the child as a repository for accumulating elements of human capital which are produced by inputs of goods and services according to some "accumulation function". Choices are made as to input mixes and output goals by parents in the early years with a growing participation by the child as it grows toward adult autonomy. But the choices are made in the context of resource constraints which vary across households and depend on existing price structures. Public policy can affect the choices by changing the distribution of disposable resources, through tax and transfer policies, by changing relative prices of "merit" goods with subsidies, and by directly providing goods and services to families with children, with or without compulsion.

A child's "accumulation function" can be specified more precisely as determining the change in a vector of stocks of various forms of human capital depending both on the current levels of such stocks and on the current flows of capital-building services. Realism might urge allowing for accidental injury or vicious practices that diminish capital stocks as well.

The next element needed could be termed a service supply function that would yield the flows of capital-building services as functions of pre-determined family variables and relevant policy parameters we shall regard as exogenous. These flow equations should be regarded as reduced form relations which subsume the household's production function for services of all kinds, the constraints coming from adult human wealth employment opportunities; public tax, transfer, and subsidy policies; plus the public's more direct provision of educational and other services, and all of these interacting with the preferences of the parent(s) who makes the allocational choices.

Now assuming that the two aforementioned sets of relationships can be specified and even estimated, we would have a means of linking individual capital accumulation patterns to parental characteristics including their human wealth and to public policy parameters. One obvious question to be considered at this point is the stability properties of the human wealth distribution. Are the transmission-of-wealth elasticities so large that, unless diluted by public policies, better endowed parents would provide an even greater relative advantage, on average, to their offspring? Similarly, would the poorest be constrained (or inclined) to leave their children even less well equipped to earn a share of society's total product? While an unstable system would provide a uniquely compelling rationale for intervention in the human capital investment process, a stable system need not move toward a satisfactory level of capital investment or toward a degree of inequality in human wealth that is acceptable on ethical or aesthetic grounds and again intervention can be justified.

Within the relations determining supply of human capital investment services there is a great deal of room for partitioning off sub-models of household choice behavior in the several areas discussed above. Particularly in the fertility and labor supply areas there is a substantial amount of theory and empirical work in existence and in progress.

Investigation of the allocation of time and expenditure budgets for families with children are clearly important parts of the "investment" function. Here it must be emphasized that major attention should be given to exploring behavioral response to variables that can be affected by public policy – that is the critical link in establishing a basis for forecasting the dynamic consequences of policy choices.

The "accumulation" function needs a lot of work. So far most of the attention has been given to only one category of inputs – schooling – and one output – cognitive ability as measured by I.Q. tests. We need to begin working with a broader range of inputs and a wider variety of outcomes or types of human capital.

Unfortunately, there is not a readily available set of measures of human capacities, nor even of concepts for which approximate indicators can be sought. No doubt my own incomplete development handicaps me in suggesting plausible categories, but I have observed that concerted efforts of psychologists and educators have not been successful so far in defining a more comprehensive set of outcomes for the Head Start program and similar compensatory efforts. There is a general agreement that "I.Q." is inadequate and rapidly loses predictive power beyond the years of formal schooling, but promising additional dimensions have not yet been found. Here, clearly, is an area that needs much more development of concepts, measures and models. It is also an area where the input of other disciplines is imperative. Economists may be able to structure the kinds of questions that need answering, but they are usually ill equipped for finding the answers.

Reverting to the original title of this essay, a word must be said about the wealth and income which ultimately result from the market's evaluation and the possessor's exercise of these elements of human capital. A complete model of wealth will have to include a demand side, and since many human investment decisions are made with long lags or gestation periods a model of expectations about future prices of human services must also be considered and implemented if we are to complete the wealth transmission process.

7. *Concluding Remarks*

To repeat, the purpose of this essay is to suggest a framework into which a large amount of contemporary micro-economic thought can be unified and tied to the notion of social progress or growth, *and* to give an economic interpretation to the recurrent notion that society ought to be concerned about what happens to children and that this concern should be a basis for ordering social priorities. In outlining this structure several gaps and lines for further study have been identified. But, perhaps more important than the ways in which "old" economic models can be reinterpreted and "new" extensions can be devised, is the focus that a concern for the human wealth endowment can give to social policy. By emphasizing the human capital investments in children we are directly in touch with the fundamental determinants of the quality and inequality of existence in future generations. We are brought more directly into confrontation with the pivotal importance of parents and families in that process. We can note further that only a small part of the adult population is involved in active "parenting" at any one time (and some never are) and that that minority gets a much smaller than proportional share of total economic resource flows with which to carry on that child-rearing process. Another interesting change of perspective takes place when one concentrates on those future adults – one is roughly four times as interested in what happens in a four-child-family than in what happens in a one-child-family. Clearly when one considers differences in family size one can find a very small minority of current adults responsible for the capital investment decisions for a majority of the new adult crop of, say, 1995, and again with a quite meager budget to allocate to those activities.

Without entering the discussion of whether more or less inequality of human wealth is desirable, it would be generally agreed that the process by which wealth is transmitted across generations *is* affected by public policy and that the quality and inequality of that wealth *is* a major determinant of social welfare. Consequently a more explicit treatment of that dynamic process would permit a more focussed discussion of policies that affect children, as well as a more sensitive indicator of social progress.

Chapter 5

Towards a Social Index of Environmental Quality

Robert DORFMAN

Not very long ago when we explained that economics studied the production and distribution of scarce goods, the standard example of an undoubted good that was not scarce was air. I don't know what example we would use today. Neither air, nor water, nor even the ozone layer in the stratosphere seems to qualify. Kittens, maybe.

A whole new range of scarce commodities, called "the environment", has seized public attention and entered the jurisdiction of economics. But they have not entered the marketplace, and their production, preservation, and distribution are not governed by the institutions that apply to the traditionally scarce commodities. There were precursors of the current awareness of the importance of environmental commodities – Pigou made factory smoke an economic topic nearly a century ago, and congestion was the subject of a famous controversy of the 1920's – but appreciation of the scale and pervasiveness of environmental commodities is novel.

Largely because these commodities have only recently become scarce we have not inherited institutions for managing them – for preserving them and allocating their use. We have not even inherited a proper vocabulary for thinking about them, but have to adapt a hodge-podge of concepts developed in other contexts.[1] At the moment societies are busy inventing the requisite institutions, and economists are working on the tools for analyzing the emergent social devices. The current situation is so unsettled that normal decision processes have become awkward to the point of paralysis.

Petroleum refineries are a case in point. They are notorious consumers (in the strict sense of the word) of clean air and clean water. Before those commodities became scarce, refineries were sited according to well-tested business principles: with an eye to cheap land, ample intake water, and access to transportation. Nowadays, though, the community, as custodian of the newly scarce commodities, becomes involved and, failing any established procedure for reconciling the plusses and minuses, the

[1]For example, we sometimes say that everyone consumes the same amount of a public good. But if "consumes" means "uses up", no one really consumes a public good at all.

decision process stalls. Clearly neither the old way of locating refineries nor the new one is tolerable.

I am not about to take on the large task of resolving such perplexities. New social decision processess will have to be evolved painfully. My concern in this paper is with only one ingredient, an important one, namely the factual basis. One reason, surely, that disputes about environmental decisions are so unresolvable is that we are substantially ignorant about the consequences of any alternative. One source of this ignorance is a remarkable deficiency of technical understanding – meteorological, hydrological, epidemiological, geological, ecological, and more – which an economist cannot help to overcome. But there is more to it than that. Even if the hard scientists knew the physical and biological facts there would remain an unsolved problem of social evaluation. These newly scarce commodities are now simply omitted from our economic accounts – for good reasons that have become obsolete. What was the point of including in GNP the services of 414 million acre-feet of fresh water a year at a value of zero per acre-foot? But now the unit value is no longer zero and, failing the traditional method of social evaluation in the marketplace, it is far from clear what the value is. That is the area in which I wish to probe.

There is, then, a well-recognized gap in the GNP accounts that leads to serious distortions. Under the current rules, if a factory increases its emissions of smoke, imposing increased medical and maintenance costs on its neighbors, GNP will rise; there is no off-setting entry for the reduced value of services of the atmosphere. But more important things are involved than tidying up our economic accounts. Protecting and improving the environment are undertakings of deep public concern. The official estimate is that an average of $20 billion a year (1973 dollars) will be spent during the next decade to carry out the federal laws and programs for environmental protection. The costs of local programs and requirements, and the opportunity costs of undertakings precluded for environmental reasons add more billions. In short, we are serious about conserving the newly scarce commodities.

In this circumstance there is clear need to monitor the state of the environment and to assess the results of the heavy expenses sustained on its behalf. The same sorts of data are needed to plan future programs and expenditures, to perform the function normally discharged by market prices. There is a limited budget available for environmental protection, and we do have to allocate it to the specific tasks where it will be most effective socially as well as technically. So we have to measure the social as well as the technical effects of various anti-pollution, anti-depletion, and anti-deterioration measures.

1. Some Recent Attempts

In this country the Council on Environmental Quality (as well as numerous other people and organizations) has long been alert to the importance of keeping tabs on the environment, and the history of their efforts is instructive. In their Third Annual Report (August 1972) the lead chapter was entitled "The Quest for Environmental Indices", and was devoted in large part to presenting a number of indices of national air and water quality that had been constructed under their sponsorship. We do not have to go into the methods used to construct those indices because in the next (Fourth Annual Report September, 1973) they were discontinued. Instead, in the measured prose appropriate to the annual reports of official agencies, there was a perceptive discussion of the conceptual problems that rendered the previous year's indices unsatisfactory, and a reaffirmation of intent to continue wrestling with the problem. The Fifth Annual Report (December 1974) initiates a more modest approach and one more consistent with the current state of competence. It includes a compendium of thirty statistical tables covering various aspects of the environment and the loads imposed on it, and offers a pilot effort toward a statistical abstract of environmental trends and conditions. No social or economic evaluations are attempted.

While the Americans are thus regrouping their forces, the Canadians are persisting with the construction of comprehensive environmental indices. Since the approach being followed in Canada is in the same general family as the American attempts, though with some significant differences, their work can be used to characterize the entire family.[2]

The result striven for is an array of indicators to depict the state of the environment in Canada as a whole and in individual provinces and metropolitan areas. For each geographic area there are separate indices for air quality, water quality, land quality, and miscellaneous aspects (meaning pesticide use and radioactivity), which can be combined into a comprehensive environmental quality index for the region.

Though the details vary, the basic strategy used to construct all these indices is uniform. The elementary unit of analysis is an annual (or monthly) average of physical measurements of some aspect of the environmental quality in some locality, say the annual average concentration of sulfur dioxide in the atmosphere of Ottawa. The ratio of the physical measurements to some objective or standard is then computed to obtain a specific aspect index, which is a dimensionless number. The

[2]The following discussion is based on Inhaber (1974). This paper reports on the work of the Federal Department of the Environment, Ottawa.

specific aspect indices are combined into a more inclusive index by computing a weighted root-mean-square, with the weights reflecting judgments of the relative importance of the different components. (Most of the American experiments used the same procedure, including root-mean-square averaging, to obtain indices of specific aspects and to average them.) Two examples will suffice.

One of the components of the air quality index is the "Index of Specific Pollutants", which is

$$I_{sp} = \sqrt{0.2I^2_{SO_2} + 0.1I^2_{SPM} + 0.1I^2_{COH} + 0.2I^2_{CO} + 0.2I^2_{NO_X}},$$

where the subscripts on the right denote sulfur dioxide, suspended particles, coefficient of haze, carbon monoxide, and nitrogen oxides, respectively. I_{SO_2}, for example, is the ratio of the observed annual average concentration of SO_2 in the atmosphere of, say, Ottawa to the prescribed atmospshetic standard.

The formula for the comprehensive index of environmental quality is

$$I_{EQI} = \sqrt{0.3I^2_{air} + 0.3I^2_{water} + 0.3I^2_{land} + 0.1I^2_{miscellaneous}}.$$

Each component of this formula is constructed by averaging subcomponents, such as I_{sp}, according to the same root-mean-square procedure.

As these formulas indicate, the environmental quality indices are in all cases composites of physical measurements, with social judgments and evaluations entering only through the selection of the weights and the standards used to convert the physical averages to dimensionless numbers. These two judgments affect the index in opposite ways. Broadly speaking, the relative importance of any component is proportional to its weight and inversely proportional to the standard used in computing it. The importance–weights are *very* rough judgments; in the American trials uniform weights were used for lack of clear reason to emphasize any aspect of the environment more than any other. The Canadian weights are equally crude, as can be seen from the formulas. The standards used to convert the physical measurements to dimensionless, and formally comparable, numbers are somewhat less arbitrary. In the American formulas, the secondary standards promulgated by the Environmental Protection Agency were used; the Canadian indices, being more comprehensive, use government standards when available and expert judgment of a satisfactory norm otherwise.

The result is an arithmetic artifact that is very difficult to interpret, and that no one cares to defend very staunchly. It shares the shortcomings of all index numbers. The absolute level is admittedly arbitrary and meaningless, but the trends exhibited by a time-series or comparisons of indices for different regions can be meaningful under proper conditions. If the components all point in pretty much the same direction, then the index constructed from them is meaningful, and the relative weights, the comparison standards, and even the formula used for averaging are all inconsequential details. If the component-by-component comparisons diverge substantially, then the weighting scheme and other technical details determine the comparative standing of the combined indices, but in that circumstance the usefulness of calculating any index at all is questionable. Sudbury has a higher SO_2 index than Ottawa while Ottawa has a higher particulate index than Sudbury; no mathematical formula can determine which city suffers more from air pollution (cet. par.) unless that formula is accepted as the definition of the degree of pollution. To put the matter starkly, an *ad hoc*, pragmatic index is either unnecessary (if all components agree) or meaningless (if they do not).

It does not appear, then, that indices of this type hold much promise for monitoring environmental trends or comparing regional conditions. Nor do such formulas appear any more suitable as guides to environmental policy. To stay with relatively proximate choices the measures that have to be taken to combat SO_2 pollution are entirely different from those that reduce NO_X. How should scarce resources be allocated between them? A mechanical formula is no guide, unless, of course, the social goal is simply to reduce the reading of the official pollution index. Since, in fact, if an index becomes official it is likely to become the measure of achievement employed by government bureaus and chambers of commerce, adopting such an index entails real dangers; the formula may usurp social judgment of the relative importance of the different components.

2. An Alternative Proposal

The upshot of the foregoing review is that a meaningful environmental quality index cannot be fabricated out of physical first-principles and a snippet of social judgment. The task is far more difficult than that. I cannot perform it, but I can suggest where to begin.

Because the environment is too big to be studied as a whole, it must be divided into segments. The approach discussed above divided it into physical components, but it seems more appropriate for purposes of social evaluation to divide it into areas of human concern. Three broad areas seem to provide a fruitful basis for division: commercial and industrial productiveness, healthfulness, and amenities. We may aspire to indices of environmental quality from each of these points of view; it does not seem reasonable to hope to combine them.

The productiveness of the environment can be measured in ordinary economic terms. Its healthfulness can be appraised in terms of its effect on vital statistics, in particular, mortality and morbidity rates. The amenities provided by the environment are a more diverse group of effects for which there does not appear to be any natural common unit. Because there is no common metric for these broad areas of concern, any consolidation into an overall measure of the quality of the environment is inherently arbitrary and none will be proposed here.

Each of these broad areas can be subdivided along physical lines into comparatively homogeneous types of physical conditions and measurement problems. Table 1 indicates the kind of schema that results. It seems feasible to construct environmental quality indices for each of the subheadings. An overall productiveness index can be constructed by combining its components without invoking arbitrary weights, as will be explained below. Overall indices of healthfulness can be constructed similarly. Beyond that it does not seem possible to go.

The categories listed in the table are self-explanatory except for the subdivision of outdoor recreation. This subdivision reflects the repeated social choice between leaving rural areas relatively undisturbed, to be used by hikers, campers, bird-watchers, and the like, or developing them with roads, picnic areas, and other facilities to make them accessible to large numbers of casual users. This is an important family of choices, and many considerations enter.

A table such as Table 1 constitutes an implicit definition of the environment and of our concerns with it, so attention should be drawn to some of its implications. "Environment" is one of the most elastic words in the dictionary. In some usages it includes the work environment, the housing environment, and much more. All such extensions are omitted from Table 1 by design. The table concentrates on the interaction between human activities and the status of non-human, natural forces and conditions. There is no intention to derogate the importance of housing, work places, schools, streets, and the other places inhabited by people. They are simply not part of the "environment" as here construed, and belong elsewhere in our thinking and social accounting.

There is no explicit mention in the table of population trends, which is heavily featured in the tables in the CEQ Fifth Annual Report, or of trends in the discharges of pesticides and other pollutants, which both the CEQ tables and the Canadian indices incorporate. These are important data, too, and are reflected in the table through their effects on environmental productiveness, healthfulness, and the other indices. To do more would be a form of double-counting. For example, if pesticide use were to increase with sufficient control so that there were no effect on healthful-

TABLE 1

MAJOR CATEGORIES OF ENVIRONMENTAL EFFECTS.

Commercial and industrial productiveness

1.1 Water (fresh, oceanic)
1.2 Air
1.3 Land and forests
1.4 Exhaustible resources

Healthfulness

2.1 Water (local public waters, global)
2.2 Troposphere
2.3 Upper atmosphere

Amenities

3.1 Urban atmospheric conditions
3.2 Urban outdoor recreation
3.3 Non-urban outdoor recreation
  3.3.1 Mass recreation facilities
  3.3.2 Specialized recreation opportunities
3.4 Integrity of nature
  3.4.1 Endangered species
  3.4.2 Natural spectacles, geological formations, etc.
  3.4.3 Wetlands, wildlife preserves, etc.

ness or the other indices, then the proposed formulation would show no deterioration of environmental quality, and properly. The motivating idea is to measure environmental quality, which is a matter of consequences, rather than causes of change.

In that same spirit, a single physical change can enter the indices in the table in several places. For example, a change in the concentration of atmospheric suspended particles may affect productiveness (item 1.2), healthfulness (item 2.2), and urban environmental amenities (item 3.1). If a change has consequences in several dimensions, each kind of consequence is accounted for separately, though the physical change itself is not recorded explicitly. As remarked above, changes in emissions and discharges of pollutants are not exhibited, though their consequences are.

Each of the categories in the table presents its individual challenges for measurement and evaluation. I shall discuss them enough to indicate the broad outlines of the approach recommended, but shall not weary us by attempting to cover every item. In every instance the aim of the index will be to measure social consequences in appropriate units rather than physical conditions. There will be no attempt to aggregate or average consequences in dissimilar units.

3. Commercial and Industrial Productiveness

The principle to be applied is that the effect of environmental conditions on commercial productiveness is measured by the difference between the net value added by a given bundle of transferrable resources in the observed environmental conditions and the value that would be added by those same resources in entirely "natural", or pristine conditions. Thus, the environmental productiveness index for any region is a comparison of its actual value of output with the value that the same resources would have yielded in a completely undeteriorated environment. This principle, of course, has to be modified in practice.

Consider the fresh water resources of a region. Their productiveness index will be built up by making an inventory of the region's lakes, rivers, and aquifers and estimating the change in the productiveness of each of them or of a representative sample. The heart of the task is to estimate the productiveness change for a single body of water.

It will not do, however, simply to study each lake or river separately and to compare the value added by the enterprises that use it with what they would have added if the water were in pristine condition. The reason is that the change in value added, so measured, depends both on the physical condition of the water and on the kinds and amounts of the resources that employ the water. An index of environmental quality should be influenced by only the first of these factors. For example, if discharges of plant nutrients reduce the dissolved oxygen concentration in a lake, we should want a measure of environmental quality to reflect this fact even though there may be no commercial use of the lake at the moment. In other words, a measure of environmental quality is conceived to measure social value or potential rather than social costs actually sustained.

For this reason, the measure of environmental quality for any body of water (or other component of the environment) has to be made with reference to some standard amount and mode of development, the same for all similar bodies in the region and for all the times to be compared. Then the first step in constructing a regional index of the productiveness of public waters is to establish a standard mode of commercial development for each class of waters (a task for an economic geographer); the second step is to estimate the effect of the water quality change on value added in these standard conditions.

The second step amounts to estimating the partial derivatives with respect to water quality of the production function of the standard mode of development. A couple of examples will indicate what is involved.

One important commercial use of water is to cool in process or exhaust streams of fluids by means of condensers, heat exchangers, and similar devices. The rate at which an industrial process can be operated is often limited by the rate at which undesired heat can be removed. The rate at which a heat exchanger of given design can remove heat (in, say, BTU per hour) is very close to proportional to the difference in temperature between the heat-source and the intake-water. For example, assuming a 400° heat-source, a 60° stream can remove 3% more heat per hour than a 70° stream. Each degree of increase in the temperature of a stream or lake therefore reduces by an easily calculable amount the rate at which industrial processes that use it for cooling can be operated. The reduction in the rate of value added per degree of increase in water temperature can therefore be computed.[3]

Things are not always, or often, that simple. Another important commercial use of public waters is fishing and shellfish culture. The size of the catch to be expected from a given level of fishing effort depends on, among other things, the temperature of the water, dissolved oxygen concentration, acidity, turbidity, salinity, and concentrations of a number of trace chemicals. Furthermore, the relationships are complex and, in spite of a great deal of research, not well enough understood to permit the kind of calculation just sketched for cooling water. Yet that is the kind of calculation that has to be made, not merely to construct environmental quality indices, but more basically to guide our management of water resources. Even at present enough is known about the environmental requirements of water life so that the various specialized research results can be pieced together into a useable estimate of a fisheries production function in which the principal dimensions of water quality enter as arguments.

To generalize: for each significant commercial use of public waters the productiveness of a standard level of cooperating resources has to be estimated as a function of the relevant physical dimensions of water quality. A meaningful index of environmental quality, for either a single body of water or all the public waters in a region, would then be the ratio between the value added under observed water quality conditions and that added under pristine conditions, expressed as a percentage of the pristine yield.

The first two components of the productiveness index relate primarily to pollution, the second two to exhaustion and depletion. Nevertheless, the same general kind of indices can be computed for all. The productive-

[3]This calculation makes no pretense to high precision. Heat-exchanger design and other aspects of operation can be adapted to the temperature of the intake-water, thus moderating the effects of changes in temperature. The basic heat-removal efficiency principles are as stated, however.

ness of agricultural land is reduced by some atmospheric pollutants, particularly sulfates and sulfur dioxide; that environmental cost is part of the air productiveness index. Agricultural productiveness is also reduced by soil erosion and by the depletion of plant nutrients. These effects belong in the productiveness index for land and forests. Forestry yields are also reduced by over-cutting. This effect can be estimated by comparing the annual economic yield of the forest as it now stands with a norm that is an estimate of the economic yield that could have been obtained if the forest had been cropped from the beginning so as to maintain its yield. A similar comparison applies to minerals and other exhaustible resources.

Thus the same general approach applies to appraising the productiveness of all components of the environment. Whether it be for the air, agricultural land, forests, or mineral resources, the relevant measure is a comparison of the annual value added by some standard level of economic effort under observed environmental conditions, with what would have been added under pristine conditions. A comprehensive index of environmental productiveness can be constructed either by summing the reductions resulting from the deterioration of the different components of the environment, or by averaging the separate indices of percentage loss, using the values added under pristine conditions as weights.[4]

4. Healthfulness

In principle, indices of the healthfulness of the environment can be constructed in much the same way, though not in terms of dollars and cents. The health costs of environmental deterioration can be measured by the mortality and morbidity experienced by a standardized population (standardized with respect to age distribution, sex, racial composition, etc.) under observed environmental conditions as compared with the same experience under pristine conditions. Table 1 suggests that separate healthfulness indices be computed for public waters, the lower atmosphere, and the upper atmosphere. Further distinctions might be made, as among urban, suburban, and rural conditions.

Though the principle is simple, the task is formidable and currently appears to be beyond our capability in spite of a vast amount of research on the effect of environmental conditions on human health. The current

[4]It seems a reasonable approximation to regard the deterioration or exhaustion of the different components of the environment as acting additively.

lack of indicators of environmental healthfulness does not indicate that they cannot be constructed; the literature that I have found deals with bits and pieces and nowhere attempts to put them together. Perhaps the best single survey of the subject is the National Academy of Sciences report (1974) *Health Effects of Air Pollutants*. This report reviews separately the health effects of carbon monoxide, nitrogen oxides, photochemical oxidants and ozone, airborne particles and sulfur oxides, and concludes with a brief digest (11 pages) of laboratory experiments in which the effects of pairs of pollutants were observed and compared with the effects of the pollutants in isolation. Instances of synergism, antagonism, and simple additivity were all observed. In the end it was concluded that the interactions among pollutants and other variables in real-life atmospheres are too complicated to permit reliable extrapolation from controlled laboratory experiments. The authors of the report did not find, or at least did not cite, any epidemiological studies of the effects of pollutants in combination. There are some well-known synergisms, for example that between sulfur dioxide and suspended particulates. Apart from them, simple additivity of effects appears to be an adequate working approximation. It seems therefore entirely feasible to construct comprehensive indices of environmental healthfulness by assembling the many studies that have been made of the effects of individual pollutants.

I should not, however, pass over the difficulties of estimating the health effects of individual pollutants, the subarea in which most relevant research has been done. Two kinds of effect have to be distinguished: acute effects, which are shown by abrupt increases in daily mortality and morbidity during episodes of exceptionally high pollution (counterbalanced by subnormal mortality and morbidity when the air is exceptionally clean), and chronic effects, which result in regularly higher death and illness rates in populations exposed to relatively high levels of pollution for long periods of time.

Acute effects have been observed frequently and measured occasionally. The type of data available is exemplified by a study by Buechley et al. (1973).[5] They compared the number of deaths in the New York–New Jersey metropolitan area on each day of the period 1962–1966 with the atmospheric concentration of SO_2 on that day and certain other atmospheric data. After allowing for the effects of other pollutants and temperature they found a close relationship between the number of deaths on each day and the logarithm of the atmospheric concentration of SO_2($R^2 = 0.92$). The relationship shows decreasing sensitivity to increases

[5]The estimates in the text are derived from a chart taken from Buechley et al. and published in a National Academy of Sciences report (1974, p. 424).

in SO_2 concentration as the concentration increases. At a concentration of 200 micrograms of SO_2 per cubic meter, which is about average for the region, the number of deaths per day increases by one per unit increase (in micrograms per cubic meter) in concentration. At a concentration of 1,200 micrograms per cubic meter, corresponding to a very bad day, the rate of increase is about a quarter that great. At least one other study confirms this general pattern – Glasser and Greenburg (1971).

Such findings of short-run effects are very suggestive but require careful interpretation to allow for peculiarities of age, socioeconomic status, and other factors in the population observed.

The effects of long periods of exposure to atmospheric pollutants are generally harder to detect. One of the frustrating aspects is that people move around a great deal and pollution concentrations vary greatly even within a single city. We therefore cannot tell from climatological data how much pollution the people who die within a given year, or who survive, have been exposed to. There are occasional exceptions. Children have comparatively small radii of operation and so can be expected to be exposed to the pollution concentrations in the neighborhoods of their homes and schools. A much cited study of second-graders in Chattanooga found that the frequency of respiratory illness rose by 0.01 cases per week per 100 children for each increase of 1 microgram per liter in the atmospheric concentration of nitrogen dioxide, up to concentrations of 150 micrograms per liter. No increase in morbidity was detected for higher concentrations.[6]

These examples suggest the kind of data one has to work with. The studies leave no room to doubt that death and illness rates increase with atmospheric pollution, but estimates of how fast they increase are few and far between. Even the examples cited are unreliable, for reasons I cannot go into.

There is probably no area where more work has been done and more remains to be done than the health effects of pollution, particularly atmospheric pollution. This work, focussed more than heretofore on quantitative estimates of the relation between pollution levels and mortality and morbidity rates, has to be accomplished before the construction of meaningful indices of environmental healthfulness.

Once the epidemiological research is in hand, the construction of healthfulness indices is straightforward. Two indices are needed, one for mortality and one for morbidity. A region's index for, say, mortality

[6]Computed from data in Shy et al. (1970). For further details and examples see the aforementioned National Academy of Sciences report (1974) and Lave and Seskin (1970).

would then be the death rate for a standardized population in a pristine atmosphere expressed as a percentage of the death rate for the same population exposed to the observed levels of pollutant concentrations.

No such indices have ever been computed, so one can have only unsubstantiated conjectures about what they would show. The fragmentary hints that I have seen suggest that few or no places in the country would have mortality indices of less than 85. Such data, if we had them, would help us form a more reasonable appreciation than we have at present of the seriousness of the environmental threat.

5. Amenities

The two previous categories were relatively homogeneous, and each gave rise to a natural measure of its aspect of environmental quality. In both cases the conceptual problem of scaling was simplified by being able to appeal to a comparison between actual and reasonably well-defined ideal conditions. None of these facilitating circumstances apply to amenities. Environmental amenities are a potpourri whose ingredients range from the absence of urban noise and haze to the availability of prospects of nature's grandeur. I see no way in which they can be added up and no uniform standard by which they can be assessed, let alone valued.

The amenity aspect of urban atmospheric conditions can perhaps be described by the kind of index described above. For example, we could compare the percentage of clear days under actual conditions with the percentage under pristine conditions in the same locality. That device, though, does not avail for recreational amenities or for the vitality of natural life.

At the moment the route already taken by the Council of Environmental Quality (1974, pp. 335–366) seems to be the only feasible one: compilation of time series to exhibit the trends in the relevant variables. The assortment of series presented, which is only preliminary and tentative, could profitably be expanded and focussed on the categories suggested in Table 1. For example, the current compilation includes only two series dealing with outdoor recreation, and both are devoted to the use of facilities rather than to availability and adequacy while neither shows any geographical detail. There are no data on the wildlife population. There are data on pesticide use, but none on fish- or bird-kills, residue concentrations, or other consequences. But it is captious to criticize the first attempt in a constructive endeavor.

6. Conclusion

The need to measure and monitor the state of the environment is widely recognized. After some forgetting, men have again come to appreciate their dependence on natural forces, and have become alarmed by realizing that now, as never before, they have the power to do irremediable harm.

The recent and current attempts to meet this need have approached the problem from a physical point of view, and have tried to describe the state of the environment in terms of formal averages of physical conditions. This approach is inherently inadequate and can be misleading. The ability of the environment to support economic activity and to contribute to the healthfulness and pleasantness of life bears no simple relation to the weight of pollutants discharged, to the ratio of pollutant concentrations to

PART II

PRIVATE EQUILIBRIUM AND PUBLIC VALUES

Chapter 6

Cournot, Bowley, Stackelberg and Fellner, and the Evolution of the Reaction Function

James W. FRIEDMAN*

Oligopoly theory is just one of the many areas of economics in which William Fellner has taken an active interest and made significant contributions. *Competition Among the Few* [Fellner (1960)] contains a very accurate and clear exposition of the work of Cournot and Stackelberg. While much of the volume is devoted to exploring cooperative equilibria, with the author leaving the clear impression that non-cooperative equilibria do not seem fruitful, non-cooperative equilibria are discussed with great thoroughness, insight and objectivity. The present paper follows the non-cooperative line, first describing the contributions of Cournot, Bowley and Stackelberg to the development of the "reaction function" models of oligopoly. Fellner's criticisms of this approach, which are next summarized, point the way toward a much better formulation of reaction function models on which I have worked and which are sketched at the end of the paper.

My purposes in writing this paper are two: First, over the years I have become convinced that there is considerable, and quite unnecessary, confusion concerning the development of the reaction function approach to oligopoly from Cournot to Stackelberg. With respect to Cournot, there is a persistent confusion of the (single-period) Cournot equilibrium and reaction function versions of his model. My hope is that a unified exposition of Cournot, Bowley and Stackelberg will make much clearer the nature of their contributions. Second, in describing the quite recent work I have done on reaction function models, which elaborates Fellner's critique of the earlier writers, the reader should be in a better position to judge whether or not the approach is a dead end. Even if it should be judged a dead end, considerable research effort will have been warranted because of the continuing popularity of reaction function models.

The idea of the "reaction function" as a description of how oligopolists

*I wish to thank Robert Becker and the editors of this volume for helpful comments, and the National Science Foundation for research support.

make their choices has been in the literature surely since Bowley's book was published in 1924 [Bowley (1960)], and perhaps since 1883 when Cournot's *Researches* . . . [Cournot (1960)] appeared. Although I am uncertain about this, the term itself may well have been coined by Fellner in *Competition Among the Few*.

The reaction function, defined briefly, is a function which determines for a firm in a given time period its action (price and/or quantity) as a function of the actions of (all) other firms during the preceding time period. For example, in a Cournot type quantity model, with 5 firms, a reaction function for firm 1 would give its quantity choice in period t as a function of the five observed quantities chosen in period t-1. Reaction functions provide an explicit way to represent the decision-making interdependence of the firms in a market, and to recognize that an oligopoly market existing over many periods of time is fundamentally different from a one-period-only market. This latter difference is very important to oligopoly. In a perfectly competitive, stationary economy it can be that a "single-period" equilibrium is Pareto optimal and if the economy is to exist over time, it will be impossible to improve upon the temporal repetition of the single-period equilibrium. In an oligopoly, one-period (non-cooperative) equilibria are, in general, not Pareto optimal, and extending the model over time may make feasible certain sorts of interesting behavior which were previously impossible.

This paper is divided into five sections. In the first, the basic market models to be used throughout the paper are presented. These are two types: a "Cournot quantity model", and a "Chamberlinian differentiated products model" [Chamberlin (1956)]. Models of either type may be used as single-period models or made the basis of dynamic models which extend over arbitrary lengths of time. Section 2 presents further discussion of Cournot's model and his results, including his particular contribution to the development of the reaction function. In Section 3, Bowley's brief contribution is taken up. Section 4 is devoted to a presentation and analysis of Stackelberg's contribution, and to a correct derivation of some of his results.

In the last section, Fellner's insight into the work of the earlier writers is discussed. Certain comments can be read as a blueprint for the way reaction function models should be formulated and for the characteristics which reaction function equilibria should possess. My own work (1971a, 1973a, 1973b) in this area, reviewed in the fifth section, is in the direction of carrying out Fellner's suggestions.

Apart from the reworking of Stackelberg, there are no new formal results in this paper. It is hoped, however, that the threads drawn together here are woven into a fabric which will afford the reader new and deeper insight.

1. Basic Market Models

1.1. Quantity Models

Cournot can be interpreted as presenting a single-period model, as well as a dynamic model. The dynamic model is not as fully specified and some of its characteristics must be inferred. In the present section, only the single-period version is discussed. Section 2 deals with one dynamic version of Cournot.

Cournot assumed a market with n firms in which each firm produced a single, perfectly homogeneous product – identical in every respect to the output of any other firm in the industry. Homogeneity, when rational consumers have full information, implies that the consumer wishes to buy from the source offering the good at the lowest price. If all charge the same price, he is indifferent from whom he buys. Another operating assumption of a Cournot model is that firms do not decide prices. They each choose a quantity to produce, and the total quantity determines the market price. If q_i denotes the output of the ith firm, p denotes the market price and

$$Q = \sum_{i=1}^{n} q_i,$$

then the demand function may be written

$$p = F(q_1 + q_2 + \ldots + q_n) = F(Q).$$

He also assumed that F has a continuous first derivative which is negative. The Cournot assumptions on demand, stated formally, are:[1]

(A.1) $F(0) = p_m$, a finite maximum possible price. There is an output level, Q^* having the properties that $F(Q^*) = 0$ and, for $Q < Q^*$, $F(Q) > 0$. If $Q > Q^*$ then $F(Q) = 0$. For Q larger than 0 and smaller than Q^*, F has continuous derivatives of any order, and $F'(Q) < 0$.

[1]To be precise about Cournot's explicit and implicit assumptions on demand [Cournot (1960, pp. 49–53)]: he assumes demand is continuous (p. 49), downward sloping (p. 50), bounded at a price of zero (p. 52) and zero for a sufficiently high price (pp. 52–53). Where he assumes demand cuts both axes, he appears somewhat ambivalent between the latter and assuming that total revenue goes to zero as price goes to zero or infinity. On cost (pp. 58–59): marginal cost is assumed positive, but not necessarily non-decreasing. He implicitly assumes derivatives exist of any order he needs. This may be seen in his chapter IV and later where he simply uses any derivatives he wishes without making any explicit statements about their existence. Any additional assumptions made in this paper, beyond those attributed to Cournot in this footnote are made by me because they are needed for the formal derivation of various results.

(A.1) states that the demand curve is downward sloping and cuts both axes. It also has derivatives of any order at positive output levels for which the market price is greater than zero. In Cournot's work and that of all writers whose work is reviewed here, a firm's sales always equals its demand. There is no provision for inventory, for backlogging demand or for firms to have more than one decision variable – either price or quantity. Denoting the total cost function of the ith firm by $C_i(q_i)$, the conditions imposed on costs are:

(A.2) $C_i(q_i)$ is defined for $0 \leq q_i \leq Q^*$. C_i has continuous derivatives of any order and $C_i(0) \geq 0$, $C_i'(q_i) > 0$, $C_i''(q_i) \geq 0$ for all q_i.

(A.2) insures that fixed cost is non-negative and marginal cost is positive and non-decreasing, as well as the cost function being infinitely differentiable.

Recall that the model set out above is a strictly one-period model. That is, it is assumed that the firms will exist in one and only one period. There is no past from which they have information to guide them and no future to which they look. Furthermore, they will be assumed to make their quantity choices simultaneously. The profit function for the ith firm is $\pi_i(q) = q_iF(Q) - C_i(q_i)$, where $q = (q_i, q_2, \ldots, q_n)$. Profit for the ith firm depends only on two variables, the firm's own output and the output of the other firms $(Q - q_i = Q_{\bar{i}})$. The Cournot equilibrium is defined as follows:

$$q^c = \text{Cournot equilibrium output vector,}$$

if

(a) $0 \leq q_i^c \leq Q^*, \qquad \text{for} \quad i = 1, \ldots, n,$

(b) $\pi_i(q^c) = \max\limits_{0 \leq q_i \leq Q^*} \pi_i(q_1^c, \ldots, q_{i-1}^c, q_i, q_{i+1}^c, \ldots, q_n^c).$

The output levels associated with the Cournot equilibrium have three fundamental properties. First, they are feasible, or allowable output levels for each firm. Second, there is no way that any one firm, by itself, could get a higher profit by choosing a different output level, given the output levels of the other firms. Finally, $\Sigma_{i=1}^n q_i^c < Q^*$. If total industry output were to exceed Q^*, and firm could increase its profit by lowering its output level. Cost would be reduced, but, until total output fell below Q^*, revenue would be unchanged (at zero).

As an equilibrium for a one-period market with simultaneous decision and in which it is *assumed* impossible for the firms to collude, it is hard to imagine one which fails to be a Cournot equilibrium. The beauty of it lies in its inherent believability. Nowhere is there false information or firms acting on the premise that their rivals are less perceptive than they. The essence of the matter is that if the ith firm chooses q_i^c and thinks that its rival will choose $q_j^c (j \neq i)$ then it will see that (a) it cannot gain by choosing some other q_i and (b) that no other firm can gain by choosing some other q_j. If a q^c exists and is unique, it is a strong equilibrium indeed; for at some other output vector, say q^*, a firm will see that either it is not doing the best it can, given the output of the others or certain other firms are not doing the best they can. In the former case, the firm's choice is not optimal and in the latter, because other firm's choices are not optimal, it is a good bet they will not choose q_j^*. Put another way, if you impose some standards of "reasonableness" on your own choice and assume others will use these standards too, then an output vector which is not a Cournot equilibrium will not look reasonable. It is crucial to the preceding discussion and assumed throughout this paper that each firm knows the profit function of every other firm.

Existence of a Cournot equilibrium is insured if

$$\frac{\partial^2 \pi_i(q)}{\partial q_i^2} = 2F'(Q) + q_i F''(Q) - C_i''(q_i) < 0, \qquad i = 1, \ldots, n,$$

when $Q < Q^*$.

Uniqueness is implied by an additional condition,[2]

$$\frac{\partial^2 \pi_i(q)}{\partial^2 q_i} + \sum_{j \neq i} \left| \frac{\partial^2 \pi_i(q)}{\partial q_i \partial q_j} \right| < 0.$$

An existence proof can be found in Frank and Quandt (1963).[3] The uniqueness condition amounts to requiring that when all firms except one change their outputs by some amount, the optimal output level of the one firm is altered by a lesser amount. Uniqueness is proved under weaker conditions in Okuguchi and Suzumura (1971). Note that the first-order

[2]This discussion of uniqueness applies to uniqueness (and existence) of Cournot equilibria at which

$$\sum_{i=1}^{n} q_i^c < Q^*.$$

If all firms had zero marginal costs it would be possible to have a Cournot equilibrium at $q^* = (q_n^*, \ldots, q_n^*)$ if

$$\sum_{j \neq i} q_j^* \geq Q^*, \qquad i = 1, \ldots, n.$$

Then, no matter what output level the ith firm chose, its profit would be $-C_i(0)$.

[3]Existence is proved by making the oligopoly model conform to the requirements of a Nash-type n-person non-zero sum game. See, for example, Debreu (1952) or Friedman (1971b) and compare to Frank and Quandt (1963).

condition for a profit maximum,

$$F(Q)+q_iF'(Q)-C_i'(q_i)=0,$$

can, when the second-order condition is met, be solved for q_i as a function of $(q_1, \ldots, q_{i-1}, q_{i+1}, \ldots, q_n)$.[4] (In fact, q_i will depend merely on $Q_{i\cdot}$.) Denoting this function $q_i = w_i(q_1, \ldots, q_{i-1}, q_{i+1}, \ldots, q_n)$, the uniqueness condition stated above implies that

$$\sum_{j\neq i}\left|\frac{\partial w_i}{\partial q_j}\right|<1.$$

This condition implies not only the uniqueness of the Cournot equilibrium, but also its "stability". There is a considerable literature in the *Review of Economic Studies* on the stability of the single-period model. Some of the references are Fisher (1961), Hahn (1961), Okuguchi (1970), Sato–Nagatani (1967) and Theocharis (1960). Stability may be understood in this way: The functions $w_1, \ldots, w_n$, taken together, form a function which maps one output vector, q', into another output vector, q''. Given the definition of the w_i, it is clear that q_i'' is the output level which would maximize the profit of firm i when other firms are choosing $(q_1', \ldots, q_{i-1}', q_{i+1}', \ldots, q_n')$. Letting $(w_1, \ldots, w_n) = w$ and $q'' = w(q')$, imagine generating an infinite sequence of output vectors: $q^3 = w(q'')$, $q^4 = w(q^3)$, etc. Uniqueness and stability guarantee that as $t \to \infty$, q^t converges to q^c, the Cournot equilibrium.[5]

1.2. Differentiated Products Price Models

Bertrand (1883) wanted to toss out Cournot's oligopoly model for two reasons: First, he thought firms would collude, making non-cooperative models irrelevant, and second, when there were only a few firms in a market, they would inevitably be price choosers, not quantity choosers, making the Cournot analysis doubly irrelevant. Edgeworth (1925) picked up the Bertrand suggestion and gave a more full analysis, and, much more recently, Shubik (1959) has given extensive attention to homogeneous product price models. It can be argued that these models are a dead end because there really are no perfectly homogeneous products. Even if that

[4]Being able to solve for q_i as a function of the other output levels rests upon the implicit function theorem, of course. See, for example, Bartle (1954).

[5]This brief discussion no doubt does not do justice to the stability literature; however, the usefulness of this literature is questionable, as it deals with stability under the quite unreasonable assumption that firms are single-period profit-maximizers and that they never learn even the most obvious lessons from information which they acquire.

view is too extreme, nearly all products made by oligopolists appear to be non-homogeneous – i.e., differentiated. Thus it may be wisest to follow Bertrand only part way and take firms to be price choosers. Doing so gets around the inherent difficulty of the Cournot models that one does not know what is the mechanism of price determination.

Much concerning differentiated products must be left up in the air, such as the way firms decide on precisely which version of a product to produce. Brems (1951) made an effort to analyze this problem, and more recently, Lancaster (forthcoming) has made some progress; however, where differentiated products models are used in this paper, it is assumed that the nature of the products are fixed and unchangeable. The firm is thought to have chosen a specific design and set of characteristics for its product. Once chosen, these are assumed unchangeable, resulting in a set of firms, no two of which produce exactly the same thing.

The important consequence for models of differentiation is that a small change in one price can never lead to an immense change in the sales of any firm. Because each product has some unique features and attracts some degree of "consumer loyalty", there is no reason why any two firms should charge the same price or why a tiny price change should ever cause a mass desertion of customers from one firm to another. To completely and sensibly characterize demand functions for firms selling differentiated products is a bit more involved than for homogeneous products.

Let p denote a *price vector* (when dealing with Cournot models, p is a price), and R^n_+ denote the "non-negative orthant" – that is, the set of all price vectors having non-negative components. It is helpful to partition R^n_+ into three (non-overlapping and exhaustive) sets for the ith firm: The demand function of the ith firm is denoted $q_i = f_i(p)$. Let $\mathring{A}_i$ be the set of all price vectors in R^n_+ which yield *strictly positive* demand for the ith firm, a_i be the set of all points which are in R^n_+, not in $\mathring{A}_i$, but which are limits of sequences of points in $\mathring{A}_i$, and let $\not{A}_i$ be the set of points which are in R^n_+ but are not in either $\mathring{A}_i$ or a_i. Thus a_i consists of the points on the boundary of $\mathring{A}_i$ at which $q_i = 0$. Formally, and on the assumption that $f_i(p) \geq 0$ for any p in R^n_+:

$$\mathring{A}_i = \{p \,|\, p \in R^n_+, \quad f_i(p) > 0\},$$

$$a_i = \{p \,|\, f_i(p) = 0, \quad p \in \text{closure of } \mathring{A}_i\},$$

$$\not{A}_i = \{p \,|\, p \in R^n_+, \quad f_i(p) = 0, \quad p \notin a_i\}.$$

For firm 1 in a two-firm market, these regions are illustrated in Figure 1. The shaded region is $\mathring{A}_1$, within which $f_1(p)$ is strictly positive. This region includes all of the vertical axis and that part of the horizontal axis from 0

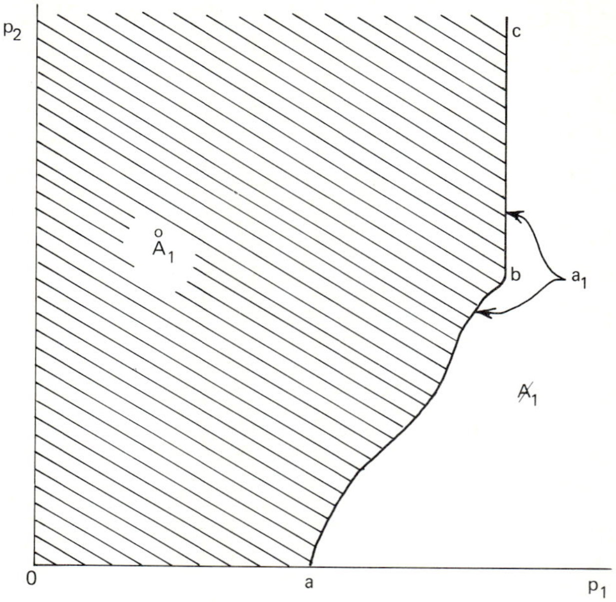

FIGURE 1

to a (not including a). The set a_1 is the curve abc, which is the boundary of $\mathring{A}_1$ on which $f_1(p)$ just reaches zero. The remainder of R^2_+ is $\not{A}_1$.

Demand functions will be assumed to obey the following conditions:

(A.3) f_i is continuous and bounded for all p in R^n_+ and has continuous partial derivatives of any order, everywhere in the interior of R^n_+ except points in $a_1 \cup a_2 \cup \ldots \cup a_n$. If $p \notin a_{k_1} \cup \ldots \cup a_{k_m}$, then f_i has continuous partial derivatives of any order with respect to $p_{k_1}, \ldots, p_{k_m}$ at p. If $p \in \mathring{A}_i \cup \mathring{A}_j$, $\partial f_i / \partial p_j > 0$ $(j \neq i)$ and if $p \in \mathring{A}_i$, $\sum_{j=1}^n \partial f_i / \partial p_j < 0$. When $p \in \not{A}_j$, $\partial f_i / \partial p_j = 0$ $(i = 1, \ldots, n)$. $\mathring{A} = \mathring{A}_1 \cup \mathring{A}_2 \cup \ldots \cup \mathring{A}_n$ is bounded.

(A.3) insures that when $f_j = 0$, the jth firm is out of the market. It cannot affect the sales of any other firm by making price changes which keep its own sales at zero. Where the ith firm has positive sales, an increase in its price will lower its own sales, an increase in the price of another firm whose sales are positive will raise its sales, and if all firms raise prices by an equal amount, all firms having positive sales will suffer a decline. Finally, the set of price vectors at which every firm, simultaneously, has positive demand is bounded. This latter condition, along with the boundedness of demand, are the counterparts of the demand function cutting both axes. For a market with two firms, these conditions are illustrated in Figure 2. The cross-hatched area is the region within which both firms have sales greater than zero. Along the curve $a'b'c'$ the amount demanded of firm 2 is constant at $q_2^0 (> 0)$. Note that in moving along this curve from a' to b', both prices increase. As p_1 rises, the amount demanded rises; hence to keep $f_2(p)$ constant, p_2 must also rise (though not by as much as p_1). As b' is approached from the left, $f_1(p)$ goes to zero. To the right of b', further increases in p_1 have no effect on $f_2(p)$; hence, keeping $f_2(p) = q_2^0$ requires no further change in p_2.

Under (A.2) and (A.3), profit functions for single-period differentiated products models may be written:

$$\pi_i(p) = p_i f_i(p) - C_i(f_i(p)).$$

There is an obvious analog in this model to the Cournot equilibrium. It will be called a "Cournot equilibrium", although, strictly speaking, the latter applies to quantity models.

$$p^c = \text{Cournot equilibrium price vector},$$

if

(a) $p_i^c \geq 0, \quad \text{for} \quad i = 1, \ldots, n,$

(b) $\pi_i(p^c) = \max_{p_i \geq 0} \pi_i(p_1^c, \ldots, p_{i-1}^c, p_i, p_{i+1}^c, \ldots, p_n^c).$

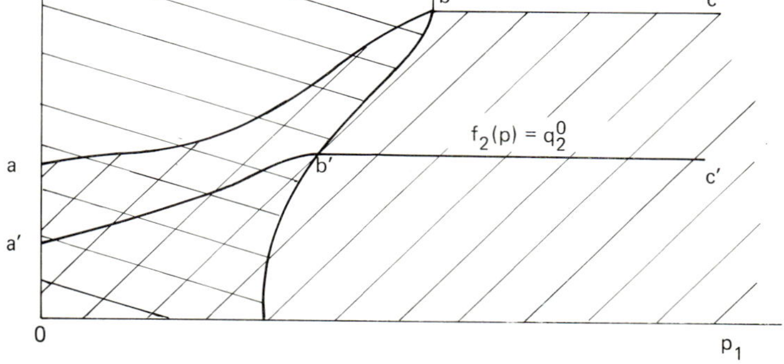

FIGURE 2

This Cournot equilibrium has the same basic properties as the corresponding equilibrium for quantity models. The prices are feasible and there is no way that any one firm, by itself, could get a higher profit by choosing a different price, given the prices of the other firms.

It is possible to give conditions for existence and uniqueness of the Cournot price equilibrium. The condition in (A.3) that $\mathring{A}$ is bounded means that $a_1 \cap \ldots \cap a_n$ is not empty. In fact, the latter consists of exactly one point p_m. This price vector is a least upper bound (or maximal price vector) for $\mathring{A}$. These properties are proved in Friedman (1972). There is never any reason for a firm to charge a price higher than p_{im} because any increase above p_{im} will have no effect whatsoever on the profit of the ith or any other firm.

The first-order conditions for a Cournot equilibrium when such an equilibrium is interior to $\mathring{A}$ are[6]

$$f_i(p) + (p_i - C_i'(f_i(p)))f_i^i(p) = 0, \qquad i = 1, \ldots, n.$$

Two additional conditions on the model which will insure that such an interior point exists are: (1) $f_i(C_i'(0), 0) > 0$, and (2) for all p in $\mathring{A}$ for which $p_i \geq C_i'(f_i(p))$, $\partial^2\pi_i/\partial p_i^2 < 0$. The former condition guarantees that, no matter what other firms do, it is never optimal to choose price so high that output will be zero. The latter is a usual second-order condition. Details may be found in Friedman (1972).

The uniqueness condition is of the same character as that given previously:

$$\frac{\partial^2\pi_i}{\partial p_i^2} + \sum_{j \neq i} \left| \frac{\partial^2\pi_i}{\partial p_i \partial p_j} \right| < 0, \qquad i = 1, \ldots, n.$$

[See Friedman (1972).]

For reasons which will be apparent when reaction function models are discussed, the uniqueness condition is much more reasonable in the price than in the quantity models.

2. A Dynamic Cournot Model

In a trivial sense, taking account of time is very easy. Just add a time subscript to the variables: $\pi_i(q_t) = q_{it}F(Q_t) - C_i(q_{it})$ for a quantity model. Of course, this is incomplete. It is necessary to specify the information conditions under which the firms operate. It will be assumed in this paper that in period t, each firm knows all the past decisions made by all firms.

[6]Partial derivatives will sometimes be denoted by the use of superscripts, such as

$$f_i^j = \partial f_i / \partial p_j \quad \text{and} \quad f_i^{jk} = \partial^2 f_i / \partial p_j p_k.$$

The second major matter is the objective function of the firm. Is the firm trying to maximize single-period profits or a discounted stream of profits?

Cournot (1960, pp. 81–83) carries on a discussion in which stability of the Cournot equilibrium is treated. The exposition seems built on a dynamic model which is incompletely specified, although it appears natural to conclude that the firms remain single-period profit-maximizers. It is these pages which suggest, or perhaps invent, the reaction function. It is not clear whether Cournot envisions that each firm makes a quantity choice in each period, or that they alternate with one firm choosing output in even numbered periods, the other in odd. Cyert and deGroot (1970) argue that Cournot intended alternating decision.[7] Whichever he intended, I believe the simultaneous decision model is much the more interesting and that is the form which will be assumed below.

In a setting of simultaneous decision, each of Cournot's firms is seeking, in period t, to choose its own current output so as to maximize its current period profits, on the assumption that all other firms will produce the same output in period t that they produced in period $t-1$. Thus, the ith firm acts on the assumption that its profit is given by

$$q_{it}F(Q_{i,t-1}+q_{it})-C_i(q_{it}),$$

and its profit maximum occurs where

$$F(Q_{i,t-1}+q_{it})+q_{it}F'(Q_{i,t-1}+q_{it})-C'_i(q_{it})=0.$$

Or, using the functions, w_i, introduced in Section 1.1, the profit-maximization condition for the ith firm may be written

$$q_{it} = w_i(Q_{i,t-1}).$$

The w_i are the reaction functions which Cournot's exposition suggests, under the simultaneous decision interpretation. They will be called "Cournot reaction functions".

There are two basic properties to be noted: First, if the Cournot reaction functions are stable, the output levels will eventually converge to the Cournot equilibrium output levels. Second, as long as output levels are not at q^c the reaction functions are obviously non-optimal for the firms using them. The reason they are not optimal is this: The reaction function for (say) firm 1 is optimal if firm 2 does not change his output. But, in general, both change their output levels in each period, making the assumption that $q_{it} = q_{i,t-1}$ untenable. If each firm knows past choices of others, then each will see that its assumptions concerning its rivals' behavior have not been correct.[8]

[7]Cyert and deGroot analyze a duopoly model of alternating decision in their work.
[8]Note that the alternate period decision formulation does not suffer from this fault.

3. Bowley's Conjectural Variation

Bowley (1960) mentions oligopoly in passing. Like Cournot, his model is not explicitly dynamic; however, unlike Cournot, no sense is to be made of it if it is not regarded as dynamic. He formulates a simple duopoly model for illustration, apparently taking the view that the essentials are represented and the reader can perform generalizations if he wishes. His model, in the notation of this paper, is

$$\pi_1 = q_1(b_1 - b_2q_1 - b_2q_2) - b_3q_1^2,$$

$$\pi_2 = q_2(b_1 - b_2q_1 - b_2q_2) - b_3q_2^2,$$

where b_1, b_2 and b_3 are positive constants. The terms in parentheses are, of course, the demand function, and the total cost functions are the terms $b_3q_1^2$. What is significant in Bowley's brief treatment is his handling of the first-order conditions for simultaneous profit-mazimization by the two firms. These are

$$\frac{\partial \pi_1}{\partial q_1} = b_1 - 2b_2q_1 - b_2q_2 - 2b_3q_1 - b_2q_1\frac{\partial q_2}{\partial q_1} = 0,$$

$$\frac{\partial \pi_2}{\partial q_2} = b_1 - 2b_2q_2 - b_2q_1 - 2b_3q_2 - b_2q_2\frac{\partial q_1}{\partial q_2} = 0.$$

He then says [Bowley (1960, p. 38)]: "To solve these we should need to know q_2 as a function of q_1, and this depends on what each producer thinks the other is likely to do." That is, the values of the "conjectural variation" terms $\partial q_2/\partial q_1$ and $\partial q_1/\partial q_2$ are not known. Were they both zero, the first-order conditions would be the same as Cournot's.

Bowley seems on the track of setting up a model in which the two firms each have two reaction functions in mind. For firm 1 the two functions are

$$q_{1t} = \phi_1(q_{2,t-1}),$$

$$q_{2t} = g_1(q_{1,t-1}),$$

where the function g_1 describes the behavior which firm 1 thinks firm 2 will follow and the function ϕ_1 is optimal for firm 1 if his assumption about firm 2's behavior is correct. There would be a similar pair of reaction functions for firm 2. While this gets around the rather wooden assumption that firm 1 thinks that $q_{2t} = q_{2,t-1}$, it shares with it a fundamental difficulty. Namely if g_1 does not, in fact, describe the behavior of firm 2, then firm 1 is sure to find out. That is, firm 1 has predictions about how firm 2 will behave. If they are wrong, firm 1 will have every opportunity to notice and alter both his estimate and his own behavior accordingly.

An equilibrium based upon the possibility that ϕ_1 is radically different from g_2 and ϕ_2 from g_1 is unappealing. The kind of equilibrium which would make sense is essentially a generalization of Cournot's equilibrium. That is the non-coperative equilbrium due to Nash (1951), which also generalized the saddle point equilibrium of von Neumann and Morgenstern (1953) for two-person zero-sum games. Denoting the "strategy" of the ith firm by s_i, his available strategy set by S_i and his "payoff function" by $P_i(s_1, s_2)$, the non-cooperative equilibrium is a strategy pair, (s_1^*, s_2^*) having the following two properties:

(a) $s_i^* \in S_i, \qquad i = 1, 2,$

(b) $P_1(s_1^*, s_2^*) = \max_{s_1 \in S_1} P_1(s_1, s_2^*)$ and $P_2(s_1^*, s_2^*) = \max_{s_2 \in S_2} P_2(s_1^*, s_2)$.

The resemblance to the Cournot equilibrium is obvious. If the P_i were single-period profits and the s_i were output levels, the model would be Cournot's single-period model. If the P_i were single-period profits, but the s_i were reaction functions, then one would be in the implied reaction function world of Cournot or Bowley.

4. The Stackelberg Model

4.1. As Found in Stackelberg

Stackelberg (1934) comes as close to an explicitly dynamic model as is humanly possible, without quite going all the way. The essence of his contribution is readily described. He deals with duopoly and, although he discusses several different versions, it is sufficient to limit presentation here to a Cournot style quantity model. He suggests there are two types of firms: "followers" and "leaders". A follower is precisely a firm which behaves as outlined in Section 2 above where the Cournot reaction function is discussed. That is, if firm 1 were a follower, he would act as if he would seek to maximize current period profits with respect to his current period output on the assumption that firm 2 would repeat in period t its output of period $t-1$. This means solving the following first-order condition for q_{1t} as a function of $q_{2,t-1}$:

$$F(q_{1t} + q_{2,t-1}) + q_{1t}F'(q_{1t} + q_{2,t-1}) - C_1'(q_{1t}) = 0.$$

This reaction function is $q_{1t} = w_1(q_{2,t-1})$. A leader is a firm which attempts to maximize profits on the assumption that his rival is a follower. The profit function for firm 2, as leader, may be written:

$$q_{2t}F(w_1(q_{2,t-1}) + q_{2t}) - C_2(q_{2t}).$$

Dropping time subscripts, the profit function of firm 2 is $q_2F(w_1(q_2)+q_2)-C_2(q_2)$. Now, if the latter is differentiated with respect to q_2 in order to get a first-order condition for the maximization of firm 2's profit, that condition is

$$\begin{aligned}&\pi_2^2(w_1(q_2), q_2)+\pi_2^1(w_1(q_2), q_2)w_1'(q_2)\\ &= F(w_1(q_2)+q_2)+q_2F'(w_1(q_2)+q_2F'(w_1(q_2)+q_2)\frac{\partial w_1}{\partial q_2}-C_2'(q_2)=0.\end{aligned} \tag{1}$$

If the latter and

$$\pi_1^1(q_1, q_2)=F(q_1+q_2)+q_1F'(q_1+q_2)-C_1'(q_1)=0$$

were simultaneously solved, the result would be the Stackelberg (leader–follower) equilibrium. There is something peculiar here, which is put somewhat in relief if the first-order condition of firm 2, with time subscripts, is written down as

$$F(q_{1t}+q_{2t})+q_{2t}F'(q_{1t}+q_{2t})+q_{2t}F'(q_{1t}+q_{2t})\frac{\partial q_{1t}}{\partial q_{2,t-1}}\frac{\partial q_{2,t-1}}{\partial q_{2t}}-C_2'(q_{2t})=0.$$

Because $q_{2,t-1}$ is chosen before q_{2t}, the partial derivative $\partial q_{2,t-1}/\partial q_{2t}=0$. Yesterday's decision, after it has been made, is not at all sensitive to today's decision. Taking account of this reduces the first-order condition of firm 2 to be *almost* that of firm 1. Two facts are clear: under these circumstances, the simultaneous solution of the (new) first-order conditions will not yield Stackelberg's leader–follower solution and q^c, the Cournot equilibrium will satisfy simultaneously the first-order conditions of the two firms.

The wary reader may be suspecting that justice is not being done Stackelberg and that what he had in mind was some sort of discounted profit-mazimization. If so, it is not explicit in his model; however, a case can be made for this view. And will be made in Section 4.2.

Before leaving Stackelberg's version of his model, the remaining two behavioral variants should be mentioned. These are follower–follower and leader–leader. The first of these boils down to the Cournot reaction function model, and the second can be dismissed because there is no way to escape inconsistency. The inconsistency arises because the solution of two leader first-order conditions (remember a leader *assumes* his rival is a follower) yields different output levels than either firm will expect. If each firm simply picked its own leader-equilibrium output level from the start, and assumed the rival will pick the follower-equilibrium output level, each will find his expectations are *not* borne out.

That is, a follower–leader equilibrium, when firm 1 is the follower, corresponds to the solution of

$$\pi_1^1(q_1, q_2) = 0,$$

$$\pi_2^2(q_1, q_2) + \pi_2^1(q_1, q_2)w_1'(q_2) = 0.$$

Call the equilibrium output levels (q_1^f, q_2^l). If firm 1 were the leader and firm 2 the follower, the equilibrium would be found by solving

$$\pi_2^2(q_1, q_2) = 0,$$

$$\pi_1^1(q_1, q_2) + \pi_1^2(q_1, q_2)w_2'(q_1) = 0.$$

Call their equilibrium output levels (q_1^l, q_2^f). If each were to decide he would be a leader, the chosen output levels would be (q_1^l, q_2^l). Firm 1 would expect to see $q_2 = q_2^f$ (not q_2^l) while firm 2 would expect to see $q_1 = q_1^f$. Some adjustment would have to take place in their behavior.

Alternatively, using a reaction function formulation, the *i*th firm as a follower would use $q_{it} = w_i(q_{j,t-1})$ while a leader would use a "leader reaction function", say $q_{it} = \phi_i(q_{j,t-1})$. If both firms were leaders, firm 1 would expect the choices of firm 2 to satisfy $q_{2t} = w_2(q_{1,t-1})$; but they would not. Instead they would satisfy $q_{2t} = \phi_2(q_{1,t-1})$. Similarly for the expectations which firm 2 would have for the behavior of firm 1.

4.2. *An Explicitly Dynamic Version of the Leader–Follower Case*

In this section a dynamic programming problem will be formulated and solved for which firm 2 is a leader, which corresponds to the leader's maximization problem when he wishes to maximize a discounted stream of profits and he can take for granted that his rival, firm 1, will behave as a follower who uses w_1, his Cournot reaction function.[9]

Denoting by α the discount parameter of firm 2, his objective function is

$$\sum_{t=1}^{T} \alpha^{t-1}\pi_2(w_1(q_{2,t-1}), q_{2t}).$$

A method of solving this problem is to start from the last period, when the "horizon" of the firm is one period, and find the optimal policy for it to follow. Then, having determined what to do in period T, step back one period and solve the two-period problem, given the optimal behavior

[9] For another Stackelberg model in which time is explicit, see Negishi and Okuguchi (1971).

already determined for the last period. Continuing in this way, a policy may be found for an horizon of any finite length. The reasons that the firm's maximization problems can be solved in this manner are: (1) The number of time periods involved is finite; hence there is a well defined end point. (2) When decisions are about to be made for a given period, say t, all past decisions and past payoffs are both known and unchangeable. Thus, at the very last time period, T, the firm faces a simple single-period maximization problem, that of maximizing $\pi_2(q_{1T}, q_{2T})$. His optimal choice will depend on some past action (in the present model, on $q_{1,T-1}$); however, the *function* describing his best policy for period T is independent of whatever his best policies may be for earlier periods. Once the best policy for period T is found, the two-period maximization problem, over $T-1$ and T, can be solved to find a best policy for period $T-1$. This latter policy must and will take account of the policy to be followed in period T.[10]

For the one period problem, where the firm wants to maximize $\pi_2(w_1(q_{2,T-1}), q_{2T})$, the first-order condition is

$$\pi_2^2(w_1(q_{2,T-1}), q_{2T}) = 0.$$

Assume this condition can be solved for q_{2T} as a function of $q_{2,T-1}$ and write the solution as $q_{2T} = \phi_1(q_{2,T-1})$. For the two-period problem, the firm seeks to maximize

$$\pi_2^2(w_1(q_{2,T-2}), q_{2,T-1}) + \alpha\pi_2^1(w_1(q_{2,T-1}), \phi_1(q_{2,T-1}))$$

with respect to $q_{2,T-1}$, and the first-order condition is

$$\pi_2^2(w_1(q_{2,T-2}), q_{2,T-1}) + \alpha\pi_2^1(w_1(q_{2,T-1}), \phi_1(q_{2,T-1}))w_1'(q_{2,T-1}).$$

Assume this condition can be expressed giving $q_{2,T-1}$ as a function of $q_{2,T-2}$,

$$Q_{2,T-1} = \phi_2(q_{2,T-2}).$$

In general, for an horizon of $s+1$ periods, with the optimal policies for horizons $1, \ldots, s$ being $\phi_1, \ldots, \phi_s$, the first-order condition is

$$\pi_2^2(w_1(q_{2,T-1}), q_{2t}) + \alpha\pi_2^1(w_1(q_{2t}), \phi_s(q_{2t}))w_1'(q_{2t}) = 0,$$

[10]The model of the firm used in this subsection is within the class dealt with in Friedman (1973b); hence, all the results of the subsection can be proved by references to this publication.

which may be rewritten as

$$q_{2t} = \phi_{s+1}(q_{2,t-1}).$$

Now make the assumption that the sequence of functions, ϕ_s, converges as s goes to infinity to a function ϕ_0, and assume further that ϕ_0 has associated with it a "fixed point". That is, an output level q_2^* such that $q_2^* = \phi_0(q_2^*)$. Then the first-order condition converges and, at q_2^*, is

$$\pi_2^2(w_1(q_2^*), q_2^*) + \alpha\pi_2^1(w_1(q_2^*), q_2^*)w_1'(q_2^*) = 0.$$

This is *almost* the original Stackelberg leader first-order condition, equation (1). If the discount parameter were unity, they would be the same. Assuming the solvability of the problem and that the limiting policy function, ϕ_0, together with w_1, form a stable system, Stackelberg's leader–follower equilibrium stands up as an equilibrium for a leader who wishes to maximize an undiscounted stream of profits and a follower whose discount parameter may be anything from zero to one (because his follower mentality makes w_1 be his chosen policy, no matter what).[11]

There remains a serious flaw in the Stackelberg model, even as amended above. The follower's behavior in the leader–follower model is no more credible than the behavior of either follower is in the follower–follower (i.e., Cournot reaction function) model. In all cases, the follower makes a demonstrably false assumption about how his rival behaves. The rival, be he follower or leader, does not keep his output unchanged from period to period – except if the initial output levels are the final equilibrium levels.[12]

There is another peculiarity in the leader–follower model, a convenient asymmetry. The leader is a very clever fellow, but the follower is an extremely naive and blind person. One knows exactly, correctly, how his rival behaves, while the other makes the most patently false and silly assumption about his rival. Unless and until solid empirical evidence is marshalled to prove the descriptive accuracy of such a model, it must be regarded as a trivial *ad hoc* variation on the Cournot theme.[13]

[11]The model must be handled differently if $\alpha = 1$, because the stated objective function will be unbounded as $T \to \infty$. An alternative is to maximize

$$\frac{1}{T}\sum_{t=1}^{T} \pi_2(q_{1t}, q_{2t}).$$

[12]Oddly, both Fellner (1960, pp. 70–71) and Leontief (1963) make the mistake of stating the follower's behavior is consistent in the sense that his expectations are borne out. This is only so at the leader–follower equilibrium, not on the way there.

[13]It should be clear, in-so-far as the leader–follower model is acceptable, it can only be generalized to n firms on the basis of one leader and $n-1$ followers.

5. Fellner and More Recent Reaction Function Models

5.1. Fellner and the Reaction Function

Competition Among the Few was published approximately a quarter century ago, and it is delightful to see how well it stands up even after all the developments in the interim. There is probably nothing in the oligopoly literature which so intelligently and helpfully discusses the general nature of oligopoly and, in so doing, underlines so well the major unsolved problems. Formal models available at the time of writing were presented, then fully discussed, and used as vehicles to indicate where new work might, hopefully, be done. So many of the unsolved problems remain untouched that *Competition Among the Few* can still be fruitfully read.

Fellner recognizes the inherent fault of a Cournot reaction function equilibrium, for example, on page 63:

> "It is essential to realize that, as long as the firms make the Cournot assumptions concerning their rivals' behavior, the analysis cannot be adjusted in such a way as to make the firms be right for the right reasons, instead of describing a situation in which they turn out to be right for the wrong reasons."

Being "right for the wrong reasons" refers to being, eventually, at the Cournot equilibrium where each firm's assumption that the other will repeat his previous output is correct. Thus he clearly sees that a satisfactory equilibrium of non-cooperative type requires that each firm's assumption concerning rival behavior be correct if they are to be verifiable.

On page 36, an explicit recognition is found that where firms exist over a long time span, it is the discounted sum of payoffs which the firms seek to maximize.

5.2. Friedman's Work on Reaction Function Models

My own work in this area is a first step at filling some of the gaps which Fellner saw in the reaction function formulations. He, after his critique, turned his own attention toward exploring the possibilities for cooperation.

Imagine a market consisting of n firms, each wishing to maximize a discounted stream of profits and each knowing that the other firms use particular reaction functions to govern their behavior. Is it possible to find n reaction functions, one for each firm, such that each is using an optimal reaction function, given correct knowledge of the functions used by the others? Were the answer "yes", the equilibrium described would be a non-cooperative equilibrium in the sense of Nash (1951), where the payoff function of the firm is its discounted profits and the strategy of a firm is its reaction function. Progress on this question was made in Friedman (1971a, 1973a, 1973b). These papers deal with differentiated products price models.

The reader interested in proofs and all the details of all assumptions is referred especially to Friedman (1973b), and to the other papers mentioned. The assumptions used are akin to (A.2) and (A.3), from Section 1, plus some additional assumptions somewhat like the conditions which insure existence of an interior, unique Cournot solution.

First the decision problem of a single firm is studied under the presumption that the firm wishes to maximize a discounted sum of profits and its rivals are known to be behaving according to specific reaction functions. Say the firm being studied is firm 1. Then its objective function is

$$\sum_{t=1}^{T} \alpha_1^{t-1} \pi_1(p_{1t}, \psi_2(p_{t-1}), \ldots, \psi_n(p_{t-1})),$$

where $\psi_j(p_{t-1})$, $j = 2, \ldots, n$, is the reaction function of the jth firm. Note that in this model, the reaction functions depend upon all prices of the preceding period – not just the prices of the *other* firms. The maximization problem can be solved in the manner indicated in Section 4.2 above. Denote by $\phi_{1s}(p_{t-1})$ the optimal reaction function for firm k, when it has an horizon of s periods. That is, for the T-period problem, firm 1 will choose $p_{11} = \phi_{1T}(p_0)$, $p_{12} = \phi_{1,T-1}(p_1), \ldots, p_{1T} = \phi_{11}(p_{T-1})$. It is found that as the horizon, s, goes to infinity, the sequence of reaction functions converges to $\phi_1(p_{t-1})$. If the ψ_j are assumed to have derivatives of any order, then the ϕ_{1s} have derivatives of any order, and if the kth order derivatives of ϕ_{1s} are bounded independently of s, then ϕ_1 has derivatives of order $k - 1$.

Existence of the limiting reaction function ϕ_1 does not insure that it (i.e., ϕ_1) is optimal for firm 1 if it wishes to maximize profit over an infinite horizon; however, in Friedman (1973a) it is shown that the limiting reaction function is optimal for the infinite horizon problem.

Now starting with a reaction function for each of the n firms, $\psi_1, \psi_2, \ldots, \psi_n$, it is possible to calculate by the methods sketched above a new vector of reaction functions, $\phi_1, \phi_2, \ldots, \phi_n$. ϕ_1 is optimal for firm 1 against $\psi_2, \ldots, \psi_n$; ϕ_2 is optimal for firm 2 against $\psi_1, \psi_3, \ldots, \psi_n$; ϕ_3 is optimal against $\psi_1, \psi_2, \psi_4, \ldots, \psi_n$; etc. The reaction functions $\psi_1, \ldots, \psi_n$

form a non-cooperative equilibrium if $\psi_i = \phi_i (i = 1, \ldots, n)$. In general, a non-cooperative equilibrium has not been shown to exist, but only an "approximate non-cooperative equilibrium". The approximate non-cooperative equilibrium is characterized by the following conditions:

(a) there is a price vector p^* such that $\psi_i(p^*) = \phi_i(p^*) = p_i^*$ for $i = 1, \ldots, n$.

(b) $\psi_i^j(p^*) = \phi_i^j(p^*)$ for $i, j = 1, \ldots, n$.

(c) $\sum_{j=1}^{n} |\phi_i^j(p^*)| < 1$ for $i = 1, \ldots, n$.

Condition (a) is that both families of reaction functions have the same steady state price vector associated with them. Condition (b) is that the two families are tangent at this price vector which means, in turn, that the ϕ_i are a close first-order approximation to the ψ_i in the neighborhood of p^*. For example, say the ith firm is behaving according to ϕ_i and thinks the others are using the ψ_j (for all j), and assume the previous price vector was "close" to p^*. The ith firm has a prediction concerning $p_{jt} - p_{j,t-1}$ $(j \neq i)$. This prediction will be approximately correct due to the tangency of the ψ_j and ϕ_j. The final condition (c) is one of local stability. Global stability conditions also appear in Friedman (1973a).

Whether reaction function models can be further developed in a fruitful way is an open question; however, I believe the work which has been outlined brings reaction function models to a stage where they are quite sophisticated and rid of some of the most damning faults.

A longstanding source of dissatisfaction with the Cournot equilibrium is that the profits associated with it are not Pareto optimal with respect to the firms. Among others, Bertrand (1883), Chamberlin (1956), and Fellner (1960) voice this, and many are led to the view that firms can effectively collude even if they cannot talk together and make formal agreements. One important implication of the reaction function models just discussed is that more profitable equilibria than the single-period Cournot can be reached on the basis of non-cooperative behavior. In Friedman (1971b) a quite different approach is taken which yields non-cooperative equilibria which are known to be Pareto optimal. Full and subtle exploration of the possibilities of non-cooperative equilibria is, in my view, very important because many market situations do not conform to conditions under which cooperative models are applicable.

Much remains to be done. Another longstanding complaint against the Cournot analysis is that it does not deal in a reasonable way with behavior out of equilibrium. None of my work does either, nor does any research in oligopoly of which I am aware. The information conditions usually assumed are too unreasonable – as a rule, that everyone knows his own and everyone else's profit function. Occasional exceptions to this complete information condition may be found; however, they suffer from faults such as thoroughly arbitrary assumptions about how one firm thinks another makes its decisions and no mechanism for a firm to change its views in the light of information which inevitably comes its way. Hopefully, future research will result in satisfactory resolutions of these problems.

6. References

Bartle, R. G., 1954, The elements of real analysis (Wiley, New York).

Betrand, J., 1883, Review of Walras' "Théorie mathématique de la richesse sociale" and Cournot's "Recherches sur les principes mathématiques de la théorie des richesses", Journal des Savants LXIII.

Bowley, A. L., 1960, The mathematical groundwork of economics (Kelley, New York).

Brems, H., 1951, Product equilibrium under monopolistic competition (Harvard University Press, Cambridge, MA).

Chamberlin, E. H., 1956, The theory of monopolistic competition, 7th ed. (Harvard University Press, Cambridge, MA).

Cournot, A. A., 1960, Researches into the mathematical principles of the theory of wealth, translated by N. T. Bacon (Kelley, New York).

Cyert, R. M. and M. deGroot, 1970, Multiperiod decision models with alternating choice as a solution to the duopoly problem, Quarterly Journal of Economics 84, Aug., pp. 410–429.

Debreu, G., 1952, A social equilibrium existence theorem, Proceedings of the National Academy of Science, pp. 886–893.

Edgeworth, F. Y., 1925, The pure theory of monopoly, Papers Relating to Political Economy I, pp. 111–142.

Fellner, W. J., 1960, Competition among the few (Kelley, New York).

Fisher, F. M., 1961, The stability of the Cournot oligopoly solution: The effects of the speeds of adjustment and increasing marginal costs, Review of Economic Studies 28, pp. 125–135.

Frank, C. R., Jr. and R. E. Quandt, 1963, On the existence of Cournot equilibrium, International Economic Review 5.

Friedman, J. W., 1971a, A non-cooperative view of oligopoly, International Ecomonic Review 12, Feb., pp. 106–122.

Friedman, J. W., 1971b, A non-cooperative equilibrium for supergames, Review of Economic Studies 38, Jan., pp. 1–12.

Friedman, J. W., 1972, On the structure of oligopoly models with differentiated products, in: H. Sauermann, Contributions to experimental economics, vol. III (J. C. B. Mohr, Tübingen).

Friedman, J. W., 1973a, On reaction function equilibria, International Economic Review 14, Oct., pp. 719–732.

Friedman, J. W., 1973b, Reaction functions as Nash equilibria, Review of Economic Studies 43, pp. 83–90.

Hahn, F. H., 1961, The stability of the Cournot oligopoly solution, Review of Economic Studies 29, pp. 329–331.

Lancaster, K., forthcoming, Socially optimal product differentiation, American Economic Review.
Leontief, W., 1963, Stackelberg on monopolistic competition, Journal of Political Economy, Aug., pp. 554–559.
Nash, J. F., 1951, Non-cooperative games, Annals of Mathematics 54, pp. 286–295.
Negishi, T. and K. Okuguchi, 1971, A model of duopoly with Stackelberg equilibrium, Zeitschrift für Nationalökonomie 32, pp. 153–162.
Neumann, J. von and O. Morgenstern, 1953, Theory of games and economic behavior, 3rd ed. (Princeton University Press, Princeton, NJ).
Okuguchi, K., 1970, Adaptive expectations in an oligopoly model, Review of Economic Studies 37, April, pp. 233–237.
Okuguchi, K. and K. Suzumura, 1971, Uniqueness of the Cournot oligopoly equilbirium, Economic Studies Quarterly XXII, April, pp. 81–84.
Sato, R. and K. Nagatani, 1967, The stability of oligopoly with conjectural variations, Review of Economic Studies 34, pp. 409–416.
Shubik, M., 1959, Strategy and market structure (Wiley, New York).
Stackelberg, H. von, 1934, Marktform und Gleichgewicht (Springer, Vienna).
Theocharis, R. D., 1960, On the stability of the Cournot solution of the oligopoly problem, Review of Economic Studies 27, pp. 133–134.

Chapter 7

Segregation on a Continuous Variable

T. C. SCHELLING

Consider an organization whose members are of varying ages and care about the ages of their associates. To be concrete, suppose the age distribution is horizontal from 20 to 70 and nobody will remain in a group whose average age exceeds his own by more than ten years or is less by more than twenty. Initially, with an even spread from 20 to 70, the mean is 45 and everybody under 35 will depart. So will everybody over 65. What happens to the group – the size of its membership and its age distribution?

Consider alternatively a group of men and women who care about the sex ratio in the group. A third of the men insist on being at least a two-thirds majority, a third will remain only if they are not a minority, and a third are willing to be outnumbered but no more than two to one. Half the women will remain as long as they are not a minority; half will remain as long as they are not outnumbered more than two to one. Initially, the group is 60 percent men and 40 percent women. What happens to the membership – its size and its sex composition?

In both cases we have people responding to an environment that consists of people who are responding to each other. As people respond they change the environments of the people they associate with, and cause further responses. Everybody's presence affects, if only slightly, the environment of everybody else. "Respond" in these cases is departure or, if we permit it, joining or rejoining. The outcomes are described in aggregates, averages and frequency distributions. But the outcomes result from *individual* decisions, unless people can commit themselves to organized or disciplined choices.

1. Models of Sorting and Mixing

These are idealized models of sorting and mixing, or segregating and integrating. We postulate a population of individuals who respond to some specified characteristics of the population itself – some ratio or average or percentage or total. We impute to the individuals certain preferences about those population characteristics, and we specify the dynamics of response.

Our interest in these models would arise from two conditions that may or may not hold. The first is that we be able to identify a model with some important social process, even if it is only a remote and abstract model that captures part of the process. The second is that the result not be trivial – that the outcomes not be so transparently related to the parameters of the model that we can proceed from postulates to results without working the model.

2. Discrete and Continuous Variables

This paper is about models in which the variable to which people respond is continuous. Discrete variables are religion, language, sex, "color", nationality, political party, and the dichotomous divisions between officers and enlisted men, faculty and students, doctors and nurses. Continuous variables are age, income, IQ, height, and skill at tennis or chess. ("Color" is in quotation marks because pigmentation is continuous in several dimensions, but for purposes of segregation "color" is discrete and nearly dichotomous in this country.) Some continuous variables, like age, are well defined, measurable and cardinal. Some, like income, can be approximately defined, if somewhat arbitrarily. Some, like IQ or skill at tennis, are susceptible only of ordinal measurement and may or may not have been calibrated on a scale. Some, like "status", may involve too many dimensions to be treated as a single variable even in an abstract model.

3. Discrete and Continuous Actions

In addition to the population characteristic, the model has to identify the action or choice. If we talk about segregation by race or by age in residential neighborhoods, we need definitions not only of "race" or "age" but of "residence" and "neighborhood". We can work with a model in which my neighbor's neighborhood is the same as mine, a "bounded neighborhood" model, or one in which my neighbor's neighborhood extends a little further in his direction and is different from mine but spatially continuous with it. Thus the "environment" can also be continuous or discrete. And the activity – association, contact, or even residence – can be an on–off variable or a continuous variable measured in proportions, frequencies, or distance.

4. The Constraining Identities

For the simplest example consider an apartment house, nursing home, or neighborhood and suppose no one is willing to stay where people on the average are older than oneself. The younger people move out; the average rises; somebody else is now younger than average and moves out; again the average rises and again somebody moves out. Eventually those who are tied for oldest are all that remain. The same would be true of a tennis club in which the poorest 10% of the players find membership unattractive.

What we have is a set of constraining "identities", mathematical conditions that cannot be evaded. For any variable by which people can be ranked or measured, in any group, half the members will be at or above the median. A quarter will be at or below the lower quartile; no more than 10% can be above the highest decile. Nobody can join or leave without changing everybody else's position. If the people above average leave, the average goes down; if they join, it goes up.

If we divide a population in two, the weighted average of the two groups has to equal the average for the population as a whole. And we cannot have the younger people in the group with the higher average, and the older in the group with the lower average, no matter how badly they all want it that way.

It is these mathematical identities that provide the "feedback loop" in our system: everybody who responds to the composition of a group affects the composition of the group.

The question of whether a grouping is possible in which everybody is satisfied is pertinent to "open-ended" models – models in which people depart if their absolute requirements are not met. In a "closed model", people move only if things are better in the place they move to; we rank people according to some variable, say age, and ask how they will distribute themselves among two or more compartments – neighborhoods, organizations, or just "compartments".

5. The Open Model

Consider now the question posed at the beginning. Initially there is an even distribution of ages from 20 to 70, with a mean of 45. Everybody under 35 is dissatisfied and will leave, as will everybody above 65. The outcome depends on the dynamics, so we have to specify whether all the dissatisfied make simultaneous decisions to depart the same day and do depart, of if they do not move simultaneously whether the young move out faster than the old and whether the 20-year-olds, who are "more discontent", move out faster than the 30-year-olds, who are discontent by only five years rather than 15.

Let all the discontent move out at once. We are left with an age spread from 35 to 65 and a mean of 50. Now everybody under 40 wants to move; the departure of more young people than old has raised the average. What about the people over 65? Do we let them back in? If we don't, the ultimate outcome will be a residual population consisting of everybody in the age range from 45 to 65. If we let back in the people who left before the average rose, and who would not have left if they had waited, we shall end up with an age range from 50 to 70.

Quite different initial conditions lead to the same result. If only the age group from 20 to 40 is initially in the organization, and if non-members can join when the age distribution appeals to them, older people will join. The younger will defect, and stability is eventually achieved with the 50–70 age group alone. People aged 40 to 50 will have joined, causing younger people to depart, only to leave in their turn as their presence attracts older members whom they cannot abide. If there had been a gap in the age distribution – nobody aged 40 to 50 – none of the older outsiders would have joined the initial 20–40 age group. Thus the intermediate ages dispossess the younger and are in turn dispossessed by the people they attract.

I leave it to the reader to work out the possible outcomes for the men and women described in the second paragraph.[1]

6. Closed Models

Suppose a group of people, differing in age, with a choice of two rooms. Everybody wants to be in the room in which the average age is nearest his own. Is there an equilibrium? How is equilibrium arrived at, and how will the process be affected by rules of movement, errors of perception, the order in which different people make their choices and the speeds with which they act, and whether adjustment is continuous or there is a limited number of attempts?

Evidently we can find an equilibrium. Spread everybody in a line by age and make a partition. The marginal person, located at the partition,

[1]This kind of analysis for dichotomous variables is explored at some length in: T. C. Schelling, Dynamic models of segregation, Journal of Mathematical Sociology 1 (1971) pp. 143–186.

prefers the older group or the younger group or is indifferent. If he prefers the older group, put him into it by moving the partition, and keep doing that until the marginal individual no longer prefers the older group. At that first partition there was some number of people, say on younger side, who preferred to be on the older side; as we move individuals from the younger group to the older, we lower the average ages in both groups. Some who were originally content to be in the younger group will prefer to move into the older, as the higher average approaches their own age and the lower average moves away. But it is easily determined that we reach an equilibrium (even if it contains only the youngest person in one room). With a few plausible assumptions about the speed with which people move and the speed with which they can estimate that parameter (arithmetic mean, for example) in which they are interested, we can generate a damped adjustment process that will converge on a division of people into the two rooms. But there are other preferences to consider.

There is the extreme case in which everybody wants to be in the room with the highest average. A possible equilibrium is that everybody ends up in one room. (Whether or not this is actually an "equilibrium" will depend on whether we let the oldest person move into an empty room, attracted by the potential average when he alone is in it.) Another possibility is that people who are above average want to be in the room with the lower average, and vice versa. There are more complicated preferences.

7. *Alternative Preferences in Closed Models*

An interesting family of preferences has the following properties. The "preferred mean age" is higher, the higher one's age, and mean ages are more preferred, the closer they are to the preferred mean. This simplified family of preferences focuses only on the arithmetic mean; and it is by no means evident that a single statistic, like a population mean, is all that people would care about. But as a warming-up exercise, it is instructive.

Let me illustrate, with as simple an example as can be created, the kinds of questions that arise and some of the answers one can get. I shall refer to "age", but at this level of abstraction any other measure would do. (Because the example uses the arithmetic mean as the motivating statistic, a cardinal measure is implied. But with horizontal distribution the mean coincides with the median.)

Imagine a population horizontally distributed between the ages of 0 and 100. There are two rooms, and everybody is free to enter the room of his choice and to change to the other room if it has the mean age that he prefers. Nobody cares about the rooms themselves; everybody cares about the ages of the people he is with. We can try some alternative preference structures.

Everybody prefers the room in which the average age is closest to his own.

Everybody prefers a room in which the average age is a little higher than his own; specifically, everybody prefers an average age that exceeds his own by a fraction of the difference between his own age and the highest age, 100; and that fraction is the same for everybody, whatever his age. (If the fraction is one-third, a 40-year-old prefers the room whose average age is nearest to 60.)

Everybody prefers the group whose average age is a little closer than his own to the population average of 50; specifically, everybody prefers a mean age closer to 50 by some uniform fraction of the difference. (If the fraction is one-fifth, a 30-year-old wants the room whose mean age is closest to 34.)

A little reflection suggests that any stable partition has to be by age, everybody above a certain age in one room, everybody below in the other. Then the first preference is easily handled: if everybody wants the room whose mean age is nearest his own there is a stable equilibrium at fifty-fifty. With a split at year 40, the mean age in one room is 20 and in the other, 70; everybody 40 to 45 would move into the younger group, raising the average in both rooms – to 22.5 and 72.5 – so that everybody 45 to 47.5 wants to move into the younger group, and so on until the division is at 50.

The second set of preferences is more complicated. Everyone wants the room whose mean age is nearest to an age that is higher than his own by a fraction of the difference between his own and 100. If everyone wants to be with a group whose mean age is older than himself by one-third of that difference, the 25-year-old will want to be in the room whose mean age is nearest 50. With a split at age 50, the means in the two rooms will be 25 and 75; and the 25-year-old is indifferent. The 30-year-old is not. He prefers the mean age closest to 53. Everybody over 25 moves into the older room, leaving a mean age of 12.5 in the younger room. Now everybody seven and older prefers the older room, and the process unravels until everybody is in the same room.

A little algebra shows that, unless that fraction – the parameter in our preference formula – is less than 0.25, there is no sustainable division into two rooms. If that fraction is less than 0.25, there is a stable division at the age given by $100(1-4a)/(2-4a)$ where a is that fraction. If the fraction is 0.2, the stable division occurs at age 16.7. If 0.1, the stable division is at 37.5. And of course if the fraction is 0, the formula gives us our fifty-fifty split.

The third preference, in which everybody prefers a group mean closer than his own age to the population mean, allows three possibilities. If the fraction of the distance from his own age to the population mean that he prefers is greater than 0.5, no split will be sustained. Everybody will be in the same room. If the fraction is less than 0.5, an even split is stable. And if the fraction exactly equals 0.5, any division by age is in neutral equilibrium.

8. A Slightly More General Formula

Keeping the horizontal distribution, which is algebraically convenient, we can examine what happens if we use some other statistic than the arithmetic mean. The mean and the median coincide, but we can ask what happens if people want to be in the group whose lower or upper quartile, or fourth or sixth decile, is closest to some preferred value – the preferred value again being their own ages or some regular displacement from their own ages. Our first preference is easily transposed into quartile or decile terms. Suppose everybody wants to be in the group whose age at the lowest quartile is nearest his own. With a horizontal distribution we can work this one in our heads. The division will occur where the marginal person – the oldest person in the younger group, and the youngest person in the older group – is equidistant in age between the lower quartiles of the two groups. Because of our horizontal distribution, this means that three quartiles in the younger group cover the same age span as one quartile in the older group. The older group therefore spans three times the years of the younger group. So the division occurs at the lower quartile of the whole population, with one-third as many people in the younger room as in the older room.

The result generalizes: for any "fractile" that people want closer to their own ages, one-tenth or two-fifths or three-quarters, the equilibrium division into two rooms occurs at that fractile. (The even split we obtained when we used the arithmetic mean was due to the coincidence of the mean with the median, which divides the population at one-half.)

A single formula takes care of these alternatives. Let everybody prefer the group whose Pth percentile is closest to the age that lies some fraction, a, of the distance from his own age to some reference age, R. If everybody wants the group whose lowest quartile is closest to one-fifth the distance from his own age, x, to age 60, P is 0.25, a is 0.2, R is 60, and he prefers the group whose 25th percentile is closest to $x + 0.2(60 - x)$. If the population is divided at age D, D is a stable dividing point if and only if

$$D + a(R - D) = \frac{PD + D + P(100 - D)}{2},$$

or

$$D = \frac{P - 2aR/100}{1 - 2a} \cdot 100.$$

Putting $P = 0.5$ for the median (mean) as before, and $R = 100$ or 50 as before, we get $D = (1 - 4a)/(2 - 4a)$ and $D = 1/2$ as before. The formula breaks down if the numerator is negative, yielding maximum values of 0.25 and 0.5 for a when $P = 0.5$ and R is equal to 100 and to 50.

The formula is not worth memorizing, since populations and preferences don't fit this idealized model. But for gaining familiarity with the way this kind of model works, the formula is suggestive.

9. A Third Room

If a third room were available, would anybody occupy it? Just as the second room will be unoccupied if the value of a is large, the third will not be occupied unless a is quite small. We can suppose an equilibrium division into two rooms and ask whether the youngest person in the younger room would move to a third room if it were available, the mean or median age in that third room then being his own. With the horizontal distribution that we are using for arithmetical convenience, the mean age in the younger room will be half the age at which the population is divided. The youngest, whose age is zero, will move into a third room if his preferred mean age, aR, is closer to zero than to a mean equal to half the age that divides the two occupied rooms. That is, if

$$4aR < \frac{P - 2aR/100}{1 - 2a} \cdot 100.$$

Using the mean (median) as the statistic of interest, $P = 0.5$, with R equal to 100, i.e., with everyone preferring a somewhat higher mean than his own age, the third room will form only if a is less than about 0.096. With R equal to 50, so that the reference age is the population mean, a third room will form with a less than 0.25.

With R equal to 100, the oldest member will always prefer to occupy the third room if it is empty. So with three rooms available, the population will settle down only if a is less than 0.096; otherwise the younger will move into upper age groups, vacating the youngest room, which then attracts the oldest again. With R equal to 50, and a less than 0.25, the vacant room will initially be occupied by the oldest or the youngest, whoever gets there first, but the end result will be the same.

10. Optimality of Division or Non-Division

Does the equilibrium division into two rooms represent some optimal, or welfare-maximizing, or collectively preferred division? We should not expect so because nobody in our model pays any heed to what he does to the average age of any group he joins.

We cannot inquire into the Pareto-optimality of any outcome, because we have only a single dimension – nothing to trade or to compensate with. But out of curiosity we can ask whether the equilibrium division minimizes the sum of the distances between actual mean ages and people's preferred mean ages. Satisfaction need not be linear in that distance, but it could be, and at least for illustration we can ask what happens to the sum of the differences between the mean ages people prefer and the mean ages they get.

With reference age R at 100, it turns out that for any positive value of a the aggregate difference is not minimized at the equilibrium division. Actually, the larger is a, the greater the disparity. Look for a moment at the situation when a is 0.25. Everybody congregates in a single room. What happens if we force the older half into one room and the younger half into another?

Everybody in the older room gains. People aged 50 have a preferred age of 62.5, which is midway between 50, the old mean, and 75, the new one. In the younger room, the youngest third – the youngest sixth of the population – is better off. They prefer their new mean of 25 to the old mean of 50. The next sixth of the population, those from the 16.7th to the 33.3rd percentile, are worse off – they prefer 50 to 25 – but they would not voluntarily move to the older room, because its mean is 75, and they prefer 25 to 75. The next sixth, from the 33.3rd percentile to the 50th, are worse off and would switch to the older group if they could, preferring a mean of 15 to 25. But if for all these people we calculate the changes in the distances between their preferred means and the means of the groups they are in, we find that division into two rooms reduces that aggregate distance. In fact, the aggregate distance is minimized when they are divided with the older 40 percent in one room, the younger 60 percent in the other.[2]

This illustrates that an equilibrium division is not likely to have any optimal properties. And it reminds us that an imposed division will benefit some, will dissatisfy some who nevertheless would not switch voluntarily, and will leave some discontent who would switch if they could.

11. The Need for Models

I return to the two circumstances in which models like these are useful. First, they must be models of *something* that matters – residence or membership or participation that involves separation or mixing of some social significance. And second, the systemic consequences of individual behaviors must not be so transparent that we can treat the aggregate as though it were a collective individual, and do without the model.

To this point I have been trying to demonstrate the second – that the outcomes are not immediately and intuitively transparent once the motivations are postulated and the population characteristics specified. If this is true, studies of aggregates will not permit inferences about individual motives, without the help of a mediating model. And knowledge of individual behaviors will not lead either to predictions of aggregate outcomes or to policies for affecting those outcomes, without attention to the intervening models that relate the micromotives of individuals to the macrophenomena that are the object of policy.

Simplified models of artificial situations can be offered for either of two purposes. One is ambitious: these are "basic models" – first approximations that can be elaborated to simulate with higher fidelity the real situations we want to examine. The second is modest: whether or not these models constitute a "starting set" on which better approximations can be built, they illustrate the *kind* of analysis that is needed, some of the phenomena to be anticipated, and some of the questions worth asking.

The more modest accomplishment is all that is claimed. The models

[2]The accounting, with everybody over 60 in one room and under 60 in the other, compared with all in one room, is as follows. Everybody over 60 prefers the separation. Everybody 40 to 60 is in the younger room and would prefer the current mean age, 80, of the older room. (These are the ones who would have to be induced to stay in the younger room.) Everybody 20 to 40 prefers the old situation – one room with a mean age of 50 – to the new, but would not be attracted to the older room with its mean of 80. Everybody under 20 prefers the new mean of his room, 30, to the old mean of 50. Sixty percent of the people gained, 40% lost; the mean displacement was 6.67 years closer (about one-third closer) to the mean of one's choice than with all in one room.

were selected for easy description, easy visualization, and easy algebraic treatment.

Even these artificial models invite further elaboration. In the closed model, for example, we could invoke a new variable, perhaps "density", and get a new division between the two rooms at a point where the greater attractiveness of the age level is balanced by the greater crowding. To do this requires interpreting "room" concretely rather than abstractly, with some physical dimension or some facility in short supply. (A child may prefer to be on the older baseball squad, but not if he gets to play less frequently; a person may prefer to travel with an older group, but not if it reduces his chances of a window seat; a person may prefer the older discussion group, but not if it means a more crowded room, more noise, fewer turns at talking and less chance of being elected chairman.) As we add dimensions to the model, and the model becomes more particular, we can be less confident that our model is of something we shall ever want to examine. And after a certain amount of heuristic experiment with building blocks, it becomes more productive to identify the actual characteristics of the phenomena we want to study, rather than to explore general properties of self-sorting on a continuous variable. Nursing homes, tennis clubs, bridge tournaments, social groupings, law firms, apartment buildings, undergraduate colleges and dancing classes may display a number of similar phenomena in their membership; and there may be a number of respects in which age, Q, walking speed, driving speed, income, seniority, body size and social distinction motivate similar behaviors. But the success of analysis eventually depends as much on identifying what is peculiar to one of them as on the insight developed by studying what is common to them.

12. Some Applications

An example that is easy to visualize, and not difficult to find, is residential homes for the elderly. These usually correspond to our "open model", a place that one can join or leave (although not costlessly). (The open model can always be recognized as a special case of the closed model, with the rest of the world as the second alternative, but so large that its population characteristics are invariant with respect to the size of membership.)

It is not feasible to compose a residential unit with elderly people of identical ages. Many are married couples. Vacancies occur irregularly through death and disability, and replacements have to be found. Markets are localized, and people seeking such housing are too few to provide stratified allocations into sizable buildings, while if the units are small they will cease to be the "units" that people identify as their environments. And age, for purposes of living together, is not strictly chronological but is a cluster of attributes, like vigor and diet and eyesight and memory, which vary at a given age and in their development over time.

So there will be a mix of ages. And the question does arise: Can there be found, among the interested population, a group of people with an age mix that every member of the group is willing to live with? As we have seen, there is no guarantee that such a group exists, even if the elderly prefer to live among the elderly. (The mathematics are like that of the freshmen class of an elite college: if nobody can bear to be in the bottom 10 percent, according to some common measure, and if everybody's percentile position is predictable, and if everybody gets to know the composition of the class before he commits himself, there will be no sustainable freshmen class.)

A related question: If people of a given age have different feelings about the groupings they are willing to live in, some willing to be youngest and others not, or some willing to be the oldest and others not, so that we can form groups that, say, all of the 80-year-olds will join but only some of the 60-year-olds, what fraction of the total elderly population can be attracted if the groupings are skillfully composed?

A third question: If with free entry and exit we cannot find viable groupings of any size, and if we can impose restrictions or inducements to lure people in or to induce them to stay out, will our problem be to bring people in or to keep people out? Or are they alternatives? (Keeping some of the old out may keep some of the younger in.)

Still another question: If a group is not viable, how large is the fraction that needs to be induced to remain in order that the rest stay voluntarily? (Remember the problem in the beginning paragraph. We ended up with the people 50 to 70. If we add the people 40 to 50, the mean age drops from 60 to 55, and the group from 45 to 50, which would not have joined on its own, will remain as long as the 40 to 45's can be induced to remain.)

Age has an interesting characteristic: it changes in a regular way with the passage of time. So for any group or cohort we can ask the above questions on a time scale. If a group is viable now, will its age mix still suit its members in five years – ten years? If it is not, but we can hold it together for a while, will it become viable? If we find a viable group with the youngest at, say 65, and replenish the group with 65-year-olds as older people die, does the age distribution generated by the mortality table represent a viable group? (If the mean age is the relevant statistic, it is equivalent to life expectancy: does life expectancy at age 65 represent a mean age that attracts everybody 65 and older?) If not, is there any age cutoff beyond which the mortality table generates a viable distribution of ages?

13. Some Other "Sorting Variables"

Students probably have preferences about the scholarship levels and the athletic proficiency of the colleges they attend. People like to excel; they like to participate; they like to be stimulated; and they like the prestige of attending a quality college or playing on a quality team. The net effect may be to prefer a college that ranks, on average, a little above one's self. Admissions policies hold down the population density of the higher ranked colleges; and if aptitude is the currency with which one buys admission, people will be stratified among colleges according to these ranking variables. (This could be incidental to the quality of the faculty and the facilities.)

14. The Structure of the Model

The simplest among these models can be described as follows. There is some population statistic to which each person relates in two ways. The person has a *preference* about that statistic, and the person *contributes* something to the statistic.

These two relations are usually distinct: being middle-aged is different from liking to associate with middle-aged people, being rich is different from liking to associate with rich people. But the two relations, though distinct, are correlated.

Without correlation people who congregated out of a common preference would be just a sample of the population, with nothing to congregate about, just like every other group. If preferences and contributions are negatively correlated, there will be a tendency toward regression. Any cluster of people who together produce a local population statistic away from the average toward either extreme will seek to join another group toward the opposite extreme, which in turn will be full of individuals seeking company like the first group. If the fat want to associate with the lean and the lean with the fat, lean and fat groups will not persist.

It is when there is positive correlation between the preferred values and the contributed values that separation can occur. If the curve showing preferred values as a function of contributed values is a rising curve, the phenomenon explored in this paper can result.

There is one statistic to which everyone contributes equally but about which their preferences may differ. That is population size, or density. Some like crowded beaches and coffeehouses, others like solitude. Leaving out body size, everybody contributes 1.0 to the statistic of his group. With no variation there is no correlation, so the principle expressed above is no help; but again let there be two rooms.

If everybody wants the less crowded room, stability will occur with equal densities; if everybody wants the more crowded room, all will be in it. If the two rooms are equal in size and all want to be in the room that more nearly contains 55% of the total, all will be in one room. (Forcibly separating anything over 10% into the other room will make everybody better off: 15 is closer to 55 than 100 is. But they won't stay there on their own because 85 is still closer.)

If people differ in the densities they prefer, the division between two rooms is governed by whoever prefers a density of exactly half the total number. (With rooms of equal size, densities are proportionate to numbers; the midpoint between the two numbers is equal to half the total.) If fewer than half the people want to be in a room with more than half, people will divide equally. If more than half want to be with more than half, they will divide where the marginal person prefers a room with just half. If among 100 people the preferences are evenly distributed from, say, 20 per room to 120 per room, 30 people prefer a room with less than 50, 70 prefer a room with more than 50, and they will divide with densities of 30 and 70. And any other distribution of preferences with the thirtieth person just preferring 50 in his room will also cause the same 30 : 70 division. If the rooms are unequal in size, the outcome will depend on whether the smaller or larger room becomes occupied by the people who like the lesser densities.[3]

15. Market Analogies

In some cases people genuinely care about their associates – about their age or income or IQ. But there are market phenomena that have many of the characteristics of these segregation models.

Consider an insurance scheme in which everybody pays the same premium and those who die or hurt themselves are compensated. The people who are least likely to die or to hurt themselves get the poorest bargain. If they know it, and if the organization is unable to discriminate

[3]If density, not numbers, is what really matters, room sizes make a difference. With rooms unequal, the outcome depends on whether people preferring the greater or the lesser densities come to occupy the larger room. With the preference distribution mentioned in the text, trebling the size of one of the rooms will cause the entire group to stay there if they start out there, the density being 100/3 or 33.3, closer than zero to the least dense preference of 20. If all start out in the smaller room, with density 100, 22.5 will migrate to the larger room, bringing the density there to 7.5, with 77.5 in the standard-size room. (When x people have migrated to the larger room, the marginal preference is for a density of $x+20$ according to the distribution mentioned. Assuming that indifference occurs at a preference midway between the densities of the two rooms, the formula is $(x+20)=\frac{1}{2}(100-x+x/3)$.)

in its premiums, they will leave to form an association of their own, one that charges lower premiums if they can identify themselves and that excludes the poorer risks. As they leave, they raise the mortality and accident rates in the organization that they leave, and the premiums have to go up. More people leave. If everybody whose expected value is negative departs, there will be nobody left. (If everybody is willing to pay a fee for insurance, the scheme may unravel until what remains is an extremely high-mortality, high-accident group that is small enough to have a mean rate of compensation that is within the fee limit of the least benefited member. But if the distribution is exponential, there is no such group.) If institutionally the groups cannot discriminate in their premiums among members, members will get sorted into different groups according to their mortality and accident classes. In this case it is not the people themselves that one cares about, but the costs they inflict by being added into the numerator of one's own group.[4]

The fact that many homes for the elderly have an annuity feature or large initiation fee, and many services are available at no cost because discrimination is difficult, adds this market dimension to the situation of the elderly.

16. Time Derivatives

What happens to the variable associated with an individual as time goes by? Age is special: age goes up by a year every year. And it does independently of the ages of the people who surround one. In the earlier years of life the age spread that one can tolerate probably widens with the passage of time. So if the age distribution in some group is not stable but can be made to wait awhile, mutual compatibility may develop. An interesting question is whether one's income is affected over time by incomes that one associates with.

A person who plays bridge or tennis improves at a rate that depends on the skill level of the people in his club. Likely there is some optimum differential between the mean skill that surrounds a person and his own skill. Then a fixed contingent of people may develop a reduced dispersion of skill over time, the better players not improving so much for lack of competition, the poorest dropping out because they can't stand the competition, and the rest showing improvement in proportion to the

[4]An excellent and original discussion of market phenomena of this type is: George A. Akerlof, The market for 'lemons': Qualitative uncertainty and the market mechanism, Quarterly Journal of Economics 84 (Aug. 1970) pp. 488–500.

difference between one's own skill and the mean skill (or some other statistic) of the group.

Status may be the same: in academic or other life, one acquires status status from associating with people of status. And just as this can be part of the motive for associating, it can diminish the dispersion of status in a group, as individuals gradually become assimilated to the status of the group.

17. Mediating Variables

I have been supposing that people of different ages, incomes, or IQ's care about the ages, incomes, or IQ's of the people they associate with. But the preferences are often about something that is a function of age, income, IQ, or skill. Among children, size and strength and age and skill are so closely associated that, when children sort themselves by age, as in baseball, the operative variables may be strength and skill. The school system sorts children by age but it can do so because age is associated with size, strength, skill, experience, and prior schooling. Adults may sort themselves by age because of family status and because of life style. People of an age to have children want to live where life is adapted to children, i.e., to families in which the parents are mostly of similar age.

People who like privacy will associate with people who like privacy, not necessarily because they like the people but because they like the privacy. People who dislike dogs are happier among people who dislike dogs, not because they like the people but because there are no dogs. People who like crowds will be crowded with people who like crowds, without necessarily liking the people who like crowds. People who want to participate in a life-annuity scheme want to participate with short-lived people, without particularly preferring to have friends who are not long for this world.

Chapter 8

Altruistic Equilibrium *

Mordecai KURZ

1. Introduction

We usually associate the notion of "altruism" with the act of transferring goods and services in our possession to other individuals or organizations without compensation. Sometimes we may think of altruism as an act of sacrificing our own utility in favor of others. There is a drastic difference between the two viewpoints since the second assumes that altruistic behavior necessarily must result in reduction of utility while the first position does not contain such an implication. In the context of utility-maximizing behavior we usually conclude that any observed altruistic transfer of goods and services from one person to the other does not result in reduced welfare to the giver but rather is a consequence of interdependency in utilities. Thus parental behavior supporting their children when unable to support themselves is interpreted as resulting from the fact that the parent's welfare rises monotonically with the welfare of their children. It appears that economic theorists have been content to regard all altruistic behavior as arising from utility interdependence and as such the notion of altruism itself is held to have no meaning: the optimizing individual simply attains maximal selfish satisfaction by helping those on whose welfare his utility function depends.[1] It is also clear that utility interdependence tends to encourage cooperative behavior giving rise to such social units as households, families, tribes and other social institutions that may function collectively due to the basic interdependencies.

Biologists and geneticists have long been interested in altruistic behavior due to its peculiar implications to natural selection and for this reason, the only generally accepted doctrine is the one which is consistent with the theory of natural selection. It was thus demonstrated [for

*This research was supported by National Science Foundation Grant GS-40104 at the Institute for Mathematical Studies in the Social Sciences at Stanford University. The author wishes to thank K. J. Arrow, R. J. Aumann, F. Hahn and R. Wilson for very valuable comments.

[1]See, however, Hammond (1975) for an approach similar to ours. I thank F. Hahn for this reference.

example, see Hamilton (1964)] that the degree of altruistic behavior between pairs of organisms is critically related to the kin relationship between the two organisms. It is argued that altruistic behavior can be explained by the deeper phenomenon of natural selection where each gene attempts to maximize the probability of its survival. More precisely, the observed altruistic behavior between related organisms is the one that maximizes the probability of survival and indicates mutual help in proportion to common genetic endowment. This is essentially the "kin selection" theory. On this basis one can argue that the observed interdependencies in utilities among members of the same family are simply reflections of the fact that these are the kind of preference orderings which have been selected for since this resulted in behavior which maximizes the probability of survival! This idea of a process of natural selection among preference orderings is rather interesting but raises some fundamental questions regarding the nature of individual preferences and their origin.

The fact does remain however, that there is extensive evidence for human altruistic behavior which cannot possibly be explained in terms of "kin selection" theory since there is absolutely no genetic relationship between the provider and the receiver. This kind of altruistic behavior is the object of our present analysis and in all the discussion below we ignore interdependencies in utility; before we define and classify this type of altruistic behavior let us re-examine the natural selection approach to the problem.

From the viewpoint of "natural selection" the mere fact that, in the long run, an organism continues to exist means that its behavior is, in fact, optimal in the sense of maximizing the probability of survival; otherwise, the observed species would not be the one to be selected for. Assuming this, it follows that the analysis of the geneticist consists mostly of trying to explain why that particular behavior does in fact provide for the maximization of the probability of survival. From this viewpoint most biologists writing on the subject tend to take the view that there is no such thing as "altruistic behavior" in the sense of a gene inducing actions which reduce its probability of survival in favor of increasing the survival probabilities of another [see, for example, Trivers (1971)]. In fact, it appears to us that in their treatment there is no observed altruistic behavior *by assumption* since the observed behavior is in fact the one maximizing the probability of survival.

It is not clear what the connection between natural selection and efficient or optimal economic behavior is. The hope of explaining non-utility interdependent altruistic behavior within the context of economic analysis is based on the simple observation that human behavior is subject to choice and alterations; to observe that a behavioral pattern is present cannot by itself be a satisfactory explanation of its private or social optimality. On the other hand, our hope to explain observed human altruistic behavior with principles of individual optimality (and without utility interdependencies) will surely rule out the existence of that pure altruistic behavior which entails the sacrifice of one's utility in favor of a different person's utility. This is in fact our view. To start with, we shall ignore in this paper any interdependencies in utility and concentrate on observed altruistic behavior without such interdependencies. We shall explain below why altruistic behavior is socially desirable and develop the theory to explain the mechanism that will make altruistic behavior individually optimal. What we are then saying is that all instances of observed altruistic behavior are in fact *equilibrium* manifestations of a complex structure of altruistic exchange. In this equilibrium individual participants maximize their benefits and in this narrow sense our individuals are in fact socially compensated and thus not acting altruistically in the pure sense mentioned earlier. Although the equilibrium provides for individual optimality it will be seen that it is a rather fragile equilibrium and due to the social benefits involved it is supplemented by the formation of social ethics and social norms which provide both the shadow price system of the equilibrium and the strategic penalties and rewards for participating or trying to "cheat" the system.

It appears to us that it is rather peculiar that most religious and social institutions preach the virtues of altruistic behavior. In addition, all such institutions promise rewards of up to eternal bliss for altruistic behavior and punishments down to eternal damnation for acts of selfishness. Moreover, this system of ethical values, rewards and punishments has been well established in our educational and psychological structure resulting in a complex system of emotional attachments, guilt feelings and social consciousness which are well known. In fact, sociologists who have studied altruistic behavior have noticed the possible connection between such behavior and the ultimate social rewards associated with it [see, for example, Friedrichs (1960) or Freedman, Wallington and Bless (1967)]. The point is that the social rewards and punishments are not the *cause* of altruism but rather the equilibrium quantities determined endogenously within the social system. In fact, at any moment of time each individual within society has to make a rational choice between acting "altruistically" and acting "selfishly" and his decision is "optimal" in some equilibrium sense. Social norms which appear to stabilize this equilibrium are thus regarded by us as endogenously determined within a broader context of an altruistic equilibrium. This paper is dedicated to making some of these concepts precise.

We start in Section 2 with the definition of altruistic behavior and explain in Section 3 the social need for such behavior. Section 4 is the main part of the paper and is devoted to an analysis of a formal model of altruistic exchange and proves a few results. Section 5 discusses the problems arising in a world of imperfect information.

2. The Definition of Altruistic Behavior

Since our view leads to the conclusion that altruistic behavior in the *strict* sense of the word does not exist, we need to define our terms more precisely.

As noted earlier, the conventional notion of altruistic behavior is based on the idea of one individual providing another individual with goods or services without being "adequately" compensated for it. In a world without interdependencies the above means that the altruistic act entails the improvement in the level of welfare of the receiving party at the expense of the welfare level of the giving party. In this strict sense an altruistic behavior cannot be based on a "fair" compensation or an expectation of a "fair" compensation.

It will become clear that the fundamental issue is related to the distinction between altruistic behavior in the above, strict, sense of the term against behavior which *looks* altruistic but in fact is a social equilibrium where the individual is compensated. Thus it will revolve around the motivation, expectations and social norms associated with this behavior. However, before dealing directly with this matter we wish to note that a normal commercial exchange, as we understand it in economic theory, leaves no room for ambiguity in the nature of the contract involved. An individual sells a commodity and receives another in return; such a transaction has the sanction of the law and the enforcement power of the state. Thus a non-altruistic behavior simply means an exchange in which the two sides engage voluntarily, reach an agreement and define a contract which is then enforced by the two parties and supported by the law of the land. We emphasize the notion of enforceability of non-altruistic contracts in order to contrast it with altruistic behavior in which no enforceable mechanism exists. For example, consider a futures contract where individual A pays B a sum of money today, and B promises to deliver a quantity X of some commodity at a later date. We always make the assumption that individual B will in fact deliver since the contract is binding and enforceable. In defining altruistic behavior individual A may give individual B something, and individual B may elect to give nothing in return. There may be an implicit or unspoken understanding between the parties but individual B has no legal obligation to compensate A, and his decision not to repay would not constitute a violation of the law. This suggests that we define altruistic behavior not on the basis of its expectations or intentions but rather on the basis of the objective protection of enforceability that the provider has. We thus define altruistic behavior as

> *an act by one person of providing goods and services to another person without any enforceable contract to receive maximal compensation for his act.*

The fundamental aspect of the above definition is that it does not distinguish between acts which are purely altruistic in the strict sense that was discussed earlier and those modes of behavior which "appear" altruistic due to the absence of enforceable contract. We shall argue below that economic principles predict an extremely wide range of behavioral patterns which are altruistic in the sense of the definition above; however, a subtle social mechanism exists to provide the set of compensations that will make this altruistic behavior individually optimal. This last condition is obviously the one which is interesting and this we shall discuss in Section 4 below. We turn now to discuss the social needs for altruistic behavior.

3. The Social Needs for Altruistic Behavior

The existence of social needs is not sufficient for the establishment of a mechanism for their satisfaction. However, by studying the reasons why altruistic behavior is desirable we can learn about individual as well as social motivation for the creation of the appropriate environment.

3.1. Cooperative Aid

Consider yourself walking in the street and noticing that the person ahead of you is being attacked by a mugger. The attacked person cries for help and you are considering your desire and ability to help. Regardless of the actual reasoning about your strength and actual willingness to help, the fact is that society as a whole will be better off if *all* people adopted a strong conviction of mutual aid. The key point in your consideration of helping the victim is based on your perception of the general social environment in which you live. If social norms of mutual aid are very strong then your inclination to help will be high and if your perception (as it is the case in some large U.S. cities) that social norms of mutual aid are very weak your tendency to help will be reduced. Thus, if you help you may feel yourself a brave and good citizen and if you don't you may feel guilty. However, it is very likely that your final action is related to the probability of your being helped if you were in place of the person attacked!

It is also clear that social norms encourage social conviction and help create that environment in which altruistic acts can take place. The point is that as in all cases of externalities, if all people accept the norm all of them are better off and if any one rejects the norm all of them are worse off. However, can we talk about an "optimal" level of mutual aid? Suppose you pass by a burning house in the second floor of which a child is screaming for help. If you do not help, the child is sure to die; if you rush to help, the probability is 90% that both of you will die since you don't have any equipment or suitable outfit for protection against fire. Under these circumstances, would you help? If very strong social norms of mutual aid existed one can visualize a situation in which the sheer force of ethics and the fear of guilt may make an individual jump into the fire and try to save the child. But one can also visualize a society with much weaker social norms and with much smaller potential penalties for anti-altruistic behavior which will make our individual *not* attempt the rescue.

The examples above show not only that altruistic behavior can be associated, through the environmental climate, to ultimate compensation but also that individual behavior is conditioned to react optimally to many situations where altruistic behavior is called for. This is precisely what one would expect a social equilibrium to mean.

3.2. Transaction Cost

In defining the behavior of individual agents we usually say that he can exchange the vector $(\boldsymbol{x} - \boldsymbol{\omega})$ of excess demands[2] among all vectors such that $\boldsymbol{p}(\boldsymbol{x} - \boldsymbol{\omega}) \leqq 0$. It is usually assumed that the exchange is binding so that the individual is committed to make the exchange via an enforceable contract. In the case of spot transactions there is no real problem since by assumption, equilibrium is a state in which each person wants to make the exchange so that we can visualize the final act of exchange as taking place

[2]Where $\boldsymbol{x}$ is a demand vector and $\boldsymbol{\omega}$ is a vector of endowment.

at a point at which all goods and services are exchanged simultaneously. There are, however, a vast number of transactions in which deliveries are not made at the same time (i.e., they are not spot exchanges) and in all such cases, the way to enforce the transaction is to write a contract and mobilize the power of the state to enforce it. Both the establishment of the contract and the mobilization of the law to enforce it are very costly and resource-consuming. As a result we observe a vast number of transactions in which no contract is written and no legal enforcement is needed. Both sides of the transaction appear to behave altruistically: the first provider seems to provide goods and services without a compensation or even a legally enforceable contract, and the other party seems to behave altruistically when he delivers his part of the bargain when, in fact, he had a chance "to get away with it". To dismiss this point as unrelated to economics is to miss a very important point. If individual 1 gives to individual 2 a sum x with the expectation of a later delivery of y units of a commodity z we would say that the transaction was made efficiently in an altruistic equilibrium if they saved the transaction cost and carried out the transaction without social resources. But what if the sum x becomes very large? There is a point at which the transaction cost to write a socially binding contract are small compared to the potential losses to individual 1 if individual 2 decides to cheat. Moreover, as the sum x increases, the incentive of individual 2 to cheat increases as well. These are the typical considerations leading to an altruistic equilibrium.

3.3. Exchange of Unmeasurables

We generally distinguish between measurable and non-measurable commodities and services. Thus we can trade oranges in established markets but we cannot have a market for loyalty. But in fact, people do exchange loyalty and love and these kinds of "trades" are the essence of marriage or friendship.[3] The point is that these exchanges are not made simultaneously and there are no enforceable contracts that will ensure the fulfillment of the provisions of the exchange. Moreover, in order to carry out the exchange there is no need for an organized market or precise measurement of the items exchanged. The parties have their own subjective evaluation of the value of the items exchanged and the prices to be paid for these exchanges and this is sufficient information.

[3]Also, see Foa (1971) who argues the same point within a different framework.

3.4. Interdependence in the Provision of Consumption

Let us first note that we are not talking about interdependence of *utilities* but rather of the interdependence in the *production* or *provision of goods and services*. Consider for example the question of why people stand in line waiting to be served one at a time. One answer is that if a person tries to be served first the others will use force to prevent him from that. This is certainly the case in a line to purchase tickets for a football game. But how about a line to buy tickets to the opera where most people will resent your action but will probably not prevent you physically? The point is that if every physically strong individual would try to crash the line the consequences to social order can be severe. This can be made more dramatic when you consider your behavior in a theater that just caught fire. An equilibrium behavior will call for an orderly departure of all people so as to maximize the number of survivors. A selfish behavior will call for a chaos in which all will attempt to get out simultaneously and end up perishing in the fire. This is perhaps a dramatic but a clear example of the incentive of each individual to "cheat" and try to save his skin when a social equilibrium calls for an orderly conduct. Note, however, that the example of the fire has a certain "once and for all" quality which the individual in panic seems to demonstrate. However, the appearance of selfish behavior by any one individual will immediately create a conflict among the rest of the crowd and in most instances will be sufficient to provide the signal that will break the altruistic equilibrium. This fragile nature of the altruistic equilibrium and the importance of signals in that state can be amplified by one more example.

Suppose you are driving in a limited-speed zone while *you are in fact in a hurry*. Also assume that you believe that limited speeding is a desirable social behavior and you are in favor of such laws. If you assume yourself to be negligible in influence your decision of how fast to drive will only depend upon the increased probability of an accident, the probability of being caught, the cost of the ticket and the value to you of arriving earlier to your destination. However, the truth of the matter is that even when you are a negligible agent in such a market the interdependence aspect is more than the increased danger to others on the road due to your speeding. That additional factor is the social signal of leadership that indicates to all other people on the road that they may join you in speeding.[4] Thus the signal in many cases is more important than your own direct individualistic influence. In case of fire in the theater you avoid

[4]This essentially creates a kind of externality which makes all agents significant rather than negligible.

running to the door not because this may crowd the others but because this would provide a signal to everybody else to do the same; you often don't speed on the freeway, not because you may endanger everybody else but because this will encourage everybody else to do the same. In fact, one can imagine people opposing speed limits who may speed *in order* to induce everybody else to do likewise and thus weaken the law itself.

It has been often stated that there is no rational reason for an individual to vote since the probability of his voting being pivotal is negligible. But people do vote and they don't do so because they expect to be pivotal. A possible interpretation of such behavior is that they vote because they regard this act to be a signal with important interdependency implications which make the democratic process more viable.

The common element of all such behavioral patterns is their amplification of the fact that individuals may regard themselves as small in relation to the market but will take into account the signals embodied in their behavior to arrive at what would be observed as altruistic behavior which would then lead to the formation of what we would call "altruistic equilibrium".

4. A Model of "Altruistic Exchange Equilibrium"

4.1. Construction

In formalizing our discussion of the different circumstances of altruistic equilibrium we cannot take into account all the factors which were discussed above. For this reason our formal treatment here will consist of a model of a special case which aims at capturing the essential nature of some of the phenomena at hand. Our object in this paper is mostly to explore the different concepts of "altruistic equilibria", characterize them and study their meaning. We want to start here with the fundamental phenomenon of altruistic equilibrium in which agents are able to execute informal contracts without the enforcement mechanism of the law. Thus our model would be called an "altruistic exchange equilibrium". To formulate the model, consider an economy $\mathscr{E}$ with n agents indexed by $i = 1, 2, \ldots, n$. Denote by $\boldsymbol{x}_i$ the k-dimensional consumption vector of agent i. This a vector indicating all the goods, services and other quantities which affect the well being of the agent. For example, component x_{ij} of the vector $\boldsymbol{x}_i$ may be the amount of affection agent i receives from his wife while the component x_{ik} may be the amount of oranges which the agent consumes. The only condition on the components of $\boldsymbol{x}_i$ is that they are measurable and divisible. Our agent i has an endowment vector $\boldsymbol{\omega}_i$ of the same dimension of $\boldsymbol{x}_i$ and thus $\boldsymbol{\omega}_i$ will usually have some zero components. Our agent has a preference ordering $>_i$ defined over vectors $\boldsymbol{x}_i$ and this ordering is represented by the monotonic and continuous utility function $u_i(\boldsymbol{x}_i)$.

Given the endowment $\boldsymbol{\omega}_i$ our agent will divide this vector into two vectors: z_i is the amount which he wishes to keep to himself, and the quantity g_i which he wishes to distribute among all other agents. Thus we have

$$\boldsymbol{\omega}_i = z_i + g_i. \tag{1}$$

Now let

y_{ij} = the vector which agent i gives to agent j;

$y_{ii} = 0$ for all i by definition;

$y_i = (y_{i1}, y_{i2}, \ldots, y_{in})$;

$$g_i = \sum_{j=1}^{n} y_{ij};$$

$$r_i = \sum_{j=1}^{n} y_{ji};$$

N = the set of agents $= \{1, 2, \ldots, n\}$.

The notation g_i was selected to indicate the totality of what i "gives", while r_i is the totality of what i "receives". The total transfers of our economy $\mathscr{E}$ can be described by a transfer matrix T which has the form

$$T = \begin{bmatrix} \mathbf{0} & y_{12} & y_{13} & \cdots & y_{1n} \\ y_{21} & \mathbf{0} & y_{23} & \cdots & y_{2n} \\ \vdots & & & & \\ y_{n1} & y_{n2} & & \cdots & \mathbf{0} \end{bmatrix} \qquad \begin{matrix} g_1 = \sum_{j=1}^{n} y_{1j} \\ g_2 = \sum_{j=1}^{n} y_{2j} \\ \vdots \\ g_n = \sum_{j=1}^{n} y_{jn} \end{matrix}$$

$$r_1 = \sum_{j=1}^{n} y_{j1} \qquad \cdots\cdots\cdots \qquad r_n = \sum_{j=1}^{n} y_{jn}. \tag{2}$$

Each agent has only one decision variable and that is the vector $y_i = (y_{i1}, y_{i2}, \ldots, y_{in})$ of what he gives to each member of the community.

Our agent has no control over how much he will receive from the rest of the society; neither does he have any enforceable contracts with any of the other agents for compensation for his deliveries y_{ij}. More precisely, our agent *cannot* make any binding contracts of exchange and there are no market prices to evaluate such transactions.

We can thus summarize the situation of agent i in the economy $\mathscr{E}$ in the following way:

Given that agents select their vectors y_j, $j = 1, 2, \ldots, n$, then agent i will

(i) receive the vector $\boldsymbol{r}_i = \sum_{j=1}^{n} y_{ji}$;

(ii) give the vector $y_i = (y_{i1}, y_{i2}, \ldots, y_{in})$ which will add up to $g_i = \sum_{j=1}^{n} y_{ij}$;

(iii) consume the vector $\boldsymbol{x}_i$ defined by

$$\boldsymbol{x}_i = \boldsymbol{\omega}_i - g_i + \boldsymbol{r}_i;$$

(iv) and enjoy the utility level

$$u_i(\boldsymbol{x}_i).$$

How should our agent i behave?

We state our immediate and rather obvious observation.

Proposition 1. *If the economy $\mathscr{E}$ takes place only once and all exchanges are made only once and if each individual aims to maximize his utility then the only equilibrium is the trivial one*:

$$\left.\begin{aligned} y_i &= 0, \\ \boldsymbol{x}_i &= \boldsymbol{\omega}_i, \end{aligned}\right\} \quad i = 1, 2, \ldots, n.$$

Thus under the specified conditions the economy degenerates into conditions of complete individualistic consumption with $\boldsymbol{x}_i = \boldsymbol{\omega}_i$. This is obviously neither efficient nor an interesting equilibrium.

Although obvious, Proposition 1 is intended to point out that within the context of a Walrasian equilibrium no altruistic behavior can be observed. Since, as we pointed out earlier, altruistic behavior *is* observed, there must exist new forces that will generate the willingness of agents to engage in altruistic exchange.

Note that the critical reason for the degeneracy in Proposition 1 is related to the fact that the exchange among our agents takes place only *once*. This proposes that we should seek the foundations of altruistic equilibrium in the *repetitive nature of the economy*. Thus the fact that the markets will reopen again and again and the relevant utility of the trader will cover all periods suggests the possibility that under these circumstances the equilibrium will not be trivial and a much richer structure will emerge. We thus assume:

Assumption I. The economy $\mathscr{E}$ is repeated an infinite number of times and neither the utility nor the endowments change from period to period. The endowment is comprised of perishable goods only.

We shall also make the following set of technical assumptions:

Assumption II. The utility functions $u_i(\boldsymbol{x}_i)$ are defined over consumption sets $X^i \subset R^k_+$. X^i are convex sets. The functions $u_i(\boldsymbol{x}_i)$ themselves are continuous, increasing and quasi-concave.

Assumption II is rather standard while Assumption I is strong and new. We make this assumption in order to simplify the analysis and discuss below its relaxation.

The idea of working with a sequence of reopening Walrasian markets is not new [see for example, Radner (1972), Hahn (1971) and Kurz (1974)]. However, the theory of sequence of markets has focused on questions of intertemporal transfers with intertemporal contracts. Moreover, all the contributions deal with a finite sequence of markets thus gaining no stability properties which will be strongly exploited below.

With the assumptions above we proceed now to reinterpret our original economy as a game. The reason for this approach is that Assumption I will allow us to examine the solution of this game with the solution of another game which consists of the original game repeated infinitely many times. This last game is called the "supergame". Contrary to the lack of theoretical development in the case of an infinite sequence of Walrasian markets, there are results related to the supergame which we shall exploit below.

Thus consider the original economy as a game $\mathscr{E}$ where each player i chooses a transfer vector (or, in this case, a strategy), $y_i = (y_{i1}, y_{i2}, \ldots, y_{in})$, where

$$y_i \in Y_i,$$

and

$$Y_i = \left\{ (y_{i1}, y_{i2}, \ldots, y_{in}) \;\middle|\; \begin{array}{l} y_{ij} \geqq 0 \\[2em] 0 \leqq \sum_{j=1} y_{ij} \leqq \omega_i. \end{array} \right\}.$$

This means that each player has a compact strategy space Y_i. For any strategy n tuple $(y_1, y_2, \ldots, y_n)$ the payoff vector is $(u_1(\boldsymbol{x}_1), \ldots, u_n(\boldsymbol{x}_n))$ where $\boldsymbol{x}_i = \boldsymbol{\omega}_i - g_i + \boldsymbol{r}_i$ and g_i, $\boldsymbol{r}_i$ are as defined above.

Before turning to the supergame suppose for a moment that the economy repeats itself only T times and $\boldsymbol{y}_i^k$ is the y vector of individual i in time period k. A strategy in this T-period game is a much more complex object involving a complete specification of what an agent does under any specific circumstances. If σ_i is the strategy of agent i then a strategy n tuple $\boldsymbol{\sigma} = (\sigma_1, \sigma_2, \ldots, \sigma_n)$ will result, for each i, in a sequence of the type

$$\{(\boldsymbol{y}_i^1, \boldsymbol{y}_i^2, \ldots, \boldsymbol{y}_i^T) | \boldsymbol{y}_i^k \in Y_i, k = 1, 2, \ldots, T\}. \tag{3}$$

This will result, for each i, in a sequence $(\boldsymbol{x}_i^1, \boldsymbol{x}_i^2, \ldots, \boldsymbol{x}_i^T)$ and a T-period utility of

$$U_i(\boldsymbol{\sigma}) = U_i(\boldsymbol{x}_i^1, \boldsymbol{x}_i^2, \ldots, \boldsymbol{x}_i^T). \tag{4}$$

Definition 1. A strategy n tuple $\boldsymbol{\sigma} = (\sigma_1, \sigma_2, \ldots, \sigma_n)$ is said to be an equilibrium (or "Nash equilibrium") if, for all i,

$$U_i(\sigma_1, \sigma_2, \ldots, \sigma_n) \geqq U_i(\sigma_1, \sigma_2, \ldots, \sigma_{i-1}, \tilde{\sigma}_i, \sigma_{i+1}, \ldots, \sigma_n)$$

to any other feasible strategy $\tilde{\sigma}_i$. Thus a Nash equilibrium is a strategy σ that no individual has an incentive to deviate from, provided he assumes that all other players do not alter their strategies. As an equilibrium concept this is a "minimal" requirement and we shall adopt it.

In order to justify our turning to the supergame we state now:

Proposition 2. *If the economy reopens a finite number of times T so that all deliveries are carried out T times, and if each agent maximizes his own utility then the only equilibrium strategy is the trivial one, i.e., it is the strategy which results in*

$$\begin{aligned} \boldsymbol{y}_i^k &= 0, \\ & \qquad i = 1, 2, \ldots, n; \quad k = 1, 2, \ldots, T. \\ \boldsymbol{x}_i^k &= \boldsymbol{\omega}_i^k, \end{aligned}$$

Proof. Suppose σ is an equilibrium strategy requiring $\boldsymbol{y}_{ij}^T \neq 0$, then agent i will certainly be better off selecting a new strategy leading to $\boldsymbol{y}_{ij}^T = 0$ for all j. Thus for a strategy to be an equilibrium it must imply $\boldsymbol{y}_{ij}^T = 0$ for all i and j. But under this condition the T-economy is equivalent to the $(T-1)$-economies with $\boldsymbol{x}_i^T = \boldsymbol{\omega}_i^T$ and thus the previous argument holds for $T-1$. This backward induction proves $y_{ij} = 0$ for all i, j and t.

The intuitive explanation of Proposition 2 brings up the fact that in a finite economy no altruistic behaviour can take place in the "last" period and in that last period the economy will degenerate back to the individualistic selfish allocation $x_i^T = \omega_i^T$. However if individual i receives nothing in period T there is no strategy which can punish i for being selfish in period $(T-1)$ since any "punishment" in period $(T-1)$ will entail action in period T at which time our individual I cannot be hurt.

It is rather interesting that no meaningful altruistic equilibrium can exist in a finite economy and that the phenomenon of the "edge effect" is applicable here as well. However, it will become clear at a later point that the existence of equilibrium requires that for each player i the coalition $N-\{i\}$ of "all the others" must always have the ability to move against i if he violates the terms of the equilibrium. It is this condition which is fulfilled in the "supergame" and thus justifies our use of this tool in the development of the theory.

Now since the supergame is nothing but a repetition of $\mathscr{E}$ an infinite number of times, a typical strategy for agent i results in an infinite sequence of the type

$$\{(y_i^1, y_i^2, \dots) | y_i^k \in Y_i, \quad k = 1, 2, 3, \dots\}. \tag{3'}$$

The utility of the player in the supergame will be defined by the mean utility of the individual components. Thus if we denote the supergame utility by $U_i(\boldsymbol{\sigma})$ then

$$U_i(\boldsymbol{\sigma}) = \lim_{m\to\infty} \frac{1}{m} \sum_{k=1}^{m} u_i(x_i^k), \tag{4'}$$

where x_i^k are the components of the allocation vectors to i in the kth play. Note that there is nothing in our discussion to ensure that the limit in (4′) exists. For analytical simplicity we shall restrict the strategy space to those n tuples of strategies that result in well-defined payoffs and consequently for any strategy n tuple σ the sequence $(1/m)\Sigma_{k=1}^m u_i(x_i^k)$ has a limit for all i. Thus in this paper whenever we talk of a supergame strategy we shall always mean a strategy for which the above limits exist. The above is a minimal restriction which we may accept with little hesitation.

We need to introduce a few definitions. First we reinterpret Definition 1 to the supergame in the obvious way:

Definition 1′. A supergame strategy n tuple $\boldsymbol{\sigma}$ is said to be an equilibrium (or "Nash equilibrium") if, for all i,

$$U_i(\sigma_1, \sigma_2, \dots, \sigma_n) \geqq U_i(\sigma_1, \sigma_2, \dots, \sigma_{i-1}, \tilde{\sigma}_i, \sigma_{i+1}, \dots, \sigma_n)$$

for any other feasible strategy $\tilde{\sigma}_i$.

Thus the interpretation of a Nash equilibrium in the supergame is the same as in any other finite game.

We introduce the following notation:

$E(\mathscr{E})$ = the set of all supergame utility allocations resulting from Nash equilibria in the supergame;
$C(\mathscr{E})$ = the set of all the core utility allocations in the game, or economy, $\mathscr{E}$.

Definition 2. A vector $\boldsymbol{x} = (\boldsymbol{x}_1, \boldsymbol{x}_2, \ldots, \boldsymbol{x}_n)$ is said to be a "*utility improving*" allocation in $\mathscr{E}$, if

$$(1) \qquad \sum_{i=1}^{n} \boldsymbol{x}_i = \sum_{i=1}^{n} \boldsymbol{\omega}_i,$$

$$i = 1, 2, \ldots, n.$$

$$(2) \qquad u_i(\boldsymbol{x}_i) \geqq u_i(\boldsymbol{\omega}_i),$$

Proposition 3. *Let $\boldsymbol{x}^*$ be any utility improving allocation in $\mathscr{E}$. Then there exists a Nash equilibrium strategy in the supergame which results in a utility allocation $\boldsymbol{U}^* = (u_i(\boldsymbol{x}_1^*), u_2(\boldsymbol{x}_2^*), \ldots, u_n(\boldsymbol{x}_n^*))$.*

Proof. Since $\boldsymbol{x}^*$ is feasible there exists a set of transfers $y^* = (y_1^*, y_2^*, \ldots, y_n^*)$ with $y_i^* \in Y_i$ such that $\boldsymbol{x}^* = \boldsymbol{\omega}_i + \boldsymbol{r}_i^* - g_i^*$.

Now define the following correlated strategy in the supergame:

$$\sigma_i = \begin{Bmatrix} \text{follow } y_i^k = y_i^* \text{ for } k = 1, 2, 3, \ldots \text{ as long as all other agents} \\ \text{follow } y_j^k = y_j^*, j \neq i, k = 1, 2, 3, \ldots \\ \text{follow } y_i^k = 0 \text{ for all } k \geqq \bar{k} \text{ where } \bar{k} \text{ is the time at which some} \\ \text{agent } j \neq i \text{ deviates from } y_j^* \end{Bmatrix}$$

We can call $\boldsymbol{\sigma} = (\sigma_1, \sigma_2, \ldots, \sigma_n)$ the "*maximal punishment*" strategy. It is clear that the strategy n tuple σ is a Nash equilibrium in the supergame. It results in the supergame allocation $(\boldsymbol{x}^*, \boldsymbol{x}^*, \boldsymbol{x}^*, \ldots)$ and a supergame utility allocation U^*.

We have used the term "altruistic equilibrium" without precisely defining this concept because *it is* an ambiguous concept. Following Proposition 1 above we propose to identify the altruistic equilibrium with the set $E(\mathscr{E})$ of Nash equilibrium points of the supergame. The reason for this is that except for the possibility of $\boldsymbol{\omega} \in E(\mathscr{E})$, any point in $E(\mathscr{E})$ gives rise to some observed altruistic behavior. Proposition 3 shows that this set is very large indeed. As an equilibrium concept this is a very weak notion and is extremely individualistic in nature; it does not allow for any explicit cooperation among individuals or coalitions. Since such equilibria are not necessarily efficient it appears that there will exist strong motivations to seek altruistic equilibria which are Pareto efficient.

To start with denote by $E^*(\mathscr{E})$ the set of all *efficient* supergame utility allocations resulting from Nash equilibria in the supergame. Thus $E^*(\mathscr{E})$ is a subset of $E(\mathscr{E})$. Since every efficient weak altruistic equilibrium can be improved upon by a point in $E^*(\mathscr{E})$ one tends to believe that social mechanisms will exist to lead to a selection of a point in $E^*(\mathscr{E})$ rather than points not in $E^*(\mathscr{E})$. Given the motivation for efficiency, we propose to regard $E^*(\mathscr{E})$ as the set of *efficient altruistic equilibria*. In studying efficient altruistic equilibria we may postulate a dynamic process by which an individual agent can begin to signal to the rest of the agents on how to improve any given allocation. There are many empirical examples of such processes and they are the "trial and error" methods by which altruistic equilibria are in fact attained. Here we do not wish to study such processes. We may note however that one way of thinking about this dynamic process may be simply statistical: an individual or a group of individuals begin to act in a certain way and they wait to find the response of the rest. By observing the pattern of the responses and keeping in mind that the supergame will continue to be played indefinitely, coalitions will simply learn to correlate their strategies. This also means that through such correlations coalitions will even learn how to take joint punitive actions against "cheaters". This obviously should not violate the condition that the resulting allocation be individually optimal in the sense of Nash equilibrium.

This discussion shows that in the supergame an individual may find himself correlating his strategies with coalitions. This gives rise to a third concept due to Aumann (1959):

Definition 3. A strategy point is said to be a *strong equilibrium point* of the supergame if no *coalition* can gain by deviating from it while the others retain the same strategy.

We denote by $S^*(\mathscr{E})$ the set of supergame utility allocations resulting from strong equilibrium points in the supergame. Being equilibrium points in the supergame members of $S^*(\mathscr{E})$ will be discussed below as a special set of altruistic equilibria.

4.2. Characterization of Altruistic Equilibria

We now turn to our main analysis.

Theorem 1. *Let* U^* *be an efficient altruistic equilibrium in* $E^*(\mathscr{E})$. *Then there exists an efficient vector* $\boldsymbol{x}^*$ *in* $\mathscr{E}$ *and a supergame strategy* $\boldsymbol{\sigma}^*$ *which results in the supergame allocation* $(\boldsymbol{x}^*, \boldsymbol{x}^*, \boldsymbol{x}^*, \ldots)$ *and thus* $\boldsymbol{U}^* = (u_1(\boldsymbol{x}_1^*), u_2(\boldsymbol{x}_2^*), \ldots, u_n(\boldsymbol{x}_n^*))$.

Proof. Let $\boldsymbol{U}^*$ be an efficient altruistic equilibrium associated with a supergame Nash equilibrium point $\boldsymbol{\sigma}^*$. This results in a sequence of allocations $\{\boldsymbol{x}^{*^k}\}_{k=1}^{\infty}$. Consider the sequence

$$\boldsymbol{z}^K = \frac{1}{K}\sum_{k=1}^{K} \boldsymbol{x}^{*^k}, \tag{5}$$

and let $\boldsymbol{z}$ be any limit point of this sequence. We shall prove that

(i) $\boldsymbol{z}$ is feasible in $\mathscr{E}$;
(ii) $\boldsymbol{U}^* = (u_1(\boldsymbol{z}_1), u_2(\boldsymbol{z}_2), \ldots, u_n(\boldsymbol{z}_n))$.

To see this note that $\boldsymbol{x}^{*^k}$ is an allocation in the kth play. Thus

$$\sum_{i=1}^{n} \boldsymbol{x}_i^{*^k} = \sum_{i=1}^{n} \boldsymbol{\omega}_i = \boldsymbol{\omega}.$$

Thus

$$\sum_{i=1}^{n} \boldsymbol{z}_i^K = \frac{1}{K}\sum_{k=1}^{K}\sum_{i=1}^{n} \boldsymbol{x}_i^{*^k} = \frac{1}{K}\sum_{k=1}^{K} \boldsymbol{\omega} = \boldsymbol{\omega}.$$

It then follows that any limit point $\boldsymbol{z}$ of $\boldsymbol{z}^K$ will have the property $\sum_{i=1}^{n} \boldsymbol{z}_i = \boldsymbol{\omega}$.

Now suppose $u_1(\boldsymbol{z}_1) \neq U_1^*$. Since $u_i(\boldsymbol{x})$ is concave we have that, for all K,

$$\frac{1}{K}\sum_{k=1}^{K} u_i(\boldsymbol{x}_i^{*^k}) \leqq u_i\left(\frac{1}{K}\sum_{k=1}^{K} \boldsymbol{x}_i^{*^k}\right).$$

Since this is also true for the subsequence which converges to $\boldsymbol{z}$ it follows that

$$U_i^* \leqq u_i(\boldsymbol{z}_i), \qquad i = 1, 2, \ldots, n,$$

and specifically,

$$U_1^* < u_1(\boldsymbol{z}_1).$$

But now, since $U_i^* \geqq u_i(\boldsymbol{\omega}_i)$ it follows that $u_i(\boldsymbol{z}_i) \geqq u_i(\boldsymbol{\omega}_i)$ and thus the allocation $\boldsymbol{z} = (\boldsymbol{z}_1, \boldsymbol{z}_2, \ldots, \boldsymbol{z}_n)$ is a "utility improving" allocation in $\mathscr{E}$ and thus by Proposition 2 the supergame allocations $(\boldsymbol{z}, \boldsymbol{z}, \boldsymbol{z}, \ldots)$ can be achieved as a Nash equilibrium with the "maximal punishment" strategy. This would result in a utility level $\boldsymbol{U} = (u_1(\boldsymbol{z}_1), u_2(\boldsymbol{z}_2), \ldots, u_n(\boldsymbol{z}_n))$. But

$u_i(z_i) \geqq U_i^*$ with $u_1(z_1) > U_1^*$. This shows that U^* is not an efficient utility allocation. This contradiction proves conditions (i) and (ii) above.

Finally select $x^* = z$ where z is any of the limit points defined above. Since $U^* = (u_1(x_1^*), \ldots, u_n(x_n^*))$ it follows that U^* can be obtained through the "maximal punishment" strategy in the supergame applied to the constant allocation sequence $(x^*, x^*, x^*, \ldots)$ and this concludes the proof.

We turn now to the characterization of any efficient altruistic equilibrium U^* with the aid of a price system. To do this recall that, since

$$x_i = \omega_i + r_i - g_i,$$

and since ω_i and r_i are given to our agent, the only decision left for him is the choice of a vector $y_i = (y_{i1}, y_{i2}, \ldots, y_{in})$ with $g_i = \sum_{j=1}^n y_{ij}$. Given a price system p and expenditure level b we can think of our agents as having a "required expenditure set",

$$\left\{ y_i \,|\, pg_i = \sum_{j=1}^n py_{ij} \geqq b, \quad y_{ij} \geqq 0 \right\}. \tag{6}$$

We thus have:

Theorem 2. *Let U^* be an efficient altruistic equilibrium in $E^*(\mathscr{E})$ associated with the Pareto efficient allocation x^* as defined in Theorem 1. Then there exists a set of prices p^* and transfer matrix T^* such that*

(i) $\sum_{i=1}^n y_i^* = \sum_{i=1}^n r_i^*$;

(ii) *for each i, given $(y_1^*, y_2^*, \ldots, y_{i-1}^*, y_{i+1}^*, \ldots, y_n^*)$ the vector y_i maximizes $u_i(x_i)$ in the expenditure set $\{y_i \,|\, p^* g_i \geqq p^* g_i^*\}$.*

Proof. Since x^* is efficient in $\mathscr{E}$ is follows from standard equilibrium theory [see, for example, Debreu (1959, Theorem 6.4, p. 95)] that there exists a price system p^* such that

(a) $\sum_{i=1}^n x_i^* = \sum_{i=1}^n \omega_i$;

(b) x_i^* maximizes $u_i(x_i)$ in the budget set $\{x_i \,|\, p^* x_i \leqq p^* x_i^*\}$.

But since $x_i^* = \omega_i + r_i^* - g_i^*$ the condition $\sum_{i=1}^n x_i^* = \sum_{i=1}^n \omega_i$ implies $\sum_{i=1}^n r_i^* = \sum_{i=1}^n g_i^*$ which proves (i).

On the other hand since agent i takes y_j^*, $j = 1$, as given then r_i^* is given.

The choice of an optimal x_i must then be made from the budget set

$$\{x_i | p^*(\omega_i + r_i^* - g_i) \leqq p^*(\omega_i + r_i^* - g_i^*)\}.$$

And this is equivalent to selecting y_i so as to maximize $u_i(x_i)$ where $x_i = \omega_i + r_i^* - g_i$ in the expenditure set

$$\{y_i | p^* g_i \geqq p^* g_i^*\},$$

which proves (ii).

The two Theorems 1 and 2 show that an efficient altruistic equilibrium is in fact an "efficiency equilibrium" with which we can associate a price system p^* that provides for the implicit exchange rates at which commodities and services are "traded" in the altruistic equilibrium. Thus an efficient altruistic equilibrium looks very much like a repeated Walrasian Pareto-optimal allocation. The only fact that prevents the altruistic equilibrium from looking like a repeated competitive equilibrium is to be found in the fact that there is nothing in the argument above to ensure that

$$p^* g_i^* = p^* r_i^*, \qquad \text{for all } i.$$

In other words the efficient altruistic equilibrium U^* may not satisfy an "equal value" condition in the sense that the value of what our agent gives will not be equal to the value of what he receives. It is clear that when this equal value condition holds (i.e., $p^* g_i^* = p^* r_i^*$, all i), then the efficiency equilibrium of Theorem 2 becomes a "competitive equilibrium".

One way of narrowing the set of equilibria is by the extension of the idea of Nash equilibrium to coalitions. The precise idea was expressed in Definition 3 above where we introduced the concept of "strong equilibrium points". If we accept this notion we have the basic result due to Aumann (1959):

Theorem 3. (*Aumann*) $S^*(\mathscr{E}) = C(\mathscr{E})$.

Proof. See Aumann (1959).

This implication of Theorem 3 is that under the conditions of Theorem 2 if $U^* \in S^*(\mathscr{E})$ then we can find a constant allocation x^* such that $(u_1(x_1^*), u_2(x_2^*), \ldots, u_n(x_n^*)) \in C(\mathscr{E})$ and thus the efficiency equilibrium in Theorem 2 is undominated.

Although appealing, the results in Theorem 3 contain some elements which are not consistent with our view of what an individualistic, altruistic equilibrium should be.

The problem must be understood in terms of the process by which *coalitions* may choose to deviate from a point in the supergame. It must be understood to take place in a world of limited information in which subtle signals are passed out seeking to correlate the strategies in the repeated economy. Thus suppose we consider a strategy n tuple $\boldsymbol{\sigma}^*$ and a coalition S attempting to form its strategy $\hat{\boldsymbol{\sigma}}_S$ so as to deviate from $\boldsymbol{\sigma}^*$ and arrive at $\hat{\boldsymbol{\sigma}} = (\hat{\boldsymbol{\sigma}}_S, \boldsymbol{\sigma}^*_{N-S})$ assuming that members of $N - S$ remain passive observers. The natural question arises: What properties should the strategy $\hat{\boldsymbol{\sigma}}_S$ have?

One way of responding to the above question is by insisting upon the "feasibility conditions" of the game. In the present case, the supergame is difficult and the informational requirements are rather extensive; this suggests that as a minimum, $\hat{\boldsymbol{\sigma}}_S$ should have a no "double-cross" property, i.e., no member of S should be able to deviate individually from $\hat{\boldsymbol{\sigma}}$. Note that strategies which are "strong equilibrium points" in the supergame do not satisfy such conditions and it is the lack of such stability properties that makes this an unsatisfactory concept of an altruistic equilibrium.

We have thus developed three basic concepts of altruistic equilibrium: Nash equilibria, $E^*(\mathscr{E})$, efficient Nash equilibria, $E(\mathscr{E})$, and strong equilibria, $S^*(\mathscr{E})$. We do not know how social organizations select among potential equilibria. Such selections appear to be related to the formation of generally accepted ethical principles of fairness and justice which may involve interpersonal comparisons. In the definition of competitive equilibrium the ethical position taken is embodied in the idea of property rights and is translated into a condition of "equal value" $\boldsymbol{p}^*\boldsymbol{g}^*_i = \boldsymbol{p}^*\boldsymbol{r}^*_i$ as a definition of social fairness.

Socially accepted ethical principles accord each participant his "rights" and thus give rise to allocations which appear to be objective and free of interpersonal comparisons. For example, to argue in favor of a core allocation one must hold the view that all coalitions should be allowed, property rights should be recognized and each agent should be paid according to his true power[5] reflected in his endowment and preferences.

The critical observation to be made is that in a pure altruistic universe analyzed in this section there is no dictator, no government and no exogenous legal system. Thus neither interpersonal weights nor legal "rights" can be established which will imply a final selection of an equilibrium point. It is therefore not surprising that without an additional structure one cannot select an equilibrium. If a complete system could be defined then the notion of equilibrium would be more narrowly defined. However, even if we accept some exogenous system of ethical principles

[5]Where "true power" is defined in terms of the capacity of blocking. This specific technical aspect is not essential here.

one must clearly distinguish between the endogenously determined value system and the ethical principles which determine the equilibrium. We discuss below the interpretation of prices as reflecting the endogenously determined system of social norms, and in Section 5 we discuss the interrelationships between ethics and punishment.

4.3. The Price Interpretation of Social Norms

We have seen above that if an altruistic equilibrium is efficient then a price system emerges which provides a universal yardstick for all altruistic exchanges. These exchange rates should be interpreted as "social norms" or "*norms of conduct*" since they state what is a "fair and proper" rate of exchange between each pair of commodities and services some of which may never be traded in a market. In accordance with our examples earlier, it is the shadow prices that state what is the degree of mutual aid that will in fact be observed and what is the degree of personal risk that an individual is "expected" to take in order to help his fellowman. These shadow prices will also state what is a "fair and proper" conduct within the family or among people standing in line for football tickets. Note that some of these prices are in fact "personal". This may happen if commodities i and j are specific to two agents who are the only ones who possess and exchange them. An example may be the loyalty of a husband to his wife. The shadow price simply reflects the social norm of what a proper reward a person should expect for being "loyal". With this interpretation the equilibrium is very similar to the equilibrium introduced by Hahn (1971) where due to transaction cost commodities may be either "named" or "anonymous". Since commodities may also be defined by the state of nature the equilibrium may therefore entail the implicit promise by individual i to help any drowning person under specified conditions and an implicit promise by all others to help i if he stands the danger of drowning under some specified conditions. The implicit set of exchange rates will also state what is the effort an individual can reasonably be expected to make in order to help other people in distress. The peculiar aspect of our equilibrium is that it is an implicit rather than explicit: there are no orderly markets, there are no explicit market prices and there is no visible means of enforcing that which is regarded as "fair and proper".

In reference to the discussion of the examples in Section 3, the present interpretation of prices shows clearly what we meant when we insisted that the observed modes of conduct and social norms should be viewed as *equilibrium quantities* rather than isolated and unrelated facts of life. The discussion still leaves open the issue raised in the sociological literature on the notion of "punishment" and its relation to the existence of altruistic equilibrium.

5. Punishment, Ethics and Imperfect Information

Perhaps the most distinct feature of our formal discussion in Section 4 is the assumption of complete information. Both the interpretation of the results and the examples discussed earlier indicate why this may not be a completely satisfactory assumption.

Under conditions of imperfect information individuals may decide that "cheating" could be a rewarding strategy since an act of cheating may not be discovered by all other participants. The point is that in an altruistic equilibrium (i.e., a Nash equilibrium in the supergame) the optimal strategies are correlated and such strategies are well-defined only when all participants have the same information. If an attempt is made to act against a violator without a complete agreement among the participants about the underlying information, the social order itself may collapse.

The above argument leads to a paradoxical conclusion: imperfect information encourages cheating policies but these lead to the application of punitive acts which are socially undesirable. This follows from the fact that punitive strategies are costly and lead to ultimate allocations which are inefficient. Moreover harsh punitive strategies (like the "maximal punishment" strategy) does not allow for remorse and for this reason optimistic estimates by any participant of the true probability of being caught, puts the entire social order in jeopardy. This does not mean that in our model above (i.e., under conditions of full information) harsh punitive actions are needed to maintain the equilibrium. In fact, if a violation takes place at a finite time points, a deterring strategy may consist of either an arbitrarily small reprisal over infinite number of times or large (and perhaps total) reprisal over a finite number of time points. We have also explored the possibility of introducing a discount factor and it appears that similar results would hold in that case as well.

From the viewpoint of society as a whole, the collapse of an altruistic equilibrium means a serious degeneracy of human social behavior. Certainly the emergence of the state legal power is a way in which the regular commercial order is institutionalized so that it will not be subject to the instability of altruistic equilibria. In addition to the legal structure society has also evolved an extremely complex structure of ethical principles and moral values. Also, a whole structure of social, religious, professional, fraternal and other institutions are functioning within the social universe with the specific purpose of encouraging and supporting man's mode of behavior which are not judged legal or illegal but are still regarded as "desirable" against "undesirable". Combined with these encouragements society also evolved a complex structure of automatic punishments of violators but almost always these punishments are "in proportion to the violation" so as to encourage remorse and return to the fold. Note that these punishments *are not* like the "maximum punishment" strategy: "excommunication" is practiced by the church only very rarely against violators of the altruistic equilibrium.

It is rather interesting that in establishing the existence of a non-trivial equilibrium it was necessary to regard the economy as being repeated forever.[6] Moreover, in considering the reasons for the existence of equilibrium we have noted that the deviator may face hostile strategies by the rest of society and these punitive actions may take place "forever". In accordance with this we find very instructive the fact that perhaps the deepest and least typical punishment that most religions impose upon the violators of the religious code is the punishment of eternal damnation while the greatest reward is the promise of heaven. To make such promises or threats effective the individual must believe in the extension of life into the infinite future. In terms of our analysis here we interpret these facts to mean that in order to force individuals not to adopt selfish or "cheating" policies that will disrupt the social order, the church essentially decreed *infinite* cost for the act of cheating. It can easily be shown that under these circumstances the pious individual will never attempt to cheat if he assumes that the probability of being caught is not necessarily 1 but is greater than zero.[7]

It is *essential* to distinguish between the endogenous social norms embodied in the price system which specifies what "fairness" means and the ethical and moral principles which induce individuals not to try and subvert the conditions of the social equilibrium. In a world of perfect information and no enforcement cost there is little need for moral principles or religious feelings to help stabilize an altruistic equilibrium. In such a world an individual cheater will *definitely* be caught and hostile strategies will *definitely* be applied against him and thus no rational individual will ever attempt to subvert the social equilibrium.

[6]However we have explored the explicit introduction of uncertainty regarding the horizon and future endowments. It appears that with this assumption we might dispose of the infinite repetition assumption.

[7]Note the similarity of this point to the celebrated "Pascal Wager" [see Pascal (1941, pp. 64–89)].

6. References

Aumann, R. J., 1959, Acceptable points in general cooperative *n*-person games, in: A. W. Tucker and R. D. Luce, eds., Contributions to the theory of games, IV, Annals of Mathematical Studies, no. 40 (Princeton University Press, Princeton, NJ) pp. 287–324.

Debreu, G., 1959, Theory of value (Wiley, New York).

Foa, U. G., 1971, Interpersonal and economic resources, Science 168, Jan., pp. 345–351.

Freedman, J. J., S. A. Wallington and E. Bless, 1967, Compliance without pressure: The effect of guilt, Journal of Personal Social Psychology 7, pp. 117–124.

Friedrichs, R. W., 1960, Alter versus ego: An exploratory assessment of altruism, American Sociological Review 25, pp. 496–508.

Hahn, F., 1971, Equilibrium with transaction costs, Econometrica 39, May, pp. 417–440.

Hamilton, W. D., 1964, The genetical evolution of social behavior, Journal of Theoretical Biology 12, pp. 12–45.

Hammond, P., 1975, Charity: Altruism or cooperative egoism? in: E. Phelps, ed., Altruism, morality and economic theory (Russell Sage Foundation, New York) pp. 115–132.

Kurz, M., 1974, Equilibrium in a finite sequence of markets with transaction cost, Econometrica 42, Jan., pp. 1–20.

Negishi, T., 1960, Welfare economics and the existence of an equilibrium for a competitive economy, Metroeconomica 12, pp. 92–97.

Pascal, B., 1941, Pensées, the provincial letters, Modern Library Edition translated by T. M'Crie (New York).

Radner, R., 1972, Existence of equilibrium of plans, prices, and price expectations in a sequence of markets, Econometrica 40, March, pp. 289–304.

Trivers, R. L., 1971, The evolution of reciprocal altruism, The Quarterly Review of Biology 46, March, pp. 35–57.

Chapter 9

Linear "Maximin" Taxation of Wage and Property Income on a "Maximin" Growth Path

Edmund S. PHELPS*

While theoretical welfare economists used to talk about social welfare, they long did very little with it – as students in the Sixties came increasingly to complain. Most studies, those in the line of Debreu and Koopmans, stayed cautiously with the notion of Paretian efficiency. And it was not apparent, not evidently to the Paretians, that the use by Samuelson and Graaff of the Bentham–Bergson social welfare function advanced the content of policy analysis much beyond the Paretian approach. The trouble lay in the neoclassical postulate of "perfect information" and its corollary, the lump-sum tax. Without allowance for disincentive effects, the distributive aspects of taxation (and public policy generally) were rendered an analytical triviality. For the maximization of social welfare, factors were to receive their marginal social products and transfers were to adjust incomes.

The face of welfare economics is now greatly changed in this respect. Mirrlees (1971) broke with the postulate of perfect information, investigating for the first time the optimal character of the graduated tax on wage income and the optimal level of the income supplement or "negative income tax". In the same year, Rawls (1971) put the finishing touches on his theory of distributive justice, which has done as much to stimulate economic research on redistributional public policies as it has to break the Benthamian habit of summing utilities. These two innovations have in a very few years loosed an outpouring of papers on the welfare theory of redistribution by actually available governmental mechanisms – such as the proportionate or graduated taxation of various kinds of income. Most of these new studies employ Mirrlees's premise of a one-dimensional continuum of abilities or advantages found predeterminedly within the population. Many also employ Rawls' "maximin" criterion – we are to maximize the opportunities of the least advantaged.

*My thanks to Janusz Ordover and John Riley for their important contributions to this paper.

The contribution here is the unavoidable offspring of two Rawlsian papers which study economies with overlapping two-period generations. A paper by Janusz Ordover and me has analyzed, for a society with exactly replicating Mirrleesian inequality of advantage, the "maximin" pair of linear tax rates on wage income and property income, respectively, on the condition that transfers and taxes combine to maintain the economy in a stationary state. This no-growth condition purposely side-stepped the question of intergeneration justice. Because the current generation is not allowed to "trade off" between the stocks of capital and public debt (the two-state variables) for mutual gain, the results obtained there must seem too special to be satisfying. A subsequent paper by John Riley and me resolved the trade-off problem by the relentless extension of the "maximin" criterion to justice among generations as well as to justice within a generation. But to solve the problem of *inter*generation "maximin" in full, the authors took refuge in the postulate that every generation is homogeneous, every member having the same productivity as well as the same tastes.

The present paper tackles one aspect of the "general" problem in which fiscal policy is Rawlsian *within* and *between* generations and each generation shows the same Mirrleesian inequality of advantages. Specifically, I develop the conditions for optimal taxation by the current generation in the manner of partial equilibrium analysis – taking as "given" in each time period the social rate of discount whose determination must await the ultimate intertemporal general equilibrium analysis.

1. Conditions for "Maximin" Taxation on a "Maximin" Path

Let $\Phi(m)$ denote the proportion of young workers in each and every generation whose ability or advantage is m or less, $m \geq 0$.

The natural specifications are

$$0 \leq \Phi(0) < 1 = \Phi(M), \qquad 0 < M \leq \infty,$$

and (1)

$$\Phi(a) < \Phi(b), \qquad \text{when} \quad 0 \leq a < b \leq M.$$

An individual of type m in generation v, $v \geq 0$, works an amount denoted e_v^m in his youth, consumes at the end of his youth an amount denoted c_v^m, and consumes in old age an amount denoted x_v^m. The corresponding amounts *per head* in this generation, all non-negative, are

$$e_v = \int_0^M e_v^m \, \mathrm{d}\Phi(m), \quad c_v = \int_0^M c_v^m \, \mathrm{d}\Phi(m), \quad x_v = \int_0^M x_v^m \, \mathrm{d}\Phi(m). \qquad (2)$$

The "effective" labor supplied by an individual depends upon his m in a proportional way, namely $l_v^m = me_v^m$. Then aggregate effective labor *per head* is

$$l_v = \int_0^M l_v^m \, \mathrm{d}\Phi(m) = \int_0^M me_v^m \, \mathrm{d}\Phi(m). \tag{3}$$

Production per head by generation v is a neoclassical function, F of effective labor per head and existing capital per head left by the previous young generation, k_{v-1}. Generations are of constant size over time, so that this generation's deposit, k_v, for the next generation is simply this period's unconsumed gross output,

$$k_v = F(k_{v-1}, l_v) - c_v - x_{v-1} \geq 0. \tag{4}$$

The production function has the property that the net marginal products, the derivatives of the net product function $Y(k, l) = F(k, l) - k$, are everywhere positive, and Y exhibits constant returns to scale.

Members of generation v all receive a demogrant, g_v, in the first period, and a further installment, h_v, in their second period. Under linear taxation of wages and interest, the budget equation for households of type m in its two-part extensive form is

$$x_v^m = h_v + (1 + \rho_v)\sigma_v^m, \tag{5a}$$

$$c_v^m = g_v + \omega_v l_v^m - \sigma_v^m. \tag{5b}$$

Here $\omega_v \geq 0$ is the after-tax reward to one unit of effort by individuals of the "standard" $m = 1$ type, and $\rho_v \geq -1$ is the after-tax rate of return to anyone's private saving.

These rates of renumeration are to be contrasted to $F_l(k_{v-1}, l_v)$, the marginal product of standard labor, and $F_k(k_v, l_{v+1}) - 1 = Y_k(k_v, l_{v+1})$, the social rate of return to investment in period v. It is natural, though inessential, to suppose that before-tax rates of remuneration, denoted w_v and r_v, are equal to these marginal products,[1]

$$w_v = F_l(k_{v-1}, l_v) > 0, \qquad r_v = F(k_{v,} l_{v+1}) - 1 > -1. \tag{6}$$

At least, F_l and $F_k - 1$ are the shadow prices of labor and saving relative to which we shall define our unit taxes, or specific tax rates,

$$t_v^w = w_v - \omega_v, \qquad t_v^r = r_v - \rho_v. \tag{7}$$

[1]In any case, under conditions of perfect markets, the before-tax wage of m_1 types would be m_1/m_2 times the before-tax wage of any other type, m_2; and all types would face the same before-tax return to saving. Hence, under linear taxation (constant proportionate rates of taxation), the after-tax wage of m_1 types would also be m_1/m_2 times the after-tax wage of m_2 types, and all types would face the same after-tax return to saving.

Each household is supposed to choose its (c^m, x^m, l^m) so as to maximize a utility function, $U(c^m, x^m, e^m)$, which is independent of m, subject to the individualized budget restraint in (5) corresponding to its m. This leads to a labor supply function, $l^m(\rho, m\omega, g, h)$, and a supply-of-wealth (or saving) function, $\sigma^m(\rho, m\omega, g, h)$, for households of type m. We may write the corresponding aggregate supply functions as

$$l = l(\rho, \omega, g, h), \qquad \sigma = \sigma(\rho, \omega, g, h). \tag{8}$$

We will require, neglecting h for a moment, that

$$\omega > 0, \quad \text{if} \quad l > 0; \qquad \rho > -1, \quad \text{if} \quad \sigma > 0, \tag{8a}$$

$$l_g < 0, \quad \text{if} \quad l > 0; \qquad \sigma_g > 0, \quad \text{if} \quad \rho > -1, \quad 1 - \sigma_g > 0, \tag{8b}$$

$$\omega l_\omega + l > 0, \qquad (1+\rho)\sigma_\rho + \sigma > 0, \tag{8c}$$

$$\sigma_\omega > 0, \qquad \omega l_\omega + l - \sigma_\omega = \partial c / \partial \omega > 0, \quad \text{if} \quad l > 0. \tag{8d}$$

The first stipulation is that work and saving are functional, not compulsive (a tall assumption). The next two conditions state that leisure and present and future consumption are normal goods. The last condition states that the rise of "lifetime" consumption resulting from a rise of ω is divided positively between present and future consumption (a plausible assumption).

Each household's maximization also leads to its maximized utility, which quantity is some function of its parameters, $V^m(\rho, m\omega, g, h)$. The "maximin" society here is concerned in particular with the least of these utilities, the utility level achievable by the generation's poorest (nonworking) members,

$$V^0(\rho, 0, g, h) = \max_{\{c^0, x^0, e^0\}} [U(c^0, x^0, e^0) \quad \text{s.t.} \quad x^0 = h + (1+\rho)(g - c^0)]. \tag{9}$$

Of course, the equations of the past two paragraphs apply to any generation so there is no need to subscript all variables by their v.

Obviously the least well-off, because they find it inoptimal to work, feel no direct effect, $\partial V^0/\partial \omega$, upon their utility from a change of ω. The latter will affect them only through its indirect effects upon g, h, and ρ. Now ρ will have a direct effect only in proportion to their saving, $\sigma^0 = g - c^0$. But the latter is arbitrary since the state is free to juggle g and h, subject to constancy of $(1+\rho)g + h$, without thereby altering people's decisions about (c^m, x^m, l^m). The larger h and the smaller g, the smaller is σ^0. For the sake of definiteness, and because the assumption appears the most natural one, I impose the condition that h is *fixed* according to

$$h = x^0(\rho, 0, g, h), \quad \text{i.e.,} \quad \sigma^0(\rho, 0, g, h) = 0, \tag{10}$$

in which the demand (or supply) functions are evaluated at the *optimal* ρ and g. Thus, for each generation, h_v is just large enough to cause zero saving by the poor (those with zero wage income) at the fiscal optimum. Hence $\partial V^0/\partial\rho = 0$ around that optimum. Finally, we have $\partial V^0/\partial g > 0$. The poor of generation v want any change of ω_v and ρ_v that offers greater g_v, given the properly fixed h_v. But too large a g_v will drive the maximum feasible $V^0(.)$ of subsequent generations below the level in generation v. Let us now formulate this intergeneration problem.

Define j_v as the maximum of the minimum $V^0(\rho_i, 0, g_i, h_i)$ over the current generation and those subsequent,

$$j_v = \max \min V^0(\rho_{v+i}, 0, g_{v+i}, h_{v+i}), \qquad i \geq 0. \tag{11}$$

Now it might be wondered whether there exists only an infimum, not a minimum, like the smallest piece of cake over infinitely many slices – size zero, though no actual piece need be so small. In that case, we would have a "max-inf" problem and an infinitude of solutions to it. However, on our assumptions of no capital saturation, $Y_k > 0$, and no utility satiation, $V_g > 0$, it is fairly obvious that the maximized minimum does indeed exist for every initial state, i.e., the infimum is attained by some or all $V^0(.)$ – provided that x_{v-1} is not too large to permit subsistence, or at any rate positive, levels of g and h for subsequent generations.

Of course, j_v is some function of the current or then-initial state, (k_{v-1}, x_{v-1}), say $j(k_{v-1}, x_{v-1})$, independent of v. Due to the happy commutative property of the minimum function, $\min(a, b, c) = \min(a, \min(b, c))$, one can write the following equation in the unknown function j:

$$j(k_{v-1}, x_{v-1}) = \max_{\{\rho_v, \omega_v, g_v\}} \{\min[V^0(\rho_v, 0, g_v, h_v), j(k_v, x_v)]\}, \tag{12}$$

subject to

$$k_v = F(k_{v-1}, l_v) - x_{v-1} - (g_v + \omega_v l_v - \sigma_v),$$

$$x_v = h_v + (1 + \rho_v)\sigma_v,$$

and h_v such that $0 = \sigma^0(\rho_v, 0, g_v, h_v)$ at maximizing $\{\rho_v, \omega_v, g_v\}$.

In a "maximin" society, whatever the $\{\rho_v, \omega_v, g_v\}$ that generation v decides upon and the current $V(\rho_v, 0, \omega_v, g_v, h_v)$ that results, the pertinent minimum over the *subsequent* $V^0(.)$ is the *maximized* minimum achievable by subsequent generations, namely $j(k_v, x_v)$; current generation will take that into account in its "maximin" endeavor.

One property of the optimal path can quickly be seen: The lifetime utility of the poor is equalized across generations. Assume that, for every v, $V^0(\rho_v, 0, g_v, h_v) = j(k_v, x_v)$; then $j(k_{v-1}, x_{v-1}) = j(k_v, x_v)$ for every v, whence $V^0(\rho_{v+i}, 0, \omega_{v+i}; g_{v+i}; h_{v+i}) = j(k_{v-1}, x_{v-1})$ for all $i = 0, 1, \ldots$. To show that $V^0(\rho_v, 0, g_v, h_v) = j(k_v, x_v)$ we argue that $j_k(k_v, x_v) > 0$, $j_x(k_v, x_v) < 0$, again on grounds of non-saturation of capital and non-satiation of utility. Then, if $V^0(.) \neq j(.)$ *were* optimal for some v, one could always raise g_v, thus raising $V^0(.)$ and reducing $j(k_v, x_v)$, or else lower g_v, thus doing the reverse; one or the other action will raise the smaller of V^0 and $j(.)$. For example, if $V^0(.)$ were optimally greater than $j(.)$, it would be better to reduce g_v, which must reduce $V^0(.)$ but raise $j(.)$ in compensation because $\partial k_v/\partial g_v < 0$ and $\partial x_v/\partial g_v > 0$; so $V^0(.)$ could not optimally be greater than $j(.)$.

The above proposition is illustrated in Figure 1, where (ρ_v, ω_v) are fixed at their optimal values and h_v according to the convention in (10). The instrument g_v can be viewed as the equalizer. Correspondingly we may view (ρ_v, ω_v) as assigned to maximizing $j(k_v, x_v)$ when evaluated at the optimal g_v and conventional h_v. In short, (ρ_v, ω_v) are aimed at maximizing future utility possibilities while g_v offers the present generation and equal share in the outcome. Eventually I shall give an interpretation of optimal (ρ_v, ω_v) in terms of total tax revenue. A more specific interpretation presents itself if we assign to ρ_v, say, the task of determining the optimal

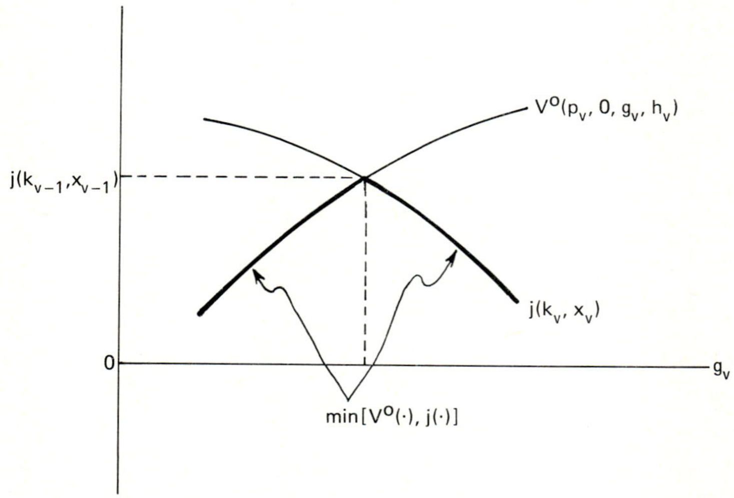

FIGURE 1

x_v: *given* that x_v, ω_v must be maximizing k_v (taking into account the accompanying variation in the required ρ_v), thus "maximizing growth" in order to maximize $j(.)$.

In view of the implied equalization of "least utility" over generations, we may formulate a new equation in our unknown function, j. In this equation, λ_v is a Lagrange multiplier; like $j(k_{v-1}, x_{v-1})$, λ_v is independent of $\{\rho_v, \omega_v, g_v\}$, being a function only of the predetermined state variables facing generation v, (k_{v-1}, x_{v-1}),

$$j(k_{v-1}, x_{v-1}) = \max_{\{\rho_v, \omega_v, g_v\}} \{V^0(\rho_v, 0, g_v; h_v) + \lambda_v[j(k_v, x_v) - j(k_{v-1}, x_{v-1})]\}, \tag{13}$$

subject to

$$k_v = F(k_{v-1}, l_v) - x_{v-1} - (g_v + \omega_v l_v - \sigma_v),$$
$$x_v = h_v + (1 + \rho_v)\sigma_v,$$
$$0 = \sigma^0(\rho_v, 0, g_v, h_v) \quad \text{at optimal } \{\rho_v, \omega_v, g_v\}.$$

The first-order conditions for an interior maximum of the right-hand side are

$$\frac{\partial V^0}{\partial \rho_v} + \lambda \left\{ j_k(k_v, x_v) \frac{\partial k_v}{\partial \rho_v} + j_x(k_v, x_v) \frac{\partial x_v}{\partial \rho_v} \right\} = 0, \tag{14a}$$

$$\frac{\partial V^0}{\partial \omega_v} + \lambda \left\{ j_k(k_v, x_v) \frac{\partial k_v}{\partial \omega_v} + j_x(k_v, x_v) \frac{\partial x_v}{\partial \omega_v} \right\} = 0, \tag{14b}$$

$$\frac{\partial V^0}{\partial g_v} + \lambda \left\{ j_k(k_v, x_v) \frac{\partial k_v}{\partial g_v} + j_k(k_v, x_v) \frac{\partial x_v}{\partial g_v} \right\} = 0. \tag{14c}$$

These conditions contain the derivatives of the unknown function j. Nevertheless we may differentiate (13) to obtain, at the fiscal optimum,

$$j_k(k_{v-1}, x_{v-1})(1 - \lambda_v) = \lambda_v j_k(k_v, x_v) F_k(k_{v-1}, l_v), \tag{15a}$$

$$j_x(k_{v-1}, x_{v-1})(1 - \lambda_v) = \lambda_v j_k(k_v, x_v)(-1). \tag{15b}$$

With $j_k(.) > 0$, therefore, we find

$$j_x(k_{v-1}, x_{v-1}) = -j_k(k_{v-1}, x_{v-1}) F_k(k_{v-1}, l_v)^{-1} < 0, \tag{16}$$

$$\frac{\lambda_v}{1 - \lambda_v} = \frac{j_k(k_{v-1}, x_{v-1})}{j_k(k_v, x_v) F_k(k_{v-1}, l_v)} > 0. \tag{17}$$

Hence, the "marginal utility" to future generations of reducing "our" x_v is equal to the "marginal utility" of our increasing "their" k_v *discounted* by

$F_k(k_v, l_{v+1})$, the gross marginal product of their initial k_v, evaluated at their optimal l_{v+1}. Also $0 < \lambda_v < 1$.

Recalling the notation $1 + r_v = F_k(k_v, l_{v+1})$, $w_v = F_l(k_{v-1}, l_v)$, the earlier results, $\partial V^0/\partial\rho = 0$, $\partial V^0/\partial\omega = 0$, and using (16) and (17), we can express the first-order conditions in the form

$$(w_v - \omega_v)\frac{\partial l_v}{\partial \rho_v} + (r_v - \rho_v)\frac{\partial \sigma^*_v}{\partial \rho_v} = \sigma^*_v, \qquad \sigma^*_v \equiv (1 + r_v)^{-1}\sigma_v, \tag{18a}$$

$$(w_v - \omega_v)\frac{\partial l_v}{\partial \omega_v} + (r_v - \rho_v)\frac{\partial \sigma^*_v}{\partial \omega_v} = l_v, \tag{18b}$$

$$(w_v - \omega_v)\frac{\partial l_v}{\partial g_v} + (r_v - \rho_v)\frac{\partial \sigma^*_v}{\partial \rho_v} = 1 - \frac{\partial V^0/\partial g_v}{\lambda_v j_k(k_v, x_v)}(<1). \tag{18c}$$

Of course the coefficients in parentheses are the tax rates, t^w_v and t^r_v.

2. Properties of the "Maximin" Tax Rates

The above result is recognizable as nominally identical to the conditions on taxation derived in Ordover and Phelps (1975), particularly in their Sections C and D where capital is variable. Much the same bag of tricks used there can be employed here to deduce the following propositions regarding the fiscal optimum. The first two of these are trivial and do not depend upon (18).

Proposition 1. *Optimal* $\omega > 0$, *thus* $t^w < w$.

Taxation of wage income is non-confiscatory because if $\omega = 0$ then $l_v = 0$, whence $k_v = 0$ which could not be "maximin".

Proposition 2. *The fiscal optimum is a corner solution, where* $\sigma = 0$, *iff* $\rho = -1$.

If $\rho = -1$ then $\sigma(.) = 0$ by hypothesis. And $\sigma(.) = 0$ implies $\rho = -1$, when $\omega > 0, g \geq 0$ and h large enough only to make $\sigma^0(.) = 0$.

Proposition 3. *At the optimum,* $\partial l/\partial\omega > 0$.

Use (18b) to write

$$F_l\frac{\partial l}{\partial \omega} = \left(l + \omega\frac{\partial l}{\partial \omega} - \frac{\partial \sigma}{\partial \omega}\right) + (1 + \rho)(1 + r)^{-1}\frac{\partial \sigma}{\partial \omega}.$$

As (8d) specifies, both terms on the right are hypothesized to be positive, like F_l, so $\partial l/\partial\omega$ must be positive.

Proposition 4. *Either $t^w > 0$ or $t^r > 0$ or both.*

In (18b), $\partial l/\partial\omega > 0$ by Proposition 3, $\partial\sigma/\partial\omega > 0$ by (8d) and $l > 0$ for maximin. Hence $\max(t^w, t^r) > 0$ for a positive left-hand side of (18b).

Proposition 5. *If the solution occurs at the propertyless corner, where $\rho = -1$, then the Hicks–Lucas effect of larger ρ, viz., $\partial l/\partial\rho > 0$, cannot be operative in that neighborhood.*

In the event of a corner maximum with respect to ρ, we have to replace (18a) by the inequality

$$(w_v - \omega_v)\frac{\partial l_v}{\partial\rho_v} + (r_v - \rho_v)\frac{\partial\sigma_v^*}{\partial\rho_v} - \sigma_v^* \leq 0. \qquad (18a')$$

Now $\sigma^* = 0$ at $\rho = -1$. Also (8c) implies $\partial\sigma/\partial\rho > 0$ at $\rho = -1$, there being no income effect to offset the substitution effect. Hence $\partial l/\partial\rho < 0$ if $w_v - \omega_v > 0$. From (18b), $(w_v - \omega_v)\,\partial l/\partial\omega = l$ at $\rho = -1$, so that $w_v - \omega_v > 0$ by Proposition 2. An interpretation: A rise of ρ, it is true, would raise x_v but only negligibly when $1 + \rho$ is close to zero; thus, since $t_w > 0$, the only cost which can explain the inoptimality of $\rho > -1$ is that, around the $\rho = -1$ optimum, the anti-Hicks–Lucas effect prevails, $\partial l/\partial\rho < 0$.

Proposition 6. *If $\partial l/\partial\rho \leq 0$ at the fiscal optimum (non-Hicks–Lucas), then $t^r \equiv r - \rho > 0$. Corollary: If optimal $t^r < 0$, the explanation depends upon the Hicks–Lucas effect.*

If $r - \rho < 0$ while $\partial l/\partial\rho \leq 0$, then the rewriting of (18a),

$$(w - \omega)\frac{\partial l}{\partial\rho} = [(1+r)^{-1} - (1+\rho)^{-1}]\cdot\left[\sigma + (1+\rho)\frac{\partial\sigma}{\partial\rho}\right] + (1+\rho)^{-1}\sigma, \qquad (18a'')$$

implies $(w - \omega) \equiv t^w < 0$. But Proposition 4 implies that if $t^r < 0$ then $t^w > 0$, a contradiction. Therefore, $r - \rho > 0$ when $\partial l/\partial\rho \leq 0$. *Interpretation*: A rise of x_v is better produced by a rise of $g + (1+\rho)^{-1}h$, in view of the needs of the poor, than by a rise of ρ. Hence if $\rho > r$ is optimal, the only explanation is *not* the effect of high ρ_v upon x_v – more $g + (1+\rho)^{-1}h$ could achieve that effect more desirably – but rather the effect upon labor supply, namely a sufficiently large $\partial l/\partial\rho > 0$.

Proposition 7. *If $\partial\sigma/\partial\rho \leq 0$ at the fiscal optimum (backward-bending segment), then t^w has the sign of $\partial l/\partial\rho$, which must be non-zero. Corollary: If $t^w \partial l/\partial\rho \leq 0$, then $\partial\sigma/\partial\rho > 0$.*

To show this, rewrite (18a) this time in the form

$$t^w \frac{\partial l}{\partial\rho} = (1+r)^{-1}\left[\sigma + (1+\rho)\frac{\partial\sigma}{\partial\rho}\right] - \frac{\partial\sigma}{\partial\rho}. \tag{18a'''}$$

Then $\partial\sigma/\partial\rho \leq 0$ implies $t^w \partial l/\partial\rho > 0$. *Interpretation*: At a trial solution on a backward-bending segment, the temptation is to reduce ρ, thus to reduce x_v and, with $\partial\sigma/\partial\rho \leq 0$, to increase k_v, given l_v. But if $t^w > 0$ and $\partial l/\partial\rho > 0$, for example, the reduction of ρ may apparently so decrease $F(k_{v-1}, l_v) - \omega_v l_v$ that k_v is reduced on balance by more than enough to offset the reduction of $x_v(1+r_v)^{-1}$.

Propositions 4, 6 and 7 may be summarized in the accompanying table:

	$\partial\sigma/\partial\rho > 0$	$\partial\sigma/\partial\rho < 0$
$\partial l/\partial\rho > 0$	$\max(t^w, t^r) > 0$	$t^w > 0$
$\partial l/\partial\rho < 0$	$t^r > 0$	$t^w < 0$ $t^r > 0$

Of course, a global analysis is required to establish rigorously that none of the cells in this matrix is in fact null, an unpopulated or empty box. Yet I see no signs that some of these cases are not true possibilities. In this connection, the following proposition is perhaps of some interest:

Proposition 8. *If first-period leisure and second-period consumption are "independent" goods or net complements for all (or sufficiently many) households at the fiscal optimum, then both tax rates are positive.*

A proof is given in the working paper preliminary to the article by Ordover and Phelps.

There is, finally, a sense in which, given the cross elasticities, the tax burden on *wage* income is comparatively greater the smaller is the wage-elasticity of labor supply. Solving for t^w and t^r from (18a) and (18b), we can obtain

$$\frac{t^r(1+\rho)^{-1}}{t^w\omega^{-1}} = \frac{\dfrac{\omega}{l}\dfrac{\partial l}{\partial\omega} - \dfrac{\omega}{\sigma}\dfrac{\partial l}{\partial\rho}}{\dfrac{1+\rho}{\sigma}\dfrac{\partial\sigma}{\partial\rho} - \dfrac{1+\rho}{l}\dfrac{\partial\sigma}{\partial\omega}}. \tag{19}$$

Note that while $\partial l/\partial \rho = 0$ is a tempting simplification, provided $\partial \sigma/\partial \rho > 0$ as Proposition 7 warns, it is not plausible to approximate (19) with the assumption that $\partial \sigma/\partial \omega = 0$.

3. Unsolved Problems

Section 1 showed that the government of generation v is to use (ρ_v, ω_v) to maximize $k_v - (1 + r_v)x_v$, evaluated at the "equalizing" g_v and given the no-saving by-the-poor convention determining h_v. An equivalent formulation of this maximand in terms of the generation's supplies of labor and wealth is

$$(w_v - \omega_v)l_v + [(1 + r_v) - (1 + \rho_v)]\sigma_v^*.$$

Thus the government belonging to the current generation can be regarded as taxing in order to maximize its socially discounted "revenue" – when labor and saving are assigned their correct shadow prices.

This observation suggests that the problem of the optimal *graduated* taxation of labor and saving, where marginal tax rates vary with the taxpayer's wage income and interest income, can be analyzed as a "straightforward" generalization of the one-dimensional wage-taxation problem. We let y denote the individual's wage income and z denote his interest income discounted by $(1 + r_v)$. Then aggregate revenue is the double integral

$$\int\int t(y, z)\, \mathrm{d}B(y, z)\, \mathrm{d}y\, \mathrm{d}z,$$

where B gives the proportion of people with earnings less than y and discounted interest less than z. $B(y, z)$ equals the proportion of people whose m's are less than the m corresponding to that (y, z). Note that the "corresponding m" is a function, say μ, involving the level and slopes of the tax schedule facing persons, thus:

$$B(y, z) \equiv \Phi[\mu(t, t_y, t_z, y, z; g, h; w, r)].$$

If I am right, we now have a well-determined problem: Find the tax function $t(y, z)$ which maximizes the revenue integral. In any case, I leave this as an intriguing – and important! – inquiry for others to pursue.

Another problem that this paper leaves outstanding is the final step in the solution of the intergeneration maximin problem. We have to determine the "right" r_v, which depends upon r_{v+1}, and so on *ad infinitum*.

There is little doubt that this problem is exceedingly difficult. Praise be to him or her who cracks it. If I were to try, I would seek to recast the intergeneration problem in terms of continuous time and a continuum of overlapping generations. It is a sheer speculation, but suppose that such a model can be reduced to two state variables, $k(t)$ and $x^*(t)$, the letter being the socially discounted volume of wealth claims by survivors at time t – including their prospective streams of $h(v, t)$ already and unrevokably committed to them. We wish to maximize the present value of the stream of transfers scheduled for new entrants, say $\beta(t)$. A "solution", for me, is an interesting characterization of the "policy functions", $\rho(k(t), x^*(t))$, $\omega(k(t), x^*(t))$ and $\beta(k(t), x^*(t))$, especially in relation to $w(k(t), x^*(t))$ and $r(k(t), x^*(t))$. (The dynamics of the resulting path, $\dot{k}(t)$ and $\dot{x}^*(t)$, are surely of interest, but not of primary interest.) This sort of problem is a differential game: The government player chooses the strategy $\{\rho(k, x^*), \ldots\}$ and households choose their strategy, both under perfect foresight regarding future states. Clearly this continuous-time problem is also going to be difficult to solve.

Fortunately, however, optimal tax analysis need not wait entirely for a full solution to the intertemporal problem, nor even for a computation of this generation's social discount, $1 + r$. Take any arbitrary (k_v^0, x_v^0) that generation v is heading for, optimally or not. More than one tax mix – more than one (ρ, ω) pair – will get it there. Which of these is optimal? What symptoms of inoptimality should be watched for?

The approach set out here makes obvious the answer. One may imagine assigning ρ_v to the target $x_v = x_v^0$, let ω_v maximize k_v while allowing g_v to rise to the point that the maximized $k_v = k_v^0$. Then "optimal" tax rates satisfy

$$0 = \max_{\{\rho_v, \omega_v\}} \{F(k_{v-1}, l_v) - x_{v-1} - g_v - \omega_v l_v - \sigma_v - k_v^0 + \theta[h_v + (1 + \rho_v)\sigma_v - x_v^0]\},$$

where θ, a Lagrange multiplier, is a constant, like g_v, a function only of the state path $\{k_{v-1}, x_{v-1}, k_v^0, x_v^0\}$. The first-order conditions to which this "sub-optimization" leads are akin to those studied in Ordover–Phelps (1975), particularly their Section A where initial and subsequent capital and wealth are both fixed. The propositions that can be deduced about this constrained tax problem are of course fewer and weaker than those obtainable when (k_v, x_v) are "optimized", one or both. Nevertheless those weaker propositions serve to weed our certain tax mixes that could not be optimal even without revision of the economy's (k_v, x_v) heading.

4. Possible Policy Ramifications

Keynes wrote of the force of ideas, Marx of the forces upon ideas. Undoubtedly the Marxians are right to say that interests can often sustain an idea when better and more accurate conceptions are producible – though Marx was not the first nor the last to jeer at the cant and myths promulgated by vested interests.

But "induced ideology" raises doubts as deep as the notion of "induced invention". Keynes and others wisely saw that technology – including economic and ethical theory – is the prime mover. Ideas develop sequentially and cumulatively, are not wholly predictable and are difficult to suppress. So tomorrow's ideas are not altogether the convenient selection by today's powerful interests; they act, from time to time, more like stochastic disturbances, thus jarring the *status quo ante* into the *status quo post.* It is a commonplace that technological developments in physical science, and the resulting opportunities for physical engineering, often alter the balance of power between competing classes. It can also be presumed that the arrival of social and economic ideas, and the inventions in social institutions they indicate, can sway the distribution of income between rich and poor, young and old, healthy and sick, white and black, male and female – just as much as discoveries of material resources.

What I am leading up to, more ponderously than I had intended, is that we may be at the start of a technological revolution in the understanding of efficient tax collection. The growth of the public sector of the past quarter century was enabled and invited by the development of the graduated income tax. The social security system needed the invention of the limited payroll tax. I wonder now whether the institution of a greatly more substantial anti-poverty program does not require a similar innovation toward greater fiscal efficiency. And I suggest that far stiffer taxation of interest income, a tax on income from new saving if not a tax on already existing wealth, perhaps coupled with lighter taxation of low-wage incomes, is the invention needed.

It could turn out that heavier taxation of saving is not the answer, that efficient reforms in the taxation of wage income are all we can rely upon. But at least we now seem to have the conceptual apparatus with which to probe this question. Like a kid one thought would never grow up, "growth theory" seems finally to have come of age and able at least to address some problems of the time.

5. Appendix

At the risk of confusing matters that seem clear to the author, let me give another derivation of the first-order conditions obtained, by the method of freezing h at its magic value, in (18). I have cribbed freely from notes sent to me by John Riley on this approach. Errors and omissions are my own.

Define $q_v \equiv (1+\rho_v)^{-1}$, $p_v \equiv (1+r_v)^{-1}$ and $\beta_v \equiv g_v + q_v h_v$. In these terms we may express new demand functions,

$$c_v = c(\beta_v, q_v, \omega_v), \quad x_v = x(\beta_v, q_v, \omega_v), \quad l_v = l(\beta_v, q_v, \omega_v).$$

Then

$$k_v = F(k_{v-1}, l(\theta_v)) - c(\theta_v) - x_{v-1}, \quad \theta_v \equiv (\beta_v, q_v, \omega_v), \tag{A.1}$$

and our functional equation involving V^0, the indirect utility function of the poor, is

$$j(k_{v-1}, x_{v-1}) = \max_{\theta_v} \min[V^0(\beta_v, q_v), \quad j(k_v, x(\theta_v))], \tag{A.2}$$

subject to (A.1).

Now form the Langrangian

$$\mathscr{L} = j_{-1} + \lambda(V^0 - j_{-1}) + \mu(j(k_v, x_v) - j_{-1}), \tag{A.3}$$

where, using households' budget constraints,

$$k_v = F(k_{v-1}, l(\theta_v)) - x_{v-1} - \omega_v l(\theta_v) + q_v x_v - \beta_v. \tag{A.4}$$

Then, assuming $c_v > 0$,

$$0 = \frac{\partial \mathscr{L}}{\partial \beta} = \lambda V_1^0(\beta, q) + \mu j_k[F_l l_1 - \omega l_1 + q x_1 - 1] + \mu j_x x_1, \tag{A.5a}$$

$$0 = \frac{\partial \mathscr{L}}{\partial q} = \lambda V_2^0(\beta, q) + \mu j_k[F_l l_2 - \omega l_2 + q x_2 + x] + \mu j_x x_2, \tag{A.5b}$$

$$0 = \frac{\partial \mathscr{L}}{\partial \omega} = \mu j_k[F_l l_3 - \omega l_3 + q x_3 - l] + \mu j_x x_3, \tag{A.5c}$$

$$0 = \frac{\partial \mathscr{L}}{\partial j_{-1}} = 1 - \lambda - \mu. \tag{A.5d}$$

Upon assuming that $j_k \geq 0$ and $j_x \leq 0$ we deduce from (A.5a) and (A.5d) that $\mu > 0$, hence $j(k_v, x_v) = j(k_{v-1}, x_{v-1})$. Assume also that $\lambda > 0$. Then, as in the text, $j_x = -p j_k$, where $p = F(k_v, l_{v+1})^{-1}$. Hence,

$$(w - \omega) l_3 + (p - q) x_3 = l > 0. \tag{A.6a}$$

Also, recalling that $V_2^0/V_1^0 = -x^0$ and introducing $\alpha = \lambda V_1^0/\mu j_k$, we have

$$(w-\omega)l_1 + (q-p)x_1 = 1-\alpha, \tag{A.6b}$$

$$(w-\omega)l_2 + (q-p)x_2 = -x + \alpha x^0. \tag{A.6c}$$

Combining these two conditions gives a new condition on q to accompany (A.6a),

$$(w-\omega)(l_2 + x^0 l_1) + (q-p)(x_2 + x^0 x_1) = -(x - x^0) \leq 0. \tag{A.6c'}$$

Equations (A.6a) and (A.6c′) are recognizable as Ordover–Phelps equations once we recollect their convention that $x = h$ and realize that *their* x_2 is $\partial x/\partial q$ with g *and* h are held constant, not with β held constant; thus, *their* x_2 is $(x_2 + x^0 x_1)$ in the present notation.

Let us express (A.6c′) in the spirit of the Ordover–Phelps notation:

$$(w-\omega)\frac{\partial l}{\partial q} + (q-p)\frac{\partial x}{\partial q} = -(x-h). \tag{A.7}$$

Then, using $d\rho/dq = -(1+\rho)^2$, $h = x^0$, $x = (1+\rho)\sigma + x^0$, and $\sigma^* = p\sigma$,

$$(1+\rho)^2\left\{t_w\frac{\partial l}{\partial \rho} + (q-p)\frac{\partial x}{\partial \rho}\right\} = (1+\rho)p^{-1}\sigma^*, \tag{A.8}$$

where $\partial x/\partial \rho = p^{-1}[\sigma^* + (1+\rho)\,\partial\sigma^*/\partial p]$. This leads to (18a) in the text. Note the $\partial x/\partial\rho$ includes the downward effect upon β of a rise of ρ, while the induced rise of x^0, thus h, at the new β, has an equal and opposite effect on $(1+\rho)\sigma$, thus no net effect upon x.

6. References

Mirrlees, J. A., 1971, An exploration in the theory of optimal income taxation, Review of Economic Studies 38, pp. 175–208.

Ordover, J. A. and E. S. Phelps, 1975, Linear taxation of wealth and wages for intragenerational lifetime justice: Some steady-state cases, American Economic Review 65.

Phelps, E. S. and J. G. Riley, 1974, Rawlsian growth, UCLA Economics Department Discussion Paper 54.

Rawls, J., 1971, A theory of economic justice (Harvard University Press, Cambridge, MA).

Chapter 10

The Income Distributional Parameter in Project Appraisal

Bela BALASSA*

1.

Recent concern with the distribution of incomes in developing countries has led to recommendations in project evaluation manuals prepared for international institutions to introduce income distributional considerations in the appraisal of investment projects undertaken by these countries. The Manual of *Industrial Project Analysis in Developing Countries*, prepared for the OECD Development Center by I. M. D. Little and J. A. Mirrlees, called for "attaching different weights to the consumption of different income groups" [Little–Mirrlees (1969, p. 42)]. In the revised volume, *Project Appraisal and Planning for Developing Countries*, it has been proposed that "these weights give expression to the objectives of the government" [Little–Mirrlees (1974, p. 234)]. Little indication is given, however, as to how these weights are to be determined on the grounds that: "In a book primarily concerned with practical applications, it would not be right to develop a theory of welfare weights in great detail" (ibid).

The UNIDO *Guidelines for Project Evaluation*, prepared by Partha Dasgupta, Stephen Marglin and Amartya Sen, put forward a rationale for the introduction of income distributional considerations in project appraisal in the following terms: "given the concern with mitigating inequalities professed by most of the developing countries, disregard of the distribution of benefits and costs from a project can be justified only if it is assumed that the desired distribution of consumption is to be achieved independently of the mix of public investment" [Dasgupta et al. (1972, p. 76)]. It is claimed that such is not the case in developing countries as "Political, institutional, and administrative obstacles prevent taxation of the rich to the point necessary to reduce consumption inequalities substantially. And, the other side of the coin is the widespread objection

*This paper was written as part of a consultant arrangement with the World Bank. For helpful comments and suggestions, the author is indebted to his colleagues and especially to Messrs Graham Pyatt and Lyn Squire.

to increasing the consumption of the poor through direct subsidies" (ibid).

Dasgupta et al. further suggested that income distributional considerations be introduced in project appraisal by weighting the consumption increments accuring to people in various income groups that result from the project's implementation (p. 77).[1] These weights are to "directly reflect political value judgments" (p. 139). They are to be derived on the basis of choices made by policy-makers in regard to particular projects and their possible variants. According to the authors of the UNIDO Guidelines, "Eventually, a consistent pattern of weighting would, it is hoped, emerge from a large number of choices" (p. 144).

The proposed World Bank Guidelines on *Economic Analysis of Projects*, written by H. G. van der Tak and L. Squire, also express the view that "if the government is unable to secure a desired redistribution of income through taxation, it can use the allocation of investment resources as an alternative method of redistributing income" [van der Tak and Squire (1975, p. 17)]. The use of distributional weights is recommended for this purpose when "Value judgments by the government determine the weights to be given . . . to benefits for different classes of income recipients . . ." (p. 26).

Distributional weights are to be derived from a utility function where the marginal utility of consumption (U_c) is taken to depend on the initial level of consumption (c) and the parameter of the utility function (n). In the formulation chosen,

$$U_c = C^{-n}, \tag{1}$$

this parameter is the (social) elasticity of the marginal utility of consumption, while the utility function itself is supposed to express the government's preferences. Thus, "the higher n the more egalitarian the government's objectives, since the higher n the higher the rate of diminishing marginal utility" (p. 63).

It is added that: "For most governments n would probably center around 1. Values close to zero or two, although possible, may be considered extreme" (ibid).[2] Within this range, it is recommended that the project analyst consider values between 0.5 and 1.5 for n (p. 103). Little

[1]The UNIDO Guidelines also consider introducing regional distribution weights (pp. 77, 78–82) and government pricing policy (pp. 82–84) but these will not be discussed in what follows.

[2]Setting the elasticity of the marginal utility of consumption equal to 1 would mean that a weight twice (one-half) of the average was assigned to a marginal increment of consumption accruing to an individual who had one-half (twice) the average consumption level. The assigned weight would be four times (one-fourth) the average if n was set at 2, while equating n to zero would mean that increments in consumption were valued equally regardless of the recipient's existing level of consumption.

justification is given, however, for the choice of the proposed range of values.

While the UNIDO Guidelines call for deriving income distributional weights on the basis of government preferences as revealed by choices of projects and project variants, according to the Bank Guidelines "if an international agency such as the World Bank conducts the analysis, it must try to arrive at an understanding with the government about [its socioeconomic goals] before the analysis is undertaken" (p. 27). It is further added that "if views diverge – with respect to the desired distribution of the gains from development, for example – the agency should analyze the proposed project relative to both its objectives and those of the government and satisfy itself that the project meets the objectives of both" (ibid).

Thus, all three project evaluation manuals call for the use of income distributional weights in project appraisal, to be derived from a social welfare function expressing governmental preferences and/or the preferences of international institutions. In so doing, they disregard private preferences that are reflected in the individual valuation of the utility of consumption.

A different approach is followed in this paper. We will take the private valuation of the utility of consumption as the basis for deriving the social elasticity of the marginal utility of consumption. The relationship between the social and the private elasticity of the marginal utility of consumption is derived below.

Assume that each individual has the same isoelastic utility function $u(i)$ and that the social welfare function is expressed as

$$W = W[u(c_1), u(c_2), \dots, u(c_n)], \tag{2}$$

with $W_i > 0$ for all i. The social elasticity of the marginal utility of consumption (n) can now be written as[3]

$$\begin{aligned} -\frac{\partial \log}{\partial \log c_i}\left\{\frac{\partial W}{\partial c_i}\right\} &= -\frac{\partial \log (W_i u'_i)}{\partial \log c_i} \\ &= -\frac{\partial \log u'_i}{\partial \log c_i} - \frac{\partial \log W_i}{\partial \log c_i} \\ &= -\frac{\partial \log u'_i}{\partial \log c_i} - \frac{c_i W_{ii} u'_i}{W_i}. \end{aligned} \tag{3}$$

The first term on the right-hand side of equation (3) will be the private

[3]The formula was originally derived by Anand (1973); the simplified derivation used here has been suggested to me by Graham Pyatt.

elasticity of the marginal utility of consumption (w), while the second term will provide an adjustment factor for deriving the social elasticity of the marginal utility of consumption from the private elasticity. As Anand (1973) shows, this term can be rewritten as the product of the elasticity of the marginal social welfare function with respect to individual i's utility and the income elasticity of individual i's utility function.

Having defined the social welfare function used in the paper, questions relating to the empirical measurement of the private elasticity of the marginal utility of consumption and the choice of adjustment factors for deriving the social elasticity will need to be considered. Section 2 of the paper provides an introduction to the measurement of the private elasticity of the marginal utility of consumption, taking as a point of departure a paper by William Fellner. In Section 3, empirical results derived in a within-country and an inter-country context will be presented. This will be followed by a discussion of the limitations of the results (Section 4). In turn, in Section 5, comments will be offered on the choice of adjustment factors for deriving the social elasticity of the marginal utility of consumption. Finally, Section 6 will examine the issue of introducing income distributional considerations in project appraisal in general terms.

2.

As Fellner reports (1967, pp. 42–43), Irving Fisher first put forward the proposition that the cardinal measurability of marginal utility depends on the independence (non-complementarity) of wants [Fisher (1892)]. The theoretical analysis underlying this proposition was further developed by Fisher himself (1927) and by Frisch (1959), who utilized the concept of the elasticity of the marginal utility of consumption or, in his terminology, the "money flexibility", in deriving a scheme for computing direct and cross demand elasticities.[4]

The first numerical estimates of the elasticity of the marginal utility of income were also made by Frisch (1932). The work of Fisher and Frisch was subsequently extended to the von Neumann–Morgenstern framework by William Fellner who also estimated the elasticity of the marginal utility of income from consumption data of U.S. cities (1967).

In the Fisher–Frisch tradition, Fellner has established the measurability of the elasticity of the marginal utility of consumption (income) on the

[4]The assumption of want independence was earlier made by Pigou (1910) in suggesting a method to derive price elasticities from income elasticities.

assumption that the individual utility function is separable into at least two additive terms, representing groups of commodities (x),

$$u = u_1(x_1) + u_2(x_2). \tag{4}$$

This permits interpreting "observable marginal rates of substitution as ratios of marginal utilities, on the assumption that if the quantity of one good is held constant and that of another is varied, then the marginal utility of the first of these goods remains unchanged" [Fellner (1967, p. 46)].

Expressing the first-order condition of utility maximization as

$$(\partial u / \partial x_i)/p_i = \lambda, \tag{5}$$

we can determine the increase in income necessary to induce the consumer to buy the same quantity of x_i at a higher price.[5] With $\partial u / \partial x_i$ being the same for the identical level of consumption of x_i in the low price–low income as well as in the high price–high income situation, Fellner suggests that, for the small income range in which we observe x to be constant, the ratio of the ith commodity's income elasticity (E_i) to its compensated own price elasticity (ϵ_i) will provide an estimate of the elasticity of the marginal utility of income.

Fellner's formula provides an approximation to the true elasticity of the marginal utility of income, which has been derived from a general model of utility maximization by Frisch (1958, p. 187),[6]

$$w = \frac{E_i(1 - \alpha_i E_i)}{\epsilon_{ii} - \alpha_i E_i} = \frac{E_i(1 - \alpha_i E_i)}{\epsilon_i}. \tag{6}$$

The difference between the results obtained with the two formulas tends to be small. Thus, Nicholas Stern has shown that Fellner's estimates of the elasticity of the marginal utility of income for the United States exceeds the true elasticity by 15 percent (1973). The difference between the results will be the smaller, the smaller is the budget share of commodity i.

Fellner's estimate of the elasticity of the marginal utility of income was based on data on incomes and on the consumption and relative price of food in a cross-section of American cities. In turn, several authors made estimates in the framework of a linear expenditure system (LES) and other models with additive specifications.[7] In the course of research

[5]In the equations, p refers to prices and λ is the marginal utility of income.

[6]In equation (6) α_i refers to the budget share of the ith commodity and ϵ_{ii} is its uncompensated own price elasticity. To express the elasticity of the marginal utility of income with a positive sign as in (3) we here followed Fellner in multiplying the compensated own price elasticity (the denominator of Frisch's original expression) by -1.

[7]For references, see Brown and Deaton (1972).

undertaken at the World Bank Development Research Center, the LES system was extended by Lluch (1973) to allow for the consumption-saving decision, and the elasticity of the marginal utility of income and consumption was estimated by Lluch and Williams (1975a, 1975b) in the framework of the extended LES system.

Equation (7) shows the relationship between the elasticity of the marginal utility of income (γ) and that of consumption (w) in the framework of the extended LES, where μ is the marginal propensity to consume [Lluch–Williams (1975a, p. 12)],

$$\gamma = \mu(1 + w) - 1. \tag{7}$$

In the following, we will briefly review available estimates of the elasticity of the marginal utility of consumption, which is the relevant concept for project appraisal.

3.

Frisch conjectured that the elasticity of the marginal utility of consumption (money flexibility) is negatively related to per capita incomes.[8] In his view [Frisch (1958, p. 189)], "we may perhaps assume that in most cases the money flexibility has values of the order of magnitude given below,

$w = 10$ for an extremely poor and apathetic part of the population;
$w = 4$ for the slightly better off but still poor part of the population with a fairly pronounced desire to become better off;
$w = 2$ for the middle income bracket, 'the median part' of the population;
$w = 0.7$ for the better off part of the population.
$w = 0.1$ for the rich part of the population with ambitions toward 'conspicuous consumption'."

Frisch further added that: "It would be a very promising research project to determine w for different countries and for different types of population. A universal 'atlas' of the values of w should be constructed. It would serve an extremely useful purpose in demand analysis" (ibid).

Estimates based on U.S. data have led Fellner (1967, p. 73) to conclude that the elasticity of the marginal utility of income is constant over a wide range of incomes in the United States at a level of about 1.5. Other

[8]Recall that we express the elasticity of the marginal utility of consumption with a positive sign while Frisch and econometric studies used a negative sign.

authors, utilizing various forms of additive utility functions, have obtained estimates clustering around 2 [Brown–Denton (1972, p. 1206)], and results reached by the so-called "Australian" [Hoa (1968)] and "Rotterdam" [Theil–Brooks (1970)] models have not provided evidence of a definite relationship between the elasticity of the marginal utility of income (consumption) and per capita incomes in a within-country context.

In turn, the application of the Extended Linear Expenditure System (ELES) to Korean data has given ambiguous results. Dividing Korean urban consumers in two groups, with incomes below and above 4000 won a year in 1970, Lluch and Williams (1975b, table 4) estimated the elasticity of the marginal utility of consumption at 3.1 in the first case and 1.9 in the second. However, the estimated elasticity is higher for urban than for rural households in Korea (6.8 and 5.3, respectively), although average incomes are two-fifths higher for the former than for the latter.

Estimates for particular countries thus do not validate Frisch's conjecture about a negative relationship between the elasticity of the marginal utility of consumption and per capita incomes in a within-country context. Brown and Denton (1972, p. 1206) extend this conclusion to inter-country relationships, suggesting the universal constancy of the elasticity of the marginal utility of consumption. This generalization is, however, contradicted by results of Lluch and Williams and Janvry, Bieri, and Nunez.

Lluch and Williams (1975a) estimated the elasticity of the marginal utility of consumption for fourteen countries chosen on the basis of data availability,[9] utilizing the extended LES system. Estimation was done by the use of equation (8), where v denotes total consumption expenditures per head, and

$$w = v\left(v - \sum p_i T_i\right)^{-1} \tag{8}$$

is the "subsistence quantity" of the ith commodity (i.e., the amount of the ith commodity consumed at the subsistence level).

Because of uncertainty as regards the level of commodity aggregation at which the additivity assumption is appropriate, for each country estimates were made at four levels of commodity aggregation (8, 4, 2, and 1 commodities).[10] The statistical significance of the results tends to be the

[9]United States, Sweden, West Germany, Australia, United Kingdom, Israel, Italy, Ireland, Greece, South Africa, Jamaica, Taiwan, Thailand, and South Korea.

[10]In the following discussion, the 1-commodity aggregation scheme has been disregarded as this corresponds to the simple Keynesian consumption function.

highest at the 8-commodity level and declines as the level of commodity aggregation increases[11] [Lluch–Williams (1975a, table 2)].

Lluch and Williams further utilized the mean estimates for the fourteen countries under study to test Frisch's hypothesis that the elasticity of the marginal utility of consumption is negatively related to per capita incomes in an inter-country framework. According to the results at the three levels of commodity aggregation, this elasticity tends to decline by about one-third of one percentage point as per capita incomes increase by one percent.

Selecting for each country the estimate with the highest level of statistical significance Lluch and Williams obtain, in a weighted regression,[12] the results shown by[13]

$$\log w = \underset{(5.49)}{1.565} - \underset{(3.51)}{0.358} \log x. \tag{9}$$

For an "average" country with incomes per head of \$3000 in 1970 prices, the elasticity of the marginal utility of consumption is shown to be 2.1 while the corresponding elasticities for countries with per capita incomes of \$1000, \$500, \$300, and \$100 are estimated at 3.1, 4.0, 4.8 and 7.0.

A greater degree of progression was found by Janvry et al. (1972), who regressed LES estimates of the elasticity of the marginal utility of consumption for the United States, Norway, Argentina, Peru and Israel on per capita incomes. For countries with per capita incomes of \$3000, \$1000, \$500, \$300, and \$100, the estimates derived from

$$\log w = \underset{(3.92)}{1.759} - \underset{(2.42)}{0.513} \log x, \qquad R^2 = 0.538, \tag{9a}$$

are 1.0, 1.7, 2.4, 3.1, and 5.5.

[11]Out of fourteen countries, the results are significant at the 5% level in twelve cases under the 8-commodity aggregation scheme and eleven cases each under the 4-commodity and the 2-commodity aggregation schemes. The number of significant results increases to fourteen in the 8-commodity aggregation scheme if a 10% level of significance is utilized [Lluch–Williams (1975a, table 2)].

[12]The regression equations estimated by combining country results obtained at the 8-, 4- and 2-commodity aggregation, respectively, are

8 commodity $\quad \log w = \underset{(3.18)}{1.338} - \underset{(2.14)}{0.302} \log x, \quad R^2 = 0.276,$

4 commodity $\quad \log w = \underset{(4.84)}{1.645} - \underset{(2.90)}{0.409} \log x, \quad R^2 = 0.518,$

2 commodity $\quad \log w = \underset{(3.22)}{1.284} - \underset{(2.27)}{0.304} \log x, \quad R^2 = 0.300.$

In the equations x refers to per capita incomes measured in U.S. dollars at the official exchange rate; t-values are shown in parentheses.

[13]The variables have been weighted by the standard error of the dependent variable.

The Lluch–Williams results can be judged superior to the estimates by Janvry et al. This is because Lluch and Williams have used data for a substantial number of countries that also exhibited large income disparities; they have applied the same model to the data of all the countries; and they have employed statistical tests to choose among results pertaining to different degrees of commodity aggregation. In turn, the Janvry–Bieri–Nunez study combines results for a smaller group of countries that exhibit lesser variations in income, and the estimates were made employing a variety of methods which did not permit making a choice on the basis of degrees of statistical significance.

4.

The Lluch–Williams, as well as the Janvry–Bieri–Nunez, results provide empirical support for Frisch's conjecture, according to which the elasticity of the marginal utility of consumption is negatively correlated with incomes in a inter-country context. The results are, however, subject to qualifications as regards the methodology employed and the applicability of the estimates to developing countries.

The measurement of the elasticity of the marginal utility of consumption necessitates an, essentially arbitrary, normalization of the utility function. In the cited studies, normalization has been accomplished by assuming additivity in utilities derived from particular product groups. Fellner suggests that the error committed thereby may not be substantial; thus, in a two-commodity group model, "we would be making excessive allowance for complementarities if we reduced our estimate [of 1.5] by 30%" [Fellner (1967, pp. 65–66)]. However, as Squire has noted (1975), in the framework of the linear expenditure system the elasticity of the marginal utility of consumption cannot be estimated if the additivity assumptions underlying the Stone–Geary formulation of individual utility functions are not made.

It should further be recalled that, in the ELES formulation, the elasticity of the marginal utility of consumption equals consumption per head divided by the difference between actual and subsistence consumption. Since, by definition, subsistence consumption cannot exceed actual consumption, the values of the elasticity will have a lower bound of 1. The elasticity values are thus constrained within certain limits by construction, excluding values hypothesized by Frisch for high-income groups. At the same time, this formulation implies a declining elasticity of the marginal utility of consumption at higher-income levels, since the share of subsistence consumption in the total tends to fall as income rises.

Further questions arise as regards the application of the inter-country results to developing countries. To begin with, while the inclusion of countries with wide differences in income levels ensured a relatively low standard error in the Lluch–Williams regressions, the large deviations between observed and estimated values for the middle-income countries reduce the applicability of the results to any particular country.

Also, differences in the economic structure and in the distribution of incomes in the mixed group of developed and developing countries for which estimates were made may conflict with the assumption of homogeneity in the pattern of consumption. The heterogeneity of the developing country group in regard to resource endowment, climatic conditions, customs and habits, and political as well as sociological factors, too, limits the applicability of the results to individual developing countries.

Furthermore, the group of countries included in the Lluch–Williams study does not comprise developing countries with a per capita income below \$140 in 1970 prices. This excludes some of the largest developing countries, such as India, Indonesia, and Pakistan, which account for three-fifths of the population of the developing world. At the same time, extrapolation outside the range of observations involves a forecasting error which increases more than proportionately as we move away from this range.

Finally, the use of exchange rates to convert national income data expressed in terms of domestic currencies into U.S. dollars imparts a systematic bias to the inter-country relationship between the elasticity of the marginal utility of consumption and per capita incomes. This will be apparent if we consider that productivity tends to increase less rapidly in the production of non-traded goods (services) than in the production of traded goods (agricultural and manufactured products), leading to a rise in the relative price of services at higher-income levels. Now, as purchasing power parities express average differences in the prices of traded *and* non-traded goods while only traded goods enter into the determination of exchange rates, the ratio of purchasing power parities to exchange rates will be positively correlated with differences in income levels.

Correspondingly, the conversion of data at exchange rates will systematically understate per capita incomes in low-income countries, and the degree of understatement will be negatively correlated with incomes per head. Taking the United States as the benchmark of comparisons, in 1960 the degree of understatement was 10% for Canada and Sweden, 20 to 30% for the United Kingdom, Norway, Belgium, Germany, and Denmark, 40 to 50% for France, Italy, and the Netherlands, and 65% for Japan [Balassa (1964, p. 588)]. The extent of understatement increases further in the developing countries, but the lack of a sufficient number of observations and the error possibilities involved in extrapolating the relationships obtained for developed countries do not permit us to estimate this quantitatively at low income levels [Balassa (1973)].

Given the systematic bias in per capita income figures, their range will be substantially smaller than estimated through conversion at exchange rates. Consequently, appropriately adjusted income data will increase the slope of the regression line between the elasticity of the marginal utility of consumption and per capita incomes.

5.

The preceding sections focused on the estimation of the private elasticity of the marginal utility of consumption that expresses valuation by individual consumers. The next question concerns the relationship between this elasticity and the social elasticity of the marginal utility of consumption. It will be discussed below by making use of equations (2) and (3).

The social welfare function shown in (2) will be strictly concave ($W_{ii} < 0$) or a straight line ($W_{ii} = 0$), depending on whether it is utilitarian or egalitarian. In the first case, social welfare is taken to be independent of the distribution of individual utilities; in the second case, the social welfare function expresses an aversion to inequality in utility levels, with diminishing marginal rate of substitution of one person's utility for another's.

The social elasticity of the marginal utility of consumption (n) will equal the private elasticity (w), if a utilitarian social welfare function is adopted which involves setting W_{ii}, and hence the second term of equation (3), to zero. In turn, the social elasticity of the marginal utility of consumption will exceed the private elasticity, if we employ an egalitarian social welfare function as negative values for W_{ii} will make the second term of equation (3) positive.

Reformulating equation (2) in an additive form under the assumption that the social welfare function is separable in individual utilities, Anand (1973) has derived the relationship between n and w under alternative assumptions as to the values taken by w. Equation (10) shows the relationship for the case when w exceeds 1,

$$n = w + m(w - 1). \tag{10}$$

In the equation, m reflects the degree of social aversion to inequalities in individual utilities.[14]

The same relationship was derived independently by Stern who has obtained a value of 4 for the social marginal utility of consumption by assuming that both w and m equal 2. The value chosen for m is said to reflect an *a priori* judgment as to the range of social elasticity of the marginal utility of income, as well as the view that "we should add something for the egalitarian position" to estimates of w [Stern (1973)]. The choice of m thus requires a value judgment and we are led back to the question of how a social welfare function could be derived.

6.

Arrow (1963) has shown the impossibility of deriving a social welfare function from individual preferences. The project evaluation manuals implicitly or explicitly substitute the government's preferences for the social welfare function. In this they appear to follow those who regard the government as the depository of the "will of the people".

Such a view has been put forward in regard to a system of representative government, which is not the case in many developing countries where one-party systems and military governments continue in power without the benefit of popular elections. It further endows the government, irrespective of how it came into power, with attributes of rationality. In particular, it is implicitly assumed that, in overruling private preferences, a government's actions will conform to what may be regarded as the well-considered interests of the community.

The proponents of introducing government preferences in project evaluation also assume that governments are monolithic and that a welfare function can be derived either from government actions with regard to projects (UNIDO Guidelines) or from government pronouncements (Bank Guidelines). Yet not even totalitarian governments are monolithic; they represent instead a conglomeration of interest groups, with continuing shifts in their power position. Also, there is rarely a single project-evaluating agency; rather, decisions on projects are taken by different ministries depending on the sector concerned and often by regional or local authorities.

If we consider the decentralization of decision-making on projects and

[14]It should be emphasized that these results depend on the assumed form of the social welfare function. As Squire shows (1975), if the welfare function is written as $W = W[F(u(c_1)), F(u(c_2)), \ldots, F(u(c_n))]$, utilitarianism does not necessarily imply that n equals w, nor does an aversion to inequality necessarily imply that n exceeds w.

changes in relative power positions over time, it will appear to be a rather futile exercise to derive welfare weights from historical decisions taken in regard to investment projects. At the same time, deriving a social welfare function from public pronouncements has the failing that such pronouncements are frequently different from the actions taken. Thus, we often find publicly expressed concern with income distribution accompanied by actions that benefit special groups which are close to the government in power. This fact may reflect differences as between intentions and realization as well as the misstating of intentions for political purposes.

Furthermore, the distinction made in project evaluation manuals between intrinsically political objectives – reducing income inequalities – and political constraints – supposedly impeding the realization of these objectives – involves an ambiguity. The problem is put essentially in black-and-white terms, with the objectives being regarded as desirable and the constraints undesirable. This may reflect a rather naive view of the decision-making process or give expression to value judgments on the part of outsiders.

The proposed use of project appraisal as a substitute for tax–expenditure policies also involves an ambiguity. Should political constraints not permit the choice of "appropriate" tax and expenditure measures, the question arises if these constraints would be inoperative in project appraisal. Were this assumed to be the case on the grounds that the complexity of project appraisal permits concealing the use of income distributional measures that would be directly apparent if they were incorporated in the government budget, one might not sufficiently appreciate the perspicacity of those affected. Alternatively, the use of income distributional weights in project evaluation may provide a convenient excuse for not proceeding with fiscal policies.

In this connection, note that in a mixed economy only some of the investment projects are evaluated by an international or governmental authority, often covering but a very small part of economic activity. This fact will limit the practical importance of introducing income distributional considerations in project appraisal. In the partial equilibrium framework used by project evaluation manuals, it also gives rise to the familiar problems of the second-best.

Second-best considerations will apply even if we limit our attention to public projects. Thus, the introduction of income distributional considerations may lead to the choice of a project with a lower increment of output, expressed in terms of income distributional weights, by reason of its effects on relative prices. In the case when producers are the "rich" and consumers the "poor" and supply is completely inelastic, a project whose output faces less elastic demand may then be favored over the one facing more elastic demand because the increment in intra-marginal transfer inherent in the fall of prices on existing consumption exceeds the loss in output.[15]

In view of the possibility of a loss in output, valued by using income distributional weights, one would need to consider alternative ways of improving the distribution of income, which may be less costly to the national economy. Such alternatives are, however, excluded by assumption, since project evaluation manuals generally take fiscal policies as given.

In judging the appropriateness of using income distributional weights in project appraisal, one would further need to consider possible effects on entrepreneurial risk-taking and on savings. The former is disregarded in project appraisal manuals while savings effects are considered by assuming fixed marginal propensities for individual income recipients and excluding possible changes in saving propensities that may result from the introduction of income distributional considerations in project evaluation.

More generally, the question needs to be raised if actions taken to reduce income inequalities necessarily improve the lot of the poor in the long run. The validity of this proposition cannot be taken for granted. Thus, we find that countries, such as Argentina and Uruguay in Latin America and Sri Lanka and India in Asia, which adopted egalitarian policies have experienced low rates of economic growth and very slow improvements, if any, in the living standards of the poor.

The experience of these countries may be contrasted with that of Hong Kong and Singapore, and subsequently Korea and Taiwan, whose policies oriented towards rapid economic growth have brought substantial increases in the income levels of the poor. In Korea, for example, it has been shown that during the 1964–1970 period the per capita incomes of the poor, whether defined as the lowest decile or the lowest four deciles of the population, increased by 58 percent, i.e., at the same rate as average incomes [Adelman–Robinson (forthcoming)].

Thus, there are situations when policies aimed at improving income distribution may be damaging for the group they are supposed to serve. This is not to say, however, that one should accept the existing distribution of incomes as given. Rather, one would need to search for methods that can improve income distribution at least cost in terms of a loss in output. The taxation of luxury goods, with the proceeds used to benefit the poor, may be more appropriate for this purpose than the introduction of income distributional weights in project appraisal.[16]

[15]I am indebted to Marcelo Selowsky on this point.
[16]On the merits of luxury taxes for reducing income inequalities, see Fellner (1960).

To begin with, luxury taxes do not have adverse effects on entrepreneurial risk-taking and savings. Also, they reduce conspicuous consumption with its unfavorable effects in the form of consumer externalities and limit the flow of domestic resources into the production of luxuries. At the same time, in the event that reliance is based on luxury taxes, one would not need to apply a complicated system of taxes and subsidies which is unavoidable in the event that income distributional considerations are introduced in project appraisal since shadow prices will diverge from market prices as a result.

It follows that the introduction of distributional considerations in project appraisal must be preceded by a study of alternative policy instruments, with attention given to their effects on efficiency, savings, and risk-taking.[17] This suggests the need to place the project appraisal process in the general framework of public decision-making rather than in isolation as the project evaluation manuals tend to do.

Finally, questions arise concerning the choice of income distributional weights in project appraisal and in policy making in general. Given the arbitrariness of leriving a social welfare function, it is suggested here that reliance be placed on the private evaluation of the elasticity of the marginal utility of consumption. This, in turn calls for further research to improve available estimates of this elasticity.

7. *References*

Adelman, I. and S. Robinson, forthcoming, A wage and price endogenous general equilibrium model of a developing country: Factors affecting the distribution of income in the short run.

Anand, S., 1973, Distributional weights in project analysis, mimeo. (International Bank for Reconstruction and Development, Washington, DC).

Arrow, K., 1963, Social choice and individual values, Cowles Foundation Monograph 12 (Wiley, New York).

Balassa, B., 1973, Just how misleading are official exchange rate conversions?, Comment, Economic Journal, Dec.

Balassa, B., 1975, The purchasing-power parity doctrine: A reappraisal, Journal of Political Economy, Dec.

Barten, A. P., 1974, Consumer demand functions under conditions of almost additive preferences, Econometrica, Jan.

Brown, A. and A. Deaton, 1972, Surveys in applied economics: Models of consumer behavior, Economic Journal, Dec.

Dasgupta, P., S. Marglin and A. Sen, 1972, Guidelines for project evaluation (United Nations Industrial Development Organization (UNIDO), New York).

Fellner, W., 1960, Rapid growth as an objective of economic policy, American Economic Review, Papers and Proceedings, May.

[17]In emphasizing need, these considerations are neglected in Sen's (1973) *On Economic Equality*, where the utilitarian position is criticized on essentially moral grounds.

Fellner, W., 1967, Operational utility: The theoretical background and a measurement, in: Ten economic studies in the tradition of Irving Fisher (Wiley, New York).
Fisher, I., 1892, Mathematical investigations in the theory of value and prices (The Connecticut Academy of Arts and Sciences).
Fisher, I., 1972, A statistical method of measuring marginal utility and the justice of the progressive income tax, in: Economic essays contributed in honor of John Bates Clark.
Frisch, R., 1932, New methods of measuring marginal utility, Beiträge zur Ökonomischen Theorie no. 3 (J. C. B. Mohr, Tübingen).
Frisch, R., 1959, A complete scheme for computing all direct and cross demand elasticities in a model with many sectors, Econometrica, April.
Hoa, T. V., 1968, Inter-regional elasticities and aggregative bias: A study of consumer demand in Australia, Australian Economic Papers.
Janvry, A. de, J. Bieri and A. Nunez, 1972, Estimation of demand parameters under consumer budgeting: An application to Argentina, American Journal of Agricultural Economics, Aug.
Little, I. M. D. and J. A. Mirrlees, 1974, Project appraisal and planning for developing countries (Heinemann Educational Books, London).
Little, I. M. D. and J. A. Mirrlees, 1965, Manual of industrial project analysis in developing countries, vol. II – Social cost benefit analysis (Development Center of the Organisation for Economic Cooperation and Development (OECD), Paris).
Lluch, C., 1973, The extended linear expenditure system, European Economic Review, April, pp. 21–32.
Lluch, C. and R. Williams, 1975a, International patterns in the elasticity of the marginal utility of income and expenditure, Development Research Center Discussion Paper no. 11 (IBRD, Washington, DC).
Lluch, C. and R. Williams, 1975b, Dualism in demand and savings patterns: The case of Korea, Economic Record, March.
Pigou, A. C., 1970, A method of determining the numerical values of elasticities of demand, Economic Journal.
Sen, A., 1973, On economic inequality (Clarendon Press, Oxford).
Squire, L., 1975, Social welfare functions and the private elasticity of the marginal utility of income, mimeo. (IBRD, Washington, DC).
Stern, N., 1973, Welfare weights and the elasticity of the marginal valuation of income, mimeo. (St. Catherine College).
Tak, H. G. van der and L. Squire, 1975, Economic analysis of projects, Published for the World Bank (Johns Hopkins University Press, Baltimore, MD).
Theil, H. and R. B. Brooks, 1970, How does the marginal utility of income change when real income changes?, European Economic Review, Winter.

PART III

MACROECONOMIC POLICIES

Chapter 11

Asset Markets and the Cost of Capital

James TOBIN and William C. BRAINARD*

A central theme of macro-economic theory throughout the twentieth century has been the sensitivity of capital formation to interest rates in financial markets. Theories of business fluctuations attribute great significance to variation in the pace of real investment, and attribute much of this variation to changes in the relative attractions for wealth-owners of physical capital, on the one hand, and money or obligations to pay money, on the other hand. Moreover, some of these changes are engineered by the monetary operations of governments and central banks; they represent a principal channel by which the authorities stabilize or destabilize the economy.

William Fellner's writings on these subjects place him in a tradition which includes, among others, Wicksell, Keynes, Schumpeter, Robertson, and Hayek. In addition to his many contributions to general macroeconomics and cycle theory, Fellner has advanced our understanding of the relation between technological change and capital formation and of business decisions with respect to risk. Our own approach to macroeconomics and its behavioral foundations has profited from our many years of contact with "Willy" at Yale.

Our paper concerns a concept which we have elsewhere baptized "q", the ratio between two valuations of the same physical asset. One, the numerator, is the market valuation: the going price in the market for exchanging existing assets. The other, the denominator, is the replacement or reproduction cost: the price in the market for newly produced commodities. We believe that this ratio has considerable macroeconomic significance and usefulness, as the nexus between financial markets and markets for goods and services.

Section 1 of the paper explains the rationale for "q", and its role in macroeconomic theory and policy. We consider also the determinants of

*Research for this paper was in part supported by grants from the National Science Foundation and the Ford Foundation. We are also grateful for expert help in computation from Roger Grawe, Jeremy Bulow, and David Hsieh.

q, both for the economy in aggregate and for specific assets and business firms.

Section 2 reports an empirical investigation of the factors determining differences in q's among non-financial corporations in the United States in each of the fifteen years 1960–1974. Although this study relies on microeconomic data, its motivation is, like that of Section 1, macroeconomic. We seek to estimate the changing market valuations of various characteristics of firms – growth, cyclical sensitivity, risk, leverage, earnings rate on replacement value of capital. From these estimates we construct measures of the cost of capital to American corporations, which we regard as better indicators of the impact of monetary policy and financial events on corporate investment than the nominal or real interest rates commonly used.

1. Valuation of Capital Stocks and their Earnings Streams

1.1. Used and New Goods

Markets for used durable producers' and consumers' goods are a central feature of capitalist economies. These may be – direct or indirect – markets for the goods themselves or for claims to the goods and to their fruits. Direct used goods markets provide everchanging market valuations both of non-reproducible real assets, like land and mineral deposits, and of reproducible assets, like buildings and equipment. In the case of reproducible assets, the current cost of producing identical or competitive goods is obviously an important factor in the valuation of an existing asset. Thus a rise in residential construction costs can be expected to raise the value of existing homes, and a rise in the price of new cars is "good" for the price of previous years' models. The reverse is also true. High valuations of existing stocks will lead both to increased production and higher prices of newly produced substitutes.

New and used prices can diverge significantly for extended periods of time, and the valuations of existing assets are more volatile than the costs or prices of their newly produced counterparts. An increase in the market valuation of houses relative to current cost of building will encourage residential construction. The incentive is the gain to be made by the excess of market price over replacement cost.

This profit is not wiped out immediately because construction takes time, and rapid construction is especially expensive, both for the individual builder and for the economy as a whole. In the longer run, however, the increase in stock brings market value into line with replacement cost, lowering the former and/or raising the latter. In equilibrium the volume of construction will meet demands for replacement and normal growth, and the size of the stock will be such that market value is the same as marginal production cost for the equilibrium volume of construction.

1.2. Business and Corporate Capital

The same mechanism applies to non-residential structures and producers' equipment. But there is an important difference. The various physical assets of a business enterprise are often designed, installed, and used in complex combinations specific to the technology. It is costly or impossible to detach and move individual assets or to apply them to alternative purposes. The valuation of the business as a whole as a going concern is generally much more relevant than the separate valuations of the assets on used goods markets.

Markets for businesses take several forms. Small unincorporated businesses are bought and sold directly or through brokers; see, for example, the advertisements in any Sunday *New York Times* or in trade journals. Corporations acquire other companies either by buying their assets or by acquiring their stock.

The most important markets, however, are those for corporate securities. In these markets ownership of corporate businesses, and other claims upon the assets, change hands daily. The securities markets provide, therefore, a continuing market valuation of the enterprise, and thus indirectly of the productive assets of the company. These markets are well organized and efficient. Their valuations are sensitive and volatile. Here, even more than in used goods markets, discrepancies arise and persist between the market valuations and the replacement costs of the assets which the market is indirectly and implicitly valuing. But here too we can expect the formation of new businesses and the expansion of existing ones to respond to such discrepancies.

As is so often the case, the point was expressed succinctly by Keynes, *General Theory* (p. 151):

> "[The] daily revaluations of the Stock Exchange, though they are primarily made to facilitate transfers of old investments between one individual and another, inevitably exert a decisive influence on the rate of current investment. For there is no sense in building up a new enterprise at a cost greater than that at which a similar existing enterprise can be purchased; whilst there is an inducement to spend

on a new project what may seem an extravagant sum, if it can be floated off on the Stock Exchange at an immediate profit."

This is the common sense justification for paying attention, as we have previously advocated,[1] to the ratio "q" of the market valuation of reproducible real capital assets to the current replacement cost of those assets. In the illustrative case of houses discussed above, q would be the ratio of market value to replacement cost, for an individual house, or for an aggregate stock. The same concept applies to a business or to corporate business in aggregate, though "replacement cost" must be interpreted to cover not only physical assets but other items on the firm's balance sheet.

Economic logic indicates that a normal equilibrium value for q is 1 for reproducible assets which are in fact being reproduced, and less than 1 for others. Values of q above 1 should stimulate investment, in excess of requirements for replacement and normal growth, and values of q below 1 discourage investment. We shall discuss below why the normal value for statistical representations of q may be different from 1.

1.3. Discounting Future Earnings

The simplest model of valuation of an earning asset says that its present value is the sum of discounted earnings at all future dates. For a house, the earnings are rents – cash or imputed, net of costs of operation and maintenance, taxes, etc. For the durable productive assets of a business, earnings are the net cash flows over their lifetimes. For a share of stock, the earnings stream includes all future dividends and other distributions.

The discount rates applied to expected earnings represent, in principle, interest costs: rates of return which the investor must pay to borrow funds to hold the asset or must sacrifice by holding smaller amounts of other assets.

The securities – debt, preferred stock, common stock – of a corporation are essentially claims to the earnings thrown off by the real productive capital assets of the business. The securities will rise in value when "the market" revises upward its expectations of future earnings, or revises downward its discount rates. Those discount rates are related to open market interest rates, which are powerfully influenced by monetary polices. The market may also take Federal Reserve actions into account

[1]See Tobin–Brainard (1968) and Tobin (1969); these are respectively Chapters 20 and 18 in Tobin (1971).

in judging future earnings. In any event it is a fact of common observation, especially in recent years, that the stock market, as well as the bond market, is highly sensitive to movements in short-term interest rates under the control of the monetary authority.

1.4. Valuations and Risks

As we stated at the outset, the margin of asset substitution between obligations to pay specified amounts of money and ownership of physical capital is an important one in macroeconomic models. Theorists have differed in the degree of substitutability assumed between bonds and capital. While Keynes' investment theory takes them as close or even perfect substitutes, we have emphasized that they are imperfect substitutes, with a margin of differential yield as important and as variable as liquidity preference theory finds between bonds and bills or bills and cash.[2] A principal reason for distinguishing, at an aggregate level, between bonds and capital is their difference in risk. The major risks on capital relate to real events – changes in technology, utilization, relative scarcities, and labor costs. The major risks on financial assets arise from uncertainties about future rates of inflation and interest.

Risk is also crucial at a disaggregated level. Differences in the magnitude and nature of risk are probably the most important factors leading to differences of required rates of return on investment in various firms and types of capital.

How would one expect valuations of assets to depend on the nature of their risks? Portfolio theory has provided some insights, which can be given precision under special assumptions [Lintner (1965), Sharpe (1964)]. The standard assumptions are that there exists a riskless asset, that investors may borrow as well as lend at the riskless rate, that they are concerned only about the mean and variance of the total return to their portfolio, and that they all agree on a joint probability distribution of asset returns. Then it can be shown that the relevant risk on any one asset is not the total variance of its return but only the "undiversifiable" part. This undiversifiable risk (which may be negative) reflects the covariation of the asset's rate of return with an overall market index of rates of return, in which assets are weighted by their relative supplies. If, for example, the asset's returns are independent of those on other assets, its "undiversifiable" risk reflects only its own weight in the index. Such an asset's own risk matters, but a single firm or particular investment in a large economy will

[2]See, for example, Tobin (1961); also Chapter 13 of Tobin (1971).

have a weight close to zero. On average, covariation of returns on business assets tends to be positive. Most assets have some undiversifiable risk.

The risk premium on a particular asset – the excess of its expected return over the riskless rate – depends on the amount of its undiversifiable risk and on a market-wide "price of risk". This common "price of risk", reflecting the aggregate supplies of the riskless and risky assets and the risk preferences of investors, provides all the information required to value the undiversifiable risk associated with any particular asset.

The simplicity of these results obviously reflects the very special nature of the underlying assumptions. Although relaxation of even one of these assumptions greatly complicates the problem of valuation, some of the qualitative characteristics of this valuation model probably survive.

For example, suppose that transactions costs limit the number of assets a typical investor can hold in his portfolio. The "undiversifiable" risk of a particular asset to him then depends on its covariation not with the entire market but with his own portfolio. Obviously an asset will be a higher proportion of the portfolios in which it is held than in the aggregate market "portfolio". Hence its own variance will be more important. In the extreme and unrealistic case where only one risky asset is held in each portfolio, its own variance is a complete and accurate measure of "undiversifiable" risk. In principle, it would be possible to relate risk premia to covariations with individualized portfolios, but as a practical matter, these are unobservable. The conclusion is that restrictions or economic limitations on the number of assets typically held in a portfolio make the estimation of undiversifiable risk difficult and increase the importance of own variance. But it is still possible to describe asset return throughout the market in terms of a riskless rate and a single "price of risk".

Relaxing other assumptions, e.g., the existence of a riskless asset, the possibility of borrowing and lending at the same rate, the homogeneity of expectations, further complicates matters. These complications not only make it difficult, both conceptually and empirically, to measure the relavant risks on particular assets. They also make it impossible to speak of, let alone estimate, a single price of risk.

In recent years there has been considerable empirical investigation of the effect of risk on the valuation of assets using the general analytic framework discussed above. Almost all of this work has focused on the market for equities. There are several conceptual difficulties with attempting to estimate the required rate of return on physical assets from equities markets alone. These have led us to look at the valuation of firms, not simply the valuation of their common stock issues.

First, even under the restrictive assumptions necessary for the simple valuation model, the list of assets should include corporate and government bonds as well as equities. Relaxation of those assumptions seems likely to make their omission even more important. In principle, even the risks on less marketable assets, such as houses, consumer durables, and human capital, are relevant to the valuation of stocks and bonds.

Second, the valuation of a firm's productive business assets may depend importantly on the firm's financial structure. It is true that the celebrated Modigliani–Miller theorem says that a firm's valuation should be independent of its financial structure, implying that a firm could theoretically estimate the required rate on a new investment just by looking in the stock market and observing the market's valuation of equities whose distribution of returns were proportional to those on the contemplated investment. But there are important reasons for believing that the valuation of a firm's physical assets and their returns cannot be divorced from its financial structure. These include corporate income taxation, which is not neutral as between debt interest and dividends; the implications of leverage for probability of bankruptcy and loss of control; economies of scale in borrowing which enable stockholders to borrow more cheaply through the corporation than individually. Looking directly at the market valuation of firms' total earnings, interest as well as common stock earnings, requires less restrictive assumptions than looking separately at the firm's various securities.

1.5. Effects of Inflation

What is the effect of inflation on the value of q? As usual, it is important to distinguish between anticipated and unanticipated inflation.

For anticipated inflation, a first approximation is (1) that q is independent of the inflation rate and (2) that q will not change over time as a result of the realization of anticipated inflation. The denominator of q moves, of course, with the prices of new capital goods in the commodity markets. The numerator will do likewise if both expected real earnings and the real interest rate used to discount them are independent of the expected rate of inflation. Stated in nominal terms, these sufficient conditions are that the dollar earnings anticipated at any future date are proportional to the price level expected at that date, and that the interest rate for that date varies point for point with the expected rate of inflation from now until then.

However, this first approximation, neutrality of inflation, fails in practice for several reasons:

Taxes are not neutral. In particular, nominal "earnings" which simply maintain the real value of an asset are taxed. Profits are overstated and over-taxed when depreciation is based on original cost.[3] This tends to lower q, but working in the other direction is the reduction of aftertax real interest rates due to the taxation of nominal interest.

Nominal interest rates do not accurately incorporate inflation premiums. Certain nominal rates are frozen or controlled – the zero rate on currency and demand deposits, the ceiling rates on savings and time deposits. Inflation expectations necessarily reduce the real rates on these assets and tend, therefore, to lower real rates in general.[4] But this q-raising effect can be offset by deliberate monetary policy.

Unanticipated inflation, or more generally upward revisions in expectations of future prices, will have additional non-neutral effects. The windfall gains of borrowers, including levered corporations, will be reflected in higher market valuations, but since similar gains cannot be expected to recur, marginal q's will not benefit. In the past, inflationary news was frequently considered a favorable sign for real business activity. Firming of prices was a symptom of strength in aggregate demand. Nowadays, however, inflationary news is more likely to be considered the harbinger of anti-inflationary policies – bringing recession, stagflation, or price controls, all damaging to the stream of earnings. Recent experience has firmly implanted this view in the market.

1.6. Market Valuation and Investment

The neoclassical theory of corporate investment is based on the assumption that the management seeks to maximize the present net worth of the company, the market value of the outstanding common shares. An investment project should be undertaken if and only if it increases the value of the shares. The securities markets appraise the project, its expected contributions to the future earnings of the company and its risks. If the value of the project as appraised by investors exceeds the cost, then the company's shares will appreciate to the benefit of existing stockholders. That is, the market will value the project more than the cash used to pay for it. If new debt or equity securities are issued to raise the cash, the prospectus leads to an increase of share prices. To state the point another way round, suppose the firm sells additional shares at the going market

[3]For empirical estimates of this and other non-neutral effects, see Shoven and Bulow (1975/6).

[4]For explanation, see Tobin (1969).

price. Will the proceeds suffice to purchase the earnings that justify that price? If they will do so, with margin to spare, then the joint operation – share issue and investment – benefits the original shareholders.

Clearly it is the q ratio *on the margin* that matters for investment: the ratio of the increment of market valuation to the cost of the associated investment. The crucial value for marginal q is 1, but this is consistent with average q values quite different from 1. A firm with monopoly power, or other sources of diminishing returns to scale, will have an average q ratio higher than its marginal q. The difference is the market's valuation of its rents or monopoly profits or "good will".

A similar but conceptually distinct problem arises from the heterogeneity of capital goods and from technological progress. The average q ratio for existing capital stocks may be a serious understatement of q for new capital goods of quite different nature. This occurs spectacularly when the new have rendered the old obsolete. The Schumpeterian phenomenon may occur within a single firm, but it is more likely to characterize whole industries or economies during periods of rapid innovation. It is at least conceivable to observe investment booms during periods when observed average q ratios are low and even declining.

Changes in factor prices make profitable new investments which promise to economize scarce factors at the same time that they lower the value of old capital goods adapted to previous prices. For example, the drastic increase in oil prices in 1973 lowered the q's for firms committed to high energy-using technologies, while making attractively profitable on the margin investments embodying energy-saving technologies.

Another dimension of heterogeneity is risk. This too can make q on the margin exceed average q. The new investments of a firm may be in a different "risk class" from the old, with different connections with the rest of the economy. They will make the firm's securities more attractive to investors by reducing the amount of undiversifiable risk they carry. Transactions costs and other limits on the sizes of individual portfolios make diversification within firms an efficient alternative to portfolio diversification across firms. This has been one of the incentives for conglomeration.

Nevertheless, the forces of continuity in the economy are strong. Especially for short-run variations of aggregate demand, we can expect that the same factors which raise or lower q on the margin likewise raise or lower q on average. This is confirmed by John Ciccolo's regressions of aggregate business fixed investment on eight quarters distributed lag values of q [Ciccolo (1975)]. These alone explain 40% of the 1953–73 quarterly variation of the ratio of gross investment to the capital stock, I/K. The eventual full effect of a 0.10 increase in q is to raise I/K by 0.08.

Investment would not be related to q if instantaneous arbitrage could produce such floods of new capital goods as to keep market values and replacement costs continuously in line. For reasons given above, such arbitrage does not occur. Discrepancies between q and its normal value do arise. The speed with which investment eliminates such discrepancies depends on the costs of adjustment and growth for individual enterprises, and for the economy as a whole on the short-run marginal costs of producing investment goods.

This is a different investment theory from what appears to be the Keynesian investment function of the *General Theory*, Keynes' condition that the marginal efficiency of capital equal the rate of interest determines not the flow of investment but the stock of capital. Specifically, it determines the capital/labor and capital/output ratios. In a stationary economy, satisfaction of the condition – at whatever level of the interest rate – means zero investment. In a growing economy, it means capital accumulation at the natural growth rate of the economy. (Since the capital stock will be larger the lower the interest rate, investment will also be larger the lower the interest rate. But this long-run steady state relationship is clearly not what Keynes had in mind in postulating an inverse relation between investment and interest rate.)

Since Keynes discusses at length independent variations in the marginal efficiency of capital and the rate of interest, he does not really imagine that investment adjusts the capital stock fast enough to keep them continuously equal. Indeed the true message is that investment is related to discrepancies between the marginal efficiency and the interest rate. This is the tradition of Wicksell and of Keynes' earlier work *The Treatise on Money*. The q ratio theory of investment follows this same tradition. Indeed under special conditions q could be equivalently defined as the ratio of the marginal efficiency of capital R to the interest rate r_k used to discount future earnings streams.[5]

[5]The marginal efficiency R is defined by the equation

$$V = \int_0^\infty E(t)\,e^{-Rt}\,dt,$$

where V is the cost of capital goods at time 0 and $E(t)$ their expected earnings.

$$\overline{MV} = \int_0^\infty E(t)\,e^{-r_k t}\,dt,$$

where $\overline{MV}$ is the market valuation of the capital goods and r_k the discount rate. If E is constant then

$$V = E/R, \qquad \overline{MV} = E/r_k, \qquad MV/V = R/r_k.$$

Several points deserve emphasis. First, the statistic q is observable as a ratio of market valuation and replacement cost, whereas R and r_k are not observable. Second, the discount rate r_k is not any observed interest rate on long-term bonds or other fixed-money-value obligations. Those interest rates are the discount factors for streams of payments with the risks and other characteristics of those instruments, while r_k is the discount rate for streams of return with the characteristics of earnings on business capital. The rates are related but not identical. Third, the rates r_k and R are in the same interest-rate numéraire. As discount for a stream of dollar earnings, they both would be nominal rates. As discount for a stream of earnings in constant dollars, they both would be real rates. The ratio q is the same either way.

The hypothesis that investment is related to the difference between R and r_k, or to the value of q, bears some resemblance to the "flexible accelerator" idea that investment is a function of the difference between a desired and actual capital stock. The desired stock appropriate to r_k is larger than the actual stock which yields R, when r_k is lower than R. Indeed the market value of the existing stock is a sort of estimate of the desired stock at replacement cost.[6]

1.7. A "q" Formulation of IS/LM Equilibrium

The investment function for a macroeconomic model could take the form $\Delta K/K = \varphi(q - \bar{q}) + g$, where $\bar{q}$ is the normal value of q, perhaps 1, $\varphi(+) = +$, $\varphi(0) = 0$, $\varphi(-) = -$, and g is the natural growth rate. Growth equilibrium occurs at that value of net output $\bar{Y}$ at which saving supports net investment gK, with $q = \bar{q}$. An "IS" locus in (q, Y) space will normally have $\partial q/\partial Y > 0$. As Y increases, saving increases at given value of q. Thus a higher value of q is required to induce additional investment, or to discourage saving. Consumer wealth rises with q, and consumption spending is stimulated by additional wealth.

An "LM" locus can also be constructed in (q, Y) space, for given *real* quantities of high-powered money and other government debts, and for a given expected rate of inflation. The financial system may contain any number of assets and determine any number of interest rates, as well as q. These outcomes will depend on Y, for the usual reason that Y affects the demands for money and for other assets. If long-run expectations of earnings, summarized in the marginal efficiency of capital, are insensitive

[6]This is exact if the elasticity of the marginal productivity of capital with respect to the stock is unity, so that $K^* r_k = KR$, where K^* is the desired stock corresponding to r_k.

to current Y, the LM locus will have $\partial q/\partial Y < 0$. Increasing transactions requirements for cash raise interest rates in general, and in particular raise the rate of discount of future earnings. But if the marginal efficiency of capital is sensitive to current Y, the sign of $\partial q/\partial Y$ may be positive: an increase in Y raises R faster than r_k. (In conventional IS/LM frameworks, this same phenomenon is usually modelled as an upward-sloping IS curve because marginal propensities to invest and to consume sum to more than one.)

Figure 1 shows these IS and LM curves. To preserve familiarity, q is measured downward on the vertical axis. Two alternative LM curves are drawn, the first on the assumption that the marginal efficiency R used in calculation of q is always $R(\bar{Y})$, based on earnings along the growth equilibrium path. The second LM curve, upward sloping, assumes R to be an increasing function of Y, $R(Y)$. Exogenous increases in R will shift the LM curve down, even though they generally raise interest rates. Expansionary monetary policy will also move the LM curve down, while lowering interest rates. Autonomous increases in consumer or government spending will, as usual, move the IS locus up.

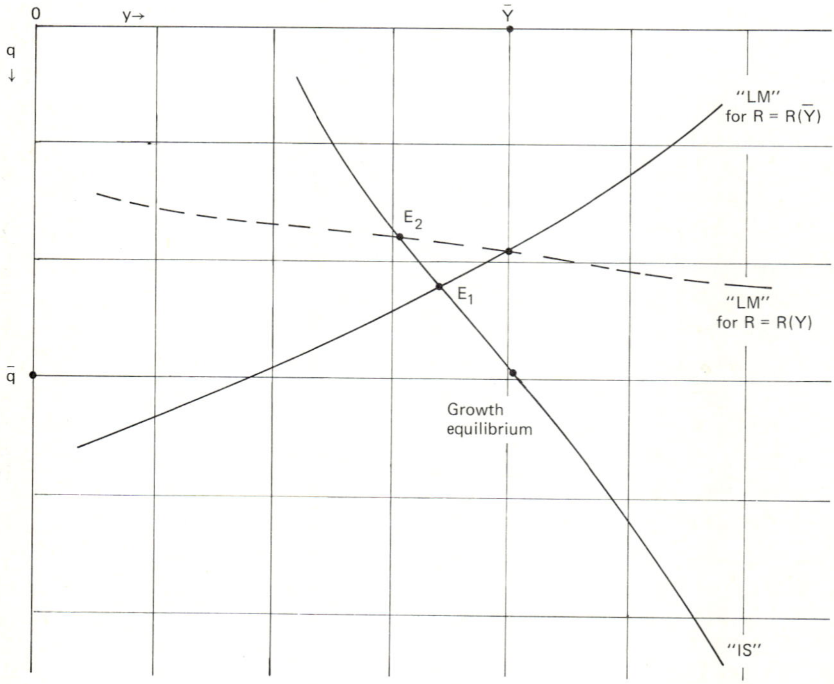

FIGURE 1. IS/LM analysis in (q, Y) space.

The above exposition embodies all the simplicities of aggregation of textbook macroeconomic models. To avoid misunderstanding, we reiterate our recognition that in fact there are many kinds of capital and accordingly many q's coexisting with different values. Moreover, there are channels other than "q's" by which monetary policies and events are transmitted to demands for goods and services. The most important of these are liquidity constraints of various kinds – credit limits, credit rationing, illiquidity of human capital and many other assets, rate ceilings, governmental restrictions on financial portfolios, etc. As these constraints are made to bind less or more tightly, spending effects occur which are inadequately modelled if related simply to prices of assets and commodities.

For these reasons, among others, it would be foolish to advocate any estimate of "q" as the sole indicator for monetary policy. But estimates of "q" are useful indicators. The fact that the indicator is in part policy-determined and in part endogenous is in this case a virtue. If "q" is low, we cannot tell whether the cause is pessimism about future profits or high discounts of future earnings, or whether, if it is the latter, the source is tight central bank policy or public asset preference. The indicated response for monetary policy is the same whichever the cause. Whether pessimistic earnings expectations, conservative asset preferences, or stingy supply of high-powered money is the reason for low q, the appropriate remedial action – and the only remedial action available to the monetary authority – is to expand the supply of bank reserves. The exceptions to the rule are the cases, discussed above, where marginal and average q's are moving in opposite directions.[7]

2. Empirical Study of Determinants of "q" 1960–74

2.1. The "Fundamental" Approach

The remainder of the paper reports a statistical investigation of stock market determinations of q's for individual industrial corporations listed on the New York Stock Exchange 1960–74. The data used were read from the Standard and Poor "Compustat" tape.

The approach is, in stock market parlance, "fundamental". That is, differences among firms in stock market prices are attributed to earnings,

[7]But the relevance of this caveat should not be exaggerated. In early 1974 the q model threw off pessimistic predictions of fixed investment. Yet it was easy to think that, given the embargo and OPEC price increase of 1973, energy-related projects would make total investment much stronger than the model predicted. This proved not to be the case.

dividends, and observable characteristics of the firms and not to previous histories of stock prices themselves.

In most studies the market value of equities is made to depend upon the characteristics of the distribution of market yields (dividends and capital gains) rather than on the more fundamental characteristics of the firm. The distribution of market yields reflects fluctuation of market discount rates as well as fluctuation in the firm's earnings. It is difficult to construct a "bootstrap" model of asset markets in which the risk characteristics of market yields used in the valuation of assets are consistent with the fluctuations in value generated by the market itself. Further, it is difficult to know how firms in making investment, and financing decisions, should react to changes in the market's valuation of risk which reflect speculative movements, or to changes in capitalization rates in response to investor preferences. For these reasons, we have taken the direct and simple expedient of asking how the market values that which the firm has to sell, the claims on prospective earnings associated with the firm's investment in physical assets.

2.2. The Variables

For each of the fifteen years 1960–74 a cross-section regression is calculated for a sample of firms. The dependent variable is q for the firm. The explanatory variables are characteristics of the firm which, theory suggests, should affect its market valuation. These characteristics, which will be defined precisely below, are as follows:

"Beta" *Growth Rate.* The prior trend of the logarithm of earnings.

"Gamma" *Cyclical Sensitivity.* Past relationship of earnings to the national unemployment rate.

"*X*" *Covariance.* Observed relationship of firm's earnings to aggregate earnings, both relative to growth trends. This is calculated for the mean unemployment rate previously observed.

"Sigma" *Earnings Volatility.* Variability of firm's earnings around trend, whether due to business cycle (as indicated by unemployment rate) or to unexplained factors.

"*PB*" *Default Probability.* Estimated probability that earnings will fall short of fixed debt service charges.

"*PD*" *Vulnerability of Dividend.* Estimated probability that earnings will fall short of fixed charges plus preferred and common dividends.

"*D/V*" *Dividend Rate.* Common dividends per dollar of capital.

"*E/V*" *Earnings Rate.* Earnings per dollar of capital.

The firm's q is measured as the ratio of market value $\overline{MV}$ to invested capital at replacement cost, V. The numerator $\overline{MV}$ includes three aggregates; common stock, preferred stock, and long-term debt. The firm's outstanding common stock is valued at its end-of-year prices. However, the tape does not provide data on market values of preferred stock and long-term debt, only book values. We were therefore not able to take account of inter-firm variations in these valuations. But we have tried to improve on the book values, by eliminating year-to-year economy-wide sources of divergence between book and market value.

We have estimated the market value of the firm's preferred stock from its reported preferred dividends for the year, dividing this quantity by the published Standard and Poor index of preferred stock yield for December. This index varies from year to year but is, for any one year, the same for all firms. A similar expedient was used to convert book value of long-term debt to market value. An economy-wide annual index of the ratio of market value of corporate debt securities to their principal value was estimated. The index was estimated from the series on gross issues from 1941 to 1974, assuming that all bonds have 20-year maturity, are issued at par with a common equal to the average Baa yield in the year of issue, and in each subsequent year are valued to yield until maturity the average Baa yield of that year.

The denominator V, invested capital at replacement cost, is the sum of the book values of common stock, preferred stock, and long-term debt, corrected by a common annual index of the ratio of replacement cost to book value. The book value of securities is not identical to the book value of physical capital assets; there are various short-term financial assets and liabilities on the balance sheet. Ignoring these items, we have corrected the book value by estimating an economy-wide index of the ratio of current replacement cost of fixed capital assets (non-residential plant and equipment) to original cost. Our index assumes exponential depreciation at 5% per year, and uses the deflator for the fixed investment component of GNP. Multiplicative correction of book values by the index is the same for all firms in any given year. But by avoiding increasing understatement of replacement value during recent years of high inflation, the correction helps to preserve comparability of results from year to year.

The "earnings" of a firm in a year include debt service and preferred stock dividends as well as the earnings attributable to common stock. Our reasons for inclusive definition both of earnings and of the capital base of earnings were explained in Section 1.

In the fifteen annual cross-section regressions, the ratio of earnings to replacement value (E/V) is, of course, the most important variable explaining q, the ratio of market value to replacement value ($\overline{MV}/V$). Dividends paid on common stock, also measured relative to V, (D/V), may also influence q.

The other six characteristics used as regressors in the cross-section regression for year T are based on a time series regression specific to the firm using observations for the years 1955 through $1955+T-1$. This regression for firm i for year T takes the form

$$\ln E_{it} = \alpha_{iT} + \beta_{iT}t + \gamma_{iT}U_t + \epsilon_{it}, \qquad t = 1, 2, \ldots, T-1. \tag{1}$$

U_t is the standard series for national unemployment rate, in percent of labor force, average for the year. Regression (1) is estimated by ordinary least squares, but with recent observations weighted more heavily. Specifically, the weights are proportional to $\exp(-0.12(T-t))$. Regression (1) attempts to simulate what market investors in year T can infer from the simple statistical history of the earnings of the firm. Clearly it does not allow for many other sources of firm-specific information.

The firm characteristics "beta" and "gamma" are the estimates of β_{iT} and γ_{iT}. These characteristics vary across firms every year, and for each firm they are re-estimated every year. To define the remaining characteristics we must consider for each firm, for each year T, expected earnings

$$\ln \hat{E}_{it} = \alpha_{iT} + \beta_{iT}t + \gamma_{iT}\bar{U}_T, \tag{2}$$

where the coefficients α, β, γ are the estimates from the weighted OLS regression (1) already described and $\bar{U}_T$ is the simple arithmetic mean value of U for the years 1 through $T-1$. Thus $\hat{E}_{it}$ is an estimate of earnings at what an investor might regard as a cyclically normal unemployment rate. Let σ_{iT} be the standard deviation of $E_{it} - \hat{E}_{it}$ over the years of the regression, each deviation weighted in the same manner as the observations for the regression itself. The characteristic "sigma" is then σ_{it}/V_T. Dividing by the capital value V eliminates scale differences between firms. Sigma is a measure of the historical volatility of the firm's earnings, whether the variability was due to the business cycle, via U, or the factors other than trend and cycle represented by ϵ in equation (1).

PB is the estimated probability that earnings E_T will not exceed fixed debt charges I_T. Let s_{iT} be the standard deviation of $\ln E_{it} - \ln \hat{E}_{it}$, computed with the same decaying exponential weights used before. PB is then calculated on the assumption that $\ln E_{iT}$ is normally distributed with mean $\ln \hat{E}_{iT}$ and standard deviation s_{iT}. PD is similarly calculated as the probability that E_T will not exceed I_T plus preferred and common dividends. Note that these probabilities, like "sigma", allow for uncertainties about business cycle developments as well as other variability in firm earnings. Since these probability measures are used in regression along with "sigma", PB is really a measure of leverage. For given "sigma", a larger PB means a higher level of fixed charges, only measured in "probits" rather than dollars. Likewise, given "sigma" and PB, a high PD means a high dividend policy, again measured in "probits".

The remaining characteristic X requires further explanation. Consider the sample of firms used in year T, and let E_t be ΣE_{it} for that sample. A weighted regression of $\ln E_t$ on t and U_t, of the same form as (1), is computed on observations $(1, 2, \ldots, T-1)$. Likewise, $\ln \hat{E}_t$ is calculated according to equation (2). Then

$$X_{iT} = \frac{\operatorname{cov}(\ln E_{it} - \ln \hat{E}_{it}, \ln E_t - \ln \hat{E}_t)}{\operatorname{var}(\ln E_t - \ln \hat{E}_t)}, \tag{3}$$

where the covariance and variance are computed with the usual weights through year $T-1$.

The characteristic X is analogous to the β commonly calculated in portfolio analysis as a measure of the relationship of the yield, including appreciation, of an individual stock to the yield of an overall market index. It is this which is multiplied by the "price of risk" to get the risk premium for an individual stock. Here, however, in keeping with our "fundamentalist" approach, the elasticity X relates the earnings of an individual firm to aggregate earnings. It is a partial elasticity to the extent that growth trends are eliminated. Theory suggests that the market will downgrade firms whose earnings move with economy-wide earnings and prize firms whose earnings move counter to the aggregate. That is, q should be negatively related to X.

2.3. The Results

The cross-section regression computed for each year T, (1960–1974 inclusive), is simply linear and has been fit by ordinary least squares,

$$\begin{aligned} q_{iT} = {} & a_{0T} + a_{1T}\beta_{iT} + a_{2T} + a_{3T}X_{iT} + a_{4T}(\sigma_{iT}/V_{iT}) + a_{5T}\overline{PB}_{iT} \\ & + a_{6T}\overline{PD}_{iT} + a_{7T}(D_{iT}/V_{iT}) + a_{8T}(E_{iT}/V_{iT}) + u_{iT}. \end{aligned} \tag{4}$$

For each year T, as many firms were included as met the following conditions:[8] Earnings were positive in all years through T, and all the data necessary to compute regression (1), E_{iT}, D_{iT}, V_{iT}, and q_{iT} were available.

Table 1 summarizes the regressions, showing the sizes of the samples in each year and the values of R^2. Table 2 reports the mean values and standard deviations of q and the eight independent variables for each year. Tables 3–10, one table for each independent variable, give the coefficients of the fifteen cross-section regressions. Tables 11 and 12, and Figures 2 and 3, record some summary measures, and it is these results we shall discuss first.

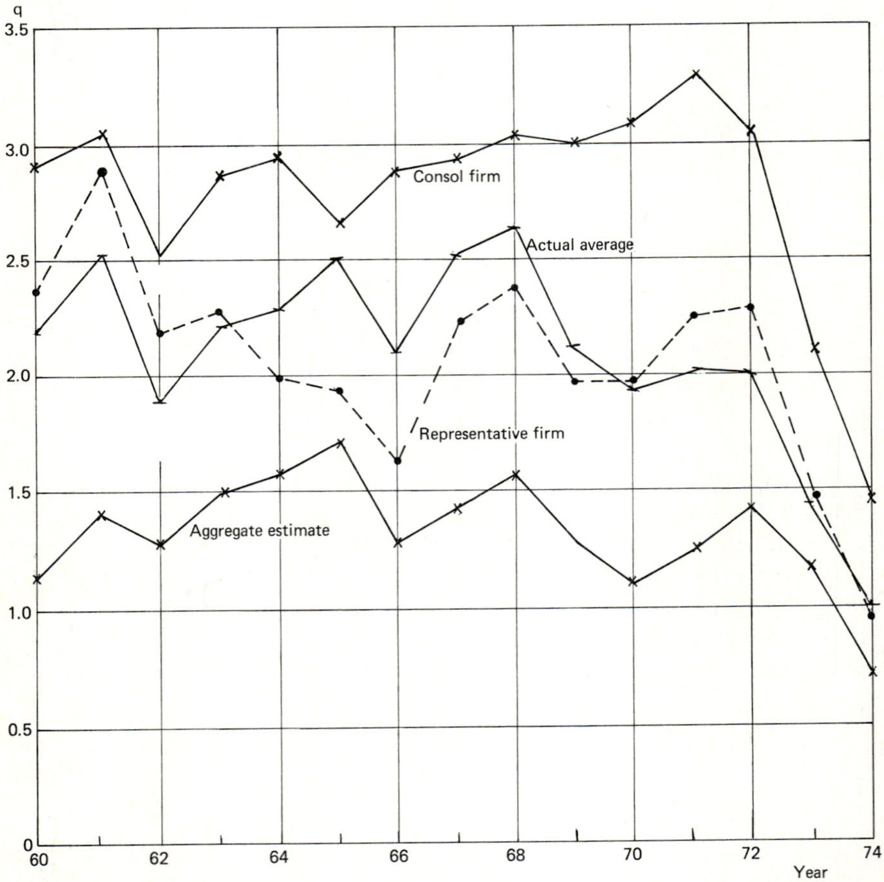

FIGURE 2. Alternative estimates of q, ratio of market to replacement value of corporate capital, 1960–74.

[8]Actually, two samples were assembled and two cross-section regressions computed for each year, one for all eligible companies, and one for dividend-paying companies only. Since the results were negligibly different, they will be presented only for the "all companies" samples.

TABLE 1

SUMMARY OF CROSS-SECTION REGRESSIONS, 1960–74.

Year	All companies No.	All companies R^2	Div.-paying companies No.	Div.-paying companies R^2	Year	All companies No.	All companies R^2	Div.-paying companies No.	Div.-paying companies R^2
1960	424	0.40	405	0.42	1968	409	0.48	399	0.50
1961	419	0.50	398	0.52	1969	406	0.46	394	0.48
1962	419	0.48	398	0.49	1970	397	0.44	383	0.47
1963	419	0.45	399	0.46	1971	395	0.49	373	0.54
1964	418	0.47	400	0.50	1972	392	0.49	370	0.54
1965	415	0.49	405	0.50	1973	392	0.36	376	0.38
1966	415	0.40	408	0.40	1974	384	0.24	371	0.30
1967	414	0.46	405	0.47					

TABLE

MEANS (STANDARD DEVIATIONS) OF

Year	q	Beta	Gamma	X
1960	2.21 (1.85)	0.104 (0.127)	−0.0925 (0.159)	1.145 (1.92)
1961	2.51 (2.10)	0.083 (0.128)	−0.0737 (0.156)	0.965 (1.92)
1962	1.88 (1.41)	0.081 (0.122)	−0.0754 (0.154)	0.983 (1.96)
1963	2.21 (1.83)	0.068 (0.105)	−0.0566 (0.146)	0.743 (1.91)
1964	2.29 (1.81)	0.069 (0.092)	−0.0574 (0.156)	0.672 (1.89)
1965	2.50 (2.25)	0.078 (0.079)	−0.0784 (0.153)	0.864 (1.67)
1966	2.11 (2.20)	0.083 (0.074)	−0.0954 (0.152)	0.990 (1.58)
1967	2.51 (2.37)	0.086 (0.072)	−0.1055 (0.150)	1.129 (1.63)
1968	2.54 (2.22)	0.084 (0.070)	−0.1007 (0.152)	1.148 (1.67)
1969	2.12 (1.88)	0.084 (0.068)	−0.0966 (0.150)	1.123 (1.68)
1970	1.92 (1.61)	0.084 (0.065)	−0.0954 (0.150)	1.130 (1.69)
1971	2.00 (1.70)	0.084 (0.066)	−0.0949 (0.132)	1.124 (1.53)
1972	1.99 (1.83)	0.087 (0.062)	−0.0840 (0.119)	1.188 (1.57)
1973	1.43 (1.84)	0.089 (0.058)	−0.0768 (0.116)	1.153 (1.54)
1974	0.97 (0.70)	0.094 (0.053)	−0.0736 (0.116)	0.965 (1.28)
Avg.[b]	2.08	0.084 (0.083)	−0.0838 (0.144)	1.021 (1.70)

[a] q = Ratio market to replacement value.
Beta = Past growth rate of earnings.
Gamma = Past relation to unemployment rate.
X = Relation firm earnings to economy earnings.
Sigma = Earnings variability.

By a "representative firm" we mean a hypothetical firm with characteristics fixed at the overall means (the simple average of the fifteen yearly means) for the period 1960–74. These are the figures in the bottom row of Table 2. By applying to these fixed characteristics the varying regression coefficients, we compute a time series of hypothetical q's for a representative American non-industrial corporation (column 1 of Table 11). This is not the same as the series of mean q's from Table 2 (also column 2 of Table 11), which apply to firms of changing characteristics. The two series generally conform, but diverge appreciably in several years. They are both plotted in Figure 2, together with Ciccolo's aggregate estimates of q. Given the differences of data base and statistical method, the *level* difference between our q's and Ciccolo's are not alarming. As should be expected, his aggregate estimate conforms better to our series of mean q than to our fixed-weight index.

To compare with the representative firm, we consider a non-existent "consol firm", with zero levels of all characteristics except the last two, D/V and E/V. They are put equal to each other and fixed at the overall mean of E/V for the period 1960–74. This theoretical consol firm is riskless, trendless, and cycle-free; it has no debt or preferred stock and pays out all its earnings at dividends. Its q series (column 3 of Table 11) is

2

REGRESSION VARIABLES, 1960–74.[a]

Sigma	*PB*	*PD*	*D/V*	*E/V*
0.0186 (0.017)	0.0106 (0.068)	0.0765 (0.155)	0.0415 (0.0301)	0.0906 (0.0456)
0.0169 (0.014)	0.0149 (0.096)	0.0726 (0.156)	0.0411 (0.0296)	0.0886 (0.0461)
0.0155 (0.014)	0.0176 (0.097)	0.0765 (0.155)	0.0380 (0.0287)	0.0846 (0.0439)
0.0144 (0.012)	0.0109 (0.068)	0.0770 (0.165)	0.0412 (0.0312)	0.0945 (0.0473)
0.0131 (0.010)	0.0106 (0.071)	0.0822 (0.168)	0.0422 (0.0324)	0.1047 (0.0496)
0.0121 (0.008)	0.0071 (0.044)	0.0730 (0.0145)	0.0428 (0.0317)	0.1107 (0.0483)
0.0122 (0.008)	0.0135 (0.072)	0.0971 (0.180)	0.0418 (0.0307)	0.1132 (0.0463)
0.0130 (0.008)	0.0218 (0.099)	0.1163 (0.200)	0.0392 (0.0285)	0.1003 (0.0449)
0.0129 (0.008)	0.0297 (0.123)	0.1433 (0.223)	0.0374 (0.0270)	0.0971 (0.0420)
0.0128 (0.007)	0.0398 (0.142)	0.1689 (0.246)	0.0353 (0.0259)	0.0944 (0.0400)
0.0127 (0.007)	0.0466 (0.151)	0.1671 (0.235)	0.0326 (0.0246)	0.0857 (0.0407)
0.0117 (0.007)	0.0355 (0.129)	0.1061 (0.176)	0.0296 (0.0236)	0.0815 (0.0388)
0.0112 (0.007)	0.0298 (0.112)	0.0763 (0.150)	0.0275 (0.0214)	0.0849 (0.0355)
0.0107 (0.007)	0.0375 (0.122)	0.1001 (0.178)	0.0262 (0.0197)	0.0949 (0.0337)
0.0103 (0.007)	0.0450 (0.131)	0.1276 (0.208)	0.0251 (0.0185)	0.0971 (0.0338)
0.0132 (0.009)	0.0247 (0.102)	0.1040 (0.183)	0.0361 (0.0269)	0.0949 (0.0424)

PB = Probability fixed charges not earned.
PD = Probability dividend not earned.
D/V = Ratio current div. to replacement value.
E/V = Ratio earnings to replacement value.
[b]Simple average of column.

also plotted in Figure 2. The consol series generally follows the contours of the other series. But the market has generally prized greater security and dividend pay-out.

Another summary form of the calculations is to compute the ratio of earnings to market value for our two hypothetical firms. These are estimates of the cost of capital to the firms. They are reported in Table 12 and Figure 3. For comparison, the Baa corporate bond rate is also plotted. Since our estimates of cost of capital are in principle *real* rates of return, the relevant comparison is with a Baa real rate, which has been computed by subtracting the geometric average inflation rate of the preceding five years.

Figure 3 makes two important points. First, the cost of capital relevant for investment decisions bears little relationship to the "real rate of interest" calculated by subtracting inflation rates from nominal interest rates. The tightness or ease of monetary policy and financial markets cannot be gauged by such naive calculations. Second, the effective real rate of interest is far from constant, contrary to a viewpoint of increasing currency.

The regression coefficients of Tables 3–10 provide some confirmations of theoretical expectations and some surprises and puzzles.

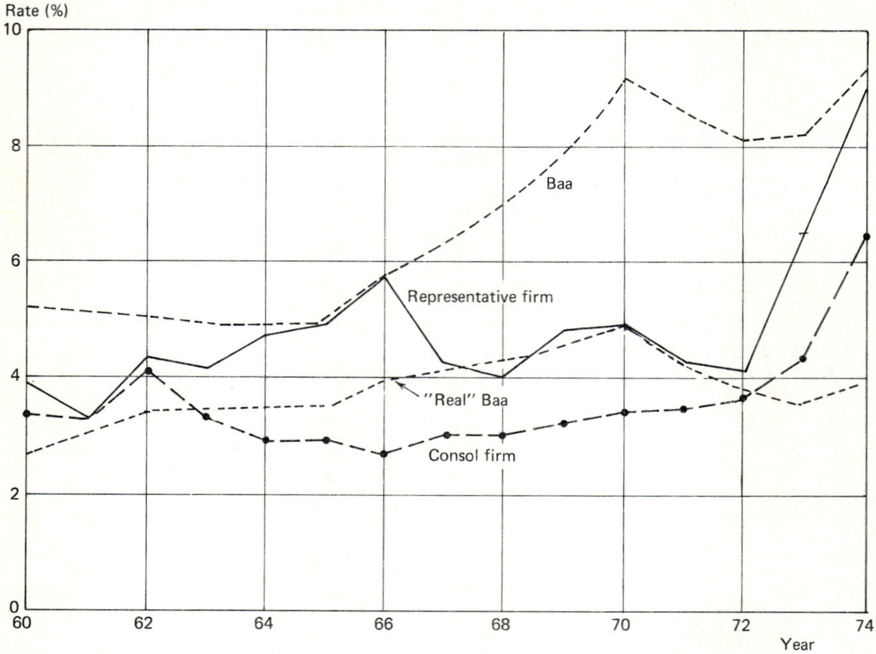

FIGURE 3. Cost of capital, alternative measures, 1960–74.

TABLE 3

EFFECT OF GROWTH RATE ON VALUATION, 1960–74; REGRESSION COEFFICIENTS OF BETA.[a]

Year	Coefficient	*t*-ratio	Variable mean (std.dev.)
1960	2.1379	2.8	0.10398 (0.127)
1961	1.0601	1.4	0.08264 (0.128)
1962	1.1837	2.1	0.08072 (0.122)
1963	1.7500	2.0	0.06778 (0.105)
1964	1.5843	1.8	0.06858 (0.092)
1965	2.1020	1.7	0.07810 (0.079)
1966	4.3793	3.0	0.08335 (0.074)
1967	6.1046	4.1	0.08576 (0.072)
1968	8.2898	5.9	0.08440 (0.070)
1969	8.6692	6.8	0.08402 (0.068)
1970	7.3217	6.3	0.08404 (0.065)
1971	7.9576	6.9	0.08400 (0.066)
1972	7.1643	5.2	0.08718 (0.062)
1973	5.2383	4.9	0.08946 (0.058)
1974	3.4282	5.0	0.09400 (0.053)

[a]In 1960 addition of one percentage point (0.01) to growth rate raises q by 0.214.

TABLE 4

EFFECT OF SENSITIVITY TO UNEMPLOYMENT ON VALUATION, 1960–74; REGRESSION COEFFICIENTS OF GAMMA.[a]

Year	Coefficient	t-ratio	Variable mean (std.dev.)
1960	−3.0713	1.5	−0.09251 (0.159)
1961	−1.5451	0.7	−0.07367 (0.156)
1962	−4.2588	2.8	−0.07540 (0.154)
1963	−4.6730	2.3	−0.05657 (0.146)
1964	−6.4126	3.2	−0.05744 (0.156)
1965	−4.9808	2.1	−0.07842 (0.153)
1966	0.4668	0.1	−0.09545 (0.152)
1967	−1.9421	0.4	−0.10548 (0.150)
1968	−8.9670	3.3	−0.10067 (0.152)
1969	−11.6678	4.1	−0.09658 (0.150)
1970	−9.3314	3.5	−0.09544 (0.150)
1971	−8.1916	2.9	−0.09489 (0.132)
1972	−4.4452	3.4	−0.08401 (0.119)
1973	−1.7786	2.5	−0.07680 (0.116)
1974	−0.2273	0.7	−0.07364 (0.116)

[a]Gamma is proportionate increase of firm earnings per percentage point unemployment. Gamma equal to −0.10 means that one more point of u reduces earnings 10%. In 1960 a firm with gamma = −0.10 has a 0.307 higher q than with gamma equal to zero.

The importance of E/V is, of course, to be expected. The striking fact in Table 10 is the sharp recent decline in the marginal value of earnings, which actually accounts for more than the observed drop in mean q from 1972 to 1974. In general, the mean value of the earning rate E/V has been quite stable compared to the regression coefficient of this variable. In terms of our discussion of section 1, r_k has moved around more than R.

As Table 9 indicates, payment of common dividends has been valued positively throughout the period, especially during the last ten years. Interpretation of this result is complicated by the fact that the alternative to common dividends may be either earnings retention or payment of debt interest and preferred dividends. According to Table 8, the market does not like dividend protection, given the dividend rate D/V. Likewise, Table 7 says that the market is indifferent or negative regarding protection of fixed debt service obligations. In combination with the expected negative coefficients on "sigma", these three results could be interpreted to mean that the stock market likes leverage (contradicting Modigliani–Miller), and for given leverage prefers pay-out of common stock earnings to their retention.

Turning now to the other three characteristics, we find significant coefficients of expected sign for "beta" and X. The market likes growth and dislikes undiversifiable risk. On the other hand, cyclical sensitivity of

TABLE 5

EFFECT OF EARNINGS COVARIANCE ON VALUATION, 1960–74; REGRESSION COEFFICIENTS OF *X*.[a]

Year	Coefficient	*t*-ratio	Variable mean (std.dev.)
1960	−0.3000	1.8	1.14480 (1.92)
1961	−0.1592	0.9	0.96503 (1.92)
1962	−0.3518	3.0	0.98342 (1.96)
1963	−0.3936	2.5	0.74344 (1.91)
1964	−0.5766	3.5	0.67228 (1.89)
1965	−0.5673	2.6	0.86427 (1.67)
1966	−0.0709	0.2	0.98973 (1.58)
1967	−0.2333	0.6	1.12853 (1.63)
1968	−0.7738	3.2	1.14776 (1.67)
1969	−0.9244	3.7	1.12272 (1.68)
1970	−0.7076	3.0	1.12995 (1.69)
1971	−0.5690	2.4	1.12376 (1.53)
1972	−0.1955	2.1	1.18810 (1.57)
1973	−0.0973	1.9	1.15283 (1.54)
1974	−0.0474	1.5	0.96502 (1.28)

[a] *X* is a measure of elasticity of firm earnings with respect to aggregate earnings. In 1960 a firm with an elasticity of one has a 0.3 lower q than a firm with zero elasticity.

TABLE 6

EFFECT OF EARNINGS VARIABILITY ON VALUATION, 1960–74; REGRESSION COEFFICIENTS OF SIGMA.[a]

Year	Coefficient	*t*-ratio	Variable mean (std.dev.)
1960	−30.3908	5.3	0.01861 (0.017)
1961	−26.3363	4.2	0.01637 (0.014)
1962	−21.3649	4.7	0.01549 (0.014)
1963	−31.1917	4.7	0.01441 (0.012)
1964	−43.1204	5.7	0.01307 (0.010)
1965	−53.2205	4.5	0.01213 (0.008)
1966	−37.3147	2.9	0.01225 (0.008)
1967	−48.0175	3.8	0.01297 (0.008)
1968	−42.4623	3.7	0.01292 (0.008)
1969	−43.8442	4.2	0.01282 (0.007)
1970	−35.2073	3.9	0.01274 (0.007)
1971	−34.7516	3.3	0.01170 (0.007)
1972	−42.0332	3.5	0.01123 (0.007)
1973	−30.0797	3.7	0.01070 (0.007)
1974	−6.6970	1.4	0.01026 (0.007)

[a] Sigma is standard deviation of firm earnings unexplained by growth trend and normal unemployment, relative to replacement value. In 1960 a firm with sigma = 0.01 would have a 0.304 lower q than a firm with sigma equal to zero.

TABLE 7

EFFECT OF DEFAULT PROBABILITY OR LEVERAGE ON VALUATION, 1960–74; REGRESSION COEFFICIENTS OF *PB*.[a]

Year	Coefficient	t-ratio	Variable mean (std.dev.)
1960	−0.0637	0.1	0.01056 (0.068)
1961	0.6858	0.6	0.01493 (0.096)
1962	0.9225	1.2	0.01761 (0.097)
1963	3.1154	2.8	0.01092 (0.068)
1964	3.3678	3.3	0.01062 (0.071)
1965	3.0404	1.5	0.00707 (0.044)
1966	1.7787	1.3	0.01351 (0.072)
1967	1.6707	1.5	0.02183 (0.099)
1968	0.0470	0.1	0.02966 (0.123)
1969	0.6882	1.1	0.03978 (0.142)
1970	0.1818	0.3	0.04660 (0.151)
1971	0.5602	0.8	0.03547 (0.129)
1972	1.8649	1.8	0.02981 (0.112)
1973	0.8353	1.3	0.03751 (0.122)
1974	−0.0526	0.1	0.04502 (0.131)

[a]*PB* is probability that firm's earnings fall short of fixed charges. In 1960 a firm with 0.01 probability has a 0.006 lower q than one with zero probability.

TABLE 8

EFFECT OF DIVIDEND VULNERABILITY ON VALUATION, 1960–74; REGRESSION COEFFICIENTS OF *PD*.[a]

Year	Coefficient	t-ratio	Variable mean (std.dev.)
1960	1.8148	3.1	0.07654 (0.155)
1961	0.8375	1.2	0.07259 (0.156)
1962	1.3898	2.8	0.07647 (0.155)
1963	1.0604	2.0	0.07704 (0.165)
1964	1.6715	3.3	0.08216 (0.168)
1965	2.9236	4.1	0.07299 (0.145)
1966	2.0829	3.3	0.09711 (0.180)
1967	3.0965	5.1	0.11628 (0.200)
1968	2.8680	5.5	0.14331 (0.223)
1969	0.9346	2.3	0.16890 (0.246)
1970	0.8780	2.2	0.16712 (0.235)
1971	1.3137	2.4	0.10612 (0.176)
1972	0.7092	0.9	0.07633 (0.150)
1973	0.3249	0.7	0.10013 (0.178)
1974	0.3420	1.4	0.12762 (0.208)

[a]*PD* is probability that earnings fall short of fixed charges plus preferred and common dividends. In 1960 a firm with 0.10 probability has a 0.18 lower q than one with zero probability.

TABLE 9

EFFECT OF DIVIDEND RATE ON VALUATION, 1960–74; REGRESSION COEFFICIENTS OF D/V.[a]

Year	Coefficient	t-ratio	Variable mean (std.dev.)
1960	6.5427	1.6	0.04148 (0.0301)
1961	0.3603	0.1	0.04109 (0.0296)
1962	5.5370	1.7	0.03797 (0.0287)
1963	7.1936	1.7	0.04120 (0.0312)
1964	10.4610	2.6	0.04225 (0.0324)
1965	5.4126	1.1	0.04282 (0.0317)
1966	21.2520	4.7	0.04177 (0.0307)
1967	14.5751	2.9	0.03923 (0.0285)
1968	17.8827	3.6	0.03741 (0.0270)
1969	21.6240	5.2	0.03532 (0.0259)
1970	23.8244	6.3	0.03261 (0.0246)
1971	25.2621	6.4	0.02959 (0.0236)
1972	17.6494	3.2	0.02754 (0.0214)
1973	14.4957	3.8	0.02625 (0.0197)
1974	10.6793	5.0	0.02513 (0.0185)

[a]In 1960 increasing D/V, rate of common dividend on replacement value, from 0 to 0.01 raises q by 0.065.

TABLE 10

EFFECT OF EARNINGS RATE ON VALUATION, 1960–74; REGRESSION COEFFICIENTS OF E/V.[a]

Year	Coefficient	t-ratio	Variable mean (std.dev.)
1960	21.5197	7.5	0.09061 (0.0456)
1961	31.7088	10.0	0.08857 (0.0461)
1962	20.1404	8.8	0.08459 (0.0439)
1963	22.3690	7.2	0.09454 (0.0473)
1964	20.3923	7.0	0.10467 (0.0496)
1965	30.2356	9.0	0.11072 (0.0483)
1966	17.6837	5.2	0.11320 (0.0463)
1967	27.1118	7.9	0.10032 (0.0449)
1968	22.6401	6.7	0.09710 (0.0420)
1969	15.6372	5.5	0.09442 (0.0400)
1970	10.3069	4.3	0.08571 (0.0407)
1971	13.8440	5.4	0.08152 (0.0388)
1972	24.1437	6.6	0.08492 (0.0355)
1973	10.9175	4.7	0.09488 (0.0337)
1974	3.9861	3.4	0.09711 (0.0338)

[a]E/V is ratio of earnings to replacement value. In 1960 increasing earnings rate from 0 to 0.10 raises q by 2.152.

TABLE 11

ESTIMATES OF q, RATIO OF MARKET TO REPLACEMENT VALUE OF CORPORATE CAPITAL, 1960–74.

Year	Actual average for year	Representative firm	Consol firm	Aggregate estimate[a]
1960	2.21	2.40	2.92	1.15
1961	2.51	2.85	3.04	1.40
1962	1.88	2.18	2.54	1.27
1963	2.21	2.27	2.85	1.48
1964	2.29	2.00	2.94	1.56
1965	2.50	1.93	2.65	1.70
1966	2.11	1.64	2.89	1.28
1967	2.51	2.23	2.93	1.41
1968	2.64	2.36	3.04	1.56
1969	2.12	1.97	2.97	1.26
1970	1.92	1.95	3.08	1.08
1971	2.00	2.24	3.27	1.21
1972	1.99	2.29	3.01	1.42
1973	1.43	1.45	2.19	1.18
1974	0.97	0.96	1.44	0.72

[a]Computed for economy as a whole by John Ciccolo, fourth quarter estimates.

TABLE 12

MEASURES OF COST OF CAPITAL, 1960–74.

Year	Representative firm	Consol firm	Corporate Baa yield[a] (Moody's)	"Real" Baa rate[a]
1960	3.96	3.39	5.19	2.63
1961	3.32	3.34	5.08	3.00
1962	4.35	4.17	5.02	3.39
1963	4.17	3.34	4.86	3.47
1964	4.75	2.93	4.83	3.46
1965	4.91	2.95	4.87	3.46
1966	5.79	2.63	5.67	3.96
1967	4.25	3.00	6.23	4.11
1968	4.02	3.03	6.94	4.29
1969	4.81	3.21	7.81	4.54
1970	4.86	3.43	9.11	5.13
1971	4.23	3.45	8.56	4.24
1972	4.14	3.66	8.16	3.82
1973	6.54	4.32	8.24	3.59
1974	9.93	6.45	9.50	3.84

[a]Corporate Baa yield less geometrical value of increase of GNP deflator (in series) over previous five years.

earnings appears – ceteris paribus – to increase q. In interpreting this result, we must remember that cyclical variability of earnings also enters "sigma" and X, and contributes there to penalizing q. The coefficients of "gamma" in Table 4 means that the market prefers that whatever covariance a firm has with the aggregate earnings of other firms be due to their common dependence on the unemployment cycle rather than to other common influences.

We conclude that the theory of asset valuation sketched in section 1 is fairly well confirmed. However, the weights the market places on the different characteristics change from year to year. The most striking empirical result is the sharp fall in q, sharp rise in cost of capital, in 1973 and 1974. This is not due to a decline in earnings but to a spectacular rise in the discount applied to earnings. Tight anti-inflationary monetary policies were undoubtedly responsible.

3. References

Ciccolo, J., 1975, A linkage between product and financial markets – Investment and q, Essay III of unpublished Ph.D. dissertation (Yale University, New Haven, CT).

Lintner, J. H., 1965, The evaluation of risk assets and the selection of risky investments in stock portfolios and capital budgets, Review of Economics and Statistics 47, Feb., pp. 13–37.

Sharpe, W. F., 1964, Capital asset prices: A series of market equilibrium under conditions of risk, Journal of Finance 19, Sept., pp. 425–442.

Shoven, J. B. and J. I. Bulow, 1975/6, Inflation accounting and non-financial corporate profits, Brookings Papers on Economic Activity 1975:3 and 1976:1.

Tobin, J., 1961, Money, capital, and other stores of value, American Economic Review 51, May, pp. 26–37.

Tobin, J., 1969, A general equilibrium approach to monetary theory, Journal of Money, Credit and Banking 1, Feb., pp. 15–29.

Tobin, J., 1971, Essays in economics, vol. 1 – Macroeconomics (North-Holland, Amsterdam).

Tobin, J. and W. C. Brainard, 1968, Pitfalls in financial model building, American Economic Review 58, May, pp. 99–122.

Chapter 12

Early Warning Signals of Inflation

Lawrence KLEIN and Sonia KLEIN*

1. Objectives

Since World War II, we have lived in an era in which inflation has been manifested in one form or another. During a time of all-out war, inflation problems are expected and endured. The analytical problem is to devise ways of dealing with this phenomenon in comparatively peaceful situations, such as the entire period since 1946. In this period, there have been some quiescent phases, but inflation has never been eradicated and is very much a living problem of the moment in the early 1970's.

The inflation picture and inflation problem have varied a good deal internationally. There have been Latin American hyperinflation, endemic British inflation, German and Japanese reconstruction inflation, and repressed inflation in the centrally planned economies. The present paper recognizes all these differences but attempts to treat the problem in the American context, using American data and referring to American conditions.

In the depressed conditions of the 1930's the critics of Keynesian type policies, especially those of the New Deal, warned about the potential inflationary consequences. Until the onset of World War II, we never achieved a close approximation to full employment, and manifestations of inflation never emerged. The period since the end of the war has been one of high employment, occasionally approaching full employment, and the carry over of wartime inflation has never been fully eradicated. The population at large has become accustomed to fairly regular increases in wage and other factor income rates. People have often borrowed in anticipation of paying off debts in depreciated dollars. Some durable goods prices have fallen, and some basic commodity prices have fluctuated up and down, but the general trend drift in prices has been upwards. This has been fully expected, but expectations and fears varied in different periods. In the fifties, the worry was over a "creeping inflation" of about two percent. In the sixties, five percent was regarded

*Insightful analysis and computational assistance from Keith Johnson and Riley Harris are gratefully acknowledged.

as a "peril point", with two or three percent considered to be good performance. Now we look upon single-digit inflation rates as highly desirable targets.

The statistical picture is one of a steady rise in the main indicators, with spurts related to the Korean War, the Vietnam War, and the food/fuel crises. In the opposite direction, there is evidence of marked slowdowns in the late fifties, early sixties, and a real shakeout in 1957–1958. The dominant upward trend is, however, so strong that little explanation is left to short- or intermediate-run analysis. Economic analysis becomes richer and more meaningful if we transform the statistical series of price indexes to *rates of change.*

In a suggestive and provocative article contributed to the Golden Anniversary Colloquia of the National Bureau of Economic Research, Moore (1972) put forward the idea that there are fairly regular cyclical movements in prices in terms of rate of change. Percentage change in price may be accepted as a plausible measure of the rate of inflation; we are led, by Moore's analysis, to consider cyclical properties of the inflation rate. In absolute form, there is little to see with the naked eye except trend movement, and cyclical analysis becomes awkward and difficult, though not impossible. In rate-of-change form, however, there are distinct and well delineated cyclical movements.

At the time of Moore's analysis, 1970, it appeared that the amplitude of cycles in the inflation rate were large right after World War II and during the Korean War, but that the amplitude regularly decreased after the initial flare up, showing fairly weak cycles since the mid fifties. The dramatic movements of 1973–1974, however, did much to restore vitality to the appearance of the charts and give the impression of a real live cycle.

If we accept the view that there is a regular cycle in the inflation rate – or periods of reduction/declination in the trend growth – it is suggestive to look for systematic patterns of differential timing in the form of leads and lags in order to have advance indicators of inflation spurts. Just as National Bureau scholars have looked for leading indicators of general cyclical movements in the economy, we might look for similar indicators of inflation. The objectives of the present paper are thus clearly understood by analogy, but the statistical methodology will be quite different.

A straightforward and natural approach would be through model building, for prices and inflation rates are among the several variables that are regularly generated in complete system simulations for prediction of the economy as a whole. Indeed, historical simulations of the Wharton Model have been shown to exhibit cyclical price behavior of the type analyzed by Geoffrey Moore [Klein (1972)]. The experience of the most recent and most serious spurt in prices, 1973–1974, was not favorable for any model builder (or any business-cycle analyst for that matter), see Klein (1974). Hopefully, past failures among all economists to predict the double-digit inflation that followed the oil embargo of 1973–1974 will teach them to be on guard and improve their systems of analysis. Repair work is vigorously going on, but a stage preliminary to model construction, involving extensive empirical investigation, may be rewarding. In this paper we carry out a number of such explorations to see if some early warning signals or advance indicators can be uncovered. These explorations should eventually lead to improvements in model construction on the price side.

The last two spurts in the rate of inflation may suggest the existence of a useful indicator, namely the rate of capacity utilization. Just prior to the Vietnam-related inflationary spurt, beginning in 1966, the Wharton Index of Capacity Utilization started to reach historic high values. Whenever the overall index gets into the 93–95% range, we can expect to see full-employment pressures building up and inflation rates rising. This was noted in 1966 and again in the spring of 1973. There are well-known differences between the Wharton and other indexes of capacity utilization, but one of the indicative features of the former is that it does appear to have given an early warning signal in periods when it significantly departed in an upward direction from the other capacity utilization indexes. These were both live situations, and the Wharton Index did not exist in the earlier periods of high inflationary pressure, although it has been reconstructed for the historical period since World War II.

For comparison with Geoffrey Moore's cyclical analysis of the inflation rate, we have made a cyclical analysis of the Wharton index of capacity utilization. To measure a single dominant period in a time series, we propose the following estimate of the angle of oscillation:

$$\theta = \cos^{-1}\frac{2-m}{2},$$

where

$$(2-m) = \frac{\sum_{t=2}^{T}(y_t + y_{t-2})y_{t-1}}{\sum_{t=2}^{T} y_{t-1}^2}.$$

The value of this ratio is obtained from least squares estimation of the autoregressive equation,

$$y_t - 2y_{t-1} + y_{t-2} = \mu y_{t-1} + e_t,$$

which is derived from a suggestion of Slutsky that sinusoidal fluctuations are found in a series in which second differences ($\Delta^2 y_t$) tend to be inversely proportional to the level, $-\mu(y_{t-1})$.[1]

These ideas for measurement of a single underlying period can be extended to estimation of superposed harmonics. In the extended case, we estimate the constrained fourth-order autoregression, by the method of least squares,

$$y_t + \lambda_1 y_{t-1} + \lambda_2 y_{t-2} + \lambda_1 y_{t-3} + y_{t-4} = e_t.$$

This gives, under mild restrictions, two conjugate complex roots with unit modulus. We therefore obtain estimates of two underlying periods.

There are no constant terms in the specifications of either the second- or fourth-order autoregressions; therefore, we measure all variables in terms of deviations from sample means. For reference, we regress

$$(C_t + C_{t-4})$$

on

$$(C_{t-1} + C_{t-3}) \quad \text{and} \quad C_{t-2},$$

where

$$C_t = \text{Wharton index of capacity utilization.}$$

The empirical result is

$$\begin{aligned}[(C_t - \bar{C}) + (C_{t-4} - \bar{C}_{-4})] = {} & 1.478[(C_{t-1} - \bar{C}_{-1}) + (C_{t-3} - \bar{C}_{-3})] \\ & (13.193) \\ & -1.199(C_{t-2} - \bar{C}_{-2}), \\ & (-5.705)\end{aligned}$$

$\bar{R}^2 = 0.925$, S.E. $= 2.627$, D.W. $= 1.669$,
Sample period: 1948.1–1974.4.

The restricted autogression obviously fits the data well and produces two pairs of conjugate complex roots with periods of oscillation,

19.77 quarters and 3.52 quarters.

The first is an estimate of the traditional U.S. business cycle and the second a short cycle.

[1]See Otsuki (1971), Howrey–Klein (1972) and Chow (1975).

Corresponding results for price change, in support of Geoffrey Moore's hypothesis, are obtained from

$$[\Delta \ln p_t + \Delta \ln p_{t-4}] = \underset{(7.826)}{0.595}[\Delta \ln p_{t-1} + \Delta \ln p_{t-3}] + \underset{(1.878)}{0.248}\Delta \ln p_{t-2},$$

$\bar{R}^2 = 0.648$, S.E. $= 0.0063$, D.W. $= 1.975$,
Sample period: 1948.2–1974.4.

The price series used is the GNP deflator, and it is understood that the variables are measured as mean deviations,

$$\Delta \ln p_t - \overline{\Delta \ln p}.$$

The first differences in logarithms are approximately the same as percentage changes.

The numerical results indicate the existence of two periods,

14.96 quarters and 2.81 quarters.

These are only slightly shorter than the oscillations in capacity utilization. It is suggestive to look upon these estimates of price periodicity as reflecting the general industrial cycle – the longer period – and a short agricultural cycle, inspired, no doubt, by "cobweb" behavior.

The fit of the price change autoregression is high and significant, but not nearly as high as the degree of fit for the capacity utilization autoregression. Nevertheless, the coefficients in the price case are highly significant, in a statistical sense. The results indicate that price cycles do exist and that they are closely related to capacity utilization cycles. This is why capacity utilization serves as a good early warning signal.

2. *Some Leads and Lags in Price Movements*

In monitoring published data on price movements, inferences about possible changes in retail, consumer, or general GNP price indexes are usually made after looking at index movements in prices at wholesale or possibly as far back as primary producers, i.e., at the farm gate. Prices usually change through the production and distribution system in a standard way, so there are recognizable patterns among different classes of indexes.

Food prices provide an excellent example of the links in a small chain. There are essentially four classes of price in the agricultural sector:

(i) prices received by farmers (this is an index of the supply price confronting farmers), *PF*;

(ii) wholesale prices of farm products, PW_F;
(iii) wholesale prices of processed foods and feeds, PW_{PF};
(iv) retail prices of food (consumer price index), PCF.

There is practically no lag between prices (i) and (ii),

$$\Delta \ln PW_F = \underset{(0.15)}{0.00016} + \underset{(34.97)}{1.011} \Delta \ln PF,$$

$R^2 = 0.917$, S.E. $= 0.0113$, D.W. $= 2.15$,
Sample period: 1947.2–1974.4.

A perfect relation between wholesale price of crude foods and prices received by farmers would have a zero constant term and a unit slope. The results here are not inconsistent, from a statistical view point, with the ideal case. The relationship is instantaneous, for the introduction of a distributed lag relationship shows no significant contribution from these sources. If a lag between $\Delta \ln PF$ and $\Delta \ln PW_F$ were to be important, this would show up in the simple fitting of a lag distribution with geometrically declining weights. But the estimate of the Koyck transformation of this case gives no plausible statistical evidence in favor of a lag effect.

$$\Delta \ln PW_F = \underset{(0.18)}{0.00020} + \underset{(33.98)}{1.013} \Delta \ln PF - \underset{(0.34)}{0.0097} \Delta(\ln PW_F)_{-1},$$

$R^2 = 0.917$, S.E. $= 0.0114$, D.W. $= 2.14$,
Sample period: 1947.3–1974.4.

The lag term is not significant nor even of the right sign.

This first link is, therefore, a direct transfer of price information between the farm gate and wholesale prices. Next we consider the relation between the wholesale price index of crude foods and of processed foods. Here, there is a significant lag distribution from the beginning,

$$\Delta \ln(PW_{PF}) = \underset{(3.15)}{0.0042} + \underset{(16.58)}{0.535} \Delta \ln(PW_F) + \underset{(2.37)}{0.122} \Delta \ln(PW_{PF})_{-1},$$

$R^2 = 0.730$, S.E. $= 0.0132$, D.W. $= 1.38$,
Sample period: 1947.3–1974.4.

If this were rewritten as a lag distribution, it would have the form

$$\Delta \ln(PW_{PF}) = \frac{0.0042}{1-0.122} + 0.535 \sum_{i=0}^{\infty} (0.122)^i \Delta \ln(PW_F)_{-i}.$$

The coefficients of current and previous values of farm product prices form the distribution sequence

$$0.535, \quad 0.535(0.122), \quad 0.535(0.122)^2, \quad 0.535(0.122)^3, \quad \ldots$$

After the 4th quarter lag (one year ago) the coefficient is less than 0.0001. Most of the effect occurs in the current and preceding quarter. Price effects are therefore mainly passed through in one-half year.

The final link is between food prices to the consumer (CPI component) and prices of manufactured foods at wholesale,

$$\Delta \ln PCF = \underset{(2.66)}{0.0027} + \underset{(13.31)}{0.493}\Delta \ln(PW_{PF}) + \underset{(3.44)}{0.196}\Delta \ln(PCF)_{-1},$$

$R^2 = 0.675$, S.E. $= 0.0095$, D.W. $= 2.25$,
Sample period: 1947.3–1974.4.

The decay factor is much slower, falling after the contemporaneous effect at the rate

$$0.2, \quad 0.04, \quad 0.008, \quad 0.0016, \quad 0.00032.$$

As the coefficient of $\Delta \ln(PW_{PF})$ is approximately 0.5, the value of the total effect four quarters ago is 0.0008. Most of the effect occurs within one year but is stretched out a bit longer than between the manufacturing stage and the original production stage.

These results are confirmed fairly well by fitting polynomial lag distributions – third-degree polynomials, covering four non-zero lags,

$$\Delta \ln(PW_{PF}) = \underset{(3.07)}{0.0040} + \underset{(15.87)}{0.530}\Delta \ln(PW_F) + \underset{(1.80)}{0.044}\Delta \ln(PW_F)_{-1}$$

$$- \underset{(2.86)}{0.060}\Delta \ln(PW_F)_{-2} + \underset{(1.38)}{0.026}\Delta \ln(PW_F)_{-3} + \underset{(4.45)}{0.110}\Delta \ln(PW_F)_{-4},$$

$R^2 = 0.724$, S.E. $= 0.013$, D.W. $= 1.35$,
Sample period: 1948.2–1974.4.

$$\Delta \ln PCF = \underset{(2.61)}{0.0025} + \underset{(12.71)}{0.460}\Delta \ln (PW_{PF}) + \underset{(5.11)}{0.143}\Delta \ln (PW_{PF})_{-1}$$

$$+ \underset{(1.64)}{0.040}\Delta \ln (PW_{PF})_{-2} + \underset{(2.25)}{0.049}\Delta \ln (PW_{PF})_{-3} + \underset{(2.46)}{0.069}\Delta \ln (PW_{PF})_{-4},$$

$R^2 = 0.701$, S.E. $= 0.0090$, D.W. $= 2.04$,
Sample period: 1948.2–1974.4.

Food prices provide a clear indication of the lead-lag process in price formation. In broader non-food categories, we find the same kinds of effects, but the lags are stretched out a bit more. We use the wholesale price index for industrial commodities, *PWI*, as an explanatory variable in these calculations. The geometric lag distributions for four cases are:

(1) *GNP Deflator, P*

$$\Delta \ln P = \underset{(5.16)}{0.0033} + \underset{(7.70)}{0.282}\Delta \ln (PWI) + \underset{(4.09)}{0.322}\Delta \ln P_{-1},$$

$R^2 = 0.657$, S.E. $= 0.0044$, D.W. $= 2.09$,
Sample period: 1947.3–1974.4.

(2) *Price Deflator of Consumer Expenditures, PC*

$$\Delta \ln PC = \underset{(4.98)}{0.0028} + \underset{(8.86)}{0.317}\Delta \ln (PWI) + \underset{(3.73)}{0.276}\Delta \ln (PC)_{-1},$$

$R^2 = 0.706$, S.E. $= 0.00417$, D.W. $= 2.04$,
Sample period: 1947.3–1974.4.

(3) *Price Deflator of Non-farm Investment, PI*

$$\Delta \ln PI = \underset{(3.05)}{0.0035} + \underset{(6.92)}{0.502}\Delta \ln (PWI) + \underset{(2.08)}{0.177}\Delta \ln (PI)_{-1},$$

$R^2 = 0.450$, S.E. $= 0.0100$, D.W. $= 1.99$,
Sample period: 1947.3–1974.4.

(4) *Consumer Price Index, CPI*

$$\Delta \ln CPI = \underset{(3.52)}{0.0024} + \underset{(6.08)}{0.264}\Delta \ln(PWI) + \underset{(5.50)}{0.428}\Delta \ln(CPI)_{-1},$$

$R^2 = 0.628$, S.E. = 0.0054, D.W. = 2.05,
Sample period: 1947.3–1974.4.

The geometric ratios of decay in the lag distributions vary approximately between 0.2 and 0.4. In comparison with the coefficients in the food case, there is more effect remaining after four quarters, although not much more. Most of the pass-through occurs in the first year of a price change, but some is left over for the second year in the non-food case.

The prolonged effect can be seen in the polynomial lag distribution for the GNP deflator, where we use a cubic polynomial with six non-zero quarterly lags,

$$\begin{aligned}\Delta \ln P = {} & \underset{(7.67)}{0.0043} + \underset{(7.46)}{0.229}\Delta \ln(PWI) + \underset{(10.25)}{0.127}\Delta \ln(PWI)_{-1} \\ & + \underset{(3.43)}{0.062}\Delta \ln(PWI)_{-2} + \underset{(1.78)}{0.026}\Delta \ln(PWI)_{-3} \\ & + \underset{(0.82)}{0.011}\Delta \ln(PWI)_{-4} + \underset{(0.37)}{0.007}\Delta \ln(PWI)_{-5} \\ & + \underset{(0.34)}{0.006}\Delta \ln(PWI)_{-6},\end{aligned}$$

$R^2 = 0.634$, S.E. = 0.0044, D.W. = 1.49,
Sample period: 1948.4–1974.4.

After four quarters, some small effects remain, but their size is uncertain, as the sampling errors are quite large. These results relating economy wide price indexes to the industrial component of the wholesale price index would not be much different, and not significantly different, if the total wholesale price index were used instead as an explanatory variable.

There is realism to the intuitive observations that movements discerned in the wholesale indexes will, with slight delay, show up in the retail or final transactions indexes. This can be spelled out in more detail by studying price transmission by stage of processing within manufacturing as well as in agriculture and other primary sectors.[2]

[2]See Popkin (1974).

3. Some Correlates of Price

Most econometric price analysis follows a structural approach, i.e., a theory of price formation is specified, and statistical equations are estimated on the basis of some parametric approximation to this theoretical equation. Two predominant specifications in contemporary thinking are:

(1) *Mark-up over unit labor costs*

$p = k(wL/X)$,
p = general price level,
w = general wage rate,
L = employment,
X = output,
k = mark-up *parameter.*

(2) *Quantity theory of money*

$p = v(M/X)$,
M = money supply,
v = velocity *parameter.*

These are crude statements and need special qualification. In a general sense, the mark-up equation is indicative of Sidney Weintraub's view and the quantity theory of Milton Friedman's view. The first depends on stability of k and the second on stability of v. In both cases, X is a value added concept; p is, therefore, a value added price, and intermediate material costs, which appear to be so important for leads and lags by stage of processing, as studied in Section 2, are "washed out" of the formulation.

To generalize the mark-up theory, we should observe that prices may not be adjusted instantaneously to labor costs, and that temporary movements, especially as a result of cyclical fluctuation in productivity, may not be considered fundamental enough to bring about a price adjustment. A more appropriate variable might be normal or long-run unit labor costs rather than actual unit labor costs. A customary specification used in macro model building is to express price level as a function of normal unit labor cost, actual unit labor cost, and one or more indicators of excess supply or demand, such as capacity utilization, order backlogs, or inventories. The latter two variables would be scaled by sales. In specifying separate price equations for individual sectors, it is clear that supply–demand balance should be a relevant variable – perhaps the only variable governing the movement of price. It is less obvious that this should be a variable in an equation for the general price level. In the case of sector prices, the balance between supply and demand can be looked upon as an indicator of competitive market forces, while the mark-up factor is indicative of the price setting power of entrepreneurs. The typical price equation represents a mixture of these two processes in an imperfectly competitive system. Another amendment to the mark-up equation is that domestic labor costs may not be the only relevant components of the total mark-up. Unit capital costs and unit import costs should also be taken into account. Since aggregate output depends on labor and capital inputs, it is clear enough that unit capital costs should be included. Intermediate materials are generally excluded from the aggregate production function since one producer's output of intermediates is another's input. This is not true, however, of imported materials. Their unit costs should be included as well as domestic labor and capital costs. If the production process is Cobb–Douglas, however, a simplification occurs: output price is proportional to any one of the unit costs alone. In a more general view of the production process and with full mark-up, however, price should depend on all three unit factor costs.

Consider now the quantity equation. It is well known that it provides a price prediction from knowledge of exogenously controlled money supply only if output is at its normal, full-use level. Monetarists have finessed this problem by asserting that nominal output values – not price level – depend on money supply,

$$pX = f(M).$$

They look to and cite money supply as the strategic indicator for the analysis of inflation and recommend policy in these terms, but their statistical analyses are now in terms of estimates of nominal output values.

To put matters in another way, the velocity parameter is unstable. It fluctuates over the course of the cycle and also has a pronounced trend drift. To correct for these difficulties, Friedman has suggested that velocity would be a stable parameter if it were re-defined as a parameter in a relation associating long-run income and long-run price. This is very much like the use of normal rather than actual unit labor costs in the mark-up equation. If we accept the Kalecki–Keynes view that velocity depends on interest rates, the whole quantity equation specification takes on a different character. It becomes a multivariate relation, as complex as the generalization of the mark-up equation.

The simplistic forms of the two basic equations, one for mark-up pricing and one for the quantity theory, are both inadequate representations of reality. In some sense, both k and v are functions of other economic variables. If one had to choose between them, and *only between them in their simplest forms*, there is no doubt that k is a more stable parameter, especially in the long run, as a cyclical average; wage movements thus provide a better early warning indicator in this sense than do movements in money supply. This may be called the "realist" as contrasted with the "monetarist" point of view.

Both simple models are inadequate; the price determination process is more complicated. Short of big system construction with all the necessary equations for sector price formation, input–output equations, flow of funds equations, income generation, and final demand, what can be done to provide quick, early warning signals? An exploratory, empirical approach using suggestive elements of both theories will be pursued here. In a sense, we shall be playing a "St. Louis" game in looking for a non-structural empirical relation. It will be different in that endogenous as well as exogenous variables will be used as regressors.

From the mark-up theory we shall select unit labor costs, separated into wage rate and productivity, rental price of capital, and import price. From the quantity theory we shall choose either velocity or money supply as a regressor. Modifications for the degree of capacity utilization and exchange depreciation will also be considered. Different indicators of current cyclical conditions such as unemployment rates, inventory–sales ratio, or orders–sales ratio could be used instead of capacity utilization, but we chose the latter because of its strong cyclical properties, as indicated by the calculations in Section 1 and its previous emissions of early warning signals in 1966, 1973.

All the estimated price regressions are in change form – first differences of logarithms except in the case of capacity utilization, which is cyclical without transformation, and has no perceptible trend. If we simply correlate the relevant variables without time lag, the result is

$$\begin{aligned}\Delta \ln p = &-\underset{-(0.23)}{0.0019} + \underset{(5.32)}{0.56}\Delta \ln w - \underset{-(5.5)}{0.27}\Delta \ln (X/L) + \underset{(3.8)}{0.08}\Delta \ln p_{\mathrm{m}}\\ &+ \underset{(1.39)}{0.09}\Delta \ln M_1 + \underset{(0.25)}{0.000026}C,\end{aligned}$$

$R^2 = 0.62$, D.W. $= 1.89$,
Sample period: 1947.2–1974.4;

p = GNP deflator, 1958: 100,
w = private compensation per man hour,
X/L = private output per man hour,
p_{m} = import deflator (goods and services), 1958: 100,
M_1 = money supply,

C = index of capacity utilization in mining, manufacturing, and utilities (Wharton).

As a first difference equation, the overall degree of correlation is pretty high. As is often the case with first difference transformations, the residuals show little evidence of serial correlation.

Wage rate and productivity are strong variables, in a correlation sense, in this regression; although they have coefficients of opposite sign, they are not of the same order of magnitude, suggesting that wage rate and productivity make distinct contributions and not necessarily in the combination of unit labor cost. The correlation contribution of import prices is very significant; money supply is just under the borderline of significance and capacity utilization is insignificant. Capital costs, when added as regressors in this equation, showed no significant contribution and made the overall results worse; therefore they were excluded, as were exchange rates, for the same reason. The influence of exchange rate changes is transmitted through p_m, however, since that index is dollar denominated by virtue of correcting foreign denominated prices by the dollar exchange rates, item-by-item.

Wage rates, productivity, and import costs crowd out any contribution to price explanation from current capacity utilization. They may not crowd out money supply completely, but they do push it to the margin of statistical significance. The magnitude of the marginal coefficient of money supply is not great, either. It states, subject to error, that money supply growth as excessive as 10% a year would add less than 100 basis points to the current inflation rate. Much stronger effects would be expected from wage changes.

In structural price equations, unit labor cost variables might be split into two components – current and normal unit labor costs. As the latter is often calculated as the ratio of current wage rates to trend values of productivity, we would not find much separate contribution from the "normal" component since the equation estimated here is in first difference form, and logarithmic first differences would tend to be fairly constant. At best, they would show a few discrete breaks in the sample period. The contemporaneous components of wage and productivity change should not, in any case, be eliminated from the equation, and it is these that tend to crowd out the capacity utilization effect.

If capacity utilization is lagged one period, its effect is not appreciably stronger. There is some indication of a lag effect in movements of p_m; this makes sense because it takes time for imported goods to have their full impact on the domestic economy when there are major international changes. This is particularly true of materials used in the production process. It is less evident from the empirical series that money supply has a stronger effect when lagged, but we try to allow for this possibility. A final regression has been estimated in which capacity utilization is dropped as a regressor and polynomial lag distributions are estimated for coefficients of p_m and M_1. The former is a quadratic polynomial with one end-point restriction zero at lag of four quarters, while the latter is a quadratic with two end-point restrictions, one at plus one and the other at minus four.

The result is

$$\begin{aligned}\Delta \ln p &= \underset{(0.89)}{0.0010} + \underset{(4.20)}{0.38}\Delta \ln w - \underset{-(4.24)}{0.18}\Delta \ln (X/L) + \underset{(2.92)}{0.05}\Delta \ln p_m \\ &+ \underset{(6.24)}{0.05}(\Delta \ln p_m)_{-1} + \underset{(3.47)}{0.03}(\Delta \ln p_m)_{-2} + \underset{(2.23)}{0.02}(\Delta \ln p_m)_{-3} \\ &+ \underset{(2.25)}{0.03}\Delta \ln M_1 + \underset{(2.25)}{0.05}(\Delta \ln M_1)_{-1} + \underset{(2.25)}{0.05}(\Delta \ln M_1)_{-2} + \underset{(2.25)}{0.03}(\Delta \ln M_1)_{-3},\end{aligned}$$

$R^2 = 0.69$, D.W. = 1.91,
Sample period: 1948.1–1974.4.

As an early warning signal, changes in M_1 appear to be only moderately powerful either in an economic or statistical sense. The economic strength of import prices is fairly high and increased over a purely contemporary correlation. To the extent to which wage changes are well signaled in advance through the collective bargaining process and productivity movements can be estimated, this correlation result suggests that we look to labor market developments, import prices, and, to a certain extent, money supply in order to get a first look at impending price movements.

4. Summary

Price movements are cyclical and readily discernible in percentage-change form. Predictions of cyclical surges in inflation rates may be signalled by strong changes in another cyclical variable, namely, the rate of capacity utilization. At least this signal appears to have been operative in recent years.

Conventional wisdom about the chain of inflationary movements from producer, to wholesaler, to retailer appears to be borne out by statistical calculation. There are some regular lag distributions, with evident lead time, in the estimation of both food or agricultural and non-food or industrial price movements.

Predicting and confirming inflationary movements is both a difficult and extremely important matter. We should, therefore, look at a variety of signals. The main correlates of price movements are changes in wage rates, productivity, import prices, and, to a certain extent, pure monetarist type variables – money supply and velocity. Sustained or well signalled movements in these correlates should be harbingers of impending price movements.

5. References

Chow, G. C., 1975, Analysis and control of dynamic economic systems (Wiley, New York).

Howrey, E. P. and L. R. Klein, 1972, Dynamic properties of nonlinear economic models, International Economic Review 13, pp. 599–618.

Klein, L. R., 1972, Price determination in the Wharton model, in: O. Eckstein, ed., The econometrics of price determination (The Federal Reserve Board, Washington, DC).

Klein, L. R., 1974, The econometrics of inflation, 1965–1974, Paper presented to the Conference for Research on Income and Wealth (Washington, DC).

Moore, G. H., 1972, The cyclical behavior of prices, in: V. Zarnowitz, ed., The business cycle today, I (Columbia University Press, New York).

Otsuki, M., 1971, Oscillations in stochastic simulation of linear systems, Economic Studies Quarterly XXII, pp. 53–71.

Popkin, J., 1974, Commodity prices and the U.S. price level, Brookings Papers on Economic Activity 1, pp. 249–259.

Chapter 13

From Multiplier to Quantity Theory

Henry C. WALLICH*

Monetarism today stands at the center of the economic scene. Ten years after the ascendancy of the "New Economics", a new doctrine is in vogue that is sharply critical of its Keynesian predecessor. Monetarism has established itself as an important part of intellectual discourse, has become influential with the press, and has captured the attention of the public. Central banks all over the world orient and explain their policies in terms of the monetary aggregates. The financial markets take their cue from data which, a few years back, were little observed and in many countries not even published. Even the nomenclature employed all over the world – M_1, M_2 – is the handiwork of Milton Friedman, the originator of monetarism.

Increasingly, monetarist prescriptions play a role in political discussions. Policy objectives are being expressed and debated in terms of growth targets of the money stock. The elected representatives of the people have discovered the attraction of monetarist doctrine because it plays down the effects of fiscal policy. Deficits can do no major damage so long as the central bank does its job right, and that is where monetarism places the ultimate responsibility. Central bankers, for the same reason, have tended to preserve a degree of faith in Keynesianism.

The trend of public discussion conceals two important facts. The first is that the present vogue of monetarism is a child of its times just as Keynesianism was. Keynesianism came out of the Depression; it followed and in some measure reflected the disappointment over monetary policy which had been held in high esteem during the 1920's, an earlier monetarist period. Monetarist doctrine – like Keynesian – has had

*I am greatly indebted to David E. Lindsey for intensive discussions and numerous suggestions in the preparation of this essay, and I also gratefully acknowledge the helpful comments received from G. L. Bach, George Clay, Robert Dugger, Milton Friedman, C. Lowell Harriss, Donald Hester, Thomas Mayer, Walter Salant, Paul Samuelson, Francis Schott, Beryl Sprinkel, Jerome Stein and John Wilson. The views expressed herein are those of the author, and do not necessarily represent the views of the Board of Governors of the Federal Reserve System.

some degree of relevance at all times. But the strong vogue of monetarism is the consequence of inflation, which has undermined many Keynesian precepts and assumptions and has lent strength to monetarist analysis. This historical evolution from unemployment to inflation is reflected in the dominant concern of the two sides, Keynesianism being oriented toward curing unemployment, monetarism predominantly toward curing inflation.

The second important fact is the narrowing, in recent years, of the analytical gap that has separated monetarists and Keynesians. Much of the debate now is not over how the economy works, but over what we want to get out of it, i.e., over values and policies. My principal purpose in this essay is to examine the process by which changes in the economic climate, from the unemployment of the 30's to the inflation of the 70's, have progressively strengthened the monetarist case. To begin with, I shall examine the coming together of the two sides in terms of their view of the economy.

1. The Keynesian Monetarist Synthesis

The long debate between Keynesians and Monetarists has reached a substantial measure of agreement. This agreement does not cover matters of policy, which often reflect value judgments. It does imply that a common view is being approached of the analytical framework of the economy. There is a common ground now as to how the economy works, what are the critical relationships. No longer do the two sides seem to speak different languages or to be looking at a different world.

What they say in the newfound common language, to be sure, still distinguishes Keynesians from Monetarists. They differ about the shape of relationships that both sides regard as important, and the magnitude of particular effects. But the analytical differences have narrowed down to the point where the difference between a fair representation of the two doctrines has been reduced by one student to the sign of a single coefficient in a large system of equations [Stein (1976)].

The process of integration has followed along two lines. On the one hand, monetarists, in developing their framework, increasingly have found themselves employing concepts and relationships originating in the Keynesian world. No longer is there a simple equation of exchange, $MV = PT$, which everybody must fill with his own analytical ideas to keep it from remaining a tautology. Money, we now clearly perceive, works mainly through interest rates, not through some mysterious black box, even though some echoes of a "direct effect" continue to reverberate. The range of interest rates and rates of return is wide, wider indeed than the original Keynesian conception, some rates being implicit rather than quoted in the market. These rates affect asset values, the wealth of consumers, the relation of market to replacement value of assets, the propensity to spend of households and firms. These effects all find their place in a sufficiently detailed version of the familiar Keynesian IS–LM framework of the economy.

On the other hand, monetarists have imposed upon the precise nature of these relationships their own particular stamp which Keynesians have largely had to accept. They say that the relation of money and interest rates is far more complex than the simple Keynesian liquidity preference doctrine implied. A difference exists between nominal and real values, which the Keynesians had tended to ignore. Under plausible assumptions, monetary policy may be more powerful than fiscal policy. The money supply rather than the interest rate may be the best intermediate target for monetary policy. Inflation may become as serious a threat to welfare as is unemployment. The Phillips Curve, the principal analytical device of the post-Keynesian era, may lose its meaning in the long run. Long lags in response to policy actions may make flexible anti-cyclical policy destabilizing. These are some of the concrete and very un-Keynesian propositions with which the monetarists have filled the essentially Keynesian analytical framework. The central bank much of the time during recent years has found itself in a crossfire between Keynesians and monetarists. Often the criticism of monetary policy coming from the Keynesian side has been less concerned with techniques than with values, e.g., the relative willingness to take risks on the side of inflation. By contrast, most of the criticism coming from the monetarist side has been over techniques, e.g., the use of interest rate vs. money supply targets, and the degree of stability of a money supply target.

The Federal Reserve itself has come a long way in the course of these discussions. After ridding itself of the sense of powerlessness that beset it during the late 30's and most of the 40's, it first moved back to the policy targets of the 1920's, based on the reserve position of banks. By gradual steps it shifted toward increasing emphasis on the monetary aggregates, as demanded by monetarist doctrine. But it has shied away from full endorsement. The monetary aggregates are not all that matters. Interest rates also are important, and so is the international value of the dollar, even under a floating regime. Accordingly, a fixed rate of money supply growth, regardless of its consequences for interest rates and exchange rates, is not practicable. At best, the monetarist emphasis on a stable – and moderate – rate of money growth can be employed to support a policy of moderation in financing budget deficits and inflation.

It would be quite wrong, however, to interpret the movement toward the present Keynesian-monetarist synthesis as a gradual discovery of immutable verities. The analytical structure, to be sure, has a considerable degree of general validity. It can be employed to explain widely differing states of the economy. But the economy has passed through a variety of states, and particularly of states of expectations, beginning with the expected unemployment of the late 30's and 40's going out to the full-employment expectations of the 50's and early 60's, and ending with the inflationary expectations of the late 60's and early 70's. In each of these phases, in my view, the behavior of the economy has been different, although capable of being represented by the same analytical relationships. The magnitudes of particular effects, the parameters and elasticities, the responses to particular policy actions, have been typically different.

These views, I realize, may be at variance with the results obtained by econometric methods. The econometric approach, to be significant, requires and implies stable relationships or at least stable changes therein. To data drawn from long periods, such as from the early 30's to the present, researchers usually apply one of the tests available to examine the stability of the structure over time. I am aware also, of course, that contemporary observation may lead to false conclusions. For a long time people believed to observe that the earth was flat.

At the same time, even well validated econometric results may be misleading. As an example, I might cite the finding that the demand for money has been very stable as a function of income and an interest rate, from which follows the conclusion that monetary policy had approximately the same expansionary power during the 1930's that it had at any other time. The demand function employed in such tests typically is a logarithmic one. If the elasticity of the demand for money with respect to the long-term interest rate then is -0.5, an increase in the money supply by 10% will bring down a long-term rate of 6% to 4.91%, and will bring down a long-term rate of 2.5% to 2.05. If the elasticity for the short-term rate (which during the 1930's reached 0.05% and during World War II was pegged at 0.375%) is -0.3, an increase in the money supply of 10% would bring down a short-term rate of 0.75 down to 0.56%. I am perfectly willing to accept these results, but I doubt that, under the conditions of the 1930's, they imply a potential for an effective monetary policy – see Khan (1974).

If the relevance and even the validity of particular propositions changes over time, an examination is called for of the evolution of Keynesian and monetarist propositions. The periods it must cover are the three periods already cited – that of expected high unemployment with prices nevertheless sticky downward, that of expected fluctuations in the neighborhood of full employment with reasonable price stability, and the final period of expected inflation combined with temporary unemployment.

2. The Demand for Money

The stability of the demand for money is a key proposition of monetarism. It is contrasted, by its sponsors, with the alleged instability of the Keynesian investment multiplier, and has been tested extensively with greater and lesser degrees of sophistication. If the demand for money is a function of both income and an interest rate, there is no reason to expect velocity (the income/money ratio) to be stable. It must be predictable, however, given the interest rate. Intuitively, one may expect this degree of predictability to have increased since the middle 1930's, for two reasons. At low rates of interest (1) a larger percentage change in the money supply is likely to be required to achieve a given absolute change in rates, and (2) the low cost of carrying idle balances leads to reduced effort in making precise adjustments in cash balances. At the very high interest rates experienced in 1974, smaller percentage changes in the money supply are likely to be associated with a given interest rate change, while efforts to economize on cash balances would be well rewarded. These observations apply particularly, of course, to M_1, and their validity does not depend on the uptrend in velocity that appears to have occurred over several decades thanks to improved payments technology, or, possibly, owing to increasing wealth.

If these considerations are valid, monetary policy in 1974 would have had more power than during earlier periods both because a given percentage change in M would produce a wider absolute swing in interest rates, and because there was less slack in the relationship. It would mean also that the money supply would have to be attuned more precisely to the desired objectives in terms of real and nominal income growth than earlier. The monetarist claim that monetary policy was not powerless during the Great Depression might have formal validity, but would have little significance given the large percentage changes in M that would have been required and the modest absolute changes in interest rates that could have been expected, as noted above. The great present power of monetary policy, under conditions of inflation, reflects no eternal verity.

3. Money and Interest Rates

The original quantity equation $MV = PT$ did not explicitly allow for the relation of interest rates and money, although it is obvious that so acute an analyst of the interest phenomenon as Irving Fisher was aware of it. Keynes remedied this by introducing "liquidity preference". During a period of expected permanent unemployment (at least in the textbooks), this seemed to be the end of the matter: an increase in money reduces the interest rate and, after allowing for a partial reversal of this effect if the ensuing rise in income is taken into account, the interest rate remains at a lower level than initially with no difference between real and nominal rates. This framework seems to make the interest rate a perfectly proper target of monetary policy.

Full employment, and eventually inflation, compel us to extend the sequence of effects, as Milton Friedman has shown. The initial decline in the interest rate leads to excess demand which eventually raises income. This increases the demand for money, causing interest rates to go up again. If prices also rise, this reduces real balances, which further raises interest rates. If inflation finally becomes imbedded in expectations, nominal interest rates rise still higher to protect real rates.

In the inflationary conditions of the 1970's, this mechanism has become widely accepted. It can reasonably be argued that the central bank has little power to reduce interest rates except for short periods. Even then, the impact is more on short-term rates, which reflect demand and supply in the money market, than on long-term rates, which reflect expectations of inflation over a much longer horizon. It has even been argued that evidence of more rapidly growing money supply causes long-term rates to go up rather than down. However, the implication that this reflects expectations of higher inflation may be spurious: rates would also rise if the market expected the acceleration of the money supply to be compensated by slower growth in the following period. One thing is clear, however: under the conditions of inflation, the only way in which the central bank can bring down interest rates lastingly is to bring down the rate of inflation. Temporarily at least, this probably requires a period of higher rates that would slow the growth of nominal and probably real GNP.

The inflationary spurts of the late 40's and the early and late 50's raise interesting questions with respect to interest rates. The response of interest rates was in no way sufficient to compensate for the inflation loss. This may be attributed to the failure of expectations of inflation to be formed. However, the decline (or reduced growth) in real balances also should have made itself felt in higher rates. Yet the effect, if any, was clearly far less pronounced than what has been experienced since the late 60's. Evidently, then, the mechanism to which monetarists rightly have pointed since that time did not fully come into play during the 40's and 50's.

4. Money Supply versus Interest Rates as Monetary Policy Target

If the relation of money and interest rates is fully known, the choice of one or the other as a target of monetary policy makes no difference. Moreover, if money affects the economy through interest rates, it would seem simpler to work directly through an interest rate target rather than a money growth target. Whether for these reasons or others, early Keynesian thinking undoubtedly focussed upon interest rates as the target and test of monetary policy. Monetarist influence gradually has brought central bankers and others around to a policy oriented toward the monetary aggregates. It is important to examine the reasons and implications.

First, emphasis on money (or its growth rate) does not mean that money affects the economy directly, rather than through interest rates, rates of return, and their impact on costs and asset values. Thus, if in a particular situation it should appear that nothing useful is to be achieved by changing these rates of interest, return, and capitalization, it is clear that, other things equal, nothing good is to be achieved by changing the money stock.

Second, the choice between an interest and a money supply target can be shown to rest upon the relative predictability of the real and financial sector. Random shocks to the real sector are best met with a stable money supply policy that allows the interest rate to vary so as to soften the shock, while shocks to financial sector can be kept from affecting the real sector by a constant interest rate policy [Poole (1970)]. The monetarist belief in the stability of the demand for money then lends support to a money supply policy. However, the belief of at least some monetarists in the stability of the private sector, which after all makes up the great part of the real sector, actually could leave some doubt as to which sector monetarists regard as inherently more stable.

Third, the choice between an interest rate and a money supply target makes a great deal of *apparent* difference to the way central bank policy *looks* during cyclical fluctuations. Since interest rates move procyclically, the endogenous forces of the economy will make the central bank look superficially right, even if it takes no action to change the money supply. Since the money supply also tends to move procyclically, the same endogenous forces under a money supply target tend to make an inactive central bank look superficially bad.

Actually, it is a mistake to judge the central bank purely on whether it takes specific action or relies on endogenous forces to achieve its objective. A driver seeking to accelerate on a downgrade may take his foot off the gas and still find himself getting up speed. A central bank may find the restraint resulting from cyclically rising interest rates sufficient for its purposes. However, there is danger that the central bank may underestimate the extent of the rise in rates required to keep the money supply from accelerating. It may then be permitting excessive expansion by looking only at rising interest rates and not at the accelerating money supply.

The signals thrown off by interest rate and money growth, respectively, may often appear to be in conflict. Financial market practitioners and monetarist economists are likely to describe in opposite terms a situation where interest rates rise while money growth accelerates, the first viewing the situation as one of "tightness", the second as one of "ease". Historically, the signals thrown off by the money supply have often been the right ones, as in 1968 and 1972. But in the first half of 1974, when interest rates signalled "tight" while the money supply had turned toward "easy", events half a year later showed that interest rates had prevailed over money supply. During the second half of 1974, when interest rates signalled "easy" and money supply "tight," the foundations actually were being laid for a bottoming out of the recession six to nine months later.

The central bank may lean toward an interest rate target, or at least toward circumscribing a money growth target with an interest constraint, because of concern about the side effects of wide rate fluctuations. The real meaning of a pure money supply target is that it produces extreme variations in interest rates. It is these extreme variations from which the special stabilizing virtues claimed by monetarists for a stable money supply policy must flow. The central bank may reasonably be skeptical of the effectiveness particularly of very low rates. In the light of the surrounding facts, the prospective gains in home construction, consumer durables purchases, inventory building, and business and plant and equipment spending may be quite moderate. Meanwhile the costs of extremely low – as well as of extremely high – rates may be severe in terms of large flows into and out of thrift institutions, international capital flows and exchange rate movements, and increases in perceived market risks. These costs may provide good reason for the central bank to back away from a stable money growth path such as monetarists might recommend. Of course, so long as it does this, the monetarist case will never be fully tested, and the central bank can always be held responsible for whatever failures occur.

There is an objective test between an interest rate target and a money growth target: what happens if the wrong target is chosen and adhered to? A wrong interest rate target will lead to expansion or contraction which eventually will cause price increases or decreases. Whichever happens, the effect of persisting in the target will be cumulative. The gap between the targeted and the equilibrium interest rate will widen, the ultimate effect will be explosive. A wrongly set money supply target does not carry this risk. It will lead to a reasonably stable rate of inflation or deflation, and will in this sense be superior to an interest rate target.

Whether any of these features would have been sufficient to gain widespread acceptance for a money supply target will always remain uncertain. The straw that broke the interest rate camel's back was inflation. The real meaning of interest rates is distorted more severely by inflation than is that of the monetary aggregates. The real interest rate, at least the long-term rate, is not observable, resting as it does on expectations. Real balances are observable.

5. Relative Importance of Fiscal and Monetary Policy

The choice between interest rates and monetary aggregates as targets of policy, which determines the meaning of a "constant monetary policy", as discussed above, is decisive for assessing the relative power of monetary and fiscal policy. In the early Keynesian period, an unchanging interest rate was the obvious and unquestioned criterion of an unchanging monetary policy. That meant that fiscal expansion would automatically be financed by monetary expansion. For the ensuing rise in GNP, fiscal policy got all the credit, monetary policy got none.

A switch of the definition of "unchanging monetary policy" to a fixed stock of money changes this drastically. Fiscal expansion now raises interest rates. At some point the resulting restraint on private expenditures offsets the fiscal stimulus. After that, fiscal policy loses its power.

The net effect of fiscal expansion even in this framework is not zero. At higher interest rates, the demand for money diminishes and a larger nominal GNP can be accommodated with a given money supply. If downward flexibility of prices were admitted, a real GNP of any size could, of course, be accommodated with a given money supply. But on that assumption, it would have to be asked why prices had not fallen before fiscal stimulus was introduced, thereby returning the economy to full employment and making fiscal stimulation unnecessary. As in all discussions of stimulative fiscal or monetary policy, there is an implicit assumption that idle resources are available, in early Keynesian doctrine without perceptible limits.

A fixed money stock in a growing economy obviously is too extreme a definition of "constant monetary policy". A growth rate of the money stock equal to the real growth rate of the economy or, if there is a technologically determined uptrend in velocity, of the "effective money stock", seems more plausible. But except for the speed with which a fiscal stimulus would be stymied, this alternative definition would make no difference. Under a money supply definition of "constant monetary policy", therefore, the allocation of responsibility for economic expansion following a fiscal stimulus remains uncertain. Monetarists are free to claim that, with a given expansion of the money supply, exactly the same economic expansion would occur with or without a fiscal stimulus. This reinterpretation raises questions, for instance, about the real effectiveness of the 1964 tax cut which was indeed accompanied by accelerated money growth.

The relative strength of fiscal and monetary policy is affected also by the exchange rate regime. The shift to floating exchange rates has strengthened monetary policy relative to fiscal policy. In a fixed rate setting with full mobility of capital, in fact, monetary policy becomes virtually powerless in a small country and loses part of its power even in a large country like the United States. Any effort to change the money supply and thereby interest rates is frustrated by international capital flows. Fiscal policy, of course, is powerful under these conditions because the interest rate effects of expansive or contractive fiscal action are compensated by international flows.

In a floating rate regime, the central bank is free to determine the money supply. Interest rate movements will still be kept within narrow bounds by international capital flows. But these flows, instead of altering the money supply as under a fixed rate regime, now alter the exchange rate. Monetary policy then becomes effective, not through the usual transmission mechanism running via rates of interest and return to investment spending, but via changes in the relative prices of domestic and foreign goods to the trade balance. Fiscal policy meanwhile loses effectiveness because its interest rate effect cause capital and consequent exchange rate movements whose impact on the trade balance offsets fiscal stimulus and restraint.

The floating regime introduced in 1973 has enhanced the relative power of monetary policy in still other ways. The main accretion of power to monetary policy has not come, indeed, from the ability of monetary policy to affect trade balances. In the normal course of events, this mechanism could become effective only with a substantial lag. But because capital mobility usually has been less than perfect, control over the money supply has meant a considerable degree of control over interest rates for most countries.

6. Expansion and Contraction

During the Keynesian years, it was generally agreed that monetary policy had some contractive power. Its critics often imputed to it a discontinuity: applied in moderation it would produce no results, because the economy was shielded against monetary pressure by its rich padding of liquidity. Vigorous application was said to threaten depression. Its expansionary powers were deemed to be minimal in an environment of high liquidity.[1]

The historical shift from unemployment with stable prices through expectations of full employment and price stability to expectations of inflation has been accompanied by rising estimates of the powers of monetary policy. On the side of contraction, it now seems to be agreed that the scale of effects need not be discontinuous. On both sides, contraction as well as expansion, the power of monetary policy has been enhanced by the effect of inflation. Interest rates in inflation can range over a much wider spectrum than during price stability, since real rates can become negative. Obviously this observation is not intended as an argument for inflation.

The question whether seeking expansion by means of monetary policy can ever be like "pushing on a string" is capable of several interpretations and answers. If it implies that very large amounts of money may be required in some conditions to produce small effects on interest rates, this has been true in conditions such as the 1930's but does not altogether deny ultimate effectiveness. The same applies if it is argued that under these conditions the lags may become very long. "Pushing on a string" might imply that the effects of monetary policy cannot usefully be pushed beyond the point where the marginal benefits diminish sharply while the marginal costs from capital and exchange market disruption mount. In this sense, the comment points to a pragmatic limitation on the useful range of monetary policy. Still another picture emerges, finally, if "pushing on a string" is interpreted to mean that the central bank finds it difficult to expand the money supply because banks receiving reserves use these to repay debt to the central bank, because recipients of currency and demand deposits convert these into time deposits, and because the banks, instead of adding to the economy's liquidity by lending to firms and households, monetize existing financial assets such as Treasury bills that are already highly liquid. Obviously the central bank can still increase the money supply even under these conditions. But the side effects from such a policy may soon outweight the benefits.

[1]See the end of Section 1 above for the reason why this view is not inconsistent with a stable demand for money function if that function is sufficiently nonlinear.

7. Real Interest Rates and Real Balances

Realized inflation separates the development of real balances from nominal balances; expected inflation separates real from nominal interest rates. The difference in the degree of observability has already been noted. Neither monetarists nor Keynesians have a monopoly on either concept. But as inflation mounted, monetarists were more successful in capitalizing on the emerging distinctions. Many Keynesians and their models were caught napping.

Keynesian doctrine always has had difficulties clearing itself of the charge of reliance on money illusion, whether the charge was levied in connection with involuntary unemployment or with the use of the Phillips Curve. The conclusion that in the long run the Phillips Curve is vertical, so that there can be no lasting trade-off between unemployment and inflation, is not an exclusive property of monetarists. But Keynesians, who have relied heavily on the Phillips Curve as the most important analytical device of the post-Keynesian era, have had much greater difficulty accepting its limitations. If to the vertical Phillips Curve there is added the tentative finding that the disturbances of high inflation reduce capacity utilization and raise unemployment, the long-run Phillips Curve acquires a tilt to the right and becomes positively sloping.

The choice between interest rates and money supply as standards of monetary policy, as already was noted, has been tilted by inflation in favor of the money supply. Real interest rates are not observable, real balances are; a wrongly set interest rate has explosive effects, a wrongly set nominal money supply target has not. In these regards, inflation has lent strength to elements of analysis and policy that carry a monetarist tinge.

This does not mean that real balances have become a helpful or readily analyzable variable.

The simple monetarist prescription for a stable growth rate of the effective money supply (which allows for velocity trend) does not translate into a similar prescription for the real money supply. Expectations of inflation reduce the demand for real balances. An effort to maintain real balances may imply an increase in nominal balances at an explosive rate. That plainly has been the lesson of the big inflations of history. The observation frequently heard in the course of 1974 that real balances were falling while prices were accelerating was no proof that the supply of nominal money was falling short of the demand. Interest rates, which at the short-term end barely managed to keep up with the rate of inflation, are a better measure.

Most of the analysis linking money and income, moreover, has been done in terms of nominal income and nominal money supply. Deflating both by the same price index would not leave the correlations undisturbed, and there appears to be no well established body of findings as to what the results would be.

8. International Developments

The shift to floating rates, itself a product largely of world inflation, has been another development lending strength to monetarists' views and policies. The preference for floating rates, while historically allied to monetarism through the person of Milton Friedman, has long been shared by many Keynesians. The simple Keynesian export multiplier mechanism, however, requires fixed exchange rates – as well as unlimited international reserves and an accommodating money supply. Fixed exchange rates, moreover, as already noted, make fiscal policy effective and monetary policy ineffective under conditions of capital mobility, although that particular setting was scarcely envisaged by early Keynesian doctrine. Floating rates reversed that relation in favor of monetary policy. Under floating rates, the power of monetary policy did not come from its influence on interest rates – given capital mobility, there could be none – but through exchange rate changes and the trade balance. More importantly for central bankers, however, floating rates restored their control over the money supply which under fixed rates was severely impaired by the need to monetize balance-of-payments surpluses. Given imperfect mobility of capital, this was quite enough to return strength to monetary policy, and of course strength of the familiar kind – through interest rates and investment. But central bankers also have meanwhile discovered, of course, that the promised freedom of monetary policy from the shackles of the balance of payments continues only so long as the central bank is willing to ignore what its domestic policies do to exchange rates.

9. Inflation

It is inflation that has finally put monetarism in the saddle. Inflation has enhanced the relevance of the doctrine, brought some of its propositions into totally new focus, and discomfited Keynesians. This does not mean, of course, that monetarists are tolerant of inflation. The opposite is the case, for a variety of analytical, historical, and idealogical reasons.

The monetarists' rejection of the Phillips Curve trade-off is one such reason. Acceptance of a natural rate of unemployment (which must be brought down by structural rather than demand oriented policies) does not by itself, to be sure, imply a preference for zero inflation. There is still a cost attached to the achievement of stable prices. When unemployment is at its natural rate, inflation continues at a constant rate – that is the meaning of "natural rate". To bring inflation down, unemployment must rise above its natural rate temporarily, until the rate of wage increases has come down to equal productivity gains, so that prices can be stable. But the social cost of this temporary excess unemployment is less than believers in a negatively sloping Phillips Curve would expect. If a positively sloping long-term Phillips Curve can be validated, positive employment gains could be expected from price stability.

High rates of inflation also are seen to impose social costs comparable to those of unemployment, even though this view is not specifically monetarist, since it stresses the unpredictability of inflation. At high rates of inflation, the variance of the inflation rate increases and so, therefore, does the income uncertainty experienced by households. This is true even when aggregate real income is unchanged, so that the gains from inflation equal losses. With risk as a negative argument in the welfare function, this becomes a demonstrable proposition.[2]

Inflation damages the market system, to which monetarists attach major importance. This is the consequence not only of inadequate anticipation of inflation but of the fact also that even with correctly anticipated inflation the real income of many market participants takes the form, in part, of unrealized appreciation in the value of non-monetary assets. This income generates no cash flow from which interest rates high enough to correctly reflect inflation can be paid, and therefore threatens these units, both home-owners and business firms, with bankruptcy.

The monetarists' predilection for the market system, in turn, seems to derive in the first place from a reading of the evidence that stresses the allocational deficiencies of the political process. More broadly, it seems to be based on a philosophical skepticism with regard to government which contrasts with the Keynesians' stress on government's role as the fiscal balance wheel of the economy and its function in remedying market imperfections.

Finally, the monetarists' view that inflation is a purely monetary

[2]For a sample containing pooled cross section-time series data for 43 countries covering the period 1956–65, the variance of inflation was shown to be a significantly positive function of the level of inflation. For a time series of U.S. data, employing the seasonally adjusted consumer price index for the years 1948–74, the same results were obtained. Likewise, the coefficient of variation was a significantly positive function of the level of variation. I am indebted to my wife for supplying the first result and to Robert Dugger for the second and third.

phenomenon helps to explain their anti-inflation orientation. If money is the source of inflation, then inflation is easy to prevent by proper monetary policies and its occurrence therefore is the responsibility largely if not exclusively of the central bank. The responsibility placed upon the central bank, to be sure, is of a peculiar sort. It arises, not necessarily from acts of commission, but also from the omission of any act that would have been required to maintain price level stability in the face of outside impulses. The central bank is responsible for failure to maintain stability in the same sense that government can be responsible for any misfortune occurring anywhere within its domain to the extent that it had the technical means of preventing it. In monetarist doctrine the central bank seems to be held responsible for inflation also if, by allowing increases in the money supply, it merely validates pressures coming from other sources, such as excessive wage demands, or monopolistic pricing at home or abroad. In such instances, the central bank's powers may be a necessary condition of inflation, but not a sufficient one, much as possession of a gun may be the necessary but not sufficient cause of a fatal shooting. It has been very difficult for central banks to find grace in the eyes of monetarists, despite their common preference for stable prices.

10. The Future of Monetarism

If monetarism has drawn much of its strength from inflation, what will be the future of the doctrine if the advice of its proponents, directed as it is toward ending inflation, is accepted and proves successful?

Monetarism is vulnerable in many respects. For a long time, it has had the advantage of being mainly in opposition, of being a critic [Johnson (1971)]. Strategically, its position remains strong, because it is unlikely that monetarist advice of hewing to a stable rate of money growth month after month and perhaps week after week will ever be literally followed, and so long as it isn't the monetarists can decline full responsibility. But such an extreme version of monetarism lacks plausibility. Monetarism will be tested and will have to take responsibility for the consequences, including the adverse side effects that central bankers fear.

Monetarism has obvious analytical weaknesses. The close relation between money and income that it deduces from historical experience is the result of a two-way relationship, the chain of causation running from income to money as well as from money to income. If the central bank breaks the causal chain running from income to money, thereby making money exogenous, will the relationship of the two still remain close? Or might there be, particularly at cyclical turning points, a parting of the ways? In the background there always lurks the concern that excessive reliance on monetarist prescriptions might some day land us in a new depression.

There are doubts also about technical matters, such as the choice among monetary aggregates, the claim that lags are long but variable, the role of non-monetary influences. The difference between real and nominal money balances is troublesome. These are problems that only further experience and research can resolve.

Problems exist also about value judgments. Monetarism is not strongly concerned about some of the side effects of its prescriptions. It relies heavily on the belief that short-run costs may have to be accepted for the sake of long-run gains.

Finally, monetarism may find some elements of future evolution difficult to take in stride. One such development is the move toward an electronic payments system. If technology makes the holding of demand deposits largely unnecessary, the usefulness of M_1 certainly will suffer. Past experience may provide little guidance as to the relationship between income and the kind of balances or overdraft facilities that may exist in an electronic payments system. Conceivably, interest rates could regain their importance as a target relative to the money stock.

A second and quite unrelated development might occur in the international sphere, if the world economy becomes more integrated. The present tolerance for wide exchange rate movements might then diminish, as it already has within the EEC. Coordination of interest rate policies might become desirable as a means of averting large international flows with their attendant changes in exchange rates. This would interfere with the use of pure money supply targets.

These are long-run possibilities. It has been part of the strength of monetarism that it has always looked to the long run, believing that if fundamentals are right, the short runs will take care of themselves. This was not the view of Keynes, who argued that in the long run we are all dead. The fact is that the number of people alive in the long run keeps increasing. It is true that the long run is nothing but a succession of short runs. But it is true also that the measures taken to deal with short-run emergencies can accrue severe long run costs. Monetarism, by stressing this fact, has helped to restore a better balance between short- and long-run objectives.

11. References

Johnson, H. G., 1971, The Keynesian revolution and the monetarist counter-revolution, American Economic Review, May, pp. 1–14.
Khan, M. S., 1974, The stability of the demand for money function in the United States, 1901–1965, Journal of Political Economy, Nov./Dec., pp. 1205–1219.
Poole, W., 1970, Optimal choice of monetary policy instruments in a simple stochastic macro model, Quarterly Journal of Economics, May, pp. 197–217.
Stein, J., 1976, Inside the monetarist black box, in: J. Stein, ed., Monetarism (North-Holland, Amsterdam).

Chapter 14

Size, Sources and Beneficiaries of International Reserve Creation: 1970–74

Robert TRIFFIN

1. International Monetary Reserves: Why and What?

National currencies have long ceased to be "commodity currencies" (primarily gold and silver) acceptable beyond a country's borders on the basis of their market value. They are paper currencies or bank deposits, without any intrinsic value whatsoever and therefore normally acceptable in final payment only within each country's political borders.

Commercial banks and international so-called "arbitrage" operators provide a market in which each national currency can be readily exchanged by traders and investors for the settlement of international transactions requiring the conversion of the payor's currency into the payee's currency. These transactions, however, do not equilibrate from day to day, nor even over fairly long periods of time, and these disequilibria could result in substantial price – i.e., exchange rate – variations often deemed unnecessary and damaging both by private traders and by the official authorities. The institutions – usually "central banks", such as the Bank of Japan, the Bank of France, etc. – entrusted with the issue of the national currency are thus often called upon to intervene in the market in order to provide or redeem the national currency of the country and avoid exchange-rate fluctuations deemed unnecessary and damaging to the national interests as well as to international traders and investors.

In older days, they usually demanded in counterpart of such sales, or offered in counterpart of such redemptions, gold or a major world currency readily convertible into gold. This system has long come to an end in practice, and the stock of international monetary reserves used for the settlement of national surpluses and deficits in each country's balance of payments now includes, besides gold, national so-called "reserve currencies" (primarily sterling in former days, but overwhelmingly dollars and Euro-dollars today), no longer convertible into gold, and reserve claims on the International Monetary Fund (including Special Drawing Rights) and on the Bank for International Settlements.

2. Size and Sources of World Reserve Creation

Table 1[1] brings out, in the simplest possible form, a number of incontrovertible and striking facts of which the man in the street is blissfully unaware, although they have an enormous and devastating impact on his daily life.

2.1. The World Inflation

The basic roots of the world inflation in which all countries are engulfed today admittedly lie outside the monetary field. They are the growing shortages of food and raw materials that have emerged from 200 years of unprecedented increases in material production, no longer interrupted and slowed down since World War II by recurring cyclical recessions, and aggravated on the contrary by the incredible explosion of world military expenditures to well over $200 billion a year.[2] "Charging what the traffic will bear" has enabled more and more sectors of the economy to raise prices, profits and wages at an accelerated pace.

This being said, it remains nevertheless clear that price and wage increases could not have been transmitted to the whole world economy if they had not been underwritten and financed by "permissive", or "accommodating", rates of national *and international* monetary and credit expansion far exceeding what could be absorbed by actual increases in production.

2.2. Size of Reserve Increases

International reserve creation plays a crucial role in this respect since it determines the sum of the monetary reserves acquired by national central banks against corresponding issues by them of "high-powered" money, multiplied in turn by their commercial banks under the traditional system of fractional reserve requirements. Reserve creation increased, in fact, the world stock of international monetary reserves, measured in SDR's, by 100 billion – from 78 billion to 178 billion – from January 1, 1970 through December 21, 1974, i.e., by 128% or about 18% at an annual rate.

[1]All estimates are in SDR units, equal to the U.S. dollar before 1971.

[2]Economic as well as political considerations make it particularly difficult to finance military expenditures in non-inflationary fashion. This is undoubtedly one of the explanations of the spectacular post-war switch from an untractable "dollar shortage" to an equally untractable "dollar glut", as the main burden of military expenditures switched from Europe and Japan to the United States.

This fantastic expansion *well preceded* the oil price explosion of Fall 1973 and fueled the worldwide inflation of which oil prices are only one – and not the major – of the components. Measured in dollars, world reserves had already more than doubled over the years 1970–72, *increasing in this short span of three years by more than in all previous years and centuries since Adam and Eve.*

This has led nearly all countries in the world to stem the flood by the adoption of floating exchange rates, but persistent inflows of dollars and Euro-currencies are continuing, nevertheless, to increase world reserves at an inflationary pace. Measured in SDR's (see first column of five bottom lines of Table 1), gross reserves increased by 30% in 1971, slowing down to 12% in 1972 and less than 3% in 1973, but rising again by 18% in 1974. (Measured in dollars, they rose, of course, much more: by 41% in 1971, 21% in 1972, 15% in 1973, and 20% in 1974.) Floating rates are, at best, a counsel of despair and do not go to the root of the problem, which remains the ability of any country whose national currency is accepted as reserves by others to flood world reserve with its own IOU's. If such a process were not arrested, it would continue to fuel world inflation even if the energy problem could be solved tomorrow.

2.3. Sources of World Reserve Increases

The first column of Table 1 breaks down the total reserve creation of the last five years (1970–74) among its three component sources: (a) gold, (b) "concerted" reserve creation by international agencies, and (c) the acceptance of *national* currencies as *international* reserves.

(a) *Gold:* Physical increases in the world stock of official gold holdings (line I) have been insignificant throughout the period: 0.3 billion, i.e., 0.3% of the total. Their revaluation at current market prices, however, would probably result in unplanned, and potentially inflationary, bookkeeping profits of about $150 billion, or SDR's 120 billion, which obviously should – but will not necessarily – be sterilized by international agreement, and released only gradually for the financing of internationally agreed objectives.

(b) *International reserve creation:* The portion of reserve creation dependent on concerted international decisions (line II.A) has also been relatively insignificant: little over 7%.

Its major component – SDR allocations (line II.A.1) – increased world reserves by 9.3 billion over the three years 1970–72, but there have been no SDR allocations since January 1, 1972.

TABLE 1

SOURCES AND BENEFICIARIES OF INTERNATIONAL RESERVE CREATION: 1970–74 (IN BILLIONS OF SDR's = U.S. DOLLARS UNTIL 1971).[a]

		Developed countries			Less developed countries		
	World	U.S.	Other	Total	Total	OPEC	Other
I. *Balance-of-payments surpluses or deficits* (–) (= III–II)	*= Gold* 0.3	–66.2	22.5	–43.7	44.0	33.6	10.4
II. *Beneficiaries of credit reserve creation*	99.6	62.4	34.0	96.4	3.2	0.2	2.9
A. *of concerted reserve creation*	*7.3*	*1.2*	*2.8*	*4.2*	*3.2*	*0.2*	*2.9*
(1) SDR allocations	9.3	2.3	4.7	7.0	2.3	0.4	2.0
(2) Net IMF lending	–1.4	–1.0	–1.2	–2.2	0.9	–0.1	1.0
(3) Net BIS–EF lending	–0.6	–	–0.6	–0.6	–	–	–
B. *of acceptance of national currencies as international reserves*	*92.3*	*61.1*	*31.2*	*92.3*	–	–	–
III. *Gross reserves* (= I + II)	99.9	–3.9	56.5	52.7	47.2	33.9	13.3
at the end of: 1969	*78.1*	*17.0*	*45.7*	*62.6*	*15.5*	*4.2*	*11.3*
1970	92.4	14.5	60.0	74.5	18.0	5.0	13.0
1971	120.0	12.1	86.8	98.9	21.1	7.7	13.4
1972	145.6	12.1	104.7	116.8	28.8	10.0	18.8
1973	150.7	11.9	103.5	115.5	35.3	12.0	23.3
1974	*178.0*	*13.1*	*102.2*	*115.3*	62.7	*38.1*	24.6

[a]*Sources and Notes:*

(1) All these estimates are derived from the "International Reserves" Tables of the January (for 1969) and May 1975 issues of *International Financial Statistics*, and regrettably exclude Communist countries for which no reliable estimates are published.

(2) Net IMF lending (line II.A.2) is the sum of IMF "gold deposits and investments" and "use of fund credit" *minus* the undistributed profits of the IMF, allotted here *pro rata* of quotas: 23% to the U.S., 49% to other developed countries, 5% to OPEC and 23% to other less developed countries.

(3) Developed countries can be assumed to be the only beneficiaries of the Bank for International Settlements (BIS) and European Fund (EF) reserve credits (= excess of gold deposit liabilities over gold holdings) and of the accumulation of their national currencies as international reserves by foreign central banks.

(4) The conservative "guesstimate" of the U.S. share of reserve currency liabilities (2nd column of line II.B) includes only those reported as direct liabilities *plus* the liabilities of foreign branches of U.S. banks to official institutions reported in Table 19b of the *Federal Reserve Bulletin*. Liabilities to the BIS and the EF are not reported separately, but are included in the line II.B estimates.

(5) Balance-of-payments surpluses or deficits (line I) are measured by the difference between the increases in countries' gross reserves (line III) and in their reserve liabilities (line II). Their net total for the world as a whole is equal, by definition, to the increase in world gold reserves, including those of the IMF, BIS, and EF.

Robert Triffin, May 1975

The other two components – net IMF (line II.A.2) and BIS and European Fund (line II.A.3) lending – have been negative for the period as a whole, although net IMF lending rose by 3.7 billion in 1974, after declining sharply in the previous three years from 4.4 billion at the end of 1969 to less than 0.3 billion at the end of 1973.

(c) *Direct financing of reserve-center countries*: The acceptance of *national* so-called "reserve currencies" in settlement of balance-of-payments surpluses and their retention by foreign central banks as *international* reserves (line II.B) accounts for most of the unplanned and inflationary reserve increases of these five years: 92.3 billion, or 92% of the 99.9 total. The generalization of floating rates, in March 1973, has not brought any change in this respect, the proportion of reserve currencies in total reserve increases continuing to hover around 90%.

3. Beneficiaries of World Reserve Creation

Line II of the fourth and fifth columns of Table 1 indicates how reserve creation was distributed between the developed and the less developed countries. The former received 96.4 billion (97%) of the 99.6 billion of loans and investments financed by international reserve creation, and the latter 3.2 billion (3%).

Particularly noteworthy is the fact that these reserve loans and investments enabled the developed countries to finance overall balance-of-payments deficits totalling 43.7 billion (as measured by their losses of *net* reserves, shown on line I), but exceeded these deficits by 52.7 billion which they added to their *gross* reserves (line III), nearly doubling them over these five years, and contributing to their domestic monetary inflation.

Published estimates unfortunately make it well nigh impossible to break down this financing between the major reserve-center countries, and particularly between the United States and the others. They identify about half ($60.6 billion) of the $120.3 billion growth of foreign exchange reserves as liabilities of the United States, and $2.2 billion as liabilities of the United Kingdom, but do not break down the residual $57.5 billion difference between recorded foreign exchange assets and liabilities increases. The breakdown presented in the second and third columns of Table 1 is therefore highly conjectural. It merely adds to reported direct U.S. liabilities to foreign official institutions the reported liabilities of foreign branches of U.S. banks to the same institutions – less than half of the "identified official Euro-dollar holdings" reported for the years

1969–1973 on p. 39 of the IMF *Annual Report* – and ascribes all the remaining residual to other developed countries.[3] This probably underestimates substantially U.S. liabilities and overestimates correspondingly the liabilities of these other countries. Yet, it shows the increase of U.S. liabilities as two thirds of the total increase in reserve currency holdings (line II.B) and the total loans and investments received by the United States (line II) as having financed more than 94% (62.4 billion) of the cumulative U.S. deficits over these five years (line I: 66.2 billion).[4]

Two striking observations emerge from this dismal record:

(1) International reserve creation – particularly the acceptance of national currencies as international reserves – has been over these years the main source, by far, of frustration of the much vaunted process of balance-of-payments adjustment, as well as a major engine of world inflation. It enabled the reserve-currency countries (primarily the United States) to run enormous and persistent deficits which they could not have sustained otherwise, and it enabled the other countries (primarily Western Europe and Japan) to run equally huge and persistent surpluses inflating their own economies, without forcing upon either group of countries timely and appropriate changes in either their domestic policies, or their exchange rates, or both.

(2) Secondly, this lending and investment pattern ran directly contrary to the often repeated pious resolutions of the United Nations calling for an acceleration of capital exports from the richest and most capitalized countries to the poorest and least capitalized ones. The lending and investment mechanism most fully controlled by national and international monetary authorities was used in exactly the reverse direction, bringing coals to Newcastle.

It admittedly contributed to the ability of the recipient countries to expand their loans and investments in the Third World,[5] but in amounts and directions determined unilaterally by them, on the basis of political as

[3]Reserve holdings of LDC's currencies may safely be assumed to have been nil or insignificant up to now, but might conceivably include in the future some "strong" OPEC currencies.

[4]In the last two years of generalized floating rates, they even overfinanced the U.S. deficits, adding 1 billion to the U.S. gross reserves. Note also that the depreciation of the dollar in terms of SDR's entailed net foreign exchange losses of $5.3 billion for the other developed countries, and of $12.4 billion for the less developed countries (as measured by the difference in their *net* foreign exchange assets calculated in U.S. dollars and in SDR's, at the end of 1974).

[5]And even to overfinance these countries' actual current account deficits, enabling them to quadruple their meager international reserves (see bottom lines of fifth column).

well as economic and humanitarian considerations. A substantial portion of these credits, moreover, could also be diverted to other aims – such as military escalation and the take-over of foreign enterprises through unrequited direct investments – which could hardly be regarded as serving the highest-priority objectives of the international community or of the main reserve lenders.

4. Policy Conclusions

These incontrovertible facts amply confirm the major conclusions around which a broad consensus among public officials had emerged, after more than ten years of debates and negotiations, about the imperative need for basic international monetary reform. In brief:

(1) Reserve creation should aim at adjusting the expansion of world reserves to the requirements of feasible, non-inflationary, real growth in world trade and production. It should take primarily the form of international reserve deposits with the IMF – broadly similar to, but more flexible and attractive than, the present SDR's – whose amounts would be collectively concerted and decided by the international community.

(2) The lending power derived from the acceptance of such IMF reserve deposits in settlement by the surplus countries should be used for collectively concerted and agreed objectives, including *among others* the financing of development of the Third World.

(3) This should entail – to use the official jargon – the "phasing out" of gold and, particularly, of *national* "reserve currencies" from the international settlement and reserve system, and help restore desirable pressures for balance-of-payments adjustment.

(4) It should also reduce to a more manageable size, and facilitate, the official "recycling" of the disruptive movements of private capital prompted by exchange-rate speculation and which are largely responsible for the wild, reversible, and excessive fluctuations of exchange rates in recent years and months.

(5) The other measures necessary to the reconstruction of a viable world monetary order could hardly be negotiated in the absence of agreement on these basic reforms. Let us note, particularly, that their earlier adoption and implementation would have prevented the wild world inflation which led to the excessive explosion of oil prices, and would have provided in any case the most appropriate mechanism for the investment and "recycling" of the temporary surpluses of the oil-exporting countries, as well as of those of all other countries.

This makes all the more bizarre and regrettable – no matter how understandable in the present context – the decision of the officials to postpone, rather than accelerate, the basic monetary reforms which they had repeatedly and rightly proclaimed to be as urgent as imperative, in view of the utter collapse of the Bretton–Woods system due to their former procrastination in this respect.

(6) In the months – and, alas, probably years – immediately ahead, we should bend all our efforts: (a) to accelerate worldwide agreement on, and implementation of, the international monetary reforms repeatedly endorsed in principle by the IMF and the Committee of XX; and (b) to spur, in the meantime, their adoption and implementation by all countries prepared to do so, and particularly, the efforts of existing, or emerging, regional groups – such as the European Community, the Central American countries, the Andean countries, the ECAFE countries, etc. – to accelerate their progress toward closer economic and monetary cooperation and integration.

The prospects for early action in all these respects are admittedly dim at the moment. We might find some encouragement, however, in the fact that the unforeseen often happens, as admitted in a notice published a few years ago by the London *Times*:

> "The meeting called for next Tuesday night by the Clairvoyance Society of Sussex must regrettably be called off because of unforeseen circumstances."

5. Statistical Annex

The people who did not begin to work on international reserve problems until 1947 – 28 years ago – are blissfully unaware of the "breakthrough" which are the publication of *International Financial Statistics* constituted for their elders.

Yet, the information lucidly and comprehensively presented in its "International Reserves" tables fails to convey to the average reader the main highlights and significance of the actual functioning of the international monetary system which broke down in 1971 and of the "system" – if it still deserves that name – which has succeeded it. The main reasons for this are that:

(1) The breakdown of international reserves into its present *components* – gold, SDR's, reserve positions in the Fund, and foreign exchange – fails to highlight the *sources* of reserve creation. Countries' SDR holdings and reserve positions in the Fund are acquired in two very different manners: (a) through international *credit* operations, i.e., the initial allocations of SDR's and the *net* loans and investments of the

TABLE 2

SOURCES AND DISTRIBUTION OF INTERNATIONAL MONETARY RESERVES: 1937–74 (IN BILLIONS OF SDR's = U.S. DOLLARS BEFORE 1971).

End of year	World	Developed countries			Less developed countries		
		U.S.	Other	Total	Total	OPEC	Other
1937							
A. *Reserve assets* (= B + C)	*27.7*	*12.8*	*12.6*	*25.4*	*2.3*		
B. *Reserve liabilities* = foreign exchange	*2.4*	*0.4*	*1.9*	*2.4*	–		
C. *Net reserves* (= A – B)	*25.3*	*12.4*	*10.6*	*23.0*	*2.3*		
1949							
A. *Reserve assets*	*46.1*	*26.0*	*11.3*	*37.4*	*8.8*	*1.2*	*7.5*
B. *Reserve liabilities*	*11.3*	3.4	*7.9*	*11.2*	*0.1*	–	*0.1*
(1) Foreign exchange	11.2	3.4	7.8	11.2	–	–	–
(2) IMF credits	0.2	–	0.1	0.1	0.1	–	0.1
(3) BIS credits	−0.1	–	−0.1	−0.1	–	–	–
C. *Net reserves*	*34.8*	*22.7*	*3.5*	*26.1*	*8.7*	*1.2*	*7.4*
1959							
A. *Reserve assets*	*57.6*	*21.5*	*26.3*	*47.8*	*9.8*	*2.7*	*7.1*
B. *Reserve liabilities*	*17.4*	*10.6*	*6.5*	*17.1*	*0.3*	–	*0.3*
(1) Foreign exchange	16.4	10.1	6.3	16.4	–	–	–
(2) IMF credits	0.8	0.5	–	0.5	0.3	–	0.3
(3) BIS–EF credits	0.1	–	0.1	0.1	–	–	–
C. *Net reserves*	*40.2*	*10.9*	*19.9*	*30.8*	*9.4*	*2.7*	*6.8*
1969							
A. *Reserve assets*	*78.1*	*17.0*	*45.7*	*62.6*	*15.5*	*4.2*	*11.3*

B. *Reserve liabilities*	*37.1*	*18.7*	*17.4*	*36.1*	*1.0*	*0.1*	*0.9*
(1) Foreign exchange	32.3	17.9	14.4	32.3	–	–	–
(2) IMF credits	4.4	0.9	2.6	3.4	1.0	0.1	0.9
(3) BIS–EF credits	0.4	–	0.4	0.4	–	–	–
C. *Net reserves*	*41.0*	*−1.8*	*28.3*	*26.5*	*14.5*	*4.1*	*10.3*
1972							
A. *Reserve assets*	*145.6*	*12.1*	*104.7*	*116.8*	*28.8*	*10.0*	*18.8*
B. *Reserve liabilities*	*104.2*	*66.5*	*34.6*	*101.1*	*3.1*	*0.5*	*2.7*
(1) Foreign exchange	94.8	64.4	30.5	94.8	–	–	–
(2) SDR allocations	9.3	2.3	4.7	7.0	2.3	0.4	2.0
(3) IMF credits	0.3	−0.2	−0.3	−0.5	0.8	0.1	0.7
(4) BIS–EF credits	−0.2	–	−0.2	−0.2	–	–	–
C. *Net reserves*	*41.4*	*−54.4*	*70.1*	*15.7*	*25.6*	*9.5*	*16.1*
1973							
A. *Reserve assets*	*150.7*	*11.9*	*103.5*	*115.5*	*35.3*	*12.0*	*23.3*
B. *Reserve liabilities*	*109.4*	*66.0*	*40.3*	*106.3*	*3.1*	*0.4*	*2.7*
(1) Foreign exchange	100.0	63.9	36.1	100.0	–	–	–
(2) SDR allocations	9.3	2.3	4.7	7.0	2.3	0.4	2.0
(3) IMF credits	0.3	−0.2	−0.3	−0.5	0.8	–	0.8
(4) BIS credits	−0.2	–	−0.2	−0.2	–	–	–
C. *Net reserves*	*41.3*	*−54.1*	*63.3*	*9.2*	*32.2*	*11.7*	*20.5*
1974							
A. *Reserve assets*	*178.0*	*13.1*	*102.2*	*115.3*	*62.7*	*38.1*	*24.6*
B. *Reserve liabilities*	*136.7*	*81.1*	*51.4*	*132.5*	*4.2*	*0.3*	*3.8*
(1) Foreign exchange	124.6	79.0	45.6	124.6	–	–	–
(2) SDR allocations	9.3	2.3	4.7	7.0	2.3	0.4	2.0
(3) IMF credits	3.0	−0.2	1.3	1.2	1.8	–	1.9
(4) BIS credits	−0.2	–	−0.2	−0.2	–	–	–
C. *Net reserves*	*41.3*	*−68.0*	*50.8*	*−17.2*	*58.5*	*37.7*	*20.7*

TABLE 3

SOURCES AND BENEFICIARIES OF INTERNATIONAL RESERVE CREATION: 1949–74 (IN BILLIONS OF SDR's = U.S. DOLLARS BEFORE 1971).

	Developed countries				Less developed countries		
	World	U.S.	Other	Total	Total	OPEC	Other
I. *Gross reserve increases*	*131.9*	*−12.9*	*90.9*	*77.9*	*53.9*	*36.9*	*17.1*
1950–59	11.5	−4.5	15.0	10.4	1.0	1.5	−0.4
1960–69	20.5	−4.5	19.4	14.8	5.7	1.5	4.2
1970–74:	*99.9*	*−3.9*	*56.5*	*52.7*	*47.2*	*33.9*	*13.3*
1970–72	67.5	−4.9	59.0	54.2	13.3	5.8	7.5
1973	5.1	−0.2	−1.2	−1.3	6.5	2.0	4.5
1974	27.3	1.2	−1.3	−0.2	27.4	26.1	1.3
II. *Credit reserve increases*	*125.4*	*77.7*	*43.5*	*121.3*	*4.1*	*0.3*	*3.7*
1950–59	6.1	7.2	−1.4	5.9	0.2	–	0.2
1960–69	19.7	8.1	10.9	19.0	0.7	0.1	0.6
1970–74:	*99.6*	*62.4*	*34.0*	*96.4*	*3.2*	*0.2*	*2.9*
1970–72	67.1	47.8	17.2	65.0	2.1	0.4	1.8
1973	5.2	−0.5	5.7	5.2	–	−0.1	–
1974	27.3	15.1	11.1	26.2	1.1	−0.1	1.1
A. *Concerted reserve creation*	*12.0*	*2.1*	*5.8*	*8.0*	*4.1*	*0.3*	*3.7*
1950–59	0.8	0.5	0.1	0.6	0.2	–	0.2
1960–69	3.9	0.4	2.9	3.2	0.7	0.1	0.6
1970–74:	*7.3*	*1.2*	*2.8*	*4.2*	*3.2*	*0.2*	*2.9*
1970–72	4.6	1.2	1.2	2.5	2.1	0.4	1.8
1973	–	–	–	–	–	−0.1	–
1974	2.7	–	1.6	1.7	1.1	−0.1	1.1

B. *Use of national currencies as international reserves*	*131.4*	*75.6*	*37.8*	*113.4*	–	–	–
1950–59	5.2	6.7	−1.5	5.2	–	–	–
1960–69	15.9	7.8	8.1	15.9	–	–	–
1970–74:	*92.3*	*61.1*	*31.2*	*92.3*	–	–	–
1970–72	62.5	46.5	16.1	62.5	–	–	–
1973	5.2	−0.5	5.6	5.2	–	–	–
1974	24.6	15.1	9.5	24.6	–	–	–
III. *Balance-of-payments surpluses or deficits* (–) (=I – II)	*6.5*	*−90.7*	*47.3*	*−43.3*	*49.8*	*36.6*	*13.4*
1950–59	5.4	−11.8	16.4	4.7	0.8	1.5	−0.6
1960–69	0.8	−12.7	8.4	−4.2	5.1	1.4	3.6
1970–74:	*0.3*	*−66.2*	*22.5*	*−43.7*	*44.0*	*33.6*	*10.4*
1970–72	0.4	−52.6	41.8	−10.8	11.1	5.4	5.8
1973	−0.1	0.3	−6.8	−6.5	6.6	2.2	4.4
1974	–	−13.9	−12.5	−26.4	26.3	26.0	0.2

Fund; (b) through mere *transfers* of previously outstanding gold and SDR reserves between member countries and the Fund, leaving *total* reserves unaffected.

(2) Nearly half of the largest component by far of reserve creation (90% or more in recent years), i.e., foreign exchange, appears as a mere "residual" item between the reported foreign exchange *assets* of member countries, on the one hand, and the reported *direct* liabilities of only the U.S. and the U.K. to foreign monetary or official institutions, on the other. This "residual" jumbles together other, *indirect* – Euro-currency or Xeno-currency – liabilities of the same two countries to the same institutions, the reserve liabilities of other countries, and all sorts of "errors and omissions".

Table 1 in the text integrates in highly simplified form:

(1) The sources – rather than the components – of reserve creation over the last five years, i.e.: (a) the increase in *world* gold reserves – including those of the IMF, the BIS and the now defunct European Fund –, (b) the full, *initial* allocations of SDR's, even if later transferred to the Fund, (c) the *net* credit and investment operations of the Fund, the BIS, and the European Fund, and (d) last, but *foremost*, the accumulation of *national* currencies as *international* reserves (labelled "foreign exchange" in IFS statistics).

(2) An attempt to break down between the United States and other – presumably developed – countries the various reserve liabilities which have fed the bulk of the gross reserve increases of the world over the last five years, and particularly the liabilities derived from the accumulation of reserve currencies.

(3) The *overall* balance-of-payments surpluses, or deficits, of the United States, other developed countries, the OPEC countries and other less developed countries, as reflected in their gains, or losses, of gross reserves, on the one hand (line III), and their decreased, or increased, reserve liabilities, on the other (line II).

The sources of these guesstimates are summarized at the bottom of Table 1, and their significance for the analysis of the functioning of the international monetary system brought out in the text.

The two "working tables" give fuller information, from which Table 1 was calculated, for various years back to 1937. Table 3, on "period changes", merely records the differences between the "end of year" estimates of Table 2.

Sources and notes would be the same as for Table 1, except that the estimates for 1949 and 1959 are taken from the *1972 Supplement* of *International Financial Statistics*, and those for 1937 from the *Supplement to 1963/1964 Issues.*

Chapter 15

*Stagflation: An Analysis of its Causes and Cures**

Gottfried HABERLER

1. Introduction

Stagflation, the combination of inflation and high and rising unemployment, which in 1974 has hit the Western industrial countries, especially the United States, is a new phenomenon as far as I know – at least on its present scale. In the past, periods of rising prices have been periods of low or falling unemployment.[1] Periods of recession or depression were characterized by falling prices. Early symptoms of the new disease – stagflation – became visible when during the post World War II recessions prices failed to decline.

Stagflation poses a disagreeable dilemma for macroeconomic policy: If it fights recession by expansionary fiscal or monetary measures, it intensifies inflation; if it fights inflation by contractive measures, it accentuates the recessions. A change in the fiscal–monetary mix in no way reduces the embarassment of the dilemma. Whether incomes policy offers a cure will be discussed later. In the old fashioned "classical" recessions and depressions the dilemma did not exist.[2] When prices were declining, macroeconomic expansionary measures counteracted the recession and merely stopped the price fall or at worst led to a mild increase in the price level.

I shall now discuss the causes of the new disease and then derive some

*Written in June 1975.

[1]In this paper when speaking of "prices", I mean consumer prices and inflation is defined in terms of the consumer price index.

[2]Owing to the typical lag of prices behind output at the upper turning point of the cycle, it is possible in some earlier cycles to identify a short period of stagflation, output and employment already falling while prices are still rising.

John R. Meyer and David H. Weinberg, in an elaborate econometric study, have found such short periods of stagflation in recent business cycles. They say, however, that "the stagflation phase seems ephemeral, not appearing in the business cycles of the mid and late 1950's . . . Omission of a stagflation phase seems even more a characteristic of the cyclical experience of the interwar years." [See Meyer and Weinberg (1975, p. 191).] This study covers the period February 1947 to September 1973, that is to say *before* stagflation on a large scale made its appearance. Broadly speaking, their findings seem to confirm my statement in the text.

conclusions about possible cures by applying the analysis to the problems confronting American policy-makers in spring of 1975.

2. The Causes of Stagflation

I maintain that stagflation is the predictable consequence of prolonged inflation. The United States and the world at large have lived under more or less continuous inflation ever since the end of the Great Depression of the 1930's. The incessant rise in the price level was only occasionally slowed down or briefly interrupted by an uneasy price stability in recessions.

It is well known that every prolonged inflation tends to become cumulative and to accelerate. This does, of course, not mean that every creeping inflation must inexorably become a trotting and a galloping one. What it does mean is that to provide the same stimulus inflation must accelerate. The reason is that prolonged inflation generates inflationary expectations: Nominal interest rates rise because borrowers and lenders expect higher prices; unions press for higher wages to protect their members from the expected price rise; businessmen place orders ahead of time and accumulate inventories, etc. Expectations of price rises may even run ahead of reality which is essentially an unstable situation. No wonder that sooner or later a stage is reached where a slowdown of the rate of inflation, or perhaps a mere reduction in its rate of acceleration, leads to unemployment and recession. If most people expect prices to rise at 15% and the actual price rise then turns out to be only 7 or 8%, the consequence for the economy will be the same as a complete stop of inflation would have had at an earlier stage. This is stagflation.[3]

Stagflation like any other inflation is a monetary phenomenon in the sense that there has never been a substantial inflation for a substantial period without a substantial increase in the quantity of money and that no inflation can be stopped without restraint on monetary growth.

But this monetarist statement has to be interpreted with care. First it does, of course, not mean that there is a precise parallelism between *M* and *P*, or between *M* and money GNP (*PT* in the quantity equation). In other words *V*, the velocity of circulation of money, is not a constant; it is subject to cyclical and other short-run changes and tends to rise in an

[3]In other words a generally *anticipated* inflation has no stimulating power. The opposite is also true: An *anticipated* deflation (decline of the price level) need not be a depressant. F. A. von Hayek has always stressed this distinction. See his comprehensive discussion of how inflation breeds depression – von Hayek (1960, ch. 21). See also the excellent interpretive article by Spencer (1975).

inflation. But it certainly is not a highly volatile or perfectly plastic substance as the Keynesians assume. It is only under extreme circumstances, such as hyperinflation or war-time rationing and price controls, that it moves out of a fairly narrow range. But this subject will not be further discussed in the present paper, because that has been done extensively in the monetary literature.

Second, the monetarist position should not preclude going behind the proximate cause of inflation, the increase in M. On the contrary it is important to identify the economic, social and political reasons why in our time the monetary authorities practically everywhere have increasingly pursued inflationary policies and why they have not successfully resisted the pressures to over-expand the money supply.

Third and last, but not least, the monetarist position should not be interpreted to mean that an effective anti-inflation or anti-recession policy should always confine itself to strictly monetary measures, that is to say to a regulation of the money supply. On the contrary, situations often arise in which an economically effective and politically acceptable and feasible anti-inflation policy must deal with some of the factors that account for the inflationary bias of monetary policy. Anti-recession policy, too, may have to go beyond monetary measures.

Several factors account for the modern inflationary bias in economic policy. The most important ones would seem to be these: There is *first* the change in the intellectual climate, especially the rise of Keynesianism with its stress on full employment and neglect of money.[4] Money and monetary policy had to be "rediscovered" in the post-war period, but the rediscovery of money was slow in coming and in some countries, especially in Great Britain, has not yet decisively influenced monetary policy.

There is, secondly, the enormous growth of the public sector in the economy. Everywhere the state absorbs a larger and larger part of total output of goods and services for its own purposes, many of them of an unproductive or counterproductive nature. In addition there are huge transfers of income through social security, welfare payments, etc. All this results in an ever-increasing tax burden.

The direct influence of this development on inflation is that the frequent large deficits of the government budget and of public enterprises often are financed by the banking system, i.e., by creating money – either because

[4]Unlike his followers, Keynes hardly wanted to relegate monetary policy to the scrap heap and at any rate would have rediscovered money before long. But it is a fact that, in Sir John Hicks' words (1974, pp. 31–32), Keynes' "followers . . . conclude from what he says [that] there is nothing important that can be done with monetary policy. . . . Keynesianism in practice has become fiscalism."

there is some real or imagined unemployment and slack in the economy which has to be counteracted, or because financing by non-inflationary means, i.e., by selling bonds to the public rather than to the banking system would drive up interest rates and "crowd out", that is reduce, private investment. Furthermore the enormous growth of the public sector and the heavy tax burden blunt incentives to save and to work and discourage enterpreneurial activities and investments – thus slowing down productivity growth and reducing the ability of the economy to provide a rising standard of living. Slower growth collides with rising aspirations of the populace for higher living standards and increasing demands of labor unions and other pressure groups for higher wages and a larger share in the national product.

This brings me to the *third* factor accounting for the inflationary tendencies in the post-war world – a factor which is especially important for explaining the new phenomenon of stagflation. It is the fact that in an ever-increasing area the price mechanism has been made inoperative or severely restrained by private monopolies, especially by labor monopolies of labor unions, and by government policies. Money wages have become almost totally rigid downward. Wage rigidity downward (even without wage push) has an inflationary effect as von Hayek (1958, pp. 147–152) and Schultze (1959) have pointed out. But wage rigidity alone is hardly sufficient to explain a high rate of inflation. For its effect on the price level could be overcome by the gradual rise in productivity. Moreover rigidity cannot explain the fact that wages often not only fail to decline, but actually rise in the face of heavy unemployment. It is the wage push, added to downward rigidity, that accounts for most of the trouble.

How about business monopolies? The answer is that as far as inflation is concerned industrial monopolies have, in principle, the same effect as labor monopolies of unions: The replacement of competition by monopoly has a one-shot inflationary effect, monopolies and oligopolies reduce output and are likely to make prices rigid (especially ologopolies and cartels).[5] But in most modern industrial countries the power of business monopolies is small compared with that of labor unions – with two important exceptions, *first* the "natural monopolies" in the public utility area, and *second* the many cases where private monopolies or quasi-monopolies are fostered, protected or created by the state.

Public utilities everywhere are either owned and operated by the government or are closely controlled by government agencies. They have become a potent source of inflation, partly because they often greatly

[5]This does, however, not mean that business monopolies and labor monopolies by unions behave exactly alike.

contribute to government deficits (along with other nationalized industries), partly because industrial monopolies, whether in private or public hands, strengthen the position of labor unions. Unions naturally wish to participate in the monopoly profits.

Governments protect and create monopolies and otherwise restrict output and raise costs and prices in many different ways. Only a few cases can be mentioned here. The oil cartel of OPEC is a glaring example. Another conspicuous example is farm price supports. Since farmers are too numerous to organize themselves in monopolies, governments step in and make them behave more or less like monopolists. The American farm price support and the agricultural policies of the European Common Market (CAP) are the best known examples. Import restrictions through tariffs, quotas, the so-called "voluntary" restrictions on foreign exports of steel, textiles, etc., are powerful creators and protectors of domestic monopolies and oligopolies. Few private monopolies and oligopolies, outside the public utility area, could survive under free trade.

Another important area of government sponsored monopolies is the direct and indirect protection and encouragement of labor unions, supplemented by minimum wage laws, generous welfare payments and unemployment benefits (which make the strike weapon much more effective) and the like. Without direct and indirect support of the government, labor unions would not have acquired and could not retain the power they now wield in many industrial countries.

In the last few years the problem of government induced or enforced price and cost increases has come under closer scrutiny [Houthakker (1974), Moore (1972), Weidenbaum (1975) and Phillips (1975)]. The overall picture that emerges is this: Labor unions and other pressure groups, organized and protected by the government, press for wage and price boosts which imply increases in the income of their members that add up to a larger national total than the economy can produce. Inflation is then the method by which the inconsistent claims on the national product are scaled down to manageable proportions. The inflation process has been accurately described in these terms by von Hayek (1967, 1974a, 1974b), Lutz (1972) and Tobin (1972). In German it is called "Anspruchsinflation", "claims inflation". Tobin takes a relaxed view; he says complacently "there are worse methods of resolving group rivalries and social conflicts". Inflation has the great merit that it works "blindly, impartially and non-politically" [Tobin (1972, p. 13)]. Hayek and Lutz as well as William Fellner are alarmed by the prospect.[6] They know that, unless it accelerates, inflation will loose its stimulating effect and its power to reconcile

[6]William Fellner expressed his concern about inflation in many publications. See, for example, Fellner (1946, 1948).

inconsistent claims. Interest rates will rise, inventories will accumulate and investments speeded up to beat the expected price rise; and if labor unions and other pressure groups see their expectations again and again frustrated by rising prices, they surely will raise their monetary claims. The accelerating inflation of the last few years and the emergence of stagflation have proved the pessimists right. Tobin's optimistic speech was delivered in 1971, before those events.

Downward rigidity of wages and prices, and wage and price increases forced by labor unions and other pressure groups with the active help and encouragement of the government are then the basic causes of stagflation. In a competitive economy stagflation would be impossible, at least on a substantial scale; for under competition, when there is heavy unemployment, wages would fall and not go on rising as they do now.

Before continuing the main line of our argument we must pause briefly to consider an important recent theoretical development. What I have in mind is the modern microeconomic theory of inflation and unemployment which deals with the border region between the ideal competitive economy where wages and prices are perfectly flexible on the one hand, and the actual present-day monopoly-ridden and government-controlled economy on the other hand, where money wages have become almost totally rigid downward and many wages and prices are pushed up by union pressure and government action.[7]

The new microeconomic theory is a theory of "frictional" or "structural" unemployment. It describes and analyses in depth the working of an imperfect market where it often takes much time and money (income foregone while gathering information and searching for a suitable job) on the part of employees to find a new job, and on the part of employers to find a suitable candidate for a job vacancy. Suppose there is a drop in demand for a particular product. The theory demonstrates that, even in the absence of unions (and of money illusion), wages will not fall immediately to the market clearing level. On the contrary there may be a more or less protracted disequilibrium period with frictional unemployment. Employees will not immediately accept a lower money wage in their old employment (if that is an option) or elsewhere before they have gathered information about other opportunities.

Now suppose there is a *general* contraction in monetary demand. Then there will be widespread frictional unemployment, many people looking for a suitable job before accepting a cut in their money wage. It stands to reason that in that period of disequilibrium, the Keynesian distinction

[7]The *locus classicus* of the new theory is Phelps (1970). Other sources are Alchian and Allen (1967), Leijonhufud (1968), and Sweeney (1974). I have briefly discussed this development in my book *Economic Growth and Stability* (1974, pp. 205–210).

between "voluntary" and "involuntary" unemployment becomes somewhat blurred. It also is clear that liberal unemployment benefits and welfare payments, apart from strengthening union power and wage push, tend to lengthen the twilight zone of disequilibrium and to increase frictional unemployment, because workers can afford to search longer for a suitable job.[8]

To describe and analyze all these frictions and imperfections of the labor market is useful and enlightening. We should always keep in mind that the perfectly competitive market, where wages rapidly adjust to the market clearing level and where (involuntary) unemployment is absent, is an ideal type. In fact, few markets are perfect, but the labor market is less perfect than others. It does not follow, however, that the fact that unions have made wages almost totally rigid downward and that they exert a powerful wage push is unimportant; nor does it follow that there is no use to compare the present state of affairs with the ideal competitive market, nor that the distinction between voluntary and involuntary unemployment should be abandoned.[9]

Returning to our main argument, I shall continue to contrast the actual state of affairs with an ideal competitive market, while keeping in mind that even in the absence of labor unions, business monopolies and government regulations which prevent or impede the smooth functioning of the market, the competitive equilibrium is not continuously maintained. After it has been disturbed, the economy has to pass through a zone of disequilibrium with frictional and structural unemployment before equilibrium is fully restored.[10]

[8]Generous unemployment and welfare payments also create more or less spurious (voluntary) unemployment, because many people who really do not care for work (are not in the labor force) apply for and receive unemployment benefits and others are tempted to remain idle and to supplement the dole by moonlighting.

[9]The new microeconomic theory of unemployment has led to a re-interpretation of what Keynes really had in mind in his famous but puzzling definition of involuntary unemployment. For reasons explained in my book *Economic Growth and Stability* (1974, pp. 207–208), I find the new interpretation quite unconvincing.

[10]It goes without saying that macroeconomic monetary and fiscal measures should be used to prevent aggregate demand from contracting. This is generally accepted. Let me recall that Pigou, whom Keynes treated as the arch-classicist, made it quite clear that he was not "in favor of attacking the problem of unemployment by manipulating wages rather than by manipulating demand" through monetary and fiscal policies. In other words he did not want to rely on the Pigou effect to end a recession. [See Pigou (1945, p. V).] True, this was a post-Keynesian book. But Pigou had taken the same position in his earlier *Industrial Fluctuations* (1927). On Pigou's views see also Hutchison (1968, pp. 277–301).

Hayek, too, has made it clear that he does not recommend that the economy be put through the wringer of a general deflation ("actual shrinkage of total demand"), to eliminate a maladjustment. But he still stresses the importance of structural unemployment due to "real maladjustments" in the structure of production. [See von Hayek (1974a, p. 116) and (1975). The latter publication reproduces also Hayek's Nobel Memorial Prize Lecture "The Pretence of Knowledge".]

Before discussing the monetary implications of, and the monetarist objections to, what has been said, I shall briefly analyze a *fourth* factor that is widely held responsible, to a large extent, for the world inflation as well as the world recession in 1973–75. This is the so-called "special factors", the enormous rise in the price of crude oil, poor harvests, the Russian wheat sale and the devaluation of the dollar. I shall concentrate on the oil price rise. What is said about that applies *mutatis mutandis* also to the other special factors.

It will be instructive first to consider how things would work out in a competitive economy. The oil price rise can be described as a deterioration of the terms of trade, a levy, tax or reparations, in short a reduction in real GNP imposed by OPEC on the oil-importing countries. For the United States this burden is comparatively small, about 1½% of GNP.[11] If the money supply is managed in such a way as to stabilize the overall price level, prices of other commodities than those of oil and oil products would have to go down a little bit, and to maintain full employment money wages would have to decline slightly. Actually in our hypothetical competitive world the decline in wages (in the United States) would be minimal. Suspending the normal growth of wages for less than a year would take care of the problem.

Next assume *money* wages to be rigid downward. In that case an attempt to keep the price level constant when the oil price goes up would result in unemployment. This is the argument Arthur Burns used. He told a Congressional committee that the Fed could have kept the price level constant by depressing other prices; but this would have caused a recession. The implication was that the only acceptable alternative was to expand the money supply and to let the price level rise in order to bring about the unavoidable reduction in real incomes by inflation.

The logic of the argument is unexceptional. But as far as oil alone is concerned, in view of the small magnitude of the problem in relation to GNP, the unemployment involved by keeping the price level stable, as well as the price rise under the alternative policy, would be minimal. If the trouble were only wage rigidity (no wage push) a rise in the price level of, say, 1½% would have taken care of the problem.

It can be argued, however, that the forced transfer to OPEC was only one of several "special factors". Others were a similar transfer to

[11]It happens to be about equal to the average annual increase for the last few years of the U.S. government's purchases of goods and services. The oil burden is temporarily lightened by the backflow of petrodollars. (The reduction in the burden could even be permanent, if the petrodollars result in a *net* increase in productive investments.) For other countries the burden is, of course, higher. But I shall not discuss in this paper the international or balance-of-payments (international transfer) aspects of the problem. This has been done elsewhere.

domestic producers of oil and other fuels and a transfer to farmers, resulting from the rise of food prices which in turn was due to a poor crop and the devaluation of the dollar.[12]

Putting matters this way demonstrates that in the final analysis the special factor problem of inflation can be regarded as a special case of Hayek–Schultze inflation caused by downward wage rigidity: The special factors cause a shift in demand and its inflationary effect stems from the assymetrical impact of that shift: Money wages and money incomes are pulled up where demand has increased, but fail to decline where demand has decreased.[13]

However, downward rigidity of wages alone, without wage push, could allow only a small fraction of the actual inflation to be attributed to the "special factors". This follows from the fact that all "special factors" together account only for a small reduction in real GNP – perhaps 3%. Therefore, an inflation of only 3% would be sufficient to take care of the real transfers involved. Those who attribute a much larger inflationary effect to the special factors must have something else in mind.

What they have in mind is, I believe this: People nowadays do not easily accept a reduction in their real incomes.[14] Concretely, organized labor and other pressure groups react to a reduction in their real disposable income due to the rise in oil or food prices (or to something else, e.g., devaluation of the dollar or higher taxes) by demanding correspondingly higher money incomes. Thus the "special factor" inflation becomes a case of the "claims inflation" which we analyzed above. It puts heavy pressure on the monetary authorities to permit an inflationary expansion of the money supply by exposing them to the dilemma either to "cause" inflation by a permissive monetary policy or to stand firm and "cause" unemployment.

It is very important to keep in mind that the dilemma would *not* exist in

[12]The devaluation of the dollar is analytically on a par with the oil price rise because it, too, involves a reduction of real GNP and a real transfer to the outside world. This real burden consists of two parts, the "improvement" in the current balance (increase in exports and/or decrease in imports implying a reduction of "absorption" fewer goods being available for domestic consumption and investment) and a possible deterioration in the terms of trade.

[13]It could be argued that an international transfer (to OPEC) is different from a domestic transfer. This could be the case under fixed exchanges, but the situation is different under floating. At any rate, OPEC is a special case, because the OPEC countries are highly specialized, wide-open economies which makes the international transfer virtually automatic. However, as mentioned, the international aspects will *not* be discussed in the present paper.

[14]This is sometimes rather inaccurately described in terms that suggest the assumption of a marginal propensity to consume of one: Consumers may refuse to cut their consumption when their real income is reduced by the oil levy. That is, of course, not impossible. But the scenario sketched in the text would seem to be more plausible.

a competitive economy. Suppose the monetary authorities stand firm and refuse to increase the money supply. Only a monopoly (union) could permanently maintain a wage level that creates much unemployment.[15] In a free, competitive labor market wages would not rise if the rise spells unemployment, or, if wages had gone up too far, unemployment would drive them down. Needless to repeat, the same holds of other pressure groups.

What could happen in free, competitive labor market is that in case real wages have to decline because of rising oil prices, some workers may work fewer hours and that others withdraw from the labor force. But it is possible that workers would work longer hours to maintain their customary living standards. In technical terms, the supply curve of labor could be either negatively inclined ("backward bending") or positively inclined. If it is positively inclined the supply of labor would shrink, when the demand for labor contracts. However, this decrease in the labor supply would *not* constitute "involuntary" unemployment. It would have to be described as "voluntary" unemployment. At any rate, considering the small reduction of GNP decreed by the special factors the effect on aggregate labor supply would probably be negligible.[16]

Now the monetary aspects: Monetarists often deny that unions and other monopolists and pressure groups have anything to do with inflation. It is important to define clearly the area of agreement and disagreement. There is agreement that stagflation and cost push inflation like any other inflation is a monetary phenomenon. It could not arise without an increase in M. Furthermore, the cost push of pressure groups is often swamped by demand inflation and wages may lag behind the rise in prices. For example the entirely unforeseen inflationary explosion in 1973 was not caused by a sudden wage push. It was a monetary demand inflation of international

[15]William Fellner, too, attributes to labor unions the major responsibility for difficulties of adjustment: "In an economy in which labor is unorganized, or in which labor unions play merely a minor role, only a faint shadow of the problem to be discussed would exist." The problem he has in mind is that of balance-of-payments adjustment under fixed exchange rates [Fellner (1973)]. It is also in the best Chicago tradition to emphasize the role of monopolies, unions, rigid prices and wages as a major source of unemployment and thus indirectly of inflation (because unemployment puts heavy pressure on the monetary authorities to expand the money supply). Speaking of the business cycle Knight (1941) said: "In a free market these differential changes [in the prices of different types of goods] would be temporary, but even then they might be serious; and with important markets as unfree as they actually are – and prices as sticky and labor and capital as immobile – the *results take on the proportion of a social disaster.*" (Italics supplied.)

[16]The reader should keep in mind the qualifications to that statement concerning disequilibrium situations, imperfect markets and frictional unemployment which were discussed above.

scope. The simultaneous strong boom in all industrial countries[17] drove up commodity prices. The acceleration of inflation had started late in 1972, *before* the enormous oil price rise. Unions were taken by surprise like everybody else and their reactions were surprisingly slow. It is also true that inflation plays into the hands of unions and other pressure groups. Union militancy in recent years has been exacerbated by inflation and would abate, if inflation were brought under control.

But it remains true that the cost push by labor unions and other pressure groups has greatly contributed to the inflationary trend and is the greatest obstacle for regaining stability. For these pressures raise the level of what the monetarists call the "natural rate of unemployment" ("equilibrium rate" would be a better term) and make it greater than modern society is prepared to accept without fighting unemployment with expansionary measures.

It is very important to keep firmly in mind that we do not live in a static Walrasian world in which general equilibrium (including "natural" unemployment) is continuously maintained or, when disturbed, rapidly restored. Of course, no market is perfect, but it stands to reason that the fragmented labor market where in many sectors wages are set by a cumbersome, time-consuming process of collective bargaining, the imperfections are greater than elsewhere and the approach to equilibrium is very slow. Monetarists like to picture the wage push by unions as a *one-shot* transition from one Walrasian equilibrium to another with a higher "natural" rate of unemployment, whenever monopolistic unions are formed (or when their "market" power is increased). In the real world the wage push becomes a continuing multi-ratchattet, self-propelling dynamic process, kept going by union rivalries and leap-frogging.[18]

Again the monetarists are right that such an inflationary process could not continue without a permissive monetary policy. But the decentralized nature of the process, involving as it does many interacting markets, some unionized others not, with different often longish overlapping lags makes it impossible to distinguish between *natural* unemployment which the authorities should *not* try to reduce by monetary measures, and *general* (disequilibrium or recession) unemployment which can legitimately be alleviated by monetary expansion.

[17]In the United States real GNP rose at the unsustainable rate of 8–9% over the last quarter of 1972 and first quarter of 1973.

[18]The situation may be somewhat different, if labor is organized in one large union and the overall wage level is determined in one, country-wide collective contract. As far as labor in the narrower sense of non-agricultural workers is concerned this state of affairs may be approached in some countries, such as Sweden. But the social contract does not, as far as I know, extend to other pressure groups, such as government officials and agriculture.

This brings us to the last topic of this paper – the question of how to cure stagflation.

3. Cures for Stagflation

To repeat, stagflation confronts the policy-maker with a nasty dilemma: Macroeconomic measures of a fiscal or monetary nature against inflation accentuate the recession and macroeconomic measures against recession intensify the inflation.

American policy and policy discussions in the last two years clearly reflect the dilemma. First let me dispose of a confusion about means and ends that frequently mars the discussion. It is often argued that recessions – unemployment and lost output – are a greater evil than rising prices. I would not question this value judgment. Confronted with the choice between, say, 10% unemployment and 20 or even 50% inflation. I would choose inflation. But the value judgment in this general form is irrelevant. For this is not the relevant choice. As was explained earlier, inflation cannot be permanently staved off by unemployment. It will either cease to stimulate or it will accelerate and then sooner or later disrupt the economy and reduce output and living standards. In technical jargon, there is no permanent trade-off between inflation and unemployment. The Phillips curve will shift. The Annual Report of the Council of Economic Advisers February 1975 demonstrates statistically that it is "difficult to defend the claim of a long-run Phillip tradeoff between inflation and unemployment" (p. 96). It was also one of the themes of the February 1974 report. Professor Fellner was the principal author of these two reports. The German Council of Economic Advisers ("Sachverständigenrat") has made this the motto for their last annual report (Annual Report for 1974/1975, Full Employment for Tomorrow ("Vollbeschäftigung für Morgen"), p. VI): "The fight against permanent inflation is nothing but an attempt to guarantee full employment for tomorrow."

Until late in 1974 the official American policy was concerned with fighting inflation. Monetary policy which had been rather expansionary in 1971 and 1972 was gradually tightened, interest rates were allowed to rise sharply in 1973 and in June 1974 the Fed stepped harder on the brake. Criticism became louder and a series of public conferences culminated in a "Summit Conference" on inflation in the White House on September 27/28, 1975.

While the debate was in full swing the mild recession which had started late in 1973 suddenly deepened in the last quarter of 1974. Industrial production slumped and unemployment shot up. This sharp contraction, the sharpest in the post-war period, was not foreseen by anybody[19] and many people, prominent economists among them, were slow to recognize it after it had started. At the time of writing (June 1975) the economy seemed to be expanding again. The rate of inflation has come down faster then was generally expected at the beginning of the year (from about 13% late in 1974 to about 7% middle 1975), despite the fact that monetary and fiscal policy had been shifted around from fighting inflation to fighting recession.

Some of the major problems confronting the policy-maker at this juncture, on which there is a good deal of controversy, are those: *First*, is the current expansionary policy inflationary? Will the huge government deficit crowd out private investment? These questions are often answered in the negative on the Keynesian ground that there is a lot of unemployment and slack in the economy. *Second*, are fiscal measures really necessary to stop the recession? Monetarists deny it. They think that steady monetary expansion is a necessary and sufficient condition for regaining stability. *Third*, is it necessary to supplement macroeconomic policies (monetary and fiscal measures) by some microeconomic policies, such as income policy in some sense?

I now shall make some comments on the three issues in the light of what has been said above about the nature of stagflation. In this discussion we should firmly keep in mind, what it is often forgotten, that every recession and depression (and every boom for that matter), if it lasts long enough, becomes cumulative and feeds on itself. Milton Friedman puts it as follows: "There are such things as chain reactions and cumulative forces . . . [An] economic collapse often has the character of a cumulative process. Let it go beyond a certain point, and it will tend for a time to gain strength from its own development as its effects spread and return to intensify the process of collapse." He continues: "Because no great strength would be required to hold back the rock that starts the landslide, it does not follow that the landslide will not be of major proportions."[20] It follows that once the landslide has assumed large proportions, great strength will be required to stop it.

I would not call the economic slide since the autumn of 1974 a "landslide of major proportions" comparable to the Great Depression of the 1930's. But that it has already lasted longer and is more severe than

[19]There are, of course, always some people around who continuously predict a severe recession. Once in a while they happen to be right.

[20]Friedman and Schwartz (1963, p. 419). The authors speak at that point of the liquidity crisis and the collapse of the American banking system in the early 1930's. But recessions and depressions become cumulative long before they degenerate into a collapse.

the earlier post-war recessions (except perhaps the 1957–58 recession), and that it has become cumulative can hardly be doubted. This amounts to saying that the business cycle is still with us.

Now to the *first* point. To say flatly that at this time monetary expansion is not inflationary because there is much unemployment and slack in the economy overlooks the fact that we still have inflation despite much slack and unemployment. We are suffering not from a "classical" recession but from an inflationary recession (stagflation). The most one can hope for is that the cumulative force of the ongoing recession will reduce the rate of inflation further despite the shift towards expansion. In other words, if not overdone the expansionary policy may *not* be inflationary in the sense that the rate of inflation may still decline. But it certainly is inflationary in the sense that it slows down the deceleration of inflation. This reasoning provides at least a partial answer to the "crowding out" question: So long as the inflation is not intensified, there is probably no "crowding out". But if inflation accelerates again, because the expansionary stimulus is too large or is applied too long, interest rates will rise, monetary policy will probably become restrictive again and private investment, especially construction, will suffer.

We should keep in mind that the coming upswing, too, will be cumulative. William Fellner has often pointed out when he was a member of the Council of Economic Advisers that after the economy has turned the corner we can count up to a point on an automatic rebound: Inventories will have to be replenished, the stock of durable and semidurable goods will have to be increased again, etc. Therefore the fiscal stimulus should not be continued for too long.[21]

All this does, however, not mean that no fiscal stimulus should be applied. The economic and political risk of relying entirely on monetary policy (see below) and on the automatic stabilizers to stop the recessionary spiral are too large, especially in as much as the automatic stabilizers have been eroded by inflation.[22] I conclude that in view of the spiralling recession a tax cut was in order. But we should not loose sight of the inflationary risks that the expansionary policy involves.

Now the *second* point. Monetarists often argue that monetary policy is all and fiscal policy is nothing as far as counteracting recession or inflation is concerned. Monetarists are right when they insist that a budget deficit will have an expansionary effect only to the extent that it is financed by the banking system that is to say in an "inflationary" (antideflationary)

[21]This does not exclude that at a later stage a "fiscal drag" may develop, because of the progressivity of the tax system. Indexation of taxes would help to avoid that danger. See Fellner et al. (1975).

[22]On the erosion of the automatic stabilizers, see Fellner et al. (1975).

manner. If the governments bonds are sold to the public there will be no expansionary effect because it will not result in an increase in the money supply and in total spending. This statement will be accepted also by non-monetarists, but it requires some minor qualifications.[23]

The specific monetarist proposition is that it makes no difference, as far as total spending is concerned, whether the additional money is injected into the economy by financing of a government deficit or by open market operations.[24] This may be true in the long run or from static point of view, but it overlooks the short-run dynamics of the problem, that is to say the business cycle. To halt a recession, once it has acquired momentum, requires strong and quick action. Recall Friedman's story of the rock that starts a landslide. To stem the slide requires much strength, even if the rock that started it could have been held back with little effort. Injecting money directly into the income stream by financing a government deficit acts quicker, than an equal increase in the money supply through open market operations. After all as a *short-run* proposition there is some truth in the phrase, so beloved by central bankers and abhorred by monetarists, that "you cannot push on a string" or that "you can take the horse to the water but cannot make him drink if he does not want to".

[23]For example, a higher interest rate resulting from the bond sales may cause a rise in *V*. Milton Friedman has mentioned this qualification which should be acceptable also to Keynesians although they shun the word "velocity of circulation of money". Or it could be argued that if in an ongoing recession the government borrows from the public merely that part of their savings that otherwise would not be invested but hoarded, it would result in a net addition to GNP, not a crowding out of private investment.

The almost generally accepted proposition that a government deficit, in order to be effective in stimulating aggregate demand, must be financed, at least partly, by the banking system, conflicts sharply with the theory of Arthur B. Laffer and Robert A. Mundell that the proper stance of macroeconomic policy in the present recession is tight money and an expansionary budget. Mundell (1975) recommends a tax cut "of at least another $30 billion . . . on top of what has already occurred", i.e., of over $50 billion (implying a deficit of $100 billion or more) and "a very drastic slowdown in Federal Reserve open market purchases of securities". Mundell says that "the recession is partly due to excessively high tax rates" and that a cut in tax rates is required "to provide incentives to production".

As a *long-run* measure to promote investment, efficiency and growth there is much to be said for that proposal. But as a *short-run* recovery measure I find it quite unacceptable. Tight money would drive up interest rates, hit investment especially in housing and deprive the tax cut of its stimulating effect.

Probably to forestall the adverse impact of the tax cut on the credit market, interest rates and private investment, Arthur Laffer has recommended (at the Clairmont Monetary Conference, March 1975) that the tax cut be combined with a cut in government expenditures. Again, as a long-run policy there is much to be said for this proposal. But as a short-run recovery measure I find it entirely unacceptable (quite apart from considerations of political feasibility.) It would be the balanced-budget multiplier in reverse. Unlike the deficit multiplier, the balanced-budget multiplier is an exceedingly weak and unreliable reed to lean on in an anti-recession policy. But in reverse the balanced-budget multiplier is even worse – it would be perverse in its action.

[24]Subject to the qualifications mentioned in the preceeding footnote.

In the end the monetary stimulus surely would pull the economy out of the recession. But relying on monetary policy alone has not only obvious *political* risks – just think what Congress might do if the recession drags on – but involves also *economic* risks: Because of the slow action of monetary policy, a large monetary overhang may well develop which later on, after the economy has turned the corner, may become troublesome. This could happen, even if from now on the monetarist prescription of a steady monetary growth were followed to the letter. This shows that the business cycle can play surprising tricks.

The *third* major problem is, should macroeconomic policies be supplemented by microeconomic measures? There is a good chance that with the help of easier money and tax cuts the U.S. economy will soon emerge from the recession. In fact it may already have done so. But the danger is that the coming cyclical upswing will start with an inflation rate of 5 or 6% and not from zero as former cyclical recoveries.[25] True, in 1975 the rate of inflation has declined faster than had been generally expected. Also wage contracts have become a little more moderate. But wages are still rising much faster than what would be compatible with stable prices. Since money illusion has been pretty much eroded by inflation and unions and other pressure groups will be very eager to make up for income lost during the recession, the pressure for higher wages and other incomes will increase and inflation will probably accelerate faster than in past recoveries. If the Fed then tries to keep the rate of inflation down by tight money the recovery will be slow at best.

How can the dismal prospect be improved? Is incomes policy the answer? Yes or no, according to what one means by this ambiguous expression. The usual meaning of incomes policy is wage and price stops or general limitations on wage increases and guidelines. Wage and price freezes are not the answer; at best they can be defended as a very short-term measure in an acute emergency. The British economy is perhaps in such a crisis. Wage guidelines that try to make the wage *level* rise in proportion to the growth of average productivity are defensible as a *target*. For in a competitive economy with stable prices, wages would in fact rise on the average approximately in proportion to the average rise in labor productivity. But unfortunately the wage *level* is not a policy variable. The government cannot make the wage *level* behave in any particular way without interfering with the structure of *relative* wages. Therefore wage guidelines and price guidelines always degenerate quickly

[25]In the post-war period cyclical recoveries have shown a clear tendency to start from successively higher inflation rates as the last annual report of the Council of Economic Advisers has pointed out.

into detailed wage and price controls. There simply is no synthetic substitute for real competition.

Realizing the shortcomings of guidelines and wage and price stops, some writers speak of incomes policy not in the conventional sense of wage freezes, guidelines and the like, but as a bundle of measures designed to bring the economy closer to the competitive ideal. Arthur Burns had this kind of incomes policy in mind when in 1970 he asked that incomes policy be used to support monetary and fiscal restraint.[26] Since the government restricts competition in dozens of ways, there are plenty of opportunities for the government to make the economy more competitive: Deregulation of industry, abolition of minimum wages and of the Davis–Bacon Act, elimination of import quotas, tariffs and "voluntary" restrictions on foreign exporters, reduction of farm price supports and many others.[27] Negative measures of eliminating government policies that restrict competition should, of course, be supplemented by positive measures to promote competition such as the anti-trust policy. But the negative measures are, both economically and administratively (though not politically) easier to apply and more important than the positive measures.

The toughest problem will be how to restrain union power. I have no new proposals to offer for the solution of that problem. But let me suggest that, since labor and business monopolies often interact and reinforce each other, since business monopolies in the public utility area and elsewhere automatically strengthen union power, a policy of making the economy more competitive through deregulation of industry, freer trade, etc., etc., would also substantially reduce the power of labor unions.[28]

Incomes policy in that sense, "Incomes Policy II", is indeed the specific cure for stagflation (keeping in mind that monetary restraint is an indispensible condition). To repeat, in a competitive economy there would be no stagflation. Keynesians and monetarists might agree on that, each group using its own mode of analysis and professional jargon. Monetarists can admit that making the economy more competitive will reduce the rate of "natural unemployment", making it easier for the authorities to keep monetary growth on an even keel. Keynesians can say

[26] I have called this type of policy "Income Policy II". See Haberler (1971, 1974).

[27] See the lists compiled by Houthakker (1974), Moore (1972) and Weidenbaum (1975).

[28] This is probably the main reason why unions are usually moderate and responsible in small countries such as the Netherlands and Switzerland where most industries heavily depend on exports. Unions understand that it is hopeless to strike against highly competitive world markets. But there are of course also striking differences in the mood and aggressiveness of labor unions in different countries which are the result of historical evolution, social structures, etc., and defy any simple explanation in terms of a single factor such as size of the market.

that "Incomes Policy II" will improve the trade-off between inflation and unemployment.[29]

Each measure on the long list compiled by the authors mentioned earlier taken in isolation, would have only a negligible effect on stagflation. But a systematic policy of freeing the economy of the fetters and restrictions which have accumulated over the years would make the economy more flexible and responsive to macroeconomic guidance.[30] It would not eliminate the cyclical recessions, but it would make them shorter and milder.

If nothing or only little is done along those lines, the prospects are that we shall have more inflation, more unemployment, continuing stop and go, and more pronounced cyclical swings around a more steeply rising price trend. Sooner or later this will lead to the imposition of wage and price controls. Since the methods of evasion of the controls are well remembered from the recent bouts with controls, the chances are that, the next time around, the controls will be quickly followed by rationing, and mandatory allocation which will lead to progressive central planning and regimentation of the economy.

4. References

Alchian, A. A. and W. R. Allen, 1967, University economics, 2nd ed. (Belmont, CA).

Fellner, W., 1946, Monetary policies and full employment (Berkeley, CA).

Fellner, W., 1948, Employment theory and business cycles, in: H. S. Ellis, Survey of contemporary economics (American Economic Association, Philadelphia, PA).

Fellner, W., 1973, Controlled floating and the confused issue of money illusion, Banca Nazionale del Lavoro Quarterly Report no. 106, Sept. Also available as: Reprint no. 22 (American Enterprise Institute, Washington, DC) pp. 22–23.

Fellner, W., K. Clarkson and J. H. Moore, 1975, Correcting taxes for inflation (American Enterprise Institute, Washington, DC).

Friedman, M. and A. J. Schwartz, 1963, Monetary history of the United States 1867–1960 (New York).

[29]This is not to say that the Phillips curve and natural unemployment are the same thing. They are not. But abstracting from the analytical superstructure, both groups seem to be aiming at the same thing.

The role of monopolies in the inflation process has been analyzed and stressed by Herbert Giersch in two important papers [Giersch (1973, 1975)].

[30]A word about indexation: Indexation of progressive taxes would be very desirable. Indexation of wages will come anyway if inflation goes on. If introduced generally in agreement with the unions it may initially moderate the wage push but the chances are that unions will soon demand indexation routinely and continue to press for a larger share in the national income pie. Indexation does not stop wage push and claims inflation; it is in no way a substitute for a policy of making the economy more competitive, of supplementing macroeconomic policy by microeconomic measures. On the limits of indexation see especially William Fellner's "The Controversial Issue of Comprehensive Indexation" in Giersch et al. (1974). As mentioned earlier Fellner is in favor of correcting taxes for inflation.

Giersch, H., 1973, Some neglected aspects of inflation in the world economy, in: Public finance (The Hague).
Giersch, H., 1975, Freer trade for higher employment and price level stability, in: F. Bergsten, ed., Towards a new world trade policy: The Maidenhead papers (Lexington, MA).
Giersch, H., M. Friedman, W. Fellner, E. M. Bernstein and A. Kafka, 1974, Essays on inflation and indexation (American Enterprise Institute, Washington, DC).
Haberler, G., 1971, Incomes policy and inflation: An analysis of basic principles (American Enterprise Institute, Washington, DC).
Haberler, G., 1974, Economic growth and stability: An analysis of economic change and policy (Los Angeles).
Hayek, F. A. von, 1958, Inflation from downward inflexibility of wages, in: Committee for Economic Development, ed., Problems of U.S. economic development, vol. I (New York). Reprinted in: F. A. von Hayek, 1967, Studies in philosophy, politics, and economics (Chicago).
Hayek, F. A. von, 1960, The constitution of liberty (Chicago).
Hayek, F. A. von, 1967, Unions, inflation and profits, in: Studies in philosophy, politics, and economics (Chicago).
Hayek, F. A. von, 1974a, Inflation – The path to unemployment, in: Inflation – Causes, consequences, cures (Institute of Economic Affairs, London).
Hayek, F. A. von, 1974b, Zwölf Thesen zur Inflationsbekämpfung, Frankfurter Allgemeine Zeitung, Aug. 19.
Hayek, F. A. von, 1975, Full employment at any price? (Institute of Economic Affairs, London).
Hicks, J., 1974, The crisis of Keynesian economics (Oxford).
Houthakker, H. S., 1974, A positive way to fight inflation, Wall Street Journal, July 30.
Hutchison, T. W., 1968, Economics and economic policy in Great Britain 1946–1966 (London).
Knight, F. H., 1941, The business cycle, interest and money, Review of Economic Statistics XXIII, no. 2, May. Reprinted in: F. H. Knight, 1956, On the history and methods of economics, Selected essays (Chicago) p. 224.
Leijonhufud, A., 1968, On Keynesian economics and the economics of Keynes (New York).
Lutz, F., 1972, Dilemmasituationen nationaler Antiinflationspolitik, in: 25 Jahre Markwirtschaft in der Bundesrepublik Deutschland (Stuttgart).
Meyer, J. R. and D. H. Weinberg, 1975, On the classification of economic fluctuations, NBER Explorations in Economic Research 2, no. 2.
Moore, T. G., 1972, Freight transportation regulation and the interstate commerce commission (American Enterprise Institute, Washington, DC).
Mundell, R. A., 1975, World money and the optimum policy mix, Special Report, May (First National Bank of Chicago).
Phelps, E. S., ed., 1970, Microeconomic foundations of employment and inflation theory (New York).
Phillips, A., ed., 1975, Promoting competition in regulated markets (Brookings Institution, Washington, DC).
Pigou, A. C., 1927, Industrial fluctuations (London).
Pigou, A. C., 1945, Lapses from full employment (London).
Schultze, C. L., 1959, Recent inflation in the United States, Study Paper no. 1, Joint Economic Committee, 86th Congress, 1st Session (Government Printing Office, Washington, DC).
Spencer, R. W., 1975, Inflation, unemployment and Hayek, Federal Reserve Rank of St. Louis Review, May.
Sweeney, R. J., 1974, A macro theory with micro foundations (Cincinnati, OH).
Tobin, J., 1972, Inflation and unemployment, American Economic Review, March.
Weidenbaum, M. L., 1975, Government mandated price increases: A neglected aspect of inflation (American Enterprise Institute, Washington, DC).

Appendix

William John Fellner: Selected Writings

Books

A Treatise on War Inflation (study undertaken from Bureau of Business and Economic Research), University of California Press, Berkeley, CA, 1942.

Monetary Policies and Full Employment, University of California Press, Berkeley, CA, 1946.

Competition Among the Few: Oligopoly and Similar Market Structures, Alfred A. Knopf, New York, 1949.

Trends and Cycles in Economic Activity: An Introduction to Problems of Economic Growth, Holt, Rinehart & Winston, New York, 1956.

Emergence and Content of Modern Economic Analysis, McGraw-Hill, New York, 1960.

Probability and Profit, Irwin, Homewood, IL, 1965.

Towards a Reconstruction of Macroeconomics: Problems of Theory and Policy, American Enterprise Institute, Washington, DC, 1976.

Co-author of:

The Problem of Rising Prices (by an International Committee of Independent Experts), Organization for European Economic Cooperation, Paris, 1961.

Articles and Essays

"Alternative monetary approaches to interest theory", *Review of Economic Statistics*, February, 1941 (jointly with Harold M. Somers).

"The technological argument of the stagnation thesis", *Quarterly Journal of Economics*, August, 1941.

"External economies and diseconomies", *American Economic Review*, September, 1943 (jointly with Howard S. Ellis); reprinted in *Readings in Price Theory*.

"Postscript on war inflation", *American Economic Review*, March, 1947; reprinted in *Readings in Fiscal Policy*.

"Prices and wages under bilateral monopoly", *Quarterly Journal of Economics*, August, 1947.

"Employment theory and business cycles", in *A Survey of Contemporary Economics I*, 1948.

"The capital–output ratio in dynamic economics", in *Money, Trade and Economic Growth*, Essays in Honor of John H. Williams, 1951.

"The influence of market structure on technological progress", *Quarterly Journal of Economics*, November, 1951; reprinted in *Readings in Industrial Organization and Public Policy.*

"Long term tendencies in private capital formation: The rate of growth and capital coefficients", in *Long-Range Economic Projection* (Studies in Income and Wealth, vol. XVI), Report of the National Bureau of Economic Research, Princeton University Press, Princeton, NJ, 1954.

"Individual investment projects in growing economies: General characteristics of the problem and comments on the conference papers", in *Investment Criteria and Economic Growth*, Papers presented at a conference sponsored jointly by the Center for International Studies and the Social Science Research Council, Center for International Studies and the Social Science Research Council, Center for International Studies, M.I.T., Cambridge, MA, 1955.

"Post-war economic tendencies in the United States", in *The Business Cycle in the Post-War World*, Erik Lundberg, ed., International Economic Association, Macmillan, London/New York, 1955.

"Relative emphasis in tax policy on encouragement of consumption or investment", in *Federal Tax Policy for Economic Growth and Stability*, Joint Committee on the Economic Report, 84th Congress, Washington, DC, 1955.

"Patinkin's integration of monetary and value theory", *American Economic Review*, December, 1956.

"The balancing of objectives under the employment act of 1946", in *The Employment Act Past and Future*, Gerhard Colm, ed., National Planning Association, Special Report no. 41, Washington, DC, 1956.

"Quantitative sufficiency of innovations and proper distribution of their factor-saving effects" ("Sur la quantité suffisante d'innovations et la distribution correcte de leurs effets quant a l'économie des facteurs de la production"), *Economie Appliquée*, Summer, 1956.

"Marxian hypotheses and observable trends under capitalism: A modernized interpretation", *The Economic Journal*, March, 1957.

"Automatic market clearance and innovations in the theory of employment and growth", *Oxford Economic Papers*, June, 1958.

"Politics, economics, and recession", *The Yale Review*, Autumn, 1958.

"Possibilities of broadening the tax base, reducing tax rates and promoting economic growth", in *Tax Revision Compendium*, vol. 1, Compendium of papers on broadcasting the tax base submitted to the Committee on Ways and Means, November 16, 1959, United States Government Printing Office, Washington, DC, 1959.

"Demand inflation, cost inflation, and collective bargaining", in *The Public Stake in Union Power*, Philip D. Bradley, ed., University of Virginia Press, Charlottesville, VA, 1959.

"Relative permanent income: Elaboration and synthesis", *The Journal of Political Economy*, October, 1959.

"Appraisal of the labour-saving and capital-saving character of innovations," in *The Theory of Capital*, Proceedings of a Conference held by the International Economic Association, Macmillan, London, 1961.

"Two propositions in the theory of induced innovations", *Economic Journal*, June, 1961.

"Rapid growth as an objective of economic policy", *American Economic Review, Papers and Proceedings*, May, 1960.

"Distortion of subjective probabilities as a reaction to uncertainty", *Quarterly Journal of Economics*, November, 1961.

"Profit-maximization, utility-maximization, and the rate and direction of innovation", *American Economic Review, Papers and Proceedings*, May, 1966.

"The slanting of subjective probabilities: Agreement on some essentials", *Quarterly Journal of Economics*, November, 1966 (jointly with K. R. W. Brewer).

"Rules of the game, vintage 1966", and "On limited flexibility of exchange rates", in *Maintaining and Restoring Balance in International Payments*, W. Fellner, F. Machlup and R. Triffin, eds., Princeton University Press, Princeton, NJ, 1966.

"Operational utility: The theoretical background and a measurement", in *Ten Economic Studies in the Tradition of Irving Fisher*, New York, 1967.

"Measures of technological progress in the light of recent growth theories", *American Economic Review*, December, 1967.

"The adaptability and lasting significance of the Chamberlinian contribution, in *Monopolistic Competition Theory: Studies in Impact*, Robert E. Kuenne, ed., Wiley, New York, 1967.

"Specific interpretations of learning by doing", *Journal of Economic Theory*, Spring, 1969.

"Trends in the activities generating technological progress", *American Economic Review*, March, 1970.

"Specific proposal for limited exchange-rate flexibility", *Weltwirtschaftliches Archiv*, March, 1970.

"A 'realistic' note on threefold flexibility of exchange rates", in *Approaches to Greater Flexibility of Exchange Rates: The Bürgenstock Papers*, George N. Halm, ed., Princeton University Press, Princeton, NJ, 1970.

"Land in Fellner's model of economic growth: A rejoinder, *American Economic Review*, September, 1970.

"Empirical support for the theory of induced innovations", *Quarterly Journal of Economics*, February, 1971.

"Phillips-type approach or acceleration?", *Brookings Papers on Economic Activity*, no. 2, 1971.

Case for Moderation in the Economic Recovery of 1971, American Enterprise Institute, Washington, DC, 1971.

"The dollar's place in the international system: Suggested criteria for the appraisal of emerging views", *Journal of Economic Literature*, June, 1972.

Employment Policy at the Crossroads: An Interim Look at Pressures to be Resisted, American Enterprise Institute, Washington, DC, 1972.

"Controlled floating and the confused issue of money illusion", *Banca Nazionale del Lavoro Quarterly Review*, no. 106, 1973.

A New Look at Inflation: Economic Policy in the Early 1970s, American Enterprise Institute, Washington, DC, 1973.

"A strange expansion", *American Economic Review, Papers and Proceedings*, May, 1974.

Discussion Paper on "The payments adjustment process and the exchange rate regime", *American Economic Review, Papers and Proceedings*, May, 1975.

Correcting Taxes for Inflation, American Enterprise Institute, Washington, DC, 1975 (jointly with Kenneth W. Clarkson and John H. Moore).

"Lessons from the failure of demand management policies: A look at the theoretical foundations", *Journal of Economic Literature*, March, 1976.

Joint Editorship

Readings in the Theory of Income Distribution, The Blakiston Company, Philadelphia, PA, 1946 (jointly with Bernard F. Haley).

Author Index

Adelman, I. 12(n), 25(n), 230, 231
Ahluwalia, M. 54
Akerlof, G. 175(n)
Alchian, A. 101, 316(n), 328
Allen, W.R. 316(n), 328
Anand, S. 219(n), 231
Arrow, K.J. 177(n), 228, 231
Aumann, R.J. 177(n), 195, 200

Bach, G. 279(n)
Balassa, B. 217, 226, 227, 231
Barten, A.P. 231
Bartle, R.G. 144(n), 159
Becker, R. 139
Bell, C. 54(n)
Benson, F.B. 135
Bernstein, E.M. 329
Bertrand, J. 144, 145, 158, 159
Bless, R. 179, 200
Bowley, A.L. 139, 140, 150, 159
Brainard, W. 235, 238(n), 262
Brems, H. 145, 159
Brooks, R.B. 223, 232
Brown, A. 221(n), 223, 231
Buechley, R.W. 131(n), 134
Bulow, J. 235(n), 242(n), 262
Burns, A. 318(n), 237

Chamberlin, E.H. 140, 158, 159
Chandarvarkar, A.G. 41(n)
Chenery, H. 32(n), 54
Chow, G.C. 266(n), 277
Ciccolo, J. 243, 254, 261(n), 262
Clark, J.M. 58(n), 101
Clarkson, K. 328
Clay, G. 279(n)
Cohen, B. 30(n), 54
Cournot, A.A. 139, 140, 141, 141(n), 142, 143, 143(n), 144, 145, 147–153, 155, 156, 195
Creason, J.P. 135
Cyert, R.M. 149, 149(n), 159

Danvry, A. 223, 225, 232
Dasgupta, P. 217, 218, 231
Deaton, A. 221(n), 223, 231
Debreu, G. 143(n), 159, 194, 200, 201
De Groot, M. 149, 149(n)
Dorfman, R. 121
Dugger, R. 279(n), 292(n)
Duloy, J.H. 54

Edgeworth, F.Y. 144, 159
Ellis, H.S. 328

Fei, J.C.H. 39(n), 55
Feller, W. 97(n), 101
Fellner, W.J. 3, 25(n), 57, 57(n), 58(n), 69(n), 101, 139, 140, 155(n), 156, 158, 159, 220, 221, 221(n), 225, 230(n), 231, 232, 235, 315, 315(n), 320(n), 322, 324, 324(n), 328, 329, 331, 333
Fisher, F.M. 59(n), 101, 144, 159, 220, 231, 232
Fisher, I. 284
Fishlow, A. 51(n), 55
Foa, U.G. 183, 200
Frank, C.R. 143(n), 159
Freedman, J.J. 179, 200
Friedman, J. 139, 143(n), 154(n), 156–159
Friedman, M. 272, 273, 279, 279(n), 284, 291, 323(n), 325, 325(n), 328, 329
Friedricks, R.W. 179, 200
Frisch, R. 220, 221(n), 222, 222(n), 224, 225, 232

Giersch, H. 328(n), 329
Gimenez, M.E. 45(n), 55
Glasser, M. 132, 135
Goldsmith, R.W. 27(n), 34, 35(n), 45, 50, 50(n), 55

Goodman, L. 55
Grawe, R. 235(n)
Greenburg, L. 132, 135
Gurley, J.G. 27(n), 55

Haberler, G. 311, 327(n), 329
Hahn, F.H. 144, 159, 177(n), 188, 197, 200
Hamilton, W.D. 178, 200
Hammond, P. 177(n), 220
Harris, L. 279(n)
Harris, R. 263(n)
Hasselblad, V. 134
Hayek, F.A. von 235, 312(n), 317(n), 319
Hester, D. 279(n)
Hicks, J. 8, 25, 209, 313(n), 329
Hoa, T.V. 232
Horner, S. 57
Houthakker, H.S. 327(n), 329
Howrey, E.P. 266(n), 277
Hsieh, D. 235(n)
Hutchison, T.W. 317(n), 329

Inhaber, H. 135

Johnson, H. 293, 295
Johnson, K. 263(n)
Jolly, R. 54

Kafka, A. 329
Kalachek, E.D. 65(n), 101
Kamien, M.J. 60(n), 101
Keynes, J. 213, 235, 237, 239, 244, 273, 284, 294, 317(n)
Khan, M.S. 282, 295
Klein, L. 263, 265, 266, 277
Klein, S. 263
Knight, F.H. 103, 103(n), 107, 320(n), 329
Kuo, S.W. 39(n), 55
Kurz, M. 177, 188, 200

Laffer, A.B. 325(n)
Lancaster, K. 145, 160
Lave, L.B. 132(n), 135
Leijonhufud, A. 316(n), 329
Leontief, W. 98(n), 101, 155(n), 160
Lindsay, D. 279(n)
Little, I.M.D. 30, 30(n), 55, 217, 232
Lluch, C. 221, 223, 224, 224(n), 225, 226, 232
Luce, R.D. 200
Lutz, F. 315, 329

Machlup, F. 333
Mansfield, E. 67(n), 101
Marglin, S. 217, 231
Marx, K. 5(n), 20, 21, 21(n), 22, 23, 23(n), 24, 25, 25(n), 213
Mayer, T. 279(n)
McClain, K.E. 135
McKinnon, R.I. 27(n), 29(n), 55
McNulty, P.J. 58, 101
Meyer, J. 211(n), 329
Mill, J.S. 3, 15, 18(n), 19, 20, 25(n)
Minami, R. 38(n), 55
Mirrlees, J.A. 201, 215(n), 217, 232
Mohr, J.C.B. 232
Montoro, A.F. 50(n), 55
Moore, G.H. 264, 265, 267, 277, 315, 329
Moore, J.H. 328
Morgenstern, O. 151, 160, 220
Mundell, R. 325(n), 329
Myint, H. 13, 13(n), 14, 25(n)

Nagatani, K. 144, 160
Nash, J.F. 151, 157, 160, 189, 190, 191–193, 196, 198
Negishi, T. 153(n), 160, 200
Nelson, R.R. 57, 65(n), 101
Nerlove, M. 106
Nevin, E. 55
Newman, J. von 151, 160, 220
Nunez, A. 223, 225, 232

Ohkawa, K. 36, 37
Okuguchi, K. 143, 144, 153(n), 160
Ordover, J. 201(n), 202, 208, 210, 212, 215, 215(n)
Otsuki, O. 266(n), 277

Parsons, R. 57
Pascal, B. 199(n), 200
Patrick H.T. 27(n), 35, 35(n), 55
Pearlman, M.E. 135
Peck, M.J. 65(n), 101
Phelps, E. 200, 201, 208, 210, 212, 215, 316(n), 329

Phillips, A. 315, 329
Pigou, A.C. 220, 232, 317(n), 329
Poole, W. 285, 295
Popkin, J. 271(n), 277
Pyatt, G. 217(n), 219(n)

Quandt, R.E. 143(n), 159
Quesnay, F. 4, 5(n), 6, 6(n), 25(n)

Radner, R. 188, 200
Ranis, G. 27, 29(n), 30(n), 31(n), 39(n), 44(n), 54, 55
Rawls, J. 201, 215
Reynolds, L. 3
Ricardo, D. 8, 15, 16, 17, 18, 25
Riggan, W.B. 134
Riley, J. 201(n), 202, 214, 215
Robbins, L.C. 4(n), 16(n), 25
Robinson, J. 24, 25
Robinson, S. 230, 231

Salant, W. 279(n)
Samuelson, P. 201, 279(n)
Sato, R. 144, 160
Schelling, T.C. 161, 164(n)
Scherer, F.M. 60(n), 101
Schott, F. 279(n)
Schultze, C.L. 314, 319, 329
Schumpeter, J. 5(n), 25, 58(n), 59, 101, 235
Schwartz, A.J. 323, 328
Schwartz, N.L. 60(n), 101
Scitovsky, T. 30, 30(n), 55
Scott, M. 30, 30(n), 55
Selowsky, M. 230(n)
Sen, A. 217, 231, 231(n), 232
Seskin, E.P. 132(n), 135
Shaw, E.S. 27(n), 43, 55
Shen, T.H. 55
Shoven, J.B. 242, 262
Shubik, M. 144, 160
Shy, C.M. 132(n), 135
Smith, A. 7, 8, 9, 11, 12, 12(n), 13–17, 20(n), 21, 25(n)
Spencer, R.W. 312(n), 329
Sprinkel, B. 279(n)
Squire, L. 217(n), 218, 225, 228(n), 232
Stackelberg, H. von 139, 140, 151, 152, 153(n), 155, 160
Stein, J. 279(n), 280, 295
Stern, N. 221, 228, 232
Suzumura, K. 143, 160
Sweeney, R.J. 316(n), 329

Temin, P. 59(n), 101
Theil, H. 223, 232
Theocharis, R.D. 144, 160
Tobin, J. 235, 238(n), 239(n), 242(n), 262, 315, 329
Triffin, R. 297, 301(n)
Trivers, R.L. 178, 200
Tucker, A.W. 200

Van Bruggen, J.B. 134
Van der Tak, H.G. 218, 232

Wallich, H. 279
Wallington, S.A. 179, 200
Watts, H. 103
Weidenbaum, M. 315, 327(n), 329
Weinberg, D. 311(n), 329
Weintraub, S. 272
Williams, J. 332
Williams, R. 221, 223, 224, 224(n), 225, 226, 232
Williamson, O.E. 95(n), 101
Wilson, J. 279(n)
Wilson, R. 177(n)
Winter, S. 57

Young, M.M. 135